# Undermining the State from Within

*Undermining the State from Within* pulls back the curtain on the counterinsurgent state to better understand how conflict dynamics affect state institutions and continue to shape political and economic development in the postwar period. Drawing on unique archival and interview data from war and postwar Central America, this book illuminates how counterinsurgent actors, under the pretext of combatting an insurgent threat, introduce alternative rules within state institutions, which undermine core activities like tax collection, public security provision, and property administration. Moreover, it uncovers how the counterinsurgent elite outmaneuvers governance reforms during democratic transition and peacebuilding to preserve the predatory wartime status quo. In so doing, this book rethinks the relationship between war and state formation, challenges existing scholarly and policy approaches to peacebuilding and post-conflict institutional reform, and contributes a new understanding of what civil war leaves behind in an institutional sense.

Rachel A. Schwartz is Assistant Professor of International and Area Studies at the University of Oklahoma.

T0381776

# Undermining the State from Within

## The Institutional Legacies of Civil War in Central America

RACHEL A. SCHWARTZ

*University of Oklahoma*

# CAMBRIDGE
## UNIVERSITY PRESS

Shaftesbury Road, Cambridge CB2 8EA, United Kingdom

One Liberty Plaza, 20th Floor, New York, NY 10006, USA

477 Williamstown Road, Port Melbourne, VIC 3207, Australia

314–321, 3rd Floor, Plot 3, Splendor Forum, Jasola District Centre, New Delhi – 110025, India

103 Penang Road, #05–06/07, Visioncrest Commercial, Singapore 238467

Cambridge University Press is part of Cambridge University Press & Assessment, a department of the University of Cambridge.

We share the University's mission to contribute to society through the pursuit of education, learning and research at the highest international levels of excellence.

www.cambridge.org
Information on this title: www.cambridge.org/9781009219938

DOI: 10.1017/9781009219907

First published 2023

*A catalogue record for this publication is available from the British Library.*

*Library of Congress Cataloging-in-Publication Data*
NAMES: Schwartz, Rachel A., 1988- author.
TITLE: Undermining the state from within : the institutional legacies of civil war in Central America / Rachel A. Schwartz.
DESCRIPTION: Cambridge, United Kingdom ; New York, NY : Cambridge University Press, 2023. | Includes bibliographical references and index.
IDENTIFIERS: LCCN 2022043287 (print) | LCCN 2022043288 (ebook)
| ISBN 9781009219938 (hardback) | ISBN 9781009219891 (paperback)
| ISBN 9781009219907 (epub)
SUBJECTS: LCSH: Civil war–Central America–History. | Counterinsurgency–Central America–History. | Political corruption–Central America. | Extrajudicial executions–Central America. | Land reform–Corrupt practices–Central America. | Central America–Politics and government–21st century.
CLASSIFICATION: LCC F1439.5 .S38 2023 (print) | LCC F1439.5 (ebook) |
DDC 320.9728–dc23/eng/20221028
LC record available at https://lccn.loc.gov/2022043287
LC ebook record available at https://lccn.loc.gov/2022043288

ISBN 978-1-009-21993-8 Hardback
ISBN 978-1-009-21989-1 Paperback

# Contents

# Figures

# Tables

# Preface

It was a Sunday afternoon in June 2015, and I was three weeks into my pre-dissertation research. As I usually do at this stage in the summer, I hopped in a taxi and headed to *la colonia* – originally a squatters' settlement on the outskirts of Guatemala City – to visit some friends I met on my first trip to Guatemala over seven years earlier.

The Guatemala of 2015 was, at once, dramatically different and eerily the same as the one I was first introduced to in 2008. The country was undergoing unprecedented social and political changes, which, at times, looked like they might wind their way right back to where they started. On April 16, 2015, Guatemalan investigators, with the help of the United Nations International Commission against Impunity (CICIG), revealed a vast corruption network within the country's customs administration, which defrauded the state of hundreds of millions of dollars. The network was named *La Línea*, after the phone line importers called to arrange customs duty adjustments. It was headed by the private secretary of then-Vice President Roxana Baldetti.

On April 25, citizens took to Guatemala City's central square in droves to demand Baldetti's resignation. They achieved it shortly thereafter. Months later, President Otto Pérez Molina, the other leader of the scheme, was forced to step down too – but not before a number of other criminal structures also came to light. There was the one in the Social Security Institute (IGSS), in which authorities negotiated shady contracts for faulty renal dialysis drugs, which killed forty-nine people and poisoned hundreds more. There was the one in the National Civilian Police (PNC), in which former agents embezzled nearly $1 million allegedly spent on vehicle repairs. There was the one in the Ministry of

Energy and Mines (MEM), in which officials accepted bribes in exchange for an electric plant concession. The list goes on.

While Guatemala felt like it had plunged into uncharted political territory, that Sunday afternoon in *la colonia*, we did what we always did when I visited. We ate lunch and played Bancopoly. Bancopoly is Guatemala's version of Monopoly, but with several apt, if unintended *chapín* twists. First, rather than buy and sell real estate properties modeled after the country's major metropolitan area, in Bancopoly, you buy and sell entire provinces. That's right, every square kilometer of Guatemalan territory is up for grabs to whoever is lucky enough to land on it and have the requisite cash in hand. In another all-too-appropriate metaphor, Guatemala's public services are also for sale. The National Institute for Electrification (INDE), the Municipal Water Company (EMPAGUA), they too can be yours, not to mention state-owned transport companies such as AVIGUA (planes) and FEGUA (trains).

And in perhaps the most apropos, if disturbing, metaphor, whenever we play Bancopoly, I, the *gringa*, always win. The game ends when one player amasses the entire country – from the coastal lowlands of Escuintla to the northernmost frontiers of the Petén. And almost every time I am that player. It's like some perverse homage to my American forerunners in Guatemala who plotted coups, armed tyrants, and white-washed genocide – all in the name of winning economic power and loyal political partners.

That smoggy June afternoon, nothing changed. Again I won. But the symbolism that had always remained latent, which had always existed just under the surface was, for the first time, spoken. Whenever any player sought to buy property, the banker, my friend's twenty-year-old son, would jokingly ask, "*¿Y donde está mi comisión?*" ("And where's my cut?"), because that's how things operate here.

More than a few times, my friend landed on Bancopoly's version of the "luxury tax" and watched her money slowly float away and into the coffers of the Superintendent of Tax Administration (SAT), in her words, "*para que los políticos lo puedan robar después*" ("So that the politicians can steal it later"). When she landed on a "chance" card and received 145 quetzales from the Social Security Institute as workers' comp, she sighed, "*Por lo menos me está devolviendo un poquito de lo que robaron*" ("At least they're giving back a tiny bit of what they stole").

"Yes," I replied. "At least, there's that."

In over a decade of fieldwork, I have had countless conversations with ordinary Guatemalans who are, on the one hand, exasperated by the daily acts of corruption that govern their lives, yet, on the other hand, acutely aware that the real problems are deep and systemic. Far from aberrations, predation and criminality constitute the "operating system" that organizes politics in Guatemala and throughout much of Central America. They are not the exception, but the rule. We will never know their true toll, but the costs are made manifest every day in the form of families living in extreme poverty, schools shuttered due to teacher shortages, understaffed hospitals that lack routine medical supplies, overcrowded prisons that foment gang violence, and the untold individuals that simply leave, risking life and limb to make it to the other side of the United States border.

As citizens throughout Central America mobilize to take back what has been stolen from them, this book seeks to illuminate why and how corruption and criminality became the region's operating system in the first place. It traces the contemporary criminalization of the state, in large part, to Central America's dark history of civil war, which empowered counterinsurgent elites and their allies to establish new institutional innovations to steal, kill, and control. Though civil war is not solely to blame for the ills that plague Central America, the bloody twentieth-century conflicts played an important role in hardwiring within state institutions the perverse, predatory logics that systematically undercut development today.

We know that armed conflicts in Central America claimed hundreds of thousands of lives. But we know less about how they irretrievably distorted the institutional landscape as well. This book seeks to tell that part of the story.

# Acknowledgments

This book reflects the kindness, generosity, and care of the many people who have contributed to my research and to my personal and intellectual growth over the years. First and foremost, I wish to thank my Guatemalan and Nicaraguan informants, friends, and colleagues whose stories and experiences fill the pages of this book and made this project possible. Though this book largely focuses on depraved acts of corruption during war, I was constantly reminded that, in the words of one Guatemalan interviewee, who has since passed away, "There are heroes in these stories too." Indeed, the only reason I was able to capture what went on in the shadows of civil war was because of the brave individuals who risked their professional standing – and sometimes their lives – to illuminate it. Out of concern for their safety and privacy, I am unable to name them here. But I will forever remain in awe of their courage and grateful for their time, their insights, and their stories. My simple hope is that the pages that follow do justice to their struggles and their sacrifices.

This book emerged out of my doctoral dissertation at the University of Wisconsin–Madison. I am deeply grateful to my dissertation committee, whose patience and guidance have been instrumental in the development of this project – and to my own development as a scholar. I cannot imagine a better advisor than Scott Straus, whose critical eye, astute feedback, and abiding support made this project – and me – better. Erica Simmons challenged me to think about political science in new ways and has given a generation of young scholars a language to describe our unconventional approaches and contributions. Her mentorship and friendship have meant so much to me. I have also been so very fortunate to count Noam Lupu as a constant source of encouragement and

xv

invaluable scholarly interlocutor and Nils Ringe as my go-to on all things "institutions." I would also like to thank Christina Ewig and Helen Kinsella, who provided critical insights and feedback during this project's early stages and profoundly influenced the course of my research. I continue to be immensely grateful to Anita Isaacs at Haverford College, who first introduced me to Guatemala and the questions that motivate this book. Anita's model of scholarship and political engagement inspires me as much today as it did as a freshman in her course fifteen years ago. None of this would have been possible without her.

At UW–Madison, I was lucky to be surrounded by a host of brilliant, kind, and fierce graduate students and colleagues, who quickly became and will forever remain my Madison family. Among them are the inimitable ladies of TWWWAT (The Women Who Write Awesome Things), Hannah Chapman, Rachel Jacobs, Anna Meier, Anna Oltman, Susanne Mueller-Redwood, and Samantha Vortherms, who have been a constant source of encouragement and laughter. I am also grateful to the members of the Latin America Colloquium (LAC), including Camila Ángulo, Nick Barnes, Casey Ehrlich, José Luis Enríquez Chiñas, David Greenwood-Sánchez, Ned Littlefield, Molly Minden, Camilla Reuterswärd, Emily Sellars, and Alberto Vargas, who provided feedback on much of this manuscript over the years. I would also like to thank the many other UW–Madison friends and colleagues who made my time in graduate school not only intellectually stimulating but loads of fun. They include Sirus Bouchat, Thomas Bunting, Evan Crawford, Mike DeCrescenzo, Desiree Desierto, Micah Dillard, Stephanie Dillon, Caleigh Glenn, Sarah Guillot, Clarence Moore, Maayan Mor, Nat Olin, Kaden Paulson-Smith, Ben Power, Michael Promisel, Megan Rowley, Ann Sojka, Mark Toukan, Degi Uvsh, Chagai Weiss, Bri Wolf, Max Wolf, Jack Van Thomme, Megan Van Thomme, Logan Vidal, Naomi Warner, Zach Warner, and Erin Zwick. Many thanks as well to David de Micheli, Min Jung Kim, Sasha Klyachkina, Nick Rush Smith, Whitney Taylor, and Vanessa van den Boogaard, who generously commented on draft chapters during the dissertation stage and beyond.

Following my time at UW–Madison, I was privileged to receive a postdoctoral fellowship at the Center for Inter-American Policy and Research (CIPR) at Tulane University, which provided an ideal intellectual environment to continue revising this manuscript. I am deeply grateful to Ludovico Feoli for his support of and feedback on this project, as well as his deep commitment to promoting scholarship on Central

America. I would also like to thank other members of the CIPR and Tulane communities, who challenged me to refine my ideas and writing and made my time in New Orleans so enjoyable. They include Caitlin Andrews-Lee, Moisés Arce, Gabriel Chouhy, David de Micheli, Sefira Fialkoff, Gonzalo Gómez Bengoechea, Stefanie Israel de Souza, Anne Mische, and Xander Slaski. In May 2020, I was fortunate to be able to hold a virtual book workshop sponsored by CIPR, which was critical to sharpening this book's theoretical and empirical contributions. Many thanks to the stellar scholars who participated, including Gustavo Flores-Macías, Reo Matsuzaki, Eduardo Moncada, Hillel Soifer, Paul Staniland, and Christine Wade, for their generosity and constructive feedback, as well as Deborah Yashar, who provided very helpful comments ahead of the workshop.

While conducting research in the field, I benefitted from a community of friends and scholars with which to share the very high highs and the very low lows of fieldwork and to explore the food, art, and beauty of Guatemala and Nicaragua. Many thanks to Kate del Valle, Catherine Flatley, Sarah Foss, Alex Galarza, Bryant Hand, Julia Hartviksen, Rachel Nolan, Fares Pérez, Jeniffer Pérez, Dan Sanders, Anna Sveinsdóttir, José Miguel Toj, and Carl the Dog. I am also immensely grateful to a number of brilliant and tireless archivists in Guatemala and Nicaragua who were instrumental to my scholarly detective work: Thelma Porres and Reyna Pérez at the Center for Mesoamerican Research (CIRMA); Hérbert Cáceres and his team at the Historical Archive of the National Police (AHPN); Patricia Ogaldes at the Guatemalan Archbishop's Office of Human Rights (ODHAG); Nelly Reyes at the General Archive of Central America (AGCA); and María Auxiliadora Estrada and María Ligia Garay at the Institute of History of Nicaragua and Central America (IHNCA).

I have also had the great fortune of working with an extraordinary team at Cambridge University Press. A huge thank you to Rachel Blaifeder, Sara Doskow, Jadyn Fauconier-Herry, and Robert Judkins for shepherding this project at various stages. Vinithan Sethumadhavan at Straive also provided invaluable assistance during the production process.

This book would not have been possible without the generous financial support of the Fulbright IIE program and the United States Institute of Peace (USIP), which allowed me to undertake a sixteen-month research stint in 2016 and 2017. I am also grateful to the UW Latin American, Caribbean, and Iberian Studies program (LACIS) and the Institute for Regional and

International Studies (IRIS), which provided summer fieldwork funding for the exploratory research that laid the foundations for this book. I received generous conference and travel support from the UW Political Science Summer Initiative Fund, supported by the Trice Family and the UW Graduate School, as well the UW–Madison Institute for Legal Studies (ILS). I am also grateful to Otterbein University's Humanities Advisory Committee (HAC) and Faculty-Scholar Development Committee (FDSC) for providing support during the homestretch of writing this book.

Parts of this manuscript are drawn from four scholarly articles that I published between 2020 and 2022. They include "Civil War, Institutional Change, and the Criminalization of the State: Evidence from Guatemala," *Studies in Comparative International Development* 55(3): 381–401; "Conjuring the Criminal State: The 'State-Idea' in Post-Conflict Reconstruction and International Statebuilding," *Journal of Global Security Studies* 6(2): 1–17; "How Predatory Informal Rules Outlast State Reform: Evidence from Postauthoritarian Guatemala," *Latin American Politics and Society* 63(1): 49–71; and "Rewriting the Rules of Land Reform: The Institutional Legacies of War in Nicaragua," *Small Wars and Insurgencies*, First View.

Finally, I owe a debt of gratitude to my family for their unwavering patience and love even when they were not entirely sure what I was doing or why I was doing it. I am so fortunate to have an extended family of aunts, uncles, cousins, and grandparents who have cheered me on every step of the way. Jamie and Ben (and Tye and Nash), thank you for keeping me laughing and for always being in the right place at the right time with a beer in hand. Hannah, thank you for building me up, for keeping me grounded, and for fixing things when they break (literally and figuratively). Yes, you can add more to the list whenever you would like. And last but not least, I would like to thank my parents, who instilled in me a penchant for asking questions and the nerve to think I might one day find answers. I hope I have made you proud.

# Abbreviations

| | |
|---|---|
| AGCA | General Archive of Central America (*Archivo General de Centroamérica*) |
| AHPN | Historical Archive of the National Police (*Archivo Histórico de la Policía Nacional*) |
| APP | Area of the People's Property (*Área de Propiedad del Pueblo*) |
| ARDE | Democratic Revolutionary Alliance (*Alianza Revolucionaria Democrática*) |
| ARENA | Nationalist Republican Alliance (*Alianza Republicana Nacionalista*) |
| AVEMILGUA | Association of Military Veterans of Guatemala (*Asociación de Veteranos Militares de Guatemala*) |
| ATC | Rural Workers' Association (*Asociación de Trabajadores del Campo*) |
| CACIF | Coordinating Committee of Agricultural, Commercial, Industrial, and Financial Associations (*Comité Coordinador de Asociaciones Agrícolas, Comerciales, Industriales y Financieras*) |
| CADEG | Anti-Communist Council of Guatemala (*Consejo Anticomunista de Guatemala*) |
| CAS | Sandinista Agricultural Cooperatives (*Cooperativas Agrícolas Sandinistas*) |
| CCS | Credit and Service Cooperatives (*Cooperativas de Crédito y Servicio*) |
| CDC | Civil Defense Committee (*Comité de Defensa Civil*) |

| | |
|---|---|
| CDS | Sandinista Defense Committee (*Comité de Defensa Sandinista*) |
| CEH | Historical Clarification Commission (*Comisión de Esclarecimiento Histórico*) |
| CEPAL | Economic Commission for Latin America and the Caribbean (*Comisión Económica para América Latina y el Caribe*) |
| CICIG | International Commission against Impunity in Guatemala (*Comisión Internacional contra la Impunidad en Guatemala*) |
| CIERA | Center for Investigations and Studies of Agrarian Reform (*Centro de Investigaciones y Estudios de la Reforma Agraria*) |
| CIRMA | Center for Mesoamerican Research (*Centro de Investigaciones Regionales de Mesoamérica*) |
| CNA | National Agrarian Commission (*Comisión Nacional Agropecuaria*) |
| CNR | National Reconciliation Commission (*Comisión Nacional de Reconciliación*) |
| CNRC | National Commission for the Revision of Confiscations (*Comisión Nacional de Revisión de Confiscaciones*) |
| COC | Joint Operations Center (*Centro de Operaciones Conjuntas*) |
| COCP | Joint Operations Center of the Police (*Centro de Operaciones Conjuntas de la Policía*) |
| DIAN | National Directorate of Taxes and Customs (*Dirección de Impuestos y Aduanas Nacionales*) |
| DIC | Department of Criminological Investigations (*Departamento de Investigaciones Criminológicas*) |
| DINC | Division of Criminal Investigations (*División de Investigaciones Criminales*) |
| DIT | Department of Technical Investigations (*Departamento de Investigaciones Técnicas*) |
| DN | National Directorate (*Dirección Nacional*) |
| EGP | Guerrilla Army of the Poor (*Ejército Guerillero de los Pobres*) |
| EM | Death Squad (*Escuadrón de la Muerte*) |
| EMP | Presidential Military Staff (*Estado Mayor Presidencial*) |
| EPS | Sandinista Popular Army (*Ejército Popular Sandinista*) |

| ESA | Secret Anti-communist Army (*Ejército Secreto Anticomunista*) |
| FAR | Rebel Armed Forces (*Fuerzas Armadas Rebeldes*) |
| FDN | Nicaraguan Democratic Front (*Frente Democrático Nicaragüense*) |
| FSLN | Sandinista National Liberation Front (*Frente Sandinista de Liberación Nacional*) |
| G-2 | Section of Military Intelligence |
| G-3 | Section of Military Operations |
| GN | National Guard (*Guardia Nacional*) |
| IGSS | Guatemalan Institute of Social Security (*Instituto Guatemalteco de Seguridad Social*) |
| IDB | Inter-American Development Bank |
| IHNCA | Institute of History of Nicaragua and Central America (*Instituto de Historia de Nicaragua y Centroamérica*) |
| INRA | Nicaraguan Institute of Agrarian Reform (*Instituto Nicaragüense de Reforma Agraria*) |
| JGRN | Government Junta of National Reconstruction (*Junta de Gobierno de Reconstrucción Nacional*) |
| MANO | Movement of Organized Nationalist Action (*Movimiento de Acción Nacionalista Organizada*) |
| MIDINRA | Ministry of Agricultural Development and Agrarian Reform (*Ministerio de Desarrollo Agropecuario y Reforma Agraria*) |
| MILPAS | Anti-Somoza Popular Militias (*Milicias Populares Anti-Somocistas*); *later* Anti-Sandinista Popular Militias (*Milicias Populares Anti-Sandinistas*) |
| MINT | Ministry of the Interior (*Ministerio del Interior*) |
| MLN | National Liberation Movement (*Movimiento de Liberación Nacional*) |
| MP | Public Prosecutor's Office (*Ministerio Público*) |
| NOA | New Anti-Communist Organization (*Nueva Organización Anticomunista*) |
| OCI | Office for the Quantification of Indemnities (*Oficina de Cuantificación de Indemnizaciones*) |
| ODHAG | Guatemalan Archbishop's Office of Human Rights |
| OOT | Office for Territorial Ordering (*Oficina de Ordenamiento Territorial*) |

| ORPA | Revolutionary Organization of People in Arms (*Organización Revolucionaria del Pueblo en Armas*) |
| PN | National Police (*Policía Nacional*) |
| PNC | National Civilian Police (*Policía Nacional Civil*) |
| REMHI | Recovery of Historical Memory Project (*Recuperación de Memoria Histórica*) |
| RN | Nicaraguan Resistance (*Resistencia Nicaragüense*) |
| SAT | Superintendent of Tax Administration (*Superintendencia de Administración Tributaria*) |
| SEM | Office of Special Ministerial Services (*Oficina de Servicios Especiales Ministeriales*) |
| SIC | Criminal Investigation Service (*Servicio de Investigación Criminal*) |
| UNAG | National Union of Agricultural Workers and Cattle Ranchers (*Unión Nacional de Agricultores y Ganaderos de Nicaragua*) |
| UNDP | United Nations Development Program |
| UNO | National Opposition Union (*Unión Nacional Opositora*) |
| URNG | Guatemalan National Revolutionary Unity (*Unidad Revolucionaria Nacional Guatemalteca*) |
| USAC | University of San Carlos (*Universidad de San Carlos*) |

PART I

FOUNDATIONS

1

# Introduction

## *Undermining the State in Civil War*

On April 16, 2015, the Guatemalan Public Prosecutor's Office (MP) alongside the UN International Commission Against Impunity in Guatemala (CICIG) uncovered a massive customs fraud network operating within the country's tax administration. Dubbed *La Línea* after the telephone line used to negotiate illegal adjustments to customs duties,[1] the network was comprised of a mix of public and private actors – customs agents, port administrators, union bosses, retail business owners, tax authorities, and, at the top, then-President Otto Pérez Molina and Vice President Roxana Baldetti.

According to wiretaps and computer files, importers contacted *La Línea* operatives to arrange adjustments through which they paid 40 percent of the customs duties they legally owed to the state and 30 percent to the criminal structure, pocketing the remaining 30 percent.[2] Recovered Excel spreadsheets, in fact, divide the customs revenue into two separate pools: "R1," the amount directed to the Superintendent of Tax Administration (SAT), and "R2," the amount captured by the illicit network.[3] Initial investigations indicated that *La Línea* siphoned off some $330,000 on a weekly basis.[4] Though the precise amount diverted from state coffers is impossible to discern, Guatemalan think tank ASIES estimates that in 2014 alone, the Guatemalan state was defrauded roughly $940 million, or 1.6 percent of its GDP.[5]

The exposure of *La Línea* prompted a series of popular protests on a scale unprecedented since Guatemala's return to civilian rule in the

---

[1] Barreto 2015.    [2] CICIG and MP 2015.    [3] De León 2015.    [4] *El Periódico* 2015.
[5] ASIES 2017: 13.

mid-1980s. Guatemalans of all political stripes converged on the capital city's *Plaza de la Constitución* with signs excoriating the country's corrupt political class and demanding "*¡Renuncia Ya!*" – that Pérez Molina and Baldetti tender their resignations immediately. Galvanizing a broader coalition of university students, indigenous Mayan communities, business elites, and urban popular sectors, the protests eventually brought down the sitting government – an achievement that many had once considered impossible in a country where impunity reigns.

The *La Línea* revelations and the resulting popular response served as a watershed moment in the country's history. However, buried within the renewed political fervor was something else equally striking: This was not the first time that a massive customs fraud network had been uncovered within Guatemala's tax administration. In fact, in September 1996, almost two decades prior and on the eve of the signing of peace accords to end Guatemala's 36-year civil war, the MP exposed a nearly identical scheme that had taken root within the Ministry of Finance. This earlier criminal structure was named the Moreno Network after the lower-ranking military intelligence agent who managed the scheme – a man by the name of Alfredo Moreno Molina.

The investigations, however, revealed that Alfredo Moreno was not the one pulling the strings. Instead the alternative, predatory institutional arrangements within the customs apparatus were devised and implemented by an elite clique of high-ranking military intelligence officers from within the president's inner circle, which had seized control of the state as the country's civil war escalated in the late 1970s. Under the pretext of leftist insurgent expansion and with significant US government backing, this narrow coterie of counterinsurgent elites crafted new procedures for fabricating customs forms and "disappearing" shipping containers to siphon off revenue destined for state coffers. At the height of the state's counterinsurgent struggle, they used their political power and discretion to introduce new institutional innovations that subverted the Guatemalan state's extractive activities on a systematic basis. The pernicious institutional arrangements are emblematic of a key concept at the heart of this book: *undermining rules*, or those that produce institutional outcomes that contravene core state activities like the collection of tax revenue. Through the wartime entrenchment and enforcement of the undermining rules, counterinsurgent leaders remade the fabric of the central state according to predatory, criminal logics that would distort development for decades to come.

Far from a new phenomenon, *La Línea* was instead an artifact of Guatemala's nearly four-decade civil war, which was brought to a close in 1996. The emergence, evolution, and consolidation of the Moreno Network and *La Línea* thus raise a series of important questions for scholars of conflict and post-conflict politics: How does civil war shape state development in the longer term? What accounts for the emergence of new, sometimes predatory procedures, or undermining rules, within the state apparatus amid civil war? How do such institutional formations survive democratic transition, peace, and postwar reforms and continue to distort political and economic development?

This book seeks to pull back the curtain on the counterinsurgent state to better understand how conflict dynamics affect state institutions and how wartime institutional transformations continue to structure state activities in the postwar period. In a turn from decades of scholarship on the causes of civil war, conflict scholars have directed increasing attention to what civil war leaves behind.[6] This burgeoning research agenda on the legacies of civil war has produced valuable insights on how the experience of conflict shapes political attitudes, identities, and participation at the individual level;[7] the lasting effects of war on local community structures;[8] and the relationship between armed conflict and broader patterns of postwar democratization and violence.[9] Yet, the machinery of the central state has been subject to less systematic scholarly inquiry. While classic theories of state formation point to the central role of foreign conflict in building the state apparatus, the institutional effects of civil war remains a nascent area of research.

Indeed, there are clear reasons to think that civil war dynamics might also spur institutional innovation and change within the state. In reorienting the power and resources of the state to eliminate an internal enemy, the existing rules governing state activity may be altered, discarded, or refashioned to facilitate counterinsurgency. This often occurs, in part, because the campaign to put down rebellion empowers new actors – specialists in information gathering, surveillance, and violence – in the process.[10] The heightened sense of threat and anxiety allows these actors to operate in the shadows and devise their own counterinsurgent methods – methods that fundamentally remake state institutions

---

[6] See Kelmendi and Rizkallah 2018.
[7] Balcells 2012; Lupu and Peisakhin 2017; Bellows and Miguel 2009; Blattman 2009.
[8] Gilligan et al. 2014; Bateson 2013.     [9] Huang 2016; Cruz 2011.
[10] Eibl et al. 2021; Slater 2020.

themselves. As a result, civil war can constitute a powerful site of institutional transformation. This project is an attempt to understand civil war
as a site of institutional creation and change within the central state and to
examine its lasting effects for state development long after the fighting
has ceased.

## THE PROBLEMS OF THE POSTWAR STATE

Though this book largely explains historical processes of wartime institutional change, it takes as its point of departure a more contemporary
problem: the woes of postwar societies and the attendant difficulties of
sustaining peace. The devastation of civil war often leaves behind a range
of social, political, and economic challenges that make postwar recovery,
at best, slow and uneven and, at worst, doomed from the outset. The
physical destruction wrought by civil war wipes out household assets,
education and health facilities, and basic infrastructure, hampering
human development. According to the World Bank, conflict-affected
and recovering states account for 77 percent of the world's school-age
children not enrolled in primary school, 61 percent of the world's population in poverty, and 70 percent of global infant mortality.[11] The
postwar obstacles to economic recovery only exacerbate these problems.
Persistent volatility within conflict and post-conflict settings often shakes
investor confidence, disrupting foreign direct investment and depressing
growth.[12]

The consequences of civil war for human and economic development
are only compounded by the social and political problems that plague
postwar countries. Formal peace at the national level does not automatically induce quotidian local peace. Post-conflict societies continue to face
staggering levels of violence, sometimes due to criminal activity by demobilized combatants.[13] The trauma experienced by individuals affected by
conflict violence has significant, often lifelong mental health consequences.[14] Wartime displacement can also trigger postwar social conflict
as internally displaced persons (IDPs) return to claim the property and
assets they were forced to abandon, only to find that others have confiscated them.[15] And, of course, the negotiated settlements or power-sharing
agreements to end war and cement stability ultimately sit atop fragile

---

[11] World Bank 2011: 63.    [12] Murdoch and Sandler 2002.
[13] Trejo et al. 2018; Daly et al. 2020; Paris 2004; World Bank 2011.
[14] Murthy and Lakshminarayana 2006.    [15] Charnysh and Finkel 2017; Steele 2017.

political coalitions and less-than-credible commitments, which may give way to perceived political inequalities and continued strife.[16]

Combined, the nagging social, political, and economic problems that hamstring postwar recovery also contribute to another well-known phenomenon: the recurrence of civil war. As Barbara Walter notes, "the problem of civil war is now almost exclusively a problem of repeat civil war."[17] Civil wars often generate a "conflict trap" in which "hatred and other rebellion-specific capital accumulates during war, making further conflict more likely."[18] Indeed, for countries approaching the end of war, the risk of returning to conflict within five years is 44 percent.[19] Of the conflicts initiated in the twenty-first century, some 90 percent took place in countries that had already experienced civil war.[20] While there is still debate on the causes of conflict onset, there is little question that once initiated, conflict begets conflict.

Why is peace so difficult to sustain following civil war? And when peace does endure, why do the developmental deficits that characterize postwar settings remain so deeply entrenched? In seeking answers to these questions, scholars and policymakers alike have overwhelmingly converged on the same common denominator: the weakness of state institutions.[21] There is a fairly broad consensus that a defining feature of fragile, war-torn countries at risk of relapsing into conflict is the state's "weak capacity to carry out basic functions of governing their population and territory."[22] Postwar state weakness is thought to fuel violence, first and foremost, because ineffective institutions are unable to peaceably channel political disagreement. But beyond this, weak state institutions are incapable of providing basic goods and services like justice, security, and healthcare, which can foster widespread grievances and empower violent, non-state actors to fill the governance void.[23]

The link between armed conflict and ineffective state institutions has prompted scholars of peacebuilding to focus increasing attention on post-conflict "statebuilding" or "governance" as the critical determinant of durable peace. For example, Paris argues that "a rudimentary network of domestic institutions" is the first imperative of peacebuilding,[24] while Walter similarly posits that "good governance" in the form of robust political and legal institutions is the answer to staving off renewed conflict

---

[16] Stedman 1997; Daly 2014.   [17] Walter 2015: 1242.
[18] Collier and Sambanis 2002: 5.   [19] Collier et al. 2003: 83.   [20] Walter 2010: 1.
[21] Steenkamp 2009; Boyle 2014.   [22] OECD 2011: 11.
[23] World Bank 2011: 7; see also, Doyle and Sambanis 2006.   [24] Paris 2004: 7.

in post-civil-war settings.[25] Similarly, Lake contends that peace is contingent upon the state's establishment of social order – rules and laws – in which society becomes invested and which, in turn, become self-enforcing.[26] Though the precise terminology varies, contemporary scholarship generally portrays statebuilding as "the *telos* (or end goal) of consolidating peace."[27]

The ineffectiveness of post-civil-war states is thus not only widely recognized but understood as the core problem underlying civil war recurrence and motivating peacebuilding agendas.[28] Yet curiously, we know very little about *why* civil war weakens states. Indeed, the wartime central state remains somewhat of a black box within contemporary conflict scholarship. And while the corrosive effect of civil war on state institutions has been corroborated by many studies,[29] these findings stand in stark contrast to the long-standing social science literature on state formation, which posits that war serves as a primary impetus for "making" the state or building administrative institutions.[30] What are the mechanisms linking civil war and "weak" states? And how does civil war shape state institutions more generally?

## THE ARGUMENT

This book departs from the conventional wisdom, which tends to assume that civil war generates ineffective states because it degrades or destroys institutions. Rather than deny the institution-building character of armed conflict, I posit that civil war is often a site of institutional innovation; however, the rules and procedures introduced amid civil war may come to undermine the formal functions of the state – as the case of the Moreno Network suggests. At its core, this book thus reexamines long-standing questions on the relationship between war and state formation through a new lens: that of institutions and institutional change. My central claim is that rather than prompting sweeping processes of statebuilding or

---

[25] Walter 2015.    [26] Lake 2016: 27–29.    [27] Sisk 2013: x.
[28] It is important to note that the empirical relationship between civil war and state weakness is very difficult to disentangle. While early studies within conflict research posited that state weakness fueled conflict onset, more recent scholarship that addresses endogeneity concerns directly finds that civil war onset induces state weakening. See Thies 2010.
[29] Besley and Persson 2008; Thies 2005, 2006, 2010.
[30] Tilly 1975, 1990; Bates 2001; Mann 1988; Rodríguez-Franco 2016.

destruction, civil war dynamics induce more minute changes at the level of state institutions, or the rules and procedures that structure behavior within core government policy arenas. These changes, in turn, distort routine state activities, like the extraction of tax revenue, control over the means of violence, and the administration of basic goods and services. Put simply, armed conflict alters the rules by which a host of state and non-state actors operate; precisely how state institutions change – the *kinds* of rules that evolve – shapes the effects of conflict on state performance.

This book focuses primarily on a particular kind of rule guided by a particular kind of institutional logic: *undermining* rules, or those that generate outcomes that contravene a given state function. Undermining rules are institutional procedures that subvert routine state activities like the extraction of tax revenue, the monopolization of coercive force, and the administration of basic goods and services, among others. Drawing on this concept, I build a new theory of wartime institutional change within the state, which accounts for how undermining rules crystallize as the escalation of the insurgent threat generates lapses in institutional enforcement and allots heightened discretion to small, insulated cliques of military leaders as the architects of counterinsurgency.

Through the empowerment of this new counterinsurgent elite or the centralization of authority in existing rulers, new, undermining rules take root within state arenas deemed key strategic sites in the struggle against rebel forces. Whether motivated by illicit profit-seeking or the preservation of political power, the absence of countervailing political forces allows this counterinsurgent elite to craft and implement new rules corresponding to their narrow interests and thus distort state activities. The trajectory of wartime state development and variation in wartime institutional logics is thus primarily a question of coalitional configurations.

Further, this book contends that the wartime institutional procedures are reproduced, become self-enforcing, and endure depending on whether the counterinsurgent elite forges a broader alliance of sectoral interests with a stake in the new institutional status quo. This broader network of actors – what I term the "distributional coalition" – often encompasses more than top military brass, bringing into the fold private sector elites who benefit from wartime economic activities, organized criminal operatives engaged in illicit wartime trades, and judicial and political officials who grant impunity for wartime abuses to maintain their power. The postwar adaptation and survival of this dominant wartime coalition dictates whether the undermining rules endure in the longer term. The reshuffling of elite political alignments, by contrast, can generate "chronic instability," which inhibits the survival of the wartime rules of the game.[31]

In sum, this approach posits a new explanation for the deleterious effects of civil war on state development through the lens of institutional change. To the extent that civil war inhibits routine state activities, it is because of the kinds of rules and procedures that civil war *creates* – rules and procedures that remake the institutional fabric of the state itself. In other words, rather than constituting the "wrong kind" of war for building states, as scholars of state formation have suggested, civil war instead often builds the "wrong kind" of state institutions. To the extent that such institutional formations survive into times of peace, they constitute a powerful legacy of counterinsurgency.[32]

### THE LIMITS OF EXISTING APPROACHES

Though various strands of social science literature address the effects of civil war on state development, on the whole, they leave us with few accounts of *how* conflict processes distort state activities – that is, how they render state institutions ineffective in carrying out core functions like the extraction of tax revenue, the control over violence within society, and the administration of public goods and services. To the extent that existing analytical approaches offer insights on this question, they fall into four camps: (1) war and statebuilding; (2) conflict, predation, and corruption; (3) wartime orders and institutions; and (4) peacebuilding and postwar governance. I address each of these analytical approaches and this book's contributions below.

### War and Statebuilding

Prominent theories of state formation hold that war plays a critical role in building the state's administrative apparatus. Notably, Charles Tilly argues that national states in Western Europe were forged through the societal mobilization, territorial consolidation, and bureaucratic development required for fighting a foreign enemy. Compelled to accumulate

---

[31] Bernhard 2015; Levitsky and Murillo 2013.
[32] This book follows Wittenberg (2015: 375) in conceptualizing historical legacies as "a phenomenon that persisted from the past," which has "at least two historical periods" and is not fully "explainable with contemporaneous causal factors." Though contemporaneous conditions may contribute to the adaption and persistence of the undermining rules rooted in civil war, they developed through wartime processes of institutional change.

greater resources for war, rulers find the public more tolerant of higher taxation amid looming security threats.[33] The accepted level of state extraction thus shifts to a "new and higher equilibrium" permitting the construction of a more robust administrative apparatus that persists long term.[34] More recent scholarship tests the applicability of this war-centered model in Africa and Latin America, lending support to Tilly's account yet through a negative focus by illustrating how the absence of external warfare, or the availability of external wartime finance, has stunted domestic taxation.[35]

While there is a broad, positive relationship between interstate war and state development, the empirical findings with respect to *intra*state war and state capacity stand as a sharp contrast. While some scholars have found that internal contention can have a similar statebuilding effect,[36] cross-national analyses largely suggest that civil war diminishes state capacity. Timothy Besley and Torsten Persson, for example, find that countries engaged in internal conflict have a tax ratio approximately 7 percent lower than countries not engaged in civil war. Conversely, states involved in external wars have a 7 percent higher share.[37] Regional analyses of Latin America and the Middle East lend further support to these results and suggest that the negative effect of civil war on state capacity is magnified by conflict severity.[38]

Beyond the more heterogeneous findings on how internal conflict shapes state development, there is also less clarity on the mechanisms driving outcomes, particularly when it comes to the state "weakening" effect of civil war. One potential explanation posits that civil wars are often more limited in scope and thus fail to mobilize society in the same way as interstate war.[39] With more circumscribed threats and greater social and territorial fragmentation, rulers cannot create the same "protection rackets" to accrue resources for statebuilding.[40] Another explanation holds that internal rivals reduce the bargaining power of rulers, lowering investments in fiscal and administrative capacity. High levels of unpredictability and shifting loyalties in conflict prompt leaders to discount the future, with adverse effects for long-term statebuilding.[41]

---

[33] Rasler and Thompson 1985.    [34] Thies 2005: 454.
[35] Herbst 1990; Centeno 2002; Rasler and Thompson 2017.
[36] Flores-Macías 2018: 2–3; Rodríguez-Franco 2016; Slater 2010; Stanley 1996.
[37] Besley and Persson 2008.    [38] Thies 2010; Thies 2005, 2006; and Lu and Thies 2013.
[39] See Centeno 2002; Herbst 2000.    [40] Tilly 1985.    [41] Collier 1999: 8.

Overall, the explanations for why civil war hinders state development adopt the same macro-structural focus as studies of interstate war, centering on processes of institutional weakening due to divided loyalties and barriers to public investment. However, they largely neglect the kind of in-depth, institution-level analysis necessary to understand what occurs within the machinery of the central state amid internal armed conflict.[42] By focusing on specific institutional procedures, this book seeks to capture the inner workings of and changes within the counterinsurgent state in a more precise and fine-grained manner.

### Civil War, Predation, and Corruption

In contrast to the statebuilding literature, scholarship on the political economy of conflict recognizes how civil war creates alternative orders characterized by corruption and criminality. Rather than represent "the breakdown of a particular system," conflict is conceptualized as "a way of creating an alternative system of profit, power, and even protection."[43] Intrastate conflict builds economies characterized by pillage, protection money, and illicit commerce.[44] Here, the perversion of the postwar state is a product of the predatory practices bred during armed conflict.

The view of war economies as generating alternative institutional orders can be traced to a broader turn from economic grievance to economic opportunity as the key driver of conflict.[45] This view portrays rebellion as a distinctive form of organized crime aimed at looting resource rents on a continuing basis to form a viable armed organization.[46] This predatory behavior contributes to a host of private actors "doing well out of war."[47] As insurgent looting generates violence and unpredictability, both governments and ordinary individuals discount the future, intensifying criminal practices for personal gain. And while existing research mostly focuses on insurgent-led criminal activities, key studies have developed concepts like the *"shadow state"*[48] and "criminalization of the state"[49] to describe the nexus of formal state authority and private power brokers that prompt or prolong conflict. The informalization of economic arrangements within conflict generates "a

---

[42] For an example of a fine-grained institutional approach to statebuilding, see Matsuzaki 2019.

[43] Keen 1998: 11.

[44] Ibid., 15; see also, Kaldor 1999; Nordstrom 2004; Ballentine and Sherman 2003.

[45] Collier and Hoeffler 2004.     [46] Collier 2000.     [47] Collier 1999.

[48] Reno 1995, 2000a.     [49] Bayart et al. 1999.

patchwork of appropriated competencies and vested interests" at the level of state institutions as well.[50]

While scholarship on the political economy of conflict has usefully identified the incentives for institutional creation and/or transformation in civil war, it exhibits two important shortcomings. First, it focuses primarily on the economic agendas tied to conflict onset and duration, rather than aftermath, revealing far less about whether and how the criminal-state structures bred in conflict evolve once the fighting ends.[51] Indeed, there is reason to believe that wartime criminal practices have an important effect on the postwar landscape. Postwar criminality is intimately tied to conflict-era structures, "exploiting and building on wartime informal trade channels and networks."[52] Corrupt activities tied to militarization often persist even after transition, as the political, military, and business elites "who have extended domains of personal control during war [...] find that the stability of peace allows them better profits."[53] Moreover, the "formal institutional engineering" of international peacebuilding interventions often empowers domestic elites to co-opt state institutions for their own personal benefit.[54] The survival of wartime predation in many postwar contexts thus suggests a more generalized pattern worth theorizing.

Second, existing empirical accounts do little to draw out the precise effects of conflict dynamics on state institutions and development. To the extent that they address the wartime "weakening" of the state, they hinge on a normative view that corruption necessarily weakens state institutions – an assumption that has been challenged by research on how institutionalized graft can bolster routine state activities.[55] Even a more rigorous account of how armed conflict foments corruption thus falls short in explaining postwar state ineffectiveness. To answer this question, we must understand precisely how the predatory institutional arrangements that emerge in conflict come to structure state outcomes.

## Wartime Orders and Institutions

Another research agenda related to wartime institutions has coalesced around the topic of rebel and paramilitary governance. Under this

[50] Schlichte 2003: 40.
[51] For some insights on this question, see Kurtenbach and Rettberg 2018; Cheng and Zaum 2011.
[52] Andreas 2008: 118.      [53] Nordstrom 2004: 201.      [54] Barma 2017.
[55] Darden 2008: 35; Engvall 2017.

approach, the relationship between civil war and weak state performance might be seen as a function of armed actor decisions to build durable local institutions and their interactions with the civilians they seek to govern. As the conditions of civil war fragment territories and populations, insurgent groups may develop "effective and legitimate governance systems."[56] In addition to generating new understandings of community and identity,[57] conflict dynamics spur institutional innovations to regulate local behavior. Through this lens, civil war does not have a uniform effect on institutional development; instead, the dynamic and endogenous processes related to controlling territory and eliciting civilian collaboration can shape local orders in diverse ways.[58] Approaches to wartime governance thus move us away from the presumption that civil war has a singular impact on political development. Instead, conflict contexts hold myriad possibilities when it comes to local institutional development.

Despite this critical insight, the literature on local order in conflict falls short in other ways. First, it focuses disproportionately on the rebel side of the wartime equation, failing to account for institutional creation and change on the part of state actors. Some insights on this question have been derived from studies of postwar Guatemala; Regina Bateson, for example, finds that where wartime violence was most intense, communities are more likely to engage in collective vigilantism because of the persistence of local civil defense patrols.[59] Overall, however, wartime state institutions have remained on the margins relative to research on rebel governance and the co-production of order by state and insurgent forces.[60] Additionally, this scholarship tends to privilege local structures and fails to account for institutional change within the machinery of the central state. The state apparatus is comprised of a host of rules and procedures that may be refashioned amid conflict. Capturing such processes is critical to understanding how conflict dynamics shape longer-term state development.

## Peacebuilding and Postwar Governance

Finally, insights on the lasting effects of civil war on postwar institutions also emerge from research on peacebuilding and postwar governance, which increasingly recognizes how peace and postwar reconstruction

---

[56] Arjona et al. 2015: 3.    [57] Bergholz 2016.    [58] Arjona 2014; Ch et al. 2018.
[59] Bateson 2013.    [60] Staniland 2012, 2021.

serve as sites of institutional continuity and allow wartime actors to secure their power and prerogatives within the new political environment.

Though conceptualizations of peacebuilding vary,[61] early approaches were unified by a central focus on the transition from a state of armed hostilities and conflict to one marked by the absence of mass killing and direct violence between military adversaries. Though early scholarly and international policy approaches focused on more immediate political, economic, and institutional measures to bring an end to violent conflict,[62] researchers and practitioners have increasingly turned to the "positive" dimensions of building peace – measures to promote "the elimination of the root causes of conflict so that actors no longer have the motive to use violence to settle their differences."[63] These measures too presuppose sweeping transformations to improve governance, address inequality, and enhance political participation and representation. Over time, contemporary international peacebuilding missions have thus assumed a more "transformative approach," which places "crafting the administrative and governance institutions to underpin lasting peace" at the center of postwar reconstruction.[64]

Peacebuilding experiences in practice, however, belie these visions of wide-ranging transformation. Instead, domestic and international peacebuilding initiatives, more often than not, produce little substantive progress toward eliminating the perverse institutional arrangements and predatory activities that characterize wartime environments, even when they do put a definitive end to the fighting. In a range of post-conflict contexts, scholars find that peacebuilding agendas often atrophy following the achievement of shorter-term procedural gains such as combatant demobilization, the resumption of civilian leadership, initial free and fair elections, and the instantiation of market reforms.[65]

Rather than constitute a "critical juncture" or dramatic break with the wartime past,[66] researchers increasingly posit that the peacebuilding moment may instead allow for the reconsolidation of previous political and economic alignments and the entrenchment of the old institutional order. Just as democratic processes can preserve "authoritarian enclaves,"[67] peacebuilding can shore up wartime institutions in numerous ways.

---

[61] See Barnett et al. 2007.
[62] For influential studies about overcoming the conflict trap, see Collier et al. 2003; Walter 2002, 2015; Doyle and Sambanis 2006; Hartzell and Hoddie 2007; Call 2012.
[63] Barnett et al. 2007.      [64] Barma 2017: 13–14.
[65] See, for example, Barnett et al. 2007; Paris 2004.      [66] Bull 2014: 119.
[67] González 2020.

Oft-overlooked local actors with a vested interest in the wartime status quo distort or co-opt peacebuilding agendas through the manipulation of international interventions.[68] Further, the failure to understand domestic power dynamics often prompt international peacebuilding missions to empower predatory political and social blocs seeking to cement their power via postwar reforms and institutions.

In contexts ranging from Central America to sub-Saharan Africa to Southeast Asia, powerful public and private sector actors use peacetime institutions to stymie the transformations sought through peacebuilding programs and further entrench their long-standing privileges. For example, through an in-depth examination of El Salvador's "captured peace," Christine Wade illustrates how the incumbent Nationalist Republican Alliance (ARENA) wielded its political advantage to stall peacebuilding reforms and safeguard its economic interests.[69] Similarly, through an analysis of the Democratic Republic of Congo, Milli Lake demonstrates how postwar legal institutions, far from reducing uncertainty and bolstering the rule of law, provided wartime elites new avenues to advance their political, economic, and military agendas, thereby securing their grip on power[70] – dynamics similar to what Naazneen Barma observes through a comparative analysis of Afghanistan, Cambodia, and East Timor. As Barma writes, "[T]he political landscape in contemporary post-conflict states is populated by elites who are attempting to solve the practical puzzle of protecting and expanding their own power bases. ... The post-conflict context has been mistakenly inferred to resemble an institutional vacuum. The reality is that the political trajectory of the past, including the conflict itself, is enormously significant for what transpires next."[71] While recognizing postwar environments as sites of continuity, such approaches to peacebuilding fall short of explicating precisely *how* conflict dynamics shape what transpires next – the process by which wartime institutional developments shape the postwar landscape.

## CONTRIBUTIONS

This book is unique in elucidating how conflict dynamics shape state institutions and why wartime institutional transformations persist and continue to distort political and economic development despite peace and democratic transition. In doing so, it contributes to several scholarly

---

[68] See, for example, Barma 2017; Lake 2017, 2022; Wade 2016; Autesserre 2014.
[69] Wade 2016; see also, Rettberg 2007.     [70] Lake 2017.     [71] Barma 2017: 52.

and policy conversations, including debates on war and state formation; state "weakness" more generally; and the legacies of conflict, peacebuilding, and postwar reconstruction.

First, at its core, this book rethinks conventional approaches to war and state formation. Rather than a question of whether conflict "builds" or "destroys" state capacity, I instead illuminate precisely how wartime dynamics reshape state institutions and elucidate the key factor that accounts for the subversion of the state amid civil war: the structure of the counterinsurgent coalition. Rather than take for granted how conflict affects state institutions – whether it prompts heightened extraction that builds the state apparatus or inhibits investment and prompts institutional erosion – this book unpacks the mechanisms of wartime institutional innovation. By focusing on specific institutional procedures, it captures the inner workings of and changes within the counterinsurgent state – the "how" of wartime statebuilding – in a more precise and fine-grained manner.

In unpacking the black box of wartime institutional change, the book also offers new conceptual tools for evaluating the state, a second key contribution. In examining the effects of civil war on state development, it introduces the concept of *undermining* rules to capture how wartime institutional innovations shape routine state activities like revenue extraction, security provision, and other administrative tasks. This conceptual framework pushes beyond the reductionist approach found within conventional understandings of state "weakness" – the state's inability to perform the tasks expected of it. This book illustrates that the failure of state actors and organizations to implement and enforce routine policy decisions does not necessarily signal their *inability* to do so.[72] Instead, what often looks like state weakness – widespread insecurity, a fragile rule of law, and deficiencies in the provision of basic goods and services – are actually manifestations of alternative logics guiding state activities. Rather than state "weakness" or "absence," such outcomes reflect the highly durable reconfiguration of state power to achieve alternative ends associated with predation or criminality.

In training our focus on these distinct state logics, this book also shifts the conversation on state capacity from a dominant focus on territorial reach and control back to institutions – the rules and procedures governing state activity. As state weakness and/or strength have become central variables in the study of politics, scholars have come to examine

---

[72] Holland 2017; for more on institutional weakness, see Brinks et al. 2019.

state authority in spatial terms[73] – its presence throughout territory – as opposed to how state institutions structure social, political, and economic life.[74] While recognizing the importance of evaluating the state's reach, this study centers the latter dimension, positing that *how* the state operates cannot simply be inferred from whether and where it is or is not present. Illuminating the institutional logics underlying the state's exercise of power is critical. On the conceptual front, this book thus reimagines prevailing analytical categories used to evaluate state activity and develops a new framework for analyzing the complex and powerful logics that underlie state (mal)functioning in many conflict and post-conflict contexts.

Finally, this book contributes to scholarly and policy debates on peacebuilding and post-conflict reconstruction by illuminating how wartime institutional innovations persist and outlast governance reforms during peace and transition. The book conceives of postwar peacebuilding as a fluid and often-fraught temporal process comprised of critical decision-making moments, yet, one that does not inevitably represent a wholesale break with the past.[75] However, in focusing on the postwar moment as a struggle between the forces of institutional continuity and change, this study goes even further, seeking to understand precisely how wartime dynamics and processes structure the postwar possibilities for institutional transformation or survival. In other words, this book illustrates how the contours of the postwar landscape are inextricably intertwined with wartime institutional transformations.[76] It also contributes a new understanding for why peace can serve as a site of institutional stability by examining how counterinsurgent elites forge a broader coalition of political officials, business leaders, and criminal operatives and co-opt new peacetime political and economic spaces to sustain the wartime rules of the game. Even if elite accommodation is a precondition of successful counterinsurgency,[77] it can be ruinous for long-term political development.

Relatedly, this book also demonstrates that post-conflict statebuilding is about much more than "the state." By uncovering the ways in which

---

[73] Herbst 2000; Mann 1984; O'Donnell 1993; Soifer 2015.
[74] Melissa Lee very usefully refers to this distinction as that between state institutionalization (strength of administrative institutions) and state consolidation (evenness over territory). See Lee 2020: 19–21.
[75] Barma 2017; Call 2012.
[76] This claim echoes Huang's (2016) approach to postwar democratization.
[77] Hazelton 2021.

counterinsurgent actors knit together a broader alliance with a stake in the wartime institutional landscape, the book demonstrates how scholars and policymakers must widen their analytical lens in devising post-conflict solutions. Approaches to postwar statebuilding must also integrate non-state economic and social spheres and capture the diverse stakeholders that sustain wartime predation and criminality in times of peace. In illustrating this approach within postwar Central America, the book provides a blueprint for reimagining the problems of the postwar landscape and for crafting policies to *undo* the wartime institutional arrangements that continue to distort state development.

## WHY CENTRAL AMERICA?

This book treats armed conflict as a particular site of institutional change, which can have long-lasting legacies for state development. It examines this phenomenon through the wartime evolution and subsequent persistence of alternative rules and procedures that have undermined state institutions in the longer term. To do so, it focuses on a particular regional context that remains understudied within conflict scholarship in political science, Central America, and draws on in-depth institution-level analysis from war to peace.

While empirical studies have focused on Central America to derive and test theories on the causes of civil war and political violence,[78] the region has also become a valuable setting to examine the broader consequences of conflict.[79] There is good reason to look to the countries of Central America[80] to assess what civil war leaves behind in the medium- and the long term. At the height of the Cold War, Central America served as a staging ground for US-backed anti-communist campaigns, which sparked civil wars in Guatemala, El Salvador, and Nicaragua to root out insurgent groups. As asymmetric conflicts in which "the rebels [privileged] small, lightly armed bands operating in rural areas," the Central American armed conflicts are emblematic of the types of irregular civil wars most

---

[78] Lehoucq 2012; Sullivan 2012; Brockett 2005; Wood 2003.
[79] Bateson 2013; Thies 2005.
[80] Following others and for the purposes of empirical study, I consider Central America as consisting of Guatemala, El Salvador, Honduras, Nicaragua, and Costa Rica. I exclude Belize, a former British colony, and Panama, which seceded from Colombia, because they were not part of the Kingdom of Guatemala ruled by Spain from the sixteenth century until independence in 1821. They thus reflect distinct historical and cultural features.

prevalent during the second half of the twentieth century,[81] allowing me to build theoretical propositions that are more likely to generalize.

In addition, the region's conflicts came to a close through negotiated settlements in the early and mid-1990s, securing formal peace that has persisted for decades. In avoiding the "conflict trap," Central America provides a unique opportunity to assess how wartime institutional changes survive even after conflict has ceased. Though the problem of civil war is very often a problem of "repeat civil war,"[82] conflict relapse is not the only possibility for war-torn states and societies. In countries that manage to clear the initial postwar hurdles to maintaining political stability, it is critical to understand why and how wartime practices and structures continue to shape political, economic, and social development in the longer term. Given the regional endurance of formal peace, Central America provides a fruitful context to probe the enduring effects of civil war on governance, and, in turn, overcome the short-term focus of most peacebuilding scholarship.[83]

Though Central America has defied the odds by overcoming the conflict trap, the region has also become emblematic of the unfulfilled promises that have characterized enduring peace. Today the countries of Central America are among the most violent, poor, and unequal in the world. In 2015, the region featured prominently within the list of countries with the highest intentional homicide rates globally, with El Salvador and Honduras occupying the first and second spots and Guatemala ranking ninth.[84] According to data from the Latin American Public Opinion Project (LAPOP), in nearly every Central American country, the proportion of the population that has been victimized by crime exceeds the global average, with the majority of citizens seeing no point in even reporting crime.[85]

Central America's three postwar countries also face abysmal levels of human development. According to 2014 data from the Economic Commission for Latin America and the Caribbean (CEPAL), roughly 68 percent of Guatemalans, 58 percent of Nicaraguans, and 41 percent of Salvadorans live in poverty. In Guatemala, nearly half of children

---

[81] Kalyvas and Balcells 2010: 418; Kalyvas 2006: 66–68.     [82] Walter 2015: 1242.
[83] See Barma 2017: 17–22.
[84] These data are from the UN Office on Drugs and Crime (UNODC) 2016, which is available at https://dataunodc.un.org/crime/intentional-homicide-victims.
[85] Cohen et al. 2017: 72–73; see also, Yashar (2018) for an in-depth examination of law and order institutions and violence in Central America.

under five are malnourished.[86] Even as the rest of Latin America reaped the benefits of a major commodities boom in the 2000s, economic growth remained stagnant in Central America, averaging just over 2 percent between 2002 and 2009.[87] A combination of violence-related and economic factors have driven Central Americans – particularly from Guatemala, El Salvador, Honduras, and more recently Nicaragua – to migrate north to seek safety and economic opportunity. According to some estimates, one in every five native-born Salvadorans now lives in the United States.[88]

A simplistic explanation of these adverse social and economic outcomes in the postwar period is weak state capacity.[89] In this view, high homicide and crime victimization rates are driven by the inability of state security forces to control extralegal violence and ensure justice when the law is violated. Similarly, underdevelopment results from the laggard provision of healthcare, education, and infrastructure – challenges exacerbated by the state's inability to extract tax revenue from the population. Indeed, a look at the conventional (if blunt) outcome- and survey-based measures of state capacity would characterize Central America's postwar states as among the most ineffective in the world. Table 1.1 provides a snapshot of these indicators for Guatemala, El Salvador, and Nicaragua fifteen years following their respective peace agreements. Even a decade and a half after peace implementation, Guatemala and El Salvador had among the lowest levels of tax revenue as a share of GDP globally. All three countries exhibited sub-par levels of political capacity relative to countries with similar populations and resources. Further, aggregate indicators for state fragility remain very high, while all three countries found themselves in the bottom-third globally with respect to perceived government effectiveness and confidence in the rule of law.

But in simply attributing present-day woes to state weakness, prevailing analyses miss a related, but separate phenomenon that characterizes contemporary Central America: undermining institutional logics. State institutions in the region do not merely lack the ability to carry out routine activities, but they are governed by alternative rules and procedures that have remade the state's institutional fabric and distorted state functions. Rather than a feature of specific governments, undermining rules in Central America transcend political party and ideology, instead

---

[86] From UNICEF data on malnutrition in children, which is available at https://data.unicef .org/topic/nutrition/malnutrition/.
[87] Casas-Zamora 2011: 9.      [88] Menjívar and Gómez Cervantes 2018.
[89] See Casas-Zamora 2011; Yashar 2018; Shifter 2012.

TABLE I.I *Measures of state capacity in Central America (15 years after conflict)*

| Country | Taxes as share of GDP (all percentages for 2008)[*] | Relative political capacity[**] | Fragile states index[***] (most fragile = 120) | Government effectiveness (percentile rank)[****] | Rule of law (percentile rank)[****] |
|---|---|---|---|---|---|
| Guatemala (2011) | 11.6 | 0.660 | 80.1 | 28.0 | 14.6 |
| El Salvador (2006) | 14.6 | 0.728 | 76.1 | 49.3 | 30.6 |
| Nicaragua (2006) | 21.7 | 0.826 | 82.4 | 20.5 | 25.3 |

[*] Casas-Zamora, Kevin. 2011. *The Travails of Development and Democratic Governance in Central America.* Policy Paper Number 28. Washington, DC: Brookings Institution.

[**] Marina Arbetman-Rabinowitz et al. 2011. "Replication data for Relative Political Capacity Dataset" https://hdl.handle.net/1902.1/16845. Harvard Dataverse, v4. Relative political capacity measures a state's actual ability to extract resources from its population relative to its predicted level of extraction given the level of economic development.

[***] The Fund for Peace. *Fragile States Index.* Accessed January 2019. Available at http://fundforpeace.org/fsi/.

[****] World Bank. Worldwide Governance Indicators. 19 October 2016. Available at https://data.worldbank.org/data-catalog/worldwide-governance-indicators.

constituting a highly stable, yet pernicious element of governance in the region. Viewing the region's primary challenge as one of chronic state "weakness" tells only a partial story; state institutions in Central America are not merely incapable of carrying out core activities, but they consist of rules and procedures that abide by different logics entirely – logics that systematically undermine extractive, coercive, and administrative functions.

Examples of these perverse institutional arrangements within the post-conflict period abound. With the late 2006 creation of Guatemala's anti-impunity commission, the CICIG, to investigate the "illicit security forces and clandestine organizations" leftover from the war, numerous state-based criminal structures were uncovered, including the customs fraud network *La Línea* described previously. The CICIG and its Guatemalan counterparts also revealed a series of illicit schemes within the Guatemalan Social Security Institute (IGSS) to negotiate multi-million-dollar state contracts with pharmaceutical companies for defective drugs in exchange for kickbacks to government officials.[90] In Honduras, local investigators exposed a similar scheme, which funneled millions in social security funds to the campaign efforts of the ruling National Party (PN). The case represents just one in a series of "kleptocratic networks" that have flourished within the Honduran state – a political setting in which predation does not reflect the malfunctioning of the state institutions but is instead the "intentional operating system" that drives state institutions.[91]

In Guatemala, other investigations pursued criminal networks within the peacetime National Civilian Police (PNC), including death squads responsible for the extrajudicial executions of prisoners in the mid-2000s. Similar extralegal activities have been uncovered within El Salvador's security forces. As in Guatemala, small, elite groups of police officers operating in the shadows carry out sweeps and extrajudicial executions of suspected gang members, who have been blamed for the staggering level of homicidal violence in the country.[92] Groups within both countries' police forces have also been involved in the theft and resale of drug shipments and other fraudulent activities.[93] Meanwhile, in Nicaragua, analysts have highlighted long-standing patterns among a group of judges of reducing sentences and authorizing releases for convicted drug traffickers.[94]

---

[90] García 2016.   [91] Chayes 2017: 2.
[92] Silva Ávalos 2014; Avelar and Martínez d'Aubuisson 2017.
[93] Ibid.; see also, CICIG 2013, 2015.   [94] Meléndez and Orozco 2013.

Across the region, undermining rules have become part of the institutional fabric of the state, distorting the extraction of tax revenue, the control of violence, and the provision of basic goods and services like justice, security, and healthcare. In light of this broader pattern, the challenge for scholars of Central American politics is not simply to explain why state institutions in the region are ineffective, but what accounts for the alternative logics that have come to define them.

Importantly, in tackling this question, this book pushes back against recent approaches to Central America that have focused on the more contemporary drivers of the region's social, political, and economic realities today. For example, leading scholarship on postwar criminal violence in Central America by experts like Deborah Yashar look to the geography of illicit economies, particularly zones of criminal competition amid a generalized environment of state co-optation, in explaining variation in regional homicide levels. As Yashar argues, "civil war transition/legacy is too specific a variable to explain the geographic scope of violence in the Americas, which extends beyond civil war cases (and is not duplicated in all post-civil war cases)."[95] Likewise, Aaron Schneider's influential work on state-building and taxation in contemporary Central America focuses on the cohesiveness of transnational elites in the postwar period, rather than the legacies of wartime institutional transformations.[96] While recognizing that the contemporary factors laid out in these studies are critical for understanding outcomes like violence and taxation, this book also contends that the history of civil war must be brought back into the conversation, particularly when considering the nature of state institutions and authority. Turning to the height of the region's armed conflicts reveals that the perverse and predatory logics that guide state activity today have remarkably deep roots, as the coming chapters will illustrate.

## EMPIRICAL APPROACH

This book traces the wartime origins of the undermining rules in Central America by examining how civil war dynamics shaped processes of institutional evolution. While not all the state-based criminal structures that have been uncovered stem directly from conflict, wartime institutional

---

[95] Yashar 2018: 32; see Cruz (2011) for a distinct approach, which does focus on civil war legacies.

[96] Importantly, at several points Schneider (2012) does address how armed conflict structured transnational elites, but this is treated more as an antecedent condition.

changes played a critical role in "making" the state according to the undermining logics present today. To explain this phenomenon, I adopt a comparative institutional approach, which looks across state sectors and leverages unique archival and interview data. Here, I describe the methodology, case selection, and data in greater detail.

## Methodology

This theory-building study departs from conventional correlational analyses, which attempt to pin down the causal effects of armed conflict on state capacity with more limited attention to fully illustrating the underlying mechanisms. To analyze how civil war dynamics shape state development, this project utilizes process tracing at the level of specific state institutions or sectors. Process tracing refers to "the analysis of evidence on processes, sequences, and conjunctures of events within a case for the purposes of either developing or testing hypotheses about causal mechanisms."[97] This project focuses primarily on the task of theory development. Given the dearth of empirical efforts to identify the underlying mechanisms, my objective is to uncover the "intensive"[98] causal process linking civil war and postwar state development to build broader theoretical propositions that can be tested in other contexts. This approach allows me to "[capture] causal mechanisms in action"[99] – to identify the building blocks of wartime institutional change and how their sequencing produces specific institutional outcomes.

Because the mechanisms linking civil war and postwar state "weakness" remain underexplored within conflict scholarship, I primarily rely on "inductive discovery" to "find new causal factors to make sense of puzzling outcomes."[100] In this sense, my analysis "traces the broad history at a fine-grained level and pulls out for special examination potential causal factors" that seem consistent across three diverse cases that all exhibit a common outcome (undermining rules).[101] At the same time, Chapter 3 also engages in a more deductive logic of inquiry, utilizing process tracing, specifically a series of hoop tests,[102] to evaluate key alternative explanations for why and how civil war produces undermining rules.

[97] Bennett and Checkel 2015: 7–8.
[98] "Intensive" causal processes focus on "the transformative sequences of events that originate after the initial cause and yield the effect of interest"; see Falleti 2016: 5.
[99] Bennett and Checkel 2015: 9.    [100] Mahoney 2015: 217.    [101] Ibid., 215.
[102] According to Mahoney (2015: 207), hoop tests "propose that a given piece of evidence from a case should be present for a hypothesis to be true. Failing a hoop test counts

Elaborating the causal process linking civil war and state development is a particularly worthy goal because it also addresses a broader deficiency within conflict research: the emphasis on "suggestive correlations [...] without understanding the casual processes that underpin associations."[103] Within conflict research, process tracing is critical for clarifying plausible causal pathways and the complex interactions between causal mechanisms. In Lyall's words, "without moving beyond correlation, we are left blind about the processes and dynamics that drive these relationships, impoverishing both our theories and our ability to contribute to policy debates."[104] By retraining our analytic lens on *how* wartime institutional evolution unfolds, this book aims to enrich our understanding of the dynamics and processes that drive the relationship between conflict and an important political phenomenon, state development.

Further, this project conceptualizes the object of analysis in a distinct fashion. Rather than drawing on typical blunt measures of state capacity, (i.e., tax revenue as share of GDP), which have been roundly criticized,[105] my approach takes specific institutional logics and the processes through which they develop as its primary focus. It thus develops a novel conceptualization of the *kinds* of wartime rules and procedures that might emerge within state institutions and seeks to uncover how those types of institutional arrangements take root.

To do this, I utilize comparative case study analysis, focusing on institutional sectors as my comparative cases. By moving beneath the national level and zeroing in on specific realms of state activity, this research heeds calls within the social sciences to move away from notions of the state as "a static, timeless territorial 'container' that encloses economic and political processes" and instead disaggregate its institutional activities and functions.[106] Further, in comparing processes of institutional development, this study follows recent work urging scholars to rethink

---

heavily against a hypothesis." See Chapter 3 for this study's use of hoop tests to assess alternative explanations for the development of undermining rules in the Guatemalan and Nicaraguan cases, including war-making strategy, ideology, and foreign support.

[103] Lyall 2015: 186.     [104] Ibid., 189.

[105] See Dargent et al. 2017; Bersch et al. 2017; Hendrix 2010; Soifer and vom Hau 2008; Centeno et al. 2017; Soifer and Vieira 2019.

[106] Brenner et al. 2003: 2; see also, Ferguson and Gupta 2002; Giraudy et al. 2019; Thelen 2004, 2014.

conventional ideas of what ought to be compared within the study of politics.[107] While most disciplinary studies define cases according to their values on the outcome of interest, valuable insights about the social and political world can also be derived by examining variation in "political processes (how things happen) [and] practices (what people do)."[108] This project embraces this more expansive approach to comparison by looking across institutional processes to understand how civil war produces distinct institutional logics.

## Case Selection

Within the Central American context, I analyze three institution-level cases: the customs administration and policing institutions in Guatemala and land tenure in Nicaragua. Each of these cases demonstrates the wartime emergence of alternative rules of the game that have similarly undermined state performance. These specific cases were selected for several reasons. First, they each reflect distinct domains of state activity (extractive, coercive, and administrative), allowing me to assess the common building blocks that characterize processes of state institutional change broadly. Second, by comparing the Guatemalan and Nicaraguan contexts, I leverage variation on core political and structural factors, which could plausibly shape processes of institutional development in different ways. Specifically, the two countries differ widely in terms of civil war antecedents, regime ideologies, war-making strategies, and the nature of foreign support. The comparison thus provides a critical opportunity to explore why we observe the emergence of similar kinds of institutional logics amid such stark differences. Finally, there are remarkable wartime archival resources that allow me to examine in detail processes of institutional change – often difficult to observe amid the shadows of war – within these sectors.

My first case analyzes the wartime institutionalization of alternative rules for capturing customs revenues in Guatemala, which systematically undermined the state's extractive performance. The structure that devised and enforced these rules, known as the Moreno Network, was forged by an elite clique of military intelligence officers, who were granted extraordinary discretion while infiltrating the state apparatus to wage counterinsurgency in the 1970s and 1980s. Insulated from broader state and

---

[107] See Simmons and Smith 2017; Simmons et al. 2018.   [108] Simmons et al. 2018: 1.

military structures, they crafted a series of new rules for siphoning off customs duties, which were enforced through violent and nonviolent forms of coercion. By forging a broader coalition of importers, security officials, and politicians, the Moreno Network ensured the survival of the predatory customs procedures even after Guatemala's transition to civilian rule.

The second case traces the emergence and consolidation of another series of undermining rules developed in the context of the Guatemalan armed conflict: those governing extrajudicial killing. In the early 1970s, the escalation of counterinsurgency led to the enhanced autonomy and special-ization of several elite investigative units within the National Police (PN). Through the fusion of these forces and privatized death squads, new insti-tutional procedures to eliminate "undesirables" through extralegal means developed and came to distort public security provision in the longer-term.

The third case turns to the Sandinista-led state in Nicaragua. It explains the introduction of undermining rules within the agrarian reform program as the rebel threat escalated and land redistribution became a tool of counterinsurgency. By 1983, the growing territorial presence of the Contra insurgency led to a dramatic reorientation of the Sandinista's initially orthodox agrarian policies, prompting much greater individual and provisional titling. These practices crystallized into rules and proced-ures that undermined the state's ability to regulate land ownership and fomented conflict and corruption.

This book focuses on three cases of undermining rules, above all, because it seeks to identify the mechanisms underlying the relationship between civil war and "weak" states. While scholars have empirically examined when and how internal conflict "makes" the state,[109] a fine-grained and systematic analysis of when and how civil war "breaks" the state is also in order, given the well-established cross-national findings discussed earlier. That analysis is the central task of this book. However, in recognizing these divergent institutional trajectories in civil war, the Conclusion probes the conditions under which conflict generates reinforcing, rather than undermining, rules through a series of brief case illustrations from Nicaragua's and Colombia's civil war contexts. In so doing, I highlight the importance of counterinsurgent coalitions in struc-turing wartime state development processes and demonstrate how coali-tional configurations can shift across time even amid conflict.

---

[109] See, most notably, Slater 2010.

## Data

This book employs fine-grained data collected from state and private archives and elite interviews conducted during a combined twenty months of fieldwork in Guatemala and Nicaragua.[110] My original archival research yielded unique primary documentation that sheds light on wartime institutional processes that have long remained in the shadows. In both Guatemala and Nicaragua, the wartime developments chronicled in this book are *"un secreto a voces"* ["an open secret"], but have too often lacked empirical substantiation. By delving into an array of state and non-state archives from the conflict periods, I illuminate precisely how civil war dynamics in the two countries gave rise to contemporary structures that have been subject to much speculation, in addition to identifying a broader class of institutional logics that emerge in civil war. These data themselves thus constitute an important empirical contribution within the study of war and postwar Guatemala and Nicaragua.

Data collection for this project also follows the burgeoning research focus on conflict archives within political science. In recent years, conflict archives have become more widely utilized resources to examine central questions within the study of political violence. As Laia Balcells and Christopher Sullivan suggest, wartime archival documentation often offers better coverage of conflict events over space and time and greater subnational disaggregation, providing unique analytical opportunities.[111] Archives can also hold advantages over other forms of qualitative data. The archival record "may detail events, actions, and perceptions in real time, overcoming some of the challenges posed by retrospective accounts."[112] Moreover, archival data collection can allow scholars to mitigate some of the physical risks associated with interviews and participant observation in conflict zones and can facilitate greater transparency.[113]

Of course, qualitative archival research also faces important challenges. These include issues of access, selection bias, and internal validity.[114] In particular, administrative records, in the words of Diana Kim, "reflect profoundly human attempts to describe and judge the lives of others, which contain and condense the biases, mistakes, and hubris of

---

[110] See Appendix for full list of interviews and archival collections. Research in Guatemala took place from May to July 2014, June to July 2015, September to November 2016, and April to December 2017. In Nicaragua, fieldwork was completed from December 2016 to March 2017.
[111] Balcells and Sullivan 2018: 139.     [112] Schwartz and Straus 2018: 226.     [113] Ibid.
[114] Ibid.

the actors who wrote them."[115] And while archives are often seen as dusty documents to which the constraints of human subjects research do not apply, nearly every facet of the archival research process can impinge on ordinary lives.[116] Efforts to uncover and share sensitive information from historical archives must also weigh the potential harms to those directly named or discussed within them, as well as others who might be affected. Within my archival research for this project, I have remained attentive to these concerns and painstakingly evaluated each piece of archival information to assess potential harms.

While the political conditions and possibilities of archival access in both countries have deteriorated since the time of field research for this book,[117] Guatemala and Nicaragua both possess substantial archival records that detail institution-level dynamics during and after their respective conflict periods. In Guatemala, I conducted research in the General Archive of Central America (AGCA), the Historical Archive of the National Police (AHPN), and the archives of the Ministry of Finance and the court system (including the collection of over 17,000 pages of court files from the Moreno Network case). I also consulted private archival collections at the Center of Regional Investigations of Mesoamerica (CIRMA) and the Recovery of Historical Memory (REMHI) project, as well as publicly available and confidential records from the CICIG, the hybrid legal body that investigated high-level criminal structures in the country until its 2019 ouster. For the Nicaraguan case, I conducted research at the Historical Institute of Nicaragua and Central America (IHNCA), Stanford University's Hoover Institution, and within the archives of the Center for Investigation and Study of Agrarian Reform (CIERA), the research arm of the Ministry of Agricultural Development and Agrarian Reform (MIDINRA). In both contexts, I also draw on declassified US government cables found within the Digital National Security Archives.

To supplement and triangulate these archival data, I also carried out semi-structured elite interviews in both countries. Given the concerns of

---

[115] Kim 2020: 26–27.
[116] See Subotić 2021; Darnton 2022; Carusi and Jirotka 2009; Davenport 2010; Wisser and Blanco-Rivera 2016.
[117] For example, in August 2018, the long-time director of the Historical Archive of the National Police (AHPN) Gustavo Meoño was abruptly removed, and the repository of some 20 million documents was placed under government control. International and domestic civil society leaders billed the move as an attempt to restrict access to sensitive materials that might contribute to human rights trials. See NSA 2018.

selection bias inherent in archival sources, interviews with individuals knowledgeable about war and postwar institutional developments allow me to probe whether the historical archives – especially those produced by state organizations – omitted, altered, or misrepresented events and dynamics as they occurred. I utilized snowball sampling to recruit interviewees, drawing on over a decade of research and professional activities in Central America. In Guatemala, I conducted 72 interviews with former intelligence officers, Ministry of Finance personnel, tax and customs officials, prosecutors, economists, security experts, and business leaders. In Nicaragua, I conducted 11 interviews with former MIDINRA and military officials, journalists, and legal experts.[118]

## ORGANIZATION OF THE BOOK

This book is organized as follows. Chapter 2 presents a theory of wartime institutional change, which accounts for why civil war can be a particular site of institutional transformation, conceptualizes undermining rules, and elaborates the causal process through which undermining rules evolve amid conflict. The latter half of the chapter tackles the question of why wartime undermining rules persist within and beyond conflict, synthesizing and explaining the mechanisms through which the alternative institutional arrangements become self-enforcing and outlast peacebuilding and state reforms.

Part II of the book (Institutional Origins) examines the causal process underlying the introduction and evolution of the undermining rules empirically within my three Central American cases. Chapter 3 provides a history of Guatemala's and Nicaragua's highly divergent conflict dynamics, but also illustrates how similarly narrow and insulated counterinsurgent coalitions emerged. Chapter 4 traces the wartime emergence of undermining rules within Guatemala's customs apparatus by the Moreno Network. Chapter 5 demonstrates the introduction of similar institutional logics within Guatemala's wartime National Police (PN), which crystallized into new rules governing extrajudicial executions. Chapter 6 turns to the case of Nicaragua's land tenure institutions, analyzing the emergence of new land titling rules that stoked land insecurity and corruption.

---

[118] Per IRB research protocol, I conducted all interviews myself, and the names of interviewees are withheld to protect their safety and privacy. I omit information revealed in interviews that attributes illegal activities to specific individuals and is not corroborated by other sources.

Part III (Institutional Persistence) turns to the second question that animates this study: how the wartime rules persist and survive periods of peacebuilding and governance reform. Chapter 7 provides a brief history of Guatemala's and Nicaragua's peace process, illustrating how the circumstances of conflict settlement and the nature of subsequent reforms set the stage for institutional persistence in Guatemala's tax and security sectors and chronic instability in Nicaragua's land administration. Chapters 8, 9, and 10 examine the three institutional arenas from Part II respectively. The chapters illustrate the extent to which the counterinsurgent elite brought other sectoral interests into the fold to forge a broader distributional coalition. It also presents the nature of postwar reforms following peace settlement and evaluates the mechanisms of institutional persistence (or instability). By comparing across the three Central American cases, I find that the persistence of the undermining rules institutionalized during conflict is driven by the enduring political power of the wartime coalition underwriting them, including its ability to adapt to new extra-state political and economic spaces.

The book's conclusion explores how the theoretical propositions derived from my comparative analysis might travel to other contexts, including non-civil-war threat environments. It also revisits my theory's scope conditions and explores how and when divergent, state-reinforcing rules emerge in civil war. Finally, it outlines key implications for the study of the state and for postwar reform efforts aimed at strengthening governance and the rule of law.

# 2

# Theorizing Wartime Institutional Change and Survival

Though research has largely focused on the destructive effects of conflict on state institutions, civil war can, in fact, be a site of institutional innovation as well. Far from merely a context of lawlessness and disorder that erodes governance, a growing literature recognizes civil war as generative of distinct social, political, and economic institutions, as well as new identities and attitudes. Even when the previous order has been dismantled, "some form of order often emerges in war zones, where clear rules are enforced."[1] Indeed, civil war often leads to the production of alternative rules of the game, which can shape patterns of social cohesion,[2] violence,[3] illicit economic activity,[4] and democratization[5] even well after conflict has ceased. Understanding civil war as a site of institutional creation is important not only for explaining different conflict processes, but also for assessing what they leave behind.

This book seeks to reconcile the competing theoretical impulses related to civil war's destructive and generative tendencies through the lens of wartime institutional change. How does civil war shape state institutions and, in turn, state performance? Specifically, under what conditions might conflict foster rules and procedures that subvert core state activities? The book puts forward a new approach to wartime institutional change within the state apparatus to explicate the mechanisms linking armed conflict and the distortion of postwar state functions.

This chapter first develops a theory of wartime institutional change then explains how and why these changes persist within and beyond

---

[1] Arjona 2014: 1362.    [2] Gilligan et al. 2014.    [3] Bateson 2013; Trejo et al. 2018.
[4] Cheng 2018; Cheng and Zaum 2011.    [5] Huang 2016.

armed conflict. The first section examines why civil war constitutes a site of institutional change – that is, the characteristics of conflict that generate institutional ambiguity and are conducive to the evolution of new rules within the state apparatus. In the second section, I conceptualize the *kinds* of rules that emerge in conflict, focusing specifically on institutional logics that are either *undermining* (generating outcomes that diverge from a given state function) or *reinforcing* (generating outcomes that bolster a given state function). In the third section, I theorize the emergence of undermining rules by laying out how the wartime escalation of the insurgent threat empowers and insulates a narrow coalition of political-military elites, who then transform state institutions. The fourth section lays out a series of alternative explanations for the emergence of undermining rules during wartime, including state war-making strategies, ideology, and foreign support. The fifth section addresses the scope conditions under which we should expect to observe such processes of wartime institutional transformation.

The sixth section turns to the questions of why and how the undermining rules devised during civil war persist within and beyond it. To reproduce the new rules and render them self-enforcing, the narrow counterinsurgent elite must draw together a broader set of sectoral interests with a vested stake in the new institutional landscape; it must forge what I call a more expansive "distributional coalition." The ability of this distributional coalition to navigate, adapt to, and survive peacebuilding and state reforms explains why the undermining rules persist long term versus when they give way to chronic instability.

## CIVIL WAR AND INSTITUTIONAL CHANGE

This book not only brings the state into burgeoning conversations on the legacies of civil war but also seeks to unpack how counterinsurgency and militarization induce processes of institutional change that distort political development in the longer term. In this section, I explain why civil war constitutes a site of institutional malleability and facilitates the introduction and enforcement of new rules structuring state activities.

The book defines institutions as the "rules and procedures that structure social interactions by constraining and enabling actors' behavior."[6] This understanding captures both formal and informal rules and procedures.[7]

---

[6] Helmke and Levitsky 2006: 5.    [7] North 1990; Carey 2000.

*State* institutions, then, are the constellations of rules and procedures that comprise the different arenas of government activity. The book focuses specifically on the extraction of revenue, control over the means of violence, and the administration of basic goods and services.[8] Though states perform numerous routine functions, these three areas reflect analytically distinct domains and are most often cited in contemporary political science scholarship.[9]

The enforcement of the rules that comprise state institutions may occur through multiple mechanisms, among them coercion, norms, and voluntary or quasi-voluntary behavior.[10] Coercion induces compliance by leveraging the use (or threat) of punishment – violent or nonviolent – to reshape behavior. Here, the exercise of power alters the costs of engaging in behavior that violates the rules – or, alternatively, presupposes rewards for compliance with the rules.[11] But compliance may also have ideational foundations. Individuals abide by the rules because of shared beliefs about what constitutes normal, appropriate, or legitimate behavior.[12] Finally, compliance can be voluntary, rendering the rules self-enforcing because they reduce uncertainty and bring increasing returns.[13] As I illustrate below, wartime institutional innovations may initially be enforced through coercion, particularly because counterinsurgent actors possess heightened coercive capacities. Yet, the long-term survival of the wartime rules hinges on them becoming self-enforcing – a process I will lay out in the latter half of this chapter.

Even as scholars of political violence focus greater attention at the institutional level, there has been relatively little theoretical discussion of what it is about civil war that generates institutional change. The presumption is that civil war – as a struggle for political control – prompts

---

[8] Soifer 2015.

[9] Ibid.; Tilly 1975; Hanson and Sigman 2013. Admittedly, this conceptualization presupposes a normative understanding of what the state *should* do – what its objectives are and who it should serve. I adopt this approach not because of a firm belief that these functions reflect the ideals toward which state organizations should strive, but because analytically it is important to begin on the same terrain as contemporary scholarly and policy conversations. Indeed, as this book will illustrate, state actors often create new institutional arrangements that deviate wildly from these governance aims in the service of elite interests. While it is this book's key contention that such actions are often governed by highly structured and well-communicated rules, most often they are treated as pernicious deviations from some norm or ideal. The conceptual framework developed here is meant to challenge this notion, while also engaging contemporary debates on state capacity and governance on their own terms.

[10] Levi 1988: 48–55.    [11] Moe 2005.    [12] March and Olsen 2011.

[13] North 1990; Pierson 2000.

armed groups to build institutions to govern, and that wartime institutional design is driven by strategic calculations and objectives, group ideologies, interactions with the civilian population, and prewar structural features, among others. But why might state institutions be prone to change during civil war in the first place?

Here, I follow James Mahoney and Kathleen Thelen in attributing institutional change to "the 'gaps' or 'soft spots' between the rule and its interpretation" and to the levels of discretion potential change agents have in refashioning the rules.[14] These two dimensions go hand in hand. Where the rules are ambiguous, actors are often afforded greater latitude in refashioning them or redirecting them toward alternative objectives. But even where the rules are less ambiguous, discretionary practices may permit the grafting of new institutions onto old ones, which can eventually bring about change.[15]

This approach envisions institutions as distributive instruments and sees institutional evolution as "a contest among actors to establish rules which structure outcomes to those equilibria for them."[16] Institutions are "created to serve the interests of those with the bargaining power to devise new rules."[17] In other words, they are products of political coalitions and conflicts. As rules that pattern behavior, institutions have "unequal implications for resource allocation" and are thus always "fraught with tensions" and vulnerable to revision, rather than inherently "sticky."[18] "Ambiguities or 'gaps' that exist by design or emerge over time" between the rules and their enforcement are exploited by political coalitions with distinct interests and, depending on the balance of power, may lead to institutional transformation.[19]

There are three important features of civil war that prompt "gaps" in the rules structuring state activities and the exploitation of these gaps by competing political and/or military actors. They emerge from the understanding of civil war as a context of "dual or divided sovereignty."[20] Though levels of violence vary, all civil wars are characterized by "the effective breakdown of the monopoly of violence by way of armed internal challenge."[21] Very often, state leaders perceive (or construct) a heightened sense of threat and vulnerability, which may alter military approaches to combating the enemy. Relatedly, the contested boundaries of sovereignty provoke uncertainties about who is an ally and who is a rebel: "civil war

---

[14] Mahoney and Thelen 2010: 14, 21.    [15] Ibid., 20.    [16] Knight 1992: 126.
[17] North 1990: 16.    [18] Mahoney and Thelen 2010: 8.
[19] Streeck and Thelen 2005: 19    [20] Kalyvas 2006: 18.    [21] Ibid.

assimilates and makes undecidable brother and enemy, inside and outside ... the killing of what is most intimate is indistinguishable from the killing of what is most foreign."[22]

As a context of divided sovereignty, civil war is a moment particularly prone to institutional change, first, because it permits the suspension of existing rules to combat a threat often perceived as serious, if not existential. Though perceptions of threat vary, the condition of dual sovereignty often prompts a "state of emergency" or "state of exception" in which the actor claiming sovereignty transcends previously established rules in the name of preserving the polity, thereby generating an institutional gray zone.[23] As Giorgio Agamben writes, "One of the paradoxes of the state of exception lies in the fact that in the state of exception, it is impossible to distinguish transgression of the law from execution of the law, such that what violates a rule and what conforms to it coincide without any remainder."[24] Indeed, the suspension of the rules in civil war, which occurs in a *de jure* sense through frequent wartime government declarations of states of emergency, creates deep institutional ambiguity, opening up space for change.

But even if civil war does not lead to the suspension of existing rules in such a dramatic fashion, it may discourage state leaders from monitoring compliance with the rules, either because such monitoring is too costly or because the existing rules contradict counterinsurgent objectives.[25] This is the second feature that makes civil war prone to institutional change. In combating an insurgency, government leaders may not have the resources or personnel to oversee compliance with tax laws or the procedures governing police conduct, land titling, or government contracting, for example. Cumbersome bureaucratic regulations may be direct obstacles to urgent wartime needs such as military acquisitions, recruitment, and surveillance. The imperative of defeating an insurgency and safeguarding the state thus alters the enforcement of existing rules because of this reorientation of goals and priorities.

Finally, institutions are particularly susceptible to transformation in civil war because state actors are typically given high levels of discretion in planning and carrying out counterinsurgent operations, which may create new rules that are then enforced through enhanced coercive capacities. The view of civil war as generative of alternative social, political, and economic orders emphasizes the license afforded to armed actors in

[22] Agamben 2015: 14–15.    [23] Schmitt 2005; Agamben 1998.
[24] Agamben 1998: 57.    [25] Collier 1999.

such contexts. The "high degree of informalization of both the economy and politics" results in systems "extremely susceptible to arbitrary decisions and instrumentalizations for ... private ends."[26] Given the imperative of eliminating an internal enemy, armed actors exploit the permissive environment to introduce new rules. Processes of militarization can allot heightened discretion to counterinsurgent actors due to "disalignment" between civilian and military leadership and the strengthening of the military's bureaucratic capacity.[27]

Military elites empowered to wage counterinsurgency possess greater capacities for coercion due to new combat and surveillance technologies and the militarization of society. This results in the concentration of an elite-level variant of what Christine Cheng terms "conflict capital" or the "wartime social connections" and "standard operating procedures" that guide violent activities.[28] These connections and capacities provide counterinsurgent elites more robust mechanisms of enforcing the new rules developed under the pretext of eradicating internal security threats. Indeed, this expansion of military control and capacity "means that the army often branches out into civilian realms of government and production," which can facilitate institutional changes even in typically civilian-controlled arenas.[29]

Given these characteristics, my approach to wartime institutional change does not envision civil war as an exogenous shock that inevitably disrupts existing institutional arrangements or as a critical juncture that sets states unwaveringly on a particular developmental path. Instead, I view the wartime introduction of new rules as reflecting an endogenous process of institutional change that is not necessarily linear, but instead varies according to coalitional dynamics among diverse actors.[30]

Of course, theories of gradual institutional change seek to explain institutional emergence, transformation, and breakdown during "normal times" – and focus disproportionately on Western, industrialized settings. In drawing on such approaches, I certainly do not mean to claim that civil war reflects "normal times." But while civil war can certainly be a source of tremendous institutional upheaval, recent political violence research points to significant variation in wartime political orders, local

---

[26] Schlichte 2003: 31, 33.    [27] Eibl et al. 2021; Slater 2020.    [28] Cheng 2018: 54–60.
[29] Eibl et al. 2021: 10.
[30] See Greif and Laitin 2004; Tsai 2006. As Gerschewski (2021) notes, we can imagine endogenous institutional ruptures in addition to more gradual forms of endogenous change. In this book, I am less concerned with the question of time horizons and more focused on the internal source of change.

institutional dynamics, and repertoires of conflict violence;[31] presuming that civil war reflects an exogenous shock that does similar work across national, and even subnational, contexts papers over this wide-ranging variation. In other words, conflict environments are not uniform. The distinct dynamics within conflict matter for processes of wartime institutional change. For this reason, I treat civil war as a setting propitious for institutional transformation but focus on specific conflict dynamics as the engines of institutional evolution itself.

## CONCEPTUALIZING WARTIME INSTITUTIONAL LOGICS

Civil war constitutes a context particularly susceptible to institutional transformation within the state apparatus for the reasons laid out above. Yet the question remains: In what ways might institutions change and with what effects? What kinds of rules and procedures might be introduced in the institutional gray area that emerges in civil war? I draw from Gretchen Helmke and Steven Levitsky's typology of informal institutions to conceptualize different kinds of rules that may emerge in the "gaps" or "soft spots" constituted in armed conflict and their distinct effects on state performance.[32] One of the two dimensions used to classify informal institutions is their degree of convergence with formal rules – that is, "whether following the informal rules produces a result substantively similar to or different from that expected from a strict and exclusive adherence to the formal rules."[33] Here, I develop a conceptual framework that disaggregates rules "convergence" into two different logics: low convergence (*undermining*) and high convergence (*reinforcing*).

This book focuses on a specific class of formal rules: those corresponding to routine state activities, which, again, will be defined here as the extraction of revenue, control over the means of violence, and the administration of basic goods and services. I thus conceptualize two types of wartime rules that might be introduced within state institutions: (1) *undermining rules*, or those that diverge and produce substantively different outcomes from a given state function, and (2) *reinforcing rules*, or those that converge with and produce substantively similar outcomes to a given state function.[34] Empirically pinpointing and categorizing these

---

[31] Staniland 2021; Arjona 2016; Gutiérrez-Sanín and Wood 2017.
[32] Helmke and Levitsky 2006: 13.    [33] Ibid.
[34] This conceptualization echoes other scholarly efforts to identify the relationships between different kinds of institutions. Lauth's (2000: 25) categorization, for example, cites

institutional logics is, of course, a tall task, particularly in the case of undermining rules, which can entail illicit activities that their architects seek to cover up. But we can identify undermining and reinforcing rules by establishing two criteria: (1) whether there are sanctions or consequences for deviating from the stipulated behavior, and (2) what behavioral outcomes result from compliance with the rules. The first benchmark establishes the "rule-bound" nature of the procedures, while the second classifies them as undermining or reinforcing.

Table 2.1 illustrates examples of undermining and reinforcing rules within commonly cited spheres of state activity, including taxation, public security, and public administration. Within the realm of taxation, undermining rules redirect revenues destined for state coffers into private hands, while similarly perverse institutional arrangements within public security agencies may contribute to widespread extrajudicial killing by security officials, paramilitaries, and other private actors, as well as systematic impunity for such abuses, thereby exacerbating insecurity and distorting the rule of law. Within administrative domains more broadly, undermining rules can inhibit the state's ability to regulate property ownership, commerce, public contracting, and population registration, among other activities. Guatemala's wartime customs fraud operations and police-led extrajudicial killing procedures, as well as Nicaragua's conflict-era provisional land titling arrangements will be examined in subsequent chapters as my primary cases of undermining rules. However, other examples abound.

For instance, Angolan military units devised new rules of taxation for the gemstone trade, undermining state revenue extraction.[35] Within the public security sector, El Salvador's wartime police force, much like Guatemala's, forged death squads that abided by alternative rules governing extrajudicial killing and social cleansing.[36] Comparable forms of crime scene manipulation and parallel investigative work were

---

"conflicting" relationships, whereby "the two systems of rules are incompatible," and "complementary" relationships, in which "they coexist side by side and mutually reinforce and support each other." Similarly, Grzymala-Busse (2010: 321, 324) points to "undermining" institutions, which "feed off and contravene emerging or existing formal institutions," and those that "support or reinforce" formal institutions. In research on Nigeria and the Democratic Republic of Congo, Meagher (2012: 1074) distinguishes between "constructive and corrosive forms of non-state order," while Hui's (2005) work on early Chinese state formation conceptualizes "self-weakening" and "self-strengthening" logics – both of which also speak to the undermining and reinforcing relationships between different forms of authority.

[35] Nordstrom 2004: 122–123.     [36] Silva Ávalos 2014; United Nations 1994.

TABLE 2.1  *Cases of undermining and reinforcing rules*

| Policy domain | Undermining rules | Reinforcing rules |
| --- | --- | --- |
| Taxation (extraction) | Guatemala: customs fraud (late 1970s and early 1980s) Angola: military gemstone taxation (early 2000s) | Colombia: Democratic Security Tax (2002) Malaysia: direct taxation (1947) Singapore: direct income tax (1947) |
| Public security and control of violence (coercion) | Guatemala: police extrajudicial killing (1960s–1970s) El Salvador: police extrajudicial killing (1980s) Colombia: military "false positives" scandal (2000s) | Nicaragua: community/ preventive policing procedures (early 1980s) Malaysia: labor registration system (1940s) |
| Provision of basic goods and services (administration) | Nicaragua: provisional land titling (mid-1980s) Guatemala: illegal adoptions (1970s and 1980s) | Colombia: land titling (1960s) Malaysia: public services and land titling within "New Villages" (1950s) Uganda: fiscal decentralization and local goods provision (1980s) |

deployed to enforce the alternative rules underlying extralegal killing.[37] In the words of Héctor Silva Ávalos, the police cliques implementing the undermining rules "[illustrate] with clarity how the police elite ... constructed fiefdoms and contributed to feeding the culture of impunity to benefit themselves or third parties."[38] Similarly, Colombia's "false positives" scandal during the 2000s revealed routinized state security procedures to increase body counts by disguising civilian executions as insurgent combatant deaths.[39]

Undermining rules have also emerged in administrative and social policy domains. In the Guatemalan context, undermining institutional logics developed within the Secretariat of Social Welfare and remade the rules governing international adoptions. Historical evidence suggests that these rules and procedures developed at the height of the counterinsurgent

[37] Silva Ávalos 2014: 135–165.    [38] Ibid., 124.
[39] Acemoglu et al. 2018; Gordon 2017.

campaign, as the Secretariat of Social Welfare, the National Police, and the armed forces abducted and adopted out the children of suspected guerrillas,[40] much like during authoritarian periods elsewhere in Latin America.[41] Wartime reforms devolved significant power to notaries to authorize adoptions, weakening formal oversight. The counterinsurgent pretext and resulting legal changes thus established alternative procedures that undermined the Guatemalan state's ability to regulate international adoptions.

We can also identify examples of reinforcing rules devised and implemented amid internal conflict. The concluding chapter will delve into some of these examples, including Colombia's wartime wealth tax established in 2002 to bolster military capacity and Nicaragua's community-oriented, preventive policing procedures following the Sandinista Revolution. Likewise, in Colombia the state expanded land titling procedures in the 1960s to shore up property rights.[42] We can also delineate numerous other empirical examples from the extractive, coercive, and administrative domains beyond Latin America. For example, Slater demonstrates how urban unrest gave rise to new rules and procedures governing direct taxation in Malaysia and Singapore during the mid-1940s.[43] In the former case, reinforcing rules also bolstered the state's control of violence through the creation of a labor registration system and expanded its administrative functions with the introduction of new procedures for public service provision and land titling within the "New Villages."[44] In Uganda, wartime village-level resistance councils (RCs) "organized food, recruits, and intelligence for the war effort," thus enhancing administrative capacity.[45]

Some additional clarifications with respect to this conceptual framework are in order. Importantly, this study brackets the "formal" or "informal" quality of the rules in question, as well as formal institutional *effectiveness* or the extent to which rules "that exist on paper are enforced or complied with in practice."[46] I make these simplifications because of my focus on the *outcomes* of wartime institutional change. On the question of informal versus formal institutions, I am not concerned with whether the rules that emerge during civil war are official or unofficial,

---

[40] SEPAZ 2009.     [41] Smith Rotabi 2014.     [42] Albertus and Kaplan 2013.
[43] Slater 2010: 82, 232.     [44] Ibid., 89.
[45] Weinstein 2005: 16; Tapscott 2021; see also, Lewis (2020: 179–188) on the role of the RC system (later called Local Councils [LCs]) in wartime intelligence-gathering.
[46] Helmke and Levitsky 2006: 13.

or whether they become so in the aftermath of conflict. As the coming chapters will illustrate, the boundary between "unwritten [rules and procedures] that are created, communicated, and enforced outside of officially sanctioned channels" and their "written" or "official" counterparts[47] is often much murkier in practice and, I would argue, less significant than the substantive outcomes they generate.

On the second question, the effectiveness of formal institutions, I similarly posit that whether alternative institutional arrangements substitute for some "weak" set of rules or coexist beside some "strong" set of rules is secondary to and may be independent of the institutional outcomes themselves. In transitional moments such as regime change and civil war "we cannot assume the strength of any particular formal institution, since these are constantly being abolished, transformed, and established anew."[48] Undermining rules can shape political outcomes whether prevailing formal institutions are strong or weak and may, in fact, influence "the emergence and transformation of formal rules" rather than the other way around.[49] For these reasons, I focus not on the purported effectiveness of the existing rules but on whether the new rules contravene or bolster the state activities identified previously.

Additionally, I distinguish undermining rules from corruption. Per conventional definitions, corruption is "the misuse of public office for private gain."[50] Though undermining rules often entail the misuse of public office for private gain, it is important that we not conflate them with corruption for two key reasons. First, corruption is not always an institution – that is, corrupt behavior is not always "organized and enforced from above" or "rooted in widely shared expectations among citizens and public officials."[51] Depending on the social and political context, corruption may instead be an anomalous activity or even a behavioral pattern that does not correspond to a set of shared rules.

Secondly, unlike the concept of undermining rules, corruption, even when rule-bound, does not necessarily imply a uniform effect on state performance. Despite the normative view that links corruption to state breakdown, some empirical accounts indicate that corruption may bolster state capacity. For example, Darden finds that, "where graft is informally institutionalized ... it provides the basis for state organizations that are effective in collecting taxes [and] maintaining public order."[52] Though

---

[47] Ibid., 5.    [48] Grzymala-Busse 2010: 313.    [49] Ibid., 314.
[50] Treisman 2000: 399.    [51] Helmke and Levitsky 2006: 7.    [52] Darden 2008: 35.

I take corruption to be a (likely) symptom of undermining rules, it is merely a subset of the phenomenon of interest within this book. Instead, my approach centers on the rules and their underlying logics.[53] And as I will demonstrate, undermining rules that entail corruption are not the only form we observe in the Central American context. In Nicaragua, for example, it was efforts to peel peasant support away from the insurgency – strategic military and political aims – that gave rise to new undermining rules within land tenure institutions.

Finally, it is worth reaffirming that I do not consider civil war to be the exclusive or even primary driver of institutional change or impetus for the creation of undermining rules within state institutions. Indeed, there is a vast social science literature that attributes institutional change to any number of exogenous shocks or to gradual processes of transformation. While I do not see civil war as the universal cause of institutional change, I do consider it to be a context particularly susceptible to institutional transformation: As military imperatives alter the interpretation and enforcement of the existing rules, conflict dynamics open up space for alternative rules to emerge. And while undermining rules that subvert state institutions may arise from numerous non-conflict-related processes, they represent an underexplored mechanism linking war and state (under)-development.

### THE WARTIME EVOLUTION OF UNDERMINING RULES

How does the development of undermining rules within the state during armed conflict unfold? Figure 2.1 lays out the basic causal sequence through which wartime institutional change occurs. As mentioned earlier, the introduction of new undermining rules is less about sweeping upheaval or the radical transformation of political structures, but instead the institutional gray zone that emerges within the gap between the interpretation and enforcement of the prevailing rules. Rather than the onset of civil war itself, I am thus primarily concerned with the key wartime condition that generates institutional ambiguity: the perceived escalation of the insurgent threat.

This perceived escalation may correspond to the actual expansion of rebel forces, rebel territorial control, and/or rebel resources; however, it need not map neatly onto some objective increase in insurgent military

---

[53] This approach is similar to Koivu's (2018: 48), in that it sees corruption as individual behavior that obscures broader group-level interactions that facilitate specific state outcomes.

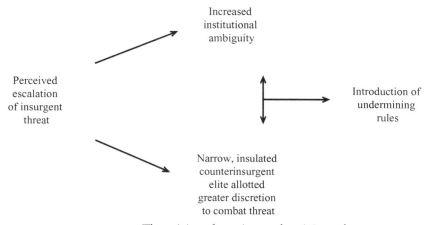

Increased
institutional
ambiguity

Perceived
escalation
of insurgent
threat

Introduction of
undermining
rules

Narrow, insulated
counterinsurgent
elite allotted
greater discretion
to combat threat

FIGURE 2.1 The origins of wartime undermining rules

capacity to be *perceived* by rulers as increased threat. It may instead correspond to a geographic shift in battle – for example, the presence of conflict violence in population centers previously untouched by the fighting. It may be fueled by the incorporation of political, ethnic, or religious groups seen as particularly dangerous within rebel organizations. Indeed, work by Paul Staniland finds that "ideological threats" drive state responses to insurgency, rather than "the size, power, or organizational characteristics of armed groups."[54] It can also stem from the anticipation of foreign intervention on behalf of the insurgency. Perceptions of threat escalation may also correspond to new vulnerabilities within the state, irrespective of changes in insurgent capability (fragmentation, coup threats, natural disasters, etc.). Threats and threat escalation can be constructed as well. Military and political leaders may exaggerate the magnitude of an insurgent threat for strategic purposes – through words or through policies like enhanced repression – to justify and facilitate elite extraction.[55] In short, rather than some measurable increase in rebel capacity, what matters is *the perception that the insurgency now poses a greater risk to the survival of the state.*

The perceived escalation of the insurgent threat prompts institutional ambiguity for the three reasons laid out in the previous section: (1) It permits the suspension of existing rules to combat a threat often perceived as serious, if not existential; (2) it discourages rulers from monitoring

[54] Staniland 2021: 2.     [55] See Stanley 1996: 35–38.

compliance with the existing rules; and (3) it grants rulers extraordinary discretion in carrying out counterinsurgent actions.

But what accounts for the emergence of new undermining rules within the institutional void constituted in conflict? How do we get from the escalation of the insurgent threat to the consolidation of alternative procedures that subvert state functions? As the perceived escalation of the insurgent threat unsettles prevailing institutional arrangements, it also empowers new political-military actors or further centralizes power in existing leaders, who, as the architects of counterinsurgency, are allotted high levels of decision-making discretion. I refer to these actors as counterinsurgent elites, defined as those government, armed forces, and police leaders in charge of designing political and combat strategies to eliminate the insurgent threat. Amid the sense of heightened vulnerability, this group of new or existing counterinsurgent elites becomes further insulated from broader political and military structures due to fears of insurgent penetration and the need to act quickly and decisively against rebel forces. The expansion of military competencies and control may even overcome internal regime opposition or civilian oversight, allowing for the concentration of political and coercive authority in an ever-narrower set of counterinsurgent elites.[56]

As a result, and under the pretext of combatting the insurgent threat, the counterinsurgent elite devises and introduces alternative rules of the game, which "stem from control of implementation [and] control over information that enables one to define the problem and identify the available options."[57] When these wartime powers are highly concentrated, the rules-making counterinsurgent elite possesses short time-horizons, and its leaders operate autonomously from broader state and military structures, the new rules are narrowly conceived and correspond to the circumscribed interests of those devising them. This is because a unified elite that possesses a high concentration of power and resources encounters few countervailing political forces to check its decision-making authority and thus seldom faces accountability. As such, it is less likely to be concerned with wielding state institutions to carry out routine activities oriented toward providing public goods and services, particularly amid the insurgent threat.[58] In this environment, the

---

[56] Eibl et al. 2021: 10.      [57] Allison and Halperin 1972: 50.

[58] This logic draws on theoretical insights from Yashar (1997) and Dahl (1971) that the concentration of power in unified elites is less likely to produce democratic outcomes, as opposed to contexts characterized by a divided elite. It is also consistent with Albertus'

counterinsurgent elite fashions and introduces distributive instruments through which benefits accrue to it narrowly, thus explaining the often-undermining logics that underlie wartime institutional arrangements.[59]

The benefits accrued through the new rules, however, need not be purely material. This project assumes that, beyond the corrupt accumulation of state economic resources, the counterinsurgent elite also introduces undermining rules intended to increase its political power or preserve its rule in the face of armed challenge. In other words, the precise *motivations* of the counterinsurgent elite often reflect a mix of opportunism and self-preservation; however, above all, it is the narrow and insulated nature of the rules-making coalition that drives the evolution of undermining institutional logics. Held together by narrow sectoral interests and shielded from potential countervailing political forces, the new rules contravene core state functions.

But when is a coalition sufficiently narrow to trigger the creation of undermining rules, and how do we know a narrow coalition when we see one? This question is difficult to answer for several reasons. It might seem natural to simply look to the identity of the actors that comprise the dominant counterinsurgent elite – whether political, ethnic, or institutional – to infer a common set of interests and thus an ability to overcome conflicting preferences and implement new rules of the game to accrue private benefits. However, this approach would also gloss over potential intra-group factions that do reflect offsetting interests and thus inhibit the implementation of undermining institutional arrangements. As I will illustrate with Guatemala's military apparatus, it was not just military control over the state, but the ascendance of a tightknit intelligence clique based on informal ties that facilitated the emergence of undermining rules. Institutions like the military are rarely unitary actors.

Therefore, this study proposes that delineating narrow coalitions requires moving beneath the broad identity categories of the relevant counterinsurgent actors to identify their specific allegiances and preferences. Where decision-making authority and discretion is vested in a unified group of counterinsurgent leaders bound by ties to one another (formal or informal), a shared ideological orientation, and the ability to

(2021: 82–85, 213) claims about how rigid decision-making hierarchies and the absence of accountability in autocracies contribute to property rights gaps.

[59] This logic follows from Bueno de Mesquita et al.'s (2003: 129–130) theoretical proposition that "a small winning coalition with a large selectorate provides the foundation for kleptocracy."

insulate themselves from or overcome the opposition of outside actors, it reflects the kind of narrow coalition that I anticipate will create and implement undermining rules. By contrast, where we see decision-makers having to incorporate the views and preferences of or answer directly to other military or civilian leadership, civil society actors (like private sector elites or grassroots social movements), or foreign governments that reflect offsetting interests, the dominant counterinsurgent coalition reflects a breadth that inhibits the introduction of undermining rules. We see this dynamic, for example, in the case of Colombia's tax sector at the height of its internal armed conflict in the early and mid-2000s, which I will discuss in the concluding chapter. Because counterinsurgent leaders depended on private sector funding for new military acquisitions – and because business leaders cared both about advances in the counterinsurgent campaign *and* that their financial contributions did not fall into corrupt hands – external influences and linkages made for a broader counterinsurgent coalition. Of course, some regime types and institutional setting are more likely to generate these broader coalitions – a question I will also return to when discussing scope conditions.

Finally, what is the nature of enforcement and compliance once the new rules of the game emerge? In the short term, the narrow counterinsurgent elite garners compliance with the undermining institutional arrangements through coercion. By controlling the means of state violence, the narrow clique of counterinsurgent leaders can use force or the threat of force to ensure compliance. Further, by seizing control of day-to-day state operations and restructuring bureaucratic functions, the counterinsurgent elite can use the threat of demotions to incentivize compliance among the public servants tasked with implementing the new rules on the ground.

## ALTERNATIVE EXPLANATIONS

Overall, this book argues that it is the structure of the wartime counterinsurgent coalition that best accounts for the emergence of undermining rules within the state. But this study also remains attentive to a series of alternative factors that might plausibly explain such wartime institutional transformations. The three primary alternatives, which are evaluated in Chapter 3, are: (1) the state's war-making strategy, (2) regime ideology, and (3) the nature of foreign support.

The first alternative explanation corresponds to Tilly's classic study of state formation, which suggests that the state's war-making strategy – its preferred mode for extracting the resources to wage war – best accounts for different trajectories of institutional development. In this account, modes of war-making can be *coercion-intensive* or *capital-intensive*. Under coercion-intensive strategies, "rulers squeezed the means of war from their own populations and others they conquered, building massive structures of extraction in the process." Meanwhile, under the capital-intensive scheme, "rulers relied on compacts with capitalists – whose interests they served with care – to rent or purchase military force, and thereby warred without building vast permanent state structures."[60] The difference between coercion-intensive and capital-intensive modes is thus whether the means of waging war are sought through the penetration of mass actors or ad hoc, often transitory, alliances with elites.

The two war-making strategies have distinct implications for the kinds of state institutions that develop. With coercion-intensive strategies, rulers sought access to "the resources [citizens] controlled through household taxation, mass conscription, censuses, police systems, and many other invasions of small-scale social life," implying "penetration and bargaining [that] laid down new state structures."[61] By contrast, capital-intensive strategies "relied on some version of indirect rule, and thus ran serious risks of disloyalty, dissimulation, corruption, and rebellion, but ... made it possible to govern without erecting, financing, and feeding a bulky administrative system."[62] In the latter case, the "bargains" struck with elites distort institutional functioning.[63] Here, it is not necessarily the nature of the rules-making coalition that determines the emergence of undermining rules in war, but the societal bases from which state leaders draw resources to wage war in the first place. By this logic, we might expect the emergence of undermining institutional formations when counterinsurgent leaders marshal wartime resources from economic elites, rather than mass actors.

---

[60] Tilly 1990: 30–31.     [61] Ibid., 25.

[62] Ibid. While Tilly's account does suggest that coercion- and capital-intensive pathways (as well as the intermediate variant, capitalized coercion) eventually converged on the formation of national states, these differences played a key role in varied state trajectories initially. See also, Hui 2005: 182.

[63] Ibid. It is also important to recognize the scope of the Tillyan model. Tilly's account draws on distinctions among a much broader range of polities found in Europe, from tribute-taking empires to city-states and federations. In other words, the starting point, for Tilly, was not states, but other political formations from the tenth to the fifteenth centuries. Yet, it is the logic of Tilly's account – that different modes of accumulating resources for war set polities on different institutional paths – that I treat as an alternative explanation for how civil war shapes state development.

A second alternative explanation focuses on the ideological orientations of the regime in power – a factor that has been shown to shape war and postwar statebuilding projects. For example, in focusing on governance by rebel groups that ascend to state power, Kai Thaler argues that those that are "programmatic," or "attempt to achieve long-term goals that extend beyond taking power to the transformation or reform of socioeconomic and political relations," are more effective statebuilders, as opposed to those that seek short-term, private benefits.[64] This is because building institutions that provide basic goods and services and expand the state's territorial reach are central to the revolutionary political and economic agenda. In exploring both rebel and paramilitary governance, Rafael Ch and co-authors similarly argue that armed actor preferences stemming from ideological commitments shape institutional logics at the local level.[65] In turn, ideology may plausibly drive the nature of wartime institutional transformations, with less programmatic and more opportunistic regimes prone to developing undermining rules within the state.

A final alternative explanation attributes the wartime development of undermining rules to foreign assistance, which further empowers predatory actors who distort the rules of the game with impunity. For example, in Mali, the diversion of US and French military assistance promoted nepotism, bribery, and other forms of illicit enrichment, empowering actors that ultimately staged a military coup in 2012.[66] Perhaps nowhere are these tendencies more clearly illustrated than in Cold War Central America, where US security aid and technical assistance "helped build up precisely those institutions within these states that were most prone to kill [and] most isolated from accountability."[67] As this book's discussion of Guatemala's wartime institutions will make clear, US security funding and training had a transformative effect not only on counterinsurgent policies and practices but military structures as well. But to what extent does foreign assistance drive the wartime development of undermining rules more broadly? This question, along with the role of state warmaking strategies and regime ideology, will be addressed in the next chapter through a comparative analysis of conflict conditions and dynamics in Guatemala and Nicaragua.

---

[64] Thaler 2018: 19.     [65] Ch et al. 2018.     [66] MacLachlan 2015.
[67] Stanley 1996: 40.

## SCOPE CONDITIONS

The above process should unfold in a subset of institutional domains within irregular civil war contexts. This framework applies to contexts of irregular civil war because it is the perceived threat posed by potential insurgent infiltration of the state apparatus that drives the institutional ambiguity and heightened discretion critical to the implementation of new undermining rules. Relatedly, rulers must perceive or construct insurgent forces as threatening enough to necessitate institutional transformations. We can thus imagine certain scenarios of low-intensity conflict and limited hostilities that would not set off the process described here.

Beyond the nature of conflict itself, this book's claims about the creation of undermining rules are most likely to apply to civil wars waged by authoritarian governments, whether institutionalized military regimes or more traditional or personalist dictatorships. This is because authoritarian contexts are more prone to bypassing institutional channels of deliberation and to the concentration of decision-making power in a narrow group of ruling elites. For this reason, it is also unlikely that the dominant counter-insurgent coalition will look dramatically different across the state apparatus. While this is theoretically possible because states are far from unitary actors, an authoritarian context presupposes centralized control, making it difficult for different sources of authority to emerge. As I will discuss in the concluding chapter, contexts of political pluralism, while not the only environments ripe for reinforcing rules, more often feature broader, multi-sectoral decision-making coalitions, which channel institutional transformations in state-reinforcing directions. Such settings might also exhibit more variation in coalitional structures across different state sectors.

Finally, this causal process plays out in institutional domains deemed vulnerable to insurgent penetration or critical to eliminating the rebel threat. This is because counterinsurgent elites must use the pretext of curbing insurgent infiltration or eliminating the "internal enemy" to justify unsettling the prevailing order and introducing new procedures. We are more likely to see this counterinsurgent pretext deployed in spheres like police and intelligence services, the justice system, migration and customs control, and population registration, while policy domains like healthcare and education are less likely to be sites of institutional innovation. However, differences in counterinsurgent elite interpretations and strategies also mean that some institutional domains not subject to the introduction of undermining rules in some conflict cases will be sites of institutional change in others.

Importantly, it is conceivable that coalitional configurations can
change across time within a civil war. As discussed above, this book treats
civil war as a dynamic and endogenous process, and so changes in
insurgent activity, military strategy, regime structures, and foreign
involvement, among other factors, can narrow or broaden the dominant
counterinsurgent coalition. We see this, for instance, in the Nicaraguan
context as the progression of the Contra campaign transformed the broad
revolutionary coalition of the early 1980s into a much narrower one,
centralized in the nine commanders of the FSLN party vanguard. In short,
just as civil wars contexts remain fluid, so too do the decision-making
coalitions waging counterinsurgency.

## HOW THE WARTIME RULES PERSIST: THEORIZING INSTITUTIONAL SURVIVAL

Civil war is a propitious site for institutional change, facilitating the
introduction of alternative rules of the game within the state apparatus.
But understanding the legacies of conflict for state development requires
more than capturing how civil war dynamics contribute to institutional
evolution; we must also understand why and how wartime institutional
innovations persist during conflict and in its aftermath. This second set of
questions is the subject of the remainder of this chapter: How are the
undermining rules developed within civil war reproduced? How do they
endure beyond conflict and continue to distort state activities, even after
substantial postwar reforms? Under what conditions do the wartime
institutional arrangements that subvert state activities remain unstable
or break down in war's aftermath?

This book contends that postwar institutional persistence or chronic
instability, much like wartime institutional change, is a question of political
coalitions. To reproduce the undermining rules, the counterinsurgent elite
must broaden the distributional coalition – the web of sectoral interests
with a vested stake in the conflict-era institutional landscape. As this
broader set of sectoral interests continues to garner political and material
benefits through the implementation of the undermining rules, they become
self-enforcing. Further, when this distributional coalition effectively adapts
to the postwar environment and continues to control political and economic power and resources, the undermining rules can survive state
reforms. By contrast, the undermining rules face chronic instability and
may be repeatedly disarticulated and replaced when there are frequent
shifts in the dominant coalition of political and economic stakeholders.

This approach to institutional persistence during and after conflict hinges on two key points. First, the dynamics of institutional persistence and instability are not epiphenomenal to *individual* wartime actors that may resurface during transition and peacebuilding and exercise continued political authority. They are instead a product of *interest groups* that seek to secure sectoral benefits and stand to gain from the endurance of the wartime rules of the game. Second, the precise mode of institutional persistence developed here does not depend on the representatives of the wartime distributional coalition continuing to occupy formal government posts; instead, these groups often find extra-state avenues of influence – spaces that often emerge through transition-era political and economic reforms themselves. This phenomenon is not simply synonymous with "state capture" – the "extraction of private benefits by incumbent office-holders from the state"[68] – but is instead much broader. A coalition-based explanation of institutional survival, therefore, must not only be attentive to how wartime interests maintain their grip on formal political authority, but also how they co-opt new spaces on the margins of the state to maintain impunity, locate strategic allies on the inside, and adjust the undermining rules of the conflict era to evade new regulations.

## REPRODUCING THE UNDERMINING RULES

While the use of coercion is enough to ensure enforcement in a short-term sense, how are the undermining rules reproduced and consolidated in the longer term? In benefitting a narrow group of institutional "winners," the new rules are vulnerable to challenges posed by those outside of the dominant counterinsurgent elite. Particularly in contexts of intrastate competition, the counterinsurgent elite must knit together a broader coalition to underwrite the new rules if they are to survive. In other words, if institutional change reflects contests to structure distributional outcomes, the counterinsurgent elite must assemble a "team" capable of prevailing in the contest, particularly as political transition becomes more likely and "the armed forces must find non-coercive ways to widen their support."[69] I refer to this "team" as the "distributional coalition" – the array of sectoral stakeholders that garners selective material and/or political benefits through the recurring implementation and enforcement of the

---

[68] Grzymala-Busse 2008: 638.     [69] Grimes and Pion-Berlin 2019: 628; Pion-Berlin 2010.

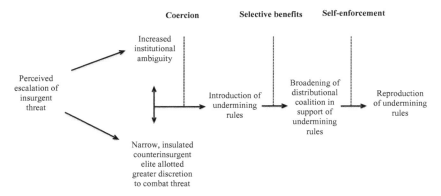

FIGURE 2.2 The origins and reproduction of wartime undermining rules

wartime institutional arrangements.[70] Often among these stakeholders are private sector elites who benefit from wartime economic activities, organized criminal operatives engaged in illicit wartime trades, and judicial and political officials who grant impunity for wartime abuses to maintain their power. The relatively circumscribed counterinsurgent elite thus seeks to bring additional sectoral interests into the fold and forge a robust coalition with a stake in the new rules, utilizing selective benefits to garner wider buy-in (see Figure 2.2).

This stage is one of institutional reproduction: As distributional benefits accrue to the broader set of sectoral interests, the undermining rules become increasingly self-enforcing. The broadening of the distributional coalition most often occurs during armed conflict itself, particularly as counterinsurgent elites' time-horizons lengthen and they look ahead to preserving the wartime status quo as conflict winds down. This stage thus lays the foundations for the survival of the undermining rules following conflict. In the remainder of the chapter, I synthesize the potential mechanisms of postwar institutional persistence and demonstrate why the wartime rules survive or face chronic instability after conflict has ceased.

---

[70] The distributional coalition is similar to that described by Schamis (1999: 242) in discussing the "winners" of economic liberalization. My conceptualization, however, includes not only economic payoffs, but political payoffs. Similar to Hazelton's (2021: 17) idea of elite accommodation in counterinsurgency, it also includes benefits "such as impunity, status, or a sinecure."

## SURVIVING PEACEBUILDING AND STATE REFORM: MECHANISMS OF INSTITUTIONAL PERSISTENCE

Scholars have increasingly noted the ways in which peacebuilding and postwar reform become sites of institutional continuity rather than change, allowing the wartime status quo to persist after the fighting has ceased.[71] But how do the undermining rules that evolve during conflict remain so resilient in the face of postwar reforms, and under what conditions might we expect them to break down following conflict? While "punctuated equilibrium" models might treat postwar state- and peacebuilding reforms as critical junctures that produce institutional change, in the "weak" institutional environments that characterize post-conflict contexts, these moments are often more conducive to institutional resilience and stability, allowing the prevailing rules and procedures to solidify or even deepen.[72]

Despite these broader postwar patterns, there have been only limited scholarly efforts to understand the precise dynamics of continuity following conflict – how these moments serve as sites of institutional stability and the mechanisms through which existing institutional arrangements outlast reforms. As Aldo Madariaga notes, "contemporary debates on causal mechanisms and institutional change have installed the idea that change is pervasive, leaving us with few alternatives to understand continuity."[73] Far from "an uninteresting or unproblematic outcome,"[74] institutional survival deserves equal analytical attention, especially in challenging conflict-ridden contexts where assumptions about political transition and reform often mask the realities of stasis and continuity.

This project focuses on three potential mechanisms of institutional persistence derived from existing research and adapted to post-conflict settings. They are: (1) the manipulation of the implementation and/or enforcement of peacebuilding and state reforms, (2) the institutionalization of cultural categories or ideas about appropriate behavior, and (3) the preservation of the dominant social and political blocs, the prevailing distributional coalitions, underwriting the previous wartime rules (see Table 2.2).

According to the first proposed mechanism, undermining rules survive because postwar political elites effectively manipulate the timing,

---

[71] Barma 2017; Wade 2016; Lake 2017, 2022.
[72] Levitsky and Murillo 2013: 94; Madariaga 2017.
[73] Madariaga 2017: 638; see also, Boas 2007.
[74] Matsuzaki 2019: 21; see also, González 2020: 30–32.

TABLE 2.2 *Mechanisms of institutional persistence*

| Mechanism | Pathway of persistence | Observable implications |
| --- | --- | --- |
| Manipulation of timing/enforcement of reform | Stalled institutional changes and/or weak enforcement of new institutions renders reforms mere window dressing, allowing the persistence of undermining rules | Incumbents hold off on implementing reforms or shelve them entirely; lack of sanctions for continued adherence to undermining rules |
| Institutionalization of collective ideas/ cultural categories | Shared beliefs about undermining rules as "appropriate" or "legitimate" allow them to outlast reforms | Undermining rules understood as a natural feature of state activity; justifications legitimating undermining rules by bureaucratic actors |
| Broadening of the wartime distributional coalition | Abiding power of dominant wartime actors maintains impunity and facilitates adjustments to undermining rules to adapt to post-reform environment | |
| *Variant 1: continued occupation of official government posts* | Continuation of impunity and institutional adaptation through wartime coalition's control of official government decision-making | Members of the wartime distributional coalition occupy many formal executive posts |
| *Variant 2: reconstitution on the margins of official political power* | Continuation of impunity and institutional adaptation through new extra- or semi-state channels (e.g., privatization, political parties) | Members of the wartime distributional coalition mostly displaced from government, but engage in political and economic activities on the margins of the state sphere |

implementation, and enforcement of postwar reforms thereby preserving the wartime status quo. Under one possible scenario, incumbents or "rule-makers" intent on preserving existing institutional arrangements outmaneuver reform coalitions by controlling the timing of changes, stalling implementation until mobilization for reform has subsided.[75] However, even when reforms are implemented, political elites can "use de jure discretion to limit enforcement" or "use de facto discretion to permit—or engage in—the violation of the rules."[76] Weak enforcement allows the undermining rules to persist because the newly reformed post-war procedures "remain on the books as window dressing" without touching the institutional status quo.[77] These explanations are premised on the same general mechanism: that the wartime undermining rules endure because of the failures of the institutional changes meant to disman-tle them, thereby leaving the perverse incentive structures that underlie them intact.[78]

A second potential mechanism focuses on the role of ideas and cultural categories. Here, undermining rules emerging from conflict endure because of abiding collective beliefs and shared understandings that they are "normal" or "legitimate."[79] Capoccia refers to this mechanism as the "institutionalization of cultural categories," a process in which stable normative understandings of rules and behaviors counteract reform.[80] Here, shared expectations among high-level state officials, low-level bureaucrats, and the general public generate "other moralities" permissive of predatory activities.[81]

A final potential mechanism, which I posit best explains the persistence of undermining rules from war to peace, focuses on the distribution of political power and resources. Undermining rules outlast post-conflict governance reforms through the influence of dominant social and political blocs, the prevailing distributional coalition, which maneuver "to defend [their] interests and policy preferences," thus preserving the institutional status quo.[82] Consistent with distributional approaches within studies of industrialized contexts,[83] informal institutions in developing contexts,[84] anti-corruption reforms,[85] and crony capitalism,[86] the resilience of under-mining rules is best attributed to the ability of the institutional "winners" within the existing system – here, those with a stake in the wartime undermining rules – to retain their political influence and prerogatives. The dominant distributional coalition ensures the stability of the undermin-ing rules by using its political clout to shield wartime allies from sanction

---

[75] Capoccia 2016.    [76] Levitsky and Murillo 2013: 101.    [77] Ibid., 102.
[78] Manion 2004; Geddes 1994; Rose-Ackerman 1999.    [79] See March and Olsen 2011.
[80] Capoccia 2016.    [81] Prasad et al. 2018: 105.    [82] Madariaga 2017: 642.
[83] Mahoney and Thelen 2010.    [84] Helmke and Levitsky 2006.    [85] Manion 2004.
[86] Kang 2002.

and through innovations, or "marginal adjustments,"[87] that allow it to outlast the reform period and evade attempted controls and regulations. In short, distributional approaches go beyond the enforcement-based mechanism described earlier. Not only do formal and *de facto* powerholders limit or manipulate the enforcement of postwar governance reforms,[88] but they also actively ensure the preservation of the undermining rules through processes of adaptation and by wielding their influence to ensure impunity.

Though such approaches focus more squarely on the question of persistence and are more attentive to the role of power, there remains a lack of clarity on the channels through which dominant distributional coalitions exercise influence to ensure the postwar stability of the undermining rules. On the one hand, studies of institutional persistence highlight the presence of hegemonic social and political blocs within official circles of power, asserting their clout through "the continuity of government posts and influence in policy-making."[89] Yet, undermining rules can survive even when wartime actors are removed from official power due to the unofficial channels through which they may continue to wield influence.

For example, wartime specialists in violence often defect to organized crime following democratization and secure impunity through previous ties.[90] Political and military elites can find alternative avenues to advance their interests through the co-optation of new rule of law institutions.[91] Further, powerful private sector leaders and firms can distort government decision-making for their own benefit. Amid worldwide democratic transitions, "the fear of the leviathan state has been replaced by a new concern about powerful oligarchs who manipulate politicians and shape institutions to advance and protect their own empires."[92] This dynamic is especially relevant in Central American bureaucracies, where undue societal influence is just as, if not more, pronounced than meddling by politicians.[93]

Postwar reforms centered on wresting control from the wartime distributional coalition by contracting out government functions similarly overlook the unofficial, informal centers of political and economic power that can serve to reinforce the previous rules of the game. Market reforms often fail to eliminate predatory activities, instead "engender[ing] changes in the modalities of corruption" by allotting leaders "discretionary power ... used to nourish corrupt networks."[94] Far from redistributing power and

---

[87] Madariaga 2017: 642.    [88] Levitsky and Murillo 2013.    [89] Madariaga 2017: 642.
[90] Trejo et al. 2018.    [91] Lake 2017; Barma 2017.    [92] Hellman et al. 2003: 752.
[93] Bowen 2017.    [94] Manzetti and Blake 1996: 685.

resources, postwar economic liberalization may create new channels of influence and exchange through which to uphold the wartime rules.

In sum, this third proposed mechanism – the survival of the wartime distributional coalition – requires further refining to better understand whether dominant social and political blocs uphold undermining rules through official government and policy-making circles or whether their endurance can occur through extra-state spaces and unofficial channels of political access. Postwar institutional persistence, in other words, must also be attentive to whether and how wartime distributional coalitions adapt to democratizing measures and maintain impunity to protect conflict-era institutional arrangements. While traditional political actors can use transitions and peace processes to secure their place within the inner circles of power, they can also do so from without.[95] Formal political turnover and bureaucratic purges are not necessarily sufficient to dismantle undermining rules if the parties with a stake in them find new political and economic spaces through which to ensure their survival.

## WARTIME INSTITUTIONS AND CHRONIC INSTABILITY

Undermining rules devised and implemented during civil war are not always effectively reproduced and may not survive periods of post-conflict peacebuilding and reform. They instead may face what Michael Bernhard terms "chronic instability," or "multiple, frequent, and connected episodes of disjunctive change."[96] Among the causes of chronic instability are changing coalitional configurations, which arise with "the entry into the system of 'actors excluded from institutional decision-making'"[97] or "where power distributions are uncertain or rapidly shifting and there is greater incongruence between the formal rule-writing process and underlying power structures."[98]

By this logic, when the wartime distributional coalition fails to adapt and survive within the new postwar environment and shifting coalitions render the distribution of power uncertain, the undermining rules experience chronic instability rather than consolidation. The latter half of the book illustrates this postwar divergence through a comparison of the Guatemalan cases, in which the rules governing customs fraud and

---

[95] Hagopian 1996.
[96] Bernhard 2015: 977; see also, what Levitsky and Murillo (2013: 95) call "serial replacement."
[97] Bernhard 2015: 982.     [98] Levitsky and Murillo 2013: 100.

extrajudicial killing persist long term, and the Nicaraguan case, where the rules within land tenure remain unstable.

## LOOKING AHEAD

This chapter outlined why civil war so often constitutes a site of institutional change and elaborated the causal process underlying the wartime development of undermining rules within the state. It also laid out when and how the wartime rules are reproduced and persist beyond conflict. Through this institutional framework, I illustrate how the perceived escalation of the insurgent threat during conflict introduces institutional ambiguity, concentrating power within a new or existing counterinsurgent elite. In the face of heightened state vulnerability, these actors then use their decision-making discretion and control over the means of coercion to implement undermining rules, which correspond to their own narrow interests. Overall, against classic war-centered explanations of statebuilding, the question is not whether war "made" the state, but *what kind* of state it made – one grounded in rules that fundamentally contravene or bolster routine state activities.

Further, the wartime rules are reproduced as the narrow counterinsurgent elite brings other actors into the fold, or forges a broader distributional coalition that garners material and political benefits through the survival of the new institutional arrangements. This stage lays the groundwork for postwar institutional persistence, whereby the dominant social and political blocs uphold the undermining rules through official government circles or through extra-state spaces and unofficial channels of political access.

Combined, this and the previous chapter provide the conceptual and theoretical foundations of the remainder of this book, which illuminates the processes of wartime institutional evolution (Part II) and war and postwar institutional persistence and instability (Part III) in three Central American cases: (1) Guatemala's tax and customs apparatus, (2) Guatemala's police forces, and (3) Nicaragua's land and property administration. But first, I turn to a brief history of Central America's Cold War-era conflicts, specifically the escalation of the insurgent threat and the resulting reconfigurations of political power.

# PART II

# INSTITUTIONAL ORIGINS

# 3

# Civil War in Central America

At the height of the Cold War, Central America served as a staging ground for US-backed counterinsurgent campaigns, which sought to eradicate burgeoning leftist revolutionary forces in the region. While US government leaders provided substantial economic, military, and political support, they operated in concert with Central America's own right-wing military factions, paramilitary allies, and landed oligarchy, prompting a series of armed conflicts. By the early 1980s, Guatemala, El Salvador, and Nicaragua had been consumed by full-scale conflict, while Honduras suffered state-sponsored repression at the hands of military dictatorship.

This book focuses on two of these settings: Guatemala's Civil War (1960–1996) and Nicaragua's Contra War (1980–1990). The longest and bloodiest of the region's wars, the Guatemalan internal armed conflict officially began in 1960, pitting the right-wing, military-led state against a series of leftist guerrilla groups. During the conflict, military leaders not only targeted urban student, labor, and political opposition leaders, but also carried out a brutal rural campaign to "drain the sea" of insurgent support, eradicating some 626 Mayan communities, according to the UN-backed Historical Clarification Commission (CEH). By war's end, an estimated 200,000 people had been killed or disappeared and 1.5 million had been displaced.[1] The CEH determined that the Guatemalan state, which committed roughly 93 percent of wartime abuses, had engaged in "acts of genocide" against five Mayan ethnolinguistic groups.[2]

---

[1] CEH 1999, Vol. 2: 318.    [2] Ibid., 417–422.

As civil war reached its most violent moment in Guatemala, Nicaragua's left-wing government initiated its own armed campaign against the US-backed Contra insurgency – a conflict that would persist through the 1980s. Having come to power in a successful revolution in 1979, the Sandinista National Liberation Front (FSLN) dismantled the repressive, oligarchic structures of the 43-year Somoza dynasty and implemented a series of transformative social and economic programs to promote health, literacy, and land redistribution.[3] But following the 1980 election of US president Ronald Reagan, the United States ramped up its support for the former Somoza forces, which organized armed resistance movements along the Honduran and Costa Rican borders. The Contra insurgency targeted Sandinista social and economic projects, triggering greater government repression. By decade's end, the Contra War had claimed some 32,000 lives and wrought nearly $4 billion in financial losses.[4]

While this book illuminates how these armed conflicts remade the rules governing routine state activities, we must begin by examining how conflict trajectories reshaped structures of political power, paving the way for the introduction of undermining rules. To do so, this chapter provides a concise history of the Guatemalan and Nicaraguan armed conflicts, beginning with the proximate causes of civil war outbreak. Within both cases, the chapter then examines the variables central to the process of wartime institutional change elaborated in Chapter 2: the perceived escalation of the insurgent threat and the creation of a narrow counterinsurgent elite coalition with heightened decision-making discretion. Rather than provide an exhaustive historical account of civil war in both cases, this chapter is instead structured to highlight these building blocks – and the connection between them – to provide the foundations for understanding the wartime implementation of undermining rules within core policy domains.

This chapter also highlights the numerous contrasts between the Guatemalan and Nicaraguan cases as a means of foregrounding the surprisingly similar trajectories of wartime institutional change that will be elaborated in Chapters 4, 5, and 6. Importantly, key divergences between

---

[3] See Núñez Soto 1991; Christian 1986; Spalding 1994; Colburn 1990; and Goodwin 2001 for histories of the Sandinista Revolution, the Contra War, and the resulting transformations.

[4] Martí i Puig 1997: 117. Casualty figures are from the Correlates of War Dataset available at www.correlatesofwar.org/data-sets/COW-war/intra-state-war-data-v4-0.

the two contexts provide evidence against the three alternative explanations for the wartime development of undermining rules elaborated in
Chapter 3: (1) state war-making strategies, (2) regime ideology, and (3) the
nature of foreign assistance. Instead, the comparable way in which the
perceived escalation of the insurgent threat restructured the dominant
political coalition explains why we see new undermining rules in the cases
at the heart of this book. In other words, this chapter endeavors to draw
out the complexities of the Guatemalan and Nicaraguan conflicts, while
underscoring the common conditions that made the wartime introduction
of perverse institutional arrangements possible.

## THE ROAD TO ARMED CONFLICT

In both Guatemala and Nicaragua, the descent into civil war came in
response to moments of revolutionary triumph and the nascent social,
political, and economic transformations that took hold thereafter. In the
Guatemalan case, however, armed conflict erupted after CIA-backed counterrevolutionary forces dismantled a decade of popular, democratic
reforms, while in Nicaragua, civil war emerged as right-wing insurgent
forces sought to derail the revolutionary project in its tracks. In this section,
I trace Guatemala's and Nicaragua's respective roads to armed conflict,
detailing how popular reforms spawned virulent anti-communist backlash.

### Guatemala (1944–1960)

The road to Guatemala's thirty-six-year civil war can – in an immediate
sense – be linked to its period of "Democratic Spring" (1944–1954),
which sought to overturn patterns of inequality and personalist caudillo
rule.[5] The decade-long window of democratic opening began with the
"October Revolution," a popular movement that overthrew the thirteen-
year dictatorship of General Jorge Ubico (1931–1944). Following continued economic stagnation, brutal repression, and the suspension of
constitutional guarantees, a broad, multi-class coalition mobilized
months of protest, eventually forcing Ubico to resign and guaranteeing
democratic elections.[6] A deepening split within military ranks facilitated
its triumph. With the creation of the military academy, the corps of junior
officers receiving professional training had grown significantly.

---

[5] Isaacs and Schwartz 2020.
[6] Gleijeses 1991: 8–29; Yashar 1997: 86–100; Handy 1994.

Disgruntled by the lack of opportunities for promotion and Ubico's subservience to US interests, this young, nationalist faction served as a reliable base of support for the opposition and blocked efforts to restore military rule following Ubico's ouster.[7]

Democratic elections instead placed civilian Juan José Arévalo (1945–1951) in power, prompting popular reforms to address the country's long-standing inequities. Among the measures implemented to promote middle- and working-class incorporation were a new labor code to protect workers' rights and a new constitution (1945) to extend suffrage and freedoms of association and expression.[8] Perhaps the most sweeping and controversial policy was Decree 900, passed in 1952 under second "Democratic Spring" president, General Jacobo Arbenz (1951–1954), the former Minister of Defense. Decree 900 would redistribute idle plantation lands to peasants. Though considered moderate in practice,[9] the measure restored communal rights to many indigenous Mayan populations and challenged the strict rural control held by the traditional oligarchy.[10]

Guatemala's landed elite and its economic and political partners in the United States vilified the reformist program advanced during the Arévalo and Arbenz administrations, providing the military's hardline, anti-communist faction with willing allies as it plotted counterreform. With mounting fears that the 1956 presidential elections could elevate the Communist Party, US advisors and large landowners mobilized the mercenary troops of the "Army of National Liberation."[11] By late 1953, the CIA had started plotting what became known as Operation Success (PBSUCCESS), a covert mission for the military overthrow of Arbenz, which succeeded in June 1954.[12]

The CIA-backed coup "thrust Guatemala's 'Democratic Spring' into reverse," swiftly dismantling the 1945 Constitution and consolidating military authoritarian rule.[13] Under the subsequent dictatorship of Colonel Carlos Castillo Armas (1954–1957), the military "purged state institutions, arguing that communists held key positions in the Presidential Palace, Ministry of Foreign Affairs, Labor Department, Social Security Office, and Congressional commissions."[14] Hardline military leaders also shuttered agencies responsible for social and economic reforms, including the land reform and labor inspection offices.

---

[7] Grieb 1979: 539–543.   [8] Yashar 1997: 103.   [9] See Gleijeses 1991.
[10] González-Izás 2014: 153.   [11] Ibid., 172.
[12] Gleijeses 1991: 242–251; Holden 2004: 141.   [13] Isaacs and Schwartz 2020.
[14] Yashar 1997: 208.

Initially, the younger, nationalist military faction did not uniformly abandon the reformist vision of the Arbenz era. They instead forged an opposition movement that challenged Castillo Armas' successor Miguel Ydígoras Fuentes (1958–1963), and eventually grew into a leftist guerrilla insurgency. Under the leadership of two army lieutenants, Marco Antonio Yon Sosa and Luis Augusto Turcios Lima, the movement led an unsuccessful revolt at the Zacapa military base in November 1960 – a rebellion propelled by 30 percent of the Guatemalan army at the time.[15] The failed uprising drove the rogue military officers further underground; however, it eventually spawned a new guerrilla organization known as the Rebel Armed Forces (FAR). The revolt, though unsuccessful, paved the way for civil war, "[provoking] a stupendous increase in what was already the isthmus' most ambitious program of US military and police collaboration, encouraging the Guatemalan military to remake itself into one of the most ruthless counterinsurgency forces in the world."[16]

## Nicaragua (1961–1979)

In contrast to Guatemala's aborted revolutionary project, the road to Nicaragua's ten-year Contra War included a successful revolution led by the Sandinista National Liberation Front (FSLN). Founded in 1961, the FSLN was forged by young political dissidents exiled in Honduras, who organized to oppose the repressive and neopatrimonial regime of Luis Somoza Debayle (1956–1963), a close US ally.[17]

Initially, the FSLN was no match for Somoza's US-backed National Guard (GN); however, a series of events in the late 1960s and early 1970s gradually turned the tide of the revolutionary struggle and eventually brought down the Somoza dictatorship.[18] In 1967, the regime organized sham elections, cementing Somoza's repressive rule. Five years later, and after Somoza amended the constitution to remain in power, Nicaragua suffered a devastating earthquake, which put on full display the regime's incompetence and corruption. And in early 1978, prominent newspaper editor and opposition figure Pedro Joaquín Chamorro was shot dead in downtown Managua, further galvanizing a broad-based anti-regime coalition. As state kleptocracy ran amok and economic conditions

---

[15] Brockett 2005: 99.    [16] Holden 2004: 149–150.
[17] His father Anastasio Somoza García (1937–1956) ruled the two decades before, and his younger brother Anastasio Somoza Debayle (1967–1979) held power for 12 years after.
[18] Goodwin 2001: 137; Spalding 1994: 57.

deteriorated, the "quasi-corporatist" relationship the Somozas had maintained with economic elites began to erode as well.[19] After several successful offensives and the unification of the different insurgent factions, the FSLN marched into Managua on July 19, 1979 and, the following day, presented the new unity government to a jubilant crowd in front of the National Palace.[20]

Following revolution, the Sandinistas, led by Daniel Ortega, launched a sweeping program to effect social and economic change on behalf of Nicaragua's working and peasant classes. They implemented an internationally recognized literacy campaign (*Cruzada Nacional de Alfabetización*), which reduced the national illiteracy rate from 50.4 to 12.9 percent in just five months.[21] They also organized the Popular Health Brigades (*Brigadistas Populares de Salud*), mobilizing some 73,000 volunteers to carry out mass anti-dengue and anti-malaria vaccination campaigns.[22] Other mechanisms to foster popular mobilization similarly flourished. By the end of 1982, 1,200 new unions had emerged,[23] and the Civil Defense Committees (CDC) formed during the revolutionary years were converted into neighborhood governance organs known as Sandinista Defense Committees (CDS).[24]

Yet, in other ways, FSLN policies in the early 1980s were less sweeping than many had anticipated. For example, while FSLN leadership envisioned the state sector as the nucleus of its economic model, it never fully abandoned the commitment to a mixed economy. The FSLN worked alongside "the progressive sectors of the bourgeoisie in order to bring their level of production in line with the standards of the new regime."[25] Despite this more moderate economic course, geopolitical developments would soon spur the growth of counterrevolutionary forces and the perceived intensification of the insurgent threat, endangering Sandinista political power and the early revolutionary gains.

### ESCALATION OF THE INSURGENT THREAT

As laid out in Chapter 2, this book distinguishes between the onset of civil war and the perceived escalation of the insurgent threat *within* civil war, treating the latter as a key impetus for wartime processes of institutional change. In this section, I chronicle two moments in the Guatemalan armed

---

[19] Spalding 1994: 51.    [20] Christian 1986: 136–138.    [21] Vilas 1984: 301.
[22] Núñez Soto 1991: 238.    [23] Vilas 1984: 247.    [24] MIDINRA 1985a.
[25] US Department of State 1986: 13; see also, Martí i Puig et al. 2011: 5.

conflict (the late 1960s and mid-1970s) and one moment in the Nicaraguan conflict (early to mid-1980s) in which state leaders perceived a marked increase in the threat posed by insurgent forces. As we will see, these escalatory dynamics correspond to somewhat different conflict processes and events. In the Guatemalan context, high-profile guerrilla violence, in one moment, and changes in the insurgency's strategic orientation and composition in another, drove perceptions of threat escalation. In Nicaragua, a shift in the makeup of counterrevolutionary forces was understood as providing rebels a greater foothold within national territory. While reflecting diverse battlefield dynamics, rulers in both cases perceived the state to be increasingly vulnerable, prompting the restructuring of wartime political power and laying the groundwork for the institutional changes to come.

## Guatemala (Late 1960s and Mid-1970s)

Over the course of thirty-six years, Guatemala's internal armed conflict witnessed multiple moments of political closure and repression by state actors, as well as various cycles of mobilization by opposition and organized insurgent forces.[26] Within the ebb and flow of armed conflict, there were two moments in which regime leaders perceived a heightened sense of insurgent threat and state vulnerability: one in the late 1960s in response to increasing urban guerrilla attacks, and one in the mid-1970s due to the reorientation of rebel strategy, specifically the increasing mobilization and territorial control within the historically marginalized Mayan highlands of the country.

The first moment of perceived threat intensification took shape after the vestiges of the first failed rebel uprising regrouped and increased targeted violence against prominent public figures in the late 1960s. In the immediate years following the revolt, the insurgent threat was seen as minimal, remaining more of an occasional nuisance than a dire risk to regime stability. For example, a US Embassy telegram from September 1963 reported that the sitting government of Enrique Peralta Azurdia (1963–1966) "continues in firm control; Communist forces in the country, which the new regime shattered in its early weeks, continue to pose no serious threat."[27] A March 1964 progress report from US officials

---

[26] See Brockett (2005) and Sullivan (2016a, 2016b) for more on the dynamics of repression and resistance in the Guatemalan armed conflict.
[27] US Embassy in Guatemala 1963: 1.

stationed in Guatemala similarly asserted that "the small, mobile bands of guerrillas that have been active in the Northeast have offered no serious threat to the stability of the Government."[28]

However, dynamics shifted during the subsequent presidency of Julio Cesár Méndez Montenegro (1966–1970), whose civilian administration was marked by escalating fears of regime vulnerability due to insurgent attacks and right-wing challenges.[29] Though small in numbers, Guatemala's primary insurgent organization at the time, the Rebel Armed Forces (FAR), demonstrated growing strength, engaging in guerrilla warfare tactics like targeted kidnappings and bombings. Comprised mostly of former military officers and soldiers, the FAR had come to represent "a major internal threat to [Guatemala's] stability for the foreseeable future," in the words of a 1968 US State Department cable.[30] Underscoring these vulnerabilities, that same year, FAR forces stormed the US Embassy in Guatemala City, murdering then-ambassador John Gordon Mein – the first US ambassador to be assassinated while serving abroad. This event was followed by a spate of similar acts in 1970, including the kidnapping of US political secretary Sean Holly, Guatemalan foreign minister Alberto Fuentes Mohr, and West German ambassador Karl von Spreti, who was eventually assassinated.[31] Though the possibilities of toppling Guatemala's military government remained distant, the high-profile acts of violence transformed perceptions of the FAR's capabilities and dramatically increased the sense of threat.

Just as the "increasing Castroite communist insurgency"[32] posed a renewed threat, extreme right-wing elements associated with anticommunist groups like the National Liberation Movement (MLN) also served as agents of government destabilization, plotting coups and backing rural vigilantism. Observers linked this increase in "right-wing terror" to covert support provided by members of the country's armed forces given their "distrust of the police and the courts as effective agents in combatting [insurgent] terror."[33] Though right-wing attempts to topple the civilian government never succeeded, such activities triggered a heightened sense of vulnerability within the Méndez Montenegro administration. According to conversations between Méndez Montenegro and US Embassy officials, the president "[admitted] that the upsurge in vigilante activity constitutes a risk to the stability of his government" and was "equally aware of the

---

[28] US Embassy in Guatemala 1964: 5.     [29] Keefe 1984: 201.
[30] US Department of State 1968: 11.
[31] Associated Press 1970a, 1970b; *The New York Times* 1970.
[32] US Department of State 1969: 7.     [33] US Department of State 1967: 2.

hazards of trying to call the military's hand on the vigilante problem," which could backfire and provoke his overthrow.

This first moment of perceived threat escalation during the Guatemalan armed conflict thus illustrates the confluence of diverse wartime dynamics. After crushing the military-led rebellion, the Guatemalan government perceived a renewed threat posed by the FAR in the late 1960s, which increasingly engaged in acts of spectacular violence targeted against prominent officials. Though the FAR's meager ranks were never capable of mounting a viable challenge to the Guatemalan state, these high-profile, selective attacks fueled the belief that the organization constituted a major internal threat. Simultaneously, the Guatemalan government faced instability and potential coup risks from radical, right-wing sectors with close ties to the most extreme elements of the military. Combined, these factors exacerbated the sense of regime instability and would provide the impetus for an initial restructuring of wartime political power to eradicate the insurgent threat.

A second, and arguably more intense, period of perceived threat escalation came in the mid-1970s, years after the early urban-based guerrilla organizations had been squashed. This escalation of rebel threat occurred when a subsequent generation of leftist insurgent groups revamped their military strategy and geographic focus. Rather than seek to build a small vanguard that would trigger broader uprising, they instead sought the direct incorporation of diverse popular organizations, ranging from urban labor groups to rural Mayan communities.[34] New organizations like the Guerrilla Army of the Poor (EGP) and the Organization of People in Arms (ORPA), which unified in 1982 under the Guatemalan National Revolutionary Unity (URNG), reflected this transformation and expanded the insurgent presence.[35]

This strategic shift had born fruit by the late 1970s and early 1980s, allowing rebel organizations to expand their support base. As Jennifer Schirmer notes, by the beginning of 1982, the ranks of the EGP had grown to an estimated 4,000 to 6,000 regular fighters, 60,000 collaborators from local clandestine committees (CCL), and some 260,000 people living in insurgent-held territory.[36] Moreover, guerrilla presence became diffuse throughout Guatemalan territory. By 1981, the insurgent movement had a presence in 16 of 22 departments of the country, and "in at least 50 municipalities, public buildings had been destroyed as a way of

---

[34] Brett 2016.    [35] Brockett 2005.    [36] Schirmer 1998a: 41.

anticipating the process of revolutionary reconstruction [...] after [the insurgency's] imminent victory."[37]

Yet, in contrast to the previous moment of perceived threat escalation, heightened fears of state vulnerability in the mid-1970s were not only triggered by an increase in insurgent presence and attacks, but by *who* was understood to be the insurgency's primary base of civilian support: indigenous Mayan communities in the northwestern highlands. Mayan claims and identities have long been perceived by the ruling *ladino* elite as challenges to the integrity of the Guatemalan nation.[38] These historical narratives suffused the counterinsurgent struggle with new meaning and reframed the sense of state vulnerability. According to records from the Operation Sofía campaign in the northwestern Ixil region,[39] military leaders understood "all of the inhabitants of the area to have been heavily indoctrinated by the subversion." The plans further asserted that the insurgency "had managed to carry out a complete job of ideological consciousness-raising among the entire population, having achieved one hundred percent support."[40] In short, beyond the dramatic expansion of the insurgency's base, this second moment of perceived threat escalation was fueled by the shifting nature and makeup of insurgent forces – their embrace and mobilization of communities long understood to challenge *"una nacionalidad guatemalteca"* [one Guatemalan nationality].[41] Beyond reshaping counterinsurgent strategy, the mounting fears of state vulnerability would also remake the structures of wartime political power.

### Nicaragua (Early to Mid-1980s)

Amid Nicaragua's Contra War, heightened fears of FSLN vulnerability in the early to mid-1980s similarly corresponded to key changes in the composition of insurgent forces, which shifted the locus of the threat from US-coordinated Somoza allies outside of national territory to peasant-led insurgent forces with deep attachments in Nicaraguan highland communities. The counterrevolutionary forces were initially comprised of former GN members that served under Somoza. Forced to flee following the 1979 revolution, they regrouped in neighboring Honduras

[37] Rosada-Granados 1999: 154.     [38] Perera 1993: 48.
[39] The Operation Sofía records are available through the National Security Archive at http:// nsarchive.gwu.edu/NSAEBB/NSAEBB297/Operation_Sofia_hi.pdf.
[40] Schwartz and Straus 2018: 230–231.     [41] Garrard-Burnett 2010: 71.

and in Miami and laid the organizational foundations of the first military movement to regain political control of Nicaragua: the National Democratic Front (FDN).

Following the 1981 inauguration of Ronald Reagan, CIA advisors became integral to FDN organizational efforts. Through classified portions of legislation passed in late 1981, the US Congress approved a $19 million program of covert military assistance to the Contra, with the goal of establishing a territorial base along the border in Honduras from which to declare a "provisional government."[42] From there, the insurgency sought to develop a social base within Nicaragua, first among Somoza-allied landowners and ex-GN family networks and then within Atlantic Coast indigenous communities and urban centers along the Pacific.[43] Though the nascent Contra groups had yet to gain a territorial foothold within Nicaragua, they did launch raids from Honduras, "systematically [terrorizing] the population" by targeting cooperatives and peasant recipients of FSLN literacy and vaccination efforts.[44]

While the counterrevolutionary resistance remained a rather homogenous force in these initial years, the Sandinista's strict control of social, political, and economic life had altered the composition of Contra forces by the mid-1980s. Disillusionment with FSLN governance fanned the flames of rebellion among peasant communities in Nicaragua's north-central highlands, contributing to a heightened sense of regime vulnerability. The Contra first began to reorganize the local guerrilla units known as the MILPAS – previously the Anti-*Somoza* Popular Militias, but now the Anti-*Sandinista* Popular Militias. With US funds, the FDN's ex-GN leaders began a robust campaign to recruit MILPAS units and members to their cause.[45] Meanwhile, new counterrevolutionary movements formed along the southern border in Costa Rica (Democratic Revolutionary Alliance, ARDE) and the largely indigenous Atlantic Coast (Miskito, Sumo, Rama Unity, MISURA, and the Nicaraguan Coast Indian Unity, KISAN).[46]

According to records from the Nicaraguan Resistance (RN), the umbrella organization that joined the FDN and ARDE, there were a reported 3,002 FDN troops in November 1982. By the beginning of 1984, that figure had nearly tripled to 8,163.[47] Based on estimates of demobilized commandos and fighters killed in action, former US State

---

[42] Serafino 1989: 1; "Los contras" 1987.    [43] "Los contras" 1987.
[44] Kruijt 2008: 120–121.    [45] Brown 2001: 88–89.    [46] Martí i Puig 1997: 72.
[47] FDN 1982, 1984.

Department liaison Timothy Brown indicates that 45,000 to 50,000 Nicaraguans may have participated in the FDN, although Contra practices of forced recruitment and kidnapping make it difficult to know what proportion joined voluntarily.[48] Archival documentation from the RN further indicates that even as early as 1982, a significant number of rebel commandos had agricultural backgrounds.[49] By 1986, forty-two of the primary one hundred Contra leaders were peasants.[50] Of the fighters who laid down their arms during the 1990–91 demobilization period, an estimated 97 percent were members of the rural peasantry.[51]

In short, the character of the conflict underwent a marked shift, culminating in "a peasant uprising, which could be considered the greatest source of erosion for the Sandinista Revolution," in the words of Orlando Núñez Soto.[52] We can see this shift in FSLN understandings of the insurgent threat within the Sandinista Popular Army's (EPS) own records. In a top-secret document, EPS leaders highlighted how in 1983 "the FDN achieved a substantial jump in its ranks [...] with the objective of deepening the presence of Contra forces within the interior of the country."[53] Former EPS major and defector, Roger Miranda, similarly elaborated how peasant militarization transformed and exacerbated the Sandinista leadership's sense of vulnerability:

Beginning in 1983, the armed activity of the FDN was transformed into a broad peasant insurrectionist movement almost impossible to eliminate militarily without annihilating the majority of the peasant population. Entire families had risen up against us in the departments of Nueva Segovia, Madriz, Matagalpa, and Jinotega, in addition to the uprisings of Miskito communities in Zelaya Norte ... and Zelaya Sur. ... Despite the concept that the FSLN had of the workers and the peasants as constituting their fundamental social forces, at least in the case of the peasants, the facts demonstrated that they had in reality become the social force that could throw them out of power.[54]

The perceived escalation of the insurgent threat can also be seen in the FSLN's reorientation of local organizational life and unprecedented military buildup. The popular programs and organizations mobilized as the vehicles of revolution were completely reoriented toward defense efforts.

---

[48] Brown (2001: 116) indicates that most of these members were voluntary; however, other accounts, such as that of former Contra fighter G. Enrique López Salinas (2011: 85), indicate that "in the final stage of the war, the counterrevolution fed its ranks, in large part, through kidnapping."

[49] RN n.d.      [50] Morales Carazo 1989: 130.      [51] Brown 2001: 116.

[52] Núñez Soto 1991: 366.      [53] Dirección de Inteligencia Militar 1987: 3.

[54] Ratliff n.d.: 80-A, 131.

As Núñez Soto describes, "being a Sandinista was no longer just a privilege with which you accessed power; it was also a cost that put your life at risk. The mobilizations were no longer just about cutting cotton or coffee ... but incorporating oneself in the defense of the country."[55] The organized proletariat, particularly those working in state-owned farms and agribusinesses, became "bastions of defense" in rural war zones.[56] Local-level FSLN organizations such as the CDS also became key instruments for detecting "counterrevolutionary sabotage" and combatting any urban Contra front.[57]

In addition to recasting the goals and activities of Sandinista-affiliated organizations, the FSLN undertook massive military expansion. According to Nicaraguan government figures, the EPS had amassed over 86,000 members by the end of the conflict.[58] According to US intelligence sources, by mid-1987, the EPS' active-duty forces numbered 74,000,[59] with its total strength, including reserve and militia units, comprising 120,000 members, or approximately 8 percent of the adult population.[60] Much of the troop buildup began in October 1983, when the government initiated conscription through the "Patriotic Military Service Law" [*Ley de Servicio Militar Patriótico, SMP*].[61] The scale and regulation of mass defense mobilization was without parallel in neighboring Guatemala and El Salvador.

## WARTIME STRUCTURES OF POWER

Despite the many divergences of Guatemala's and Nicaragua's wartime settings, this book argues that the perceived growth of the rebel threat and heightened fears of state vulnerability in both cases had a remarkably similar effect on the wartime structures of political power: It prompted the counterinsurgent elite – those government, armed forces, and police leaders in charge of designing political and combat strategies to eliminate the insurgent threat – to become narrower and further insulated from broader state and military structures under the pretext of staving off

---

[55] Núñez Soto et al. 1998: 202.    [56] Ibid., 292.    [57] MIDINRA 1985a: 25.

[58] Ejército de Nicaragua 2009: 90.

[59] By comparison, Guatemala had just over 32,000 active-duty members, less than half the number in Nicaragua. El Salvador had nearly 45,000, roughly 60 percent. See US Department of State and Department of Defense 1987: 5.

[60] Ibid., 3.    [61] JGRN 1983.

insurgent penetration and annihilating the internal enemy. As elaborated in Chapter 2, it is this process that best accounts for the wartime creation and implementation of new undermining rules within the state. This section chronicles the reconfiguration of wartime structures of political power in both cases as state leaders sought to combat the mounting insurgent threat.

## Guatemala

Following the two moments of perceived threat escalation – the rise in selective attacks by the FAR in the late 1960s and the expansion of the EGP and ORPA within the Mayan highlands in the mid-1970s – Guatemalan military leaders forged highly specialized, elite units within state security forces, a strategy meant to enhance their ability to root out guerrilla forces embedded within the population. Under the guise of combatting insurgent infiltration, overcoming intra-agency mistrust, and strengthening counterinsurgent capacities, political and military power was concentrated in the hands of high-level intelligence officers that operated in the shadows and eventually devised new institutional procedures that would undermine core state functions, like tax collection and public security provision. Here, I chronicle how the escalation of the insurgent threat in the late 1960s and mid-1970s translated into new structures of wartime power, focusing first on military intelligence and then on the National Police's (PN) Detective Corps.

### *Military Intelligence*

As fears mounted in the late 1960s, the Guatemalan military, with critical US assistance, undertook serious measures to professionalize its ranks, which focused, above all, on strengthening the intelligence apparatus. A relatively young organization that only developed a national identity following World War II, the Guatemalan military remained woefully unprepared to take on the sophisticated tasks required of irregular warfare. Assessments from US military advisors suggest that the field of intelligence was particularly in need of strengthening due to widespread deficiencies within the army's intelligence division, known as the G-2. One declassified US cable from 1968 claimed that, "within the armed forces the quantity and quality of intelligence gathered by the G-2 is minimal. Evaluation and analysis is nearly non-existent. ... The quality of intelligence produced is fair to poor. The caliber of agents is poor, the amount of money is low, and the systematic intelligence collation and assessment is poor."[62] An evaluation by Department of Defense officials nearly four years later was even more damning. It claimed that the army's intelligence section:

>...is relatively small and ineffective. Attempts by conscientious intelligence officers to improve its functions and capabilities have been met with little support from the Army and Government leaders, due in large part to suspicion and antipathy resulting from the former role of the G-2 in conducting investigations of a personal nature. ... Other reasons for lack of effectiveness stem from a lack of proper selection of agency personnel ... and poor source administration and control.[63]

The strategy for tackling the weaknesses in the view of US military advisors consisted of streamlining and strengthening intelligence gathering and analysis as well as empowering elite intelligence units thought to have fewer links the politicized practices of the past. In response to the first moment of perceived threat escalation, the military government of Carlos Manuel Arana Osorio (1970–1974) established the US-backed Joint Operations Center (COC)[64] to "serve as the *one* location where *all* intelligence on insurgent personalities and their activities is collected and collated."[65] The centralization of intelligence was also combined with enhanced training and resources. In 1980, following insurgent expansion in the northwestern highlands, the military established its Intelligence School (*Escuela de Inteligencia*) and in 1983, with CIA support, created an advanced intelligence training course.[66] By 1983, the Guatemalan army had some 2,000 new intelligence officers.[67]

In addition to the streamlining and enhanced training, Guatemalan political leadership came to vest greater power in more specialized elite intelligence units, a response to distrust of the G-2. One such intelligence outfit, which will be the focus of Chapter 4, was known first as the *Centro Regional de Telecomuncaciones* (Regional Telecommunications Center) or "*La Regional*" and then later as the *Sección de Archivo General y Servicios de Apoyo* (General Archive and Support Services Section) or "*El Archivo*."[68] *El Archivo* was tied to the Presidential Military Staff (EMP),

---

[62] USAID 1968: 2–3.    [63] DIA 1972: 1.

[64] In 1979 under the regime of Lucas García, a similar intelligence center called the "Information-Gathering and Operations Center," or CRIO *(Centro de Recopilación de Información y Operaciones)*, was created; see Vela 2002: 78.

[65] USAID 1968: 11.    [66] Vela 2002: 78.    [67] Ibid.; see also, Isaacs and Schwartz 2020.

[68] I will refer to this organization as "EMP intelligence" or "*El Archivo*," since the latter was the name used at the height of the unit's autonomy and political power. Based on my interviews and conversations, it is also the name most Guatemalans associate with it.

a personal military advisory body that responded directly to the president. Though some version of a presidential guard can be traced back to Guatemala's early postindependence period, *El Archivo* was first established under the military government of Enrique Peralta Azurdia in 1964. It was an initiative of the United States' Office of Public Safety, which sought to strengthen the military's capacity to identify and eliminate "internal enemies" attempting to destabilize the domestic order.[69] US advisors chose to focus their resources and energy on *El Archivo* and "dismiss the army's own intelligence structure due to mistrust between the US government and Guatemalan authorities" – mistrust that stemmed from continued suspicions of US intervention among the more nationalist factions of the Guatemalan military.[70]

*El Archivo* was formally tasked with "the collection and analysis of information on individuals considered enemies of the political interests of the government."[71] But in practice its activities were far broader. The CEH notes that *El Archivo* operations extended well beyond presidential security and came to include "developing counterinsurgent activities, advancing political espionage, and elaborating analysis on individual citizens."[72] While the activities of the G-2 intelligence section of the Guatemalan army largely corresponded to combat in conflict zones, the smaller, specialized staff of *El Archivo* played a more overtly political role, selectively targeting political opposition to the regime.[73] It wove a vast network of civilian informants and controlled other state security organizations, like the investigative divisions of the National Police (PN).[74] *El Archivo* also served as an architect of misinformation campaigns to cover up extralegal activities and manipulate the population.[75]

With its increasing specialization and discretion, *El Archivo* became a key perpetrator of human rights abuses and developed extensive links to right-wing death squads. Particularly under Arana Osorio, whose regime was heavily backed by the extremist MLN, EMP intelligence effectively "served as a security command center to coordinate 'a covert program of selective assassination,'"[76] with *El Archivo* officers granted the freedom

---

[69] Schirmer 1998a: 157.
[70] See Dirección de los Archivos de Paz 2011: 102. Efforts to strengthen *El Archivo* through technical assistance were also supported by other foreign partners, including the Israeli and Argentine governments; see CEH 1999, Vol. 2: 99.
[71] CEH 1999, Vol. 2: 101.    [72] Ibid., 109.
[73] Vela 2002: 75–76; see also, Schirmer 1998a.    [74] CEH 1999, Vol. 2: 75–76, 86–89.
[75] Ibid., 80–82, 100.    [76] Schirmer 1998a: 158; McClintock 1985: 170.

"to apprehend, hold, interrogate, and dispose of suspected guerrillas as they saw fit," in the words of one CIA cable.[77]

But the discretion allotted to *El Archivo*, particularly in the second moment of perceived threat escalation in the mid-1970s, went beyond the use of violence and came to encompass political control of a broad array of government agencies. Per the CEH, "beginning in 1978, members of intelligence ... had penetrated various public entities, including the postal service, telephone service, immigration, customs, the courts, the Ministry of Finance, [and] the Public Prosecutor's Office."[78] What began as "simple infiltration" turned into "the total incorporation" of intelligence officers within these offices.[79] In sum, the perceived escalation of the insurgent threat not only concentrated counterinsurgent strategy and operations in the hands of a narrow corps of counterinsurgent elites, but it further empowered them to infiltrate non-defense-related agencies framed as vulnerable to insurgent incursion.

### The Detective Corps

A very similar story can be told about Guatemala's National Police (PN), which became tightly linked with the military intelligence apparatus. As fears of state vulnerability mounted with the surge in FAR attacks in the late 1960s, the PN was deemed incapable of the internal security tasks necessary to stem insurgent revival. Though it had been brought under the umbrella of the General Directorate of National Security in 1956,[80] its persistent deficiencies with respect to countering guerrilla activity were widely noted by US public security advisors. As one explained, the "police forces have a limited capacity to face up to any large-scale internal subversion, rioting or guerrilla warfare that might be fomented by Castro-Communists or to act as an effective deterrent."[81]

On the one hand, the existing deficiencies were structural, stemming from the absence of professional training, poor personnel and budget administration, limited equipment, and low morale.[82] On the other hand, the obstacles had to do with leadership and political will. By the mid-1960s, US efforts to strengthen the police had continually been "thwarted by the [Government of Guatemala's] failure to give the police minimal

---

[77] CIA 1983: 1; see also, Amnesty International 2003: 4–5.
[78] CEH 1999, Vol. 2: 100–101.      [79] Ibid.      [80] US Embassy in Guatemala 1956.
[81] US Embassy in Guatemala 1961: 4.
[82] International Cooperation Administration 1956: 3–4.

budget and administrative support"[83] and "to furnish the police the material and other resources necessary to make it an effective organization."[84]

Under the direction of US advisors and top Guatemalan military brass, the National Police underwent reorganization to expand police coverage, institutionalize the PN's counterinsurgent role under military control, and enhance internal security and intelligence capabilities. In the early 1970s, new police stations and substations were created throughout the country. Particular attention was focused on Guatemala City, with four new police divisions established within delimited operational zones.[85] The size of the police force nearly doubled over a decade, increasing from 3,000 agents in 1965 to 5,368 in 1974.[86]

Moreover, much like the evolution of Guatemalan military intelligence, a core measure undertaken to strengthen police counterinsurgent capabilities was the empowerment of narrow, elite investigative units, whose operational discretion far exceeded their formal duties. The most powerful of these groups within the PN was known as the *Cuerpo de Detectives*, or the Detective Corps.[87] The Detective Corps was formally established on November 3, 1970 under the Arana Osorio government; however, it originated from a series of police investigative units created in 1925, when the PN first achieved organizational coherence.[88] Formally, the Detective Corps was charged with tasks "in support of prosecutors and judges in order to obtain, compile, secure, and study judicial evidence."[89] In accordance with its legislative origins, its sole institutional function was that of criminal investigation: "to study the causes and circumstances under which a criminal act occurred."[90]

The nature of the PN's investigative division, however, underwent a categorical shift with the formal creation of the Detective Corps in 1970 in response to the surge in selective FAR attacks in the late 1960s. This shift involved two related elements: (1) greater specialization in investigative and intelligence techniques, which transformed the Detective Corps into an "elite" police organ; and (2) the insulation of

---

[83] US Embassy in Guatemala 1963: 1–2.     [84] US Embassy in Guatemala 1964: 5.
[85] AVANCSO 2013: 52.     [86] McClintock 1985: 157.
[87] Prior to 1955, the Detective Corps was called the "Section of Investigations," the "Security Police," and then the "Judicial Guard." Following the 1982 coup, the Detective Corps transitioned into the "Department of Technical Investigations." In 1986, it was renamed the "Brigade of Special Investigations and Narcotics." And finally, from 1988 onward, it was called the "Department of Criminal Investigations;" see AHPN 2009: 9.
[88] AHPN 2009: 19.     [89] AVANCSO 2013: 62.     [90] AHPN 2009: 27.

the Detective Corps from the broader police apparatus and its operational autonomy under the military intelligence elite.

First, the Detective Corps was envisioned not merely as a repressive force that operated at the whims of the president, but instead as a highly trained group capable of counteracting urban guerrilla activity. In a conversation between President Arana Osorio and US diplomats months prior to its creation, the Detective Corps was conceived of as "an elite police corps to deal with urban terrorism" and a "new high-level security force [that would use] the latest scientific techniques within the legal framework."[91] While its predecessor, the Judicial Police, carried out repression against political opponents, it lacked the investigative and intelligence capacity necessary to wage targeted counterinsurgent operations. The transition to the Detective Corps was thus a means of bringing the PN's investigative apparatus into the fold of the state's elite intelligence efforts.

By the early 1970s, the Guatemalan government invested increasing resources in developing within the Detective Corps the requisite manpower, surveillance techniques, and intelligence collection and analysis capacities to serve as "a source of information that complemented the government's intelligence apparatus."[92] Toward this aim, the Arana Osorio government created the Detective Corps Academy in 1971,[93] which more than doubled the number of agents from 150 in 1962 to 324 by 1974.[94] The concept of police intelligence was also more clearly delineated and aligned with the US-driven National Security Doctrine, which guided the Guatemalan state's counterinsurgent struggle. According to documentation from the Historical Archives of the National Police (AHPN):

Police intelligence is designed to protect the government against insurrectionist elements that try to subvert and undermine the internal security of the state. . . . Within the framework of the counter-insurrection, police intelligence is the information concerning the subversive activities and the attitude of the population, which permits the police or other counterinsurgent forces to determine the existence of a climate of discontent, identify the tendencies, identify the leaders and members of the clandestine guerrilla organizations, know the places where they are found, their movements and methods of operation, and the terrain in which they act.[95]

---

[91] US Department of State 1970: 1.     [92] AHPN 2009: 103.     [93] Ibid., 48.
[94] US Embassy in Guatemala 1962: 1; McClintock 1985: 157.     [95] AHPN 1980: 1.

The institutional functions of police intelligence thus acquired a new level of specialization. Rather than operating as "goon squads"[96] to face down political dissidents on the streets, the Detective Corps engaged in the more technically sophisticated tasks related to intelligence collection and analysis, which elevated its role within the PN.

As a result, the Detective Corps became entirely insulated from other police structures and was instead empowered to operate from the shadows, under the thumb of Guatemala's military intelligence elite. This is the second key change that occurred in the early 1970s. As a means of fending off guerrilla infiltration, the Detective Corps enjoyed *de facto* separation from the PN Directorate and instead operated as an arm of the elite military intelligence cliques controlling executive decision-making. According to the prevailing view at the time, such entities "constituted the [insurgency's] favorite targets, given that, from within them, [the insurgency] can destroy discipline and secure greater freedom to develop clandestine activities."[97] As a result, officials urged that, "the intelligence unit should have a certain degree of autonomy to reduce the possibility of compromising its confidential operations."[98]

This autonomy from the PN command structure brought the Detective Corps under the umbrella of military intelligence, a move further facilitated by the creation of the Joint Operations Center of the Police (COCP) in 1972. The COCP was an interinstitutional agency formally tasked with "the elaboration of statistical analysis and the systematization of registered information" gathered from police patrols and activities. The COCP served as the main link between Detective Corps activities and the intelligence work of military officials.[99] It shifted the Detective Corps' institutional locus from the formal police organization to the powerful cliques of military intelligence elites.

The Guatemalan case thus illustrates how the perceived escalation of the insurgent threat in two distinct moments prompted the restructuring of wartime political power within the military and police, narrowing the dominant counterinsurgent coalition and insulating it from potential countervailing forces within other state structures. This reconfiguration of wartime power would be critical to the institutional changes to come.

---

[96] US Embassy in Guatemala 1962: 1–2.     [97] Ibid., 11.     [98] Ibid., 2.
[99] AVANCSO 2013: 23.

## Nicaragua

By the mid-1980s, Nicaragua had witnessed a similar restructuring of wartime political power – the creation of a narrow coalition of counter-insurgent elites empowered to introduce wartime institutional innovations. Here, I detail how, amid the perceived growth of the Contra threat, Nicaragua's postrevolutionary government gave way to a circumscribed and insulated clique of FSLN elites that would remake the rules of state administration in perverse and corrosive ways.

Upon the 1979 triumph of the Sandinista Revolution, Nicaraguan leaders initially forged a broad unity government that reflected the cross-class anti-Somoza coalition that facilitated political change. The multi-sectoral nature of the revolutionary coalition – a feature promoted by the more pragmatic *Tercerista* faction – readily translated into a governance model that allowed the Sandinistas "to pursue a controlled form of pluralism involving an alliance between classes" once in power.[100] We can see the manifestations of this "controlled form of pluralism" within the two key governing institutions established in 1979: the Government Junta of National Reconstruction (JGRN) and the Council of State. The former, encompassed the FSLN; the United People's Movement (MPU), "an umbrella organization of anti-Somocistas dominated by the *Terceristas*;" and the business groups that had come to align with the revolutionary coalition.[101] The five-member transitional government included FSLN leader Daniel Ortega, leftist activists Sergio Ramírez and Moisés Hassan, and more conservative anti-Somoza opposition figures Violeta Barrios de Chamorro and Alfonso Robelo. Meanwhile, the Council of State represented the diverse corporate interests even more explicitly, consisting of delegates from distinct political parties, women's associations, unions, youth organizations, indigenous communities, and the organized private sector, represented by the Higher Council of Private Enterprise (COSEP).

Initial postrevolutionary governing structures thus resembled a corporatist regime channeling multiple countervailing forces, rather than the revolutionary vanguard that would emerge. As Robert Chisholm notes, "[T]he FSLN's program of national unity under popular hegemony bore a great deal of resemblance to corporatist ideals of national consensus, the elimination of conflictual competition, and the mediation of group conflict by a state which incorporates all social groups within it. . . . The FSLN

---

[100] Chisholm 1991: 32; see also, Wright 1990: 41–44.     [101] Chisholm 1991: 33.

accepted the articulation of conflicting interests within certain limits rather than attempt to destroy groups that remained outside the state and party."[102]

Yet the plural nature of the early revolutionary coalition gave way to FSLN dominance – a process that accelerated with the escalation of the Contra insurgent threat. The executive structures described above were understood as merely one facet of "State of National Reconstruction" – "the socio-political superstructure of transition between the neo-colonial capitalist state and the popular Sandinista state."[103] Alongside the JGRN stood the FSLN's National Directorate (DN), the party vanguard comprised of nine revolutionary commanders and understood to be the "undisputed leadership" empowered to "[carry] out political directives with complete autonomy."[104] In fact, it became common to hear at political rallies and assemblies the call *"¡Dirección Nacional ordene!"* [By order of the National Directorate!].[105]

Despite framing the JGRN as comprised of "the distinct political and social sectors of the country," FSLN leadership affirmed the JGRN's subordination to the decision-making authority of the DN. According to a 1980 FSLN document on "The Structure and Functioning of the Government Junta of National Reconstruction":

The sovereignty of the State of National Reconstruction resides in the Sandinista people and is represented in the current moment by their vanguard. ... This fact, in addition to the correlation of national and international political forces resulting from the popular victory on July 19, has determined that in Nicaragua hegemonic political power resides in the National Directorate (DN) of the FSLN. ... The legitimacy of the DN's direction of the country is indisputable. It is based in the representation of the popular sovereignty of the Sandinista people by its organized vanguard. ... The ends of the Government Junta of National Reconstruction is to direct National Reconstruction socially, politically, and economically, within the political directives determined by the National Directorate of the FSLN.[106]

The DN also ensured the FSLN's strict control over key government posts and agencies, including the Ministry of the Interior (MINT) and the Ministry of Agricultural Development and Agrarian Reform (MIDINRA). With the formation of the Sandinista Popular Army (EPS),

---

[102] Ibid., 38–9.    [103] FSLN 1980: 7.
[104] Martí i Puig 2010: 83. The members of the DN included Bayardo Arce, Tomás Borge, Luis Carrión, Daniel Ortega, Humberto Ortega, Carlos Núñez, Henry Ruiz, Víctor Tirado, and Jaime Wheelock.
[105] Ibid.    [106] FSLN 1980: 7.

whose institutional identity was directly linked to the party movement, the FSLN secured the fusion of the party, state, and military and consolidated full political control.[107] Opposition leaders Chamorro and Robelo eventually stepped down from the JGRN, further narrowing the dominant political coalition.

Though the nine DN leaders professed the importance of popular participation, in practice, state authority was highly concentrated in the Sandinista vanguard, especially by the mid-1980s. In the words of revolutionary commander Bayardo Arce, FSLN governance was anchored in "democratic centralism." But as the Contra War wore on, the conditions became ripe for "the strengthening of control, centralization, and verticalism." Arce admitted that military and economic necessities pushed the revolutionary commanders to become "more centralist than democratic."[108]

As part of this centralizing tendency, the DN suspended civil and political rights through the State of Emergency first decreed in 1982 and again revived in 1985. These decrees represented the "tightening of political space" in response to Contra gains.[109] In the wake of increased regime vulnerability, the DN also undertook several measures to limit the autonomy of postrevolutionary mass organizations, "[subordinating] their demands to the government's defense requirements" and cementing their role as "merely appendices to the party apparatus."[110]

The administrative reorganization of the country had a similar effect, reducing the decision-making latitude of local-level Sandinista cadre. Amid greater Contra control within highland peasant and coastal indigenous communities, FSLN leaders divided Nicaraguan territory into six discrete regions and three special zones to better coordinate defensive efforts. This reorganization, however, subordinated community leadership to the regional representatives of the Sandinista Assembly, the legislative body that operated as a rubberstamp for DN decision-making.[111]

In sum, following a fleeting period of "controlled pluralism," the perceived escalation of the Contra threat triggered the further centralization of political power and decision-making authority in the narrow, nine-member DN – the purported FSLN vanguard empowered to defend the revolutionary project at all costs. Once the "imperialist aggression" acquired a more internal and rural character, the DN consolidated its vertical structure and subsumed any remaining local autonomy in the name of national defense. This narrowing of Nicaragua's counterinsurgent elite in the mid-1980s is

---

[107] Cajina 1997: 75–119.     [108] Invernizzi et al. 1986: 65, 86.
[109] Williams 1994: 177.     [110] Ibid., 174.     [111] Martí i Puig 1997: 85–86.

comparable to the restructuring of wartime political power in Guatemala, where fears of state vulnerability spawned a small and insulated intelligence elite granted broad decision-making discretion.

### ASSESSING ALTERNATIVE EXPLANATIONS

In addition to underscoring the similar ways in which the wartime escalation of the perceived insurgent threat restructured political power, the comparison of the Guatemalan and Nicaraguan contexts also provides important sources of variation that allow me to evaluate the three alternative explanations outlined in Chapter 2: (1) state war-making strategies, (2) regime ideology, and (3) foreign support.

First, the Guatemalan and Nicaraguan conflicts reflect stark contrasts in how the state waged war, specifically the kinds of resources it marshalled to mount its counterinsurgent campaign. In Guatemala, political and military leaders forged tight linkages with oligarchic elites – a form of war-making consistent with Tilly's "capital-intensive" mode whereby state-economic elite bargaining "made it possible to govern without erecting, financing, and feeding a bulky administrative system."[112] By contrast, Nicaragua's mode of accruing the means of war against the Contra is best characterized as "coercion-intensive" in that rulers sought access to "the resources [citizens] controlled through household taxation, mass conscription, censuses, police systems, and many other invasions of small-scale social life," implying "penetration and bargaining [that] laid down new state structures."[113] The reorientation of popular organizations toward defensive efforts and the mass military buildup, including mandatory conscription, might predict processes of contestation and bargaining that generate robust administrative structures. In other words, the resulting institutions would bolster and reinforce the extractive, coercive, and regulatory functions of the Nicaraguan state. Yet, as Chapter 6 will illustrate, my analysis of wartime changes within Nicaragua's land reform institutions suggests the opposite, casting doubt on this alternative explanation.

The nature of the two wartime regimes also provides evidence against the idea that regime ideology best accounts for trajectories of institutional change within the state amid conflict – the second alternative explanation. Along with the foundations of regime support, the ideological orientations of the military-led governments in Guatemala and the FSLN ruling

---

[112] Tilly 1990: 25.    [113] Ibid.

coalition in Nicaragua were remarkably distinct. Guatemala's military dictatorship enjoyed robust private sector backing and wielded state power on behalf of the country's most reactionary societal forces, while Nicaragua's wartime ruling party pursued sweeping socialist-inspired policies on behalf of the masses. Though the FSLN's ideological commitments and programmatic focus might predict a more effective postrevolutionary statebuilding campaign,[114] land reform and tenure institutions indicate that these effects were not uniform across distinct policy arenas, challenging the explanatory leverage of an ideology-based approach alone.

Finally, the Nicaraguan and Guatemalan conflicts varied on another key dimension linked to the third alternative explanation: the role of foreign influence and, in this case, the most significant international actor at the time, the US government. After Reagan's 1980 election, the US government undertook an extensive economic and technical assistance program to arm and train anti-Sandinista rebels. US intelligence organizations were also involved in anti-Sandinista military activities in a more direct sense. For example, the CIA oversaw the mining of three Nicaraguan ports in late 1983. Amid US opposition, the Sandinista regime did enjoy moderate economic and technical assistance from the Soviet bloc; however, aid dwindled by the mid-1980s and was never any match for US Contra support.[115]

By contrast, in Guatemala, the United States figured on the opposite side of the playing field. As discussed above, the Guatemalan government received significant US financial and technical support. Though this funding was well below that provided to El Salvador, Guatemala still received $620.4 million in US aid between 1981 and 1988.[116] These contrasting roles played by the United States in Nicaragua and Guatemala, while having important effects on the balance of military capabilities, also cast doubt on the idea that the nature and extent of foreign support best accounts for the wartime emergence of undermining rules in the cases examined within this book.

## LOOKING AHEAD

In many ways, the armed conflicts that ravaged Guatemala and Nicaragua in the latter part of the twentieth century are emblematic of the irregular "proxy wars" that made "the developing world into the hot

---

[114] Thaler 2018.     [115] Kinzer 1984.     [116] GAO 1989: 11.

frontline of the Cold War"[117] – albeit with key differences in the align-
ment of forces. While Guatemala's armed conflict occurred after counterrevolution reinstalled right-wing military dictatorship and spurred
insurgent mobilization, the outbreak of war in Nicaragua followed the
successful rise of a leftist revolutionary movement to state power and
subsequent backlash to reforms.

Further, the nearly four-decade-long trajectory of the Guatemalan
internal armed conflict witnessed two distinct moments in which
US-backed military rulers perceived an increase in the leftist insurgent threat:
one in the late 1960s in response to the spectacular, targeted violence waged
by the FAR, and one in the mid-1970s as new insurgent organizations
expanded their territorial base among the country's highland indigenous
communities. In Nicaragua, FSLN leaders perceived that the US-funded
Contra insurgency constituted a serious threat when it transformed from a
group of Somoza-allied elites to a force of primarily peasant producers
disillusioned with FSLN rule.

Despite these differences, however, the perceived escalation of the
insurgent threat in both cases had a similar effect: It centralized
decision-making authority in a narrow counterinsurgent elite empowered
to introduce new rules and procedures to annihilate the rebel threat. In the
Guatemalan case, this occurred through the creation of elite military and
police intelligence units, like *El Archivo* and the Detective Corps, which
were allotted extraordinary discretion to infiltrate and control non-
defense-related agencies. Moreover, these narrow blocs of counterinsurgent leaders remain shielded from broader political and military forces,
allowing them to evade external oversight and accountability. Similarly,
in Nicaragua, rising Contra attacks and support prompted the FSLN
vanguard, the DN, to further centralize power and subordinate subnational organizations to its strict, vertical control. With the empowerment
of a circumscribed clique of counterinsurgent elites in both contexts, the
rules of the game within state institutions were ripe for change.

Building on these foundations, I now turn to analyzing three cases of
wartime institutional change, within distinct state arenas: Guatemala's
customs apparatus (Chapter 4), Guatemala's policing institutions
(Chapter 5), and Nicaragua's land tenure administration (Chapter 6).

---

[117] Kalyvas and Balcells 2010: 416.

# 4

## The Wartime Institutionalization of Customs Fraud in Guatemala

At 6 am on September 14, 1996, investigators from Guatemala's Public Prosecutor's Office (MP), accompanied by military intelligence and National Police (PN) agents, surrounded the home of Alfredo Moreno Molina, the alleged leader of a criminal network within the customs administration. Located in a secluded zone of the Guatemala City suburb Mixco, Moreno's residence was protected by dozens of private security guards and PN officers, who reportedly fled to the surrounding ravines when investigators arrived.[1] Authorities on the scene began a search that lasted five hours, seizing computers, personnel files, and more than fifty IDs issued to Moreno by different state entities.[2] The judge that authorized the raid eventually arrived to inspect the piles of evidence. Finding sufficient proof of contraband and tax evasion, he ordered Moreno's immediate detention.[3]

As they put the pieces together, investigators uncovered a vast series of institutional arrangements within the Ministry of Finance and the General Directorate of Customs, which they believed defrauded the Guatemalan state up to $30 million on a monthly basis for nearly twenty years. The mounting evidence not only revealed the fraudulent customs operations coordinated by Moreno but shed light on the extensive web of associates he had woven in the process – individuals positioned at the highest levels of government. Just days after Moreno's capture, five police chiefs, four customs administrators, and nine top military officials, including the vice

---

[1] *El Gráfico* 1996a; Letter from the PN's Office of Professional Responsibility (ORP) to the Public Prosecutor's Office (MP) from September 27, 1996 (Organismo Judicial 2003).
[2] *Siglo Veintiuno* 1996a.     [3] Hernández S. 1996a.

minister of defense, were forced to resign for suspected connections to the criminal structure.[4] Moreno was charged with customs fraud, contraband, bribery, and tampering with evidence.[5]

Moreno's capture and the unmasking of the "Moreno Network" was an extraordinary feat for the government of Álvaro Arzú (1996–2000), which was concluding a lengthy peace process to end Guatemala's thirty-six-year internal armed conflict. The case had been in the making for months and was nearly sabotaged multiple times due to leaks from within the investigative agencies. But the highly distorted levels of customs revenue had reached a tipping point, according to top Ministry of Finance authorities.[6] Growing pressure from US intelligence officials – who had identified Moreno as the capo of customs at least five years earlier[7] – pushed the Guatemalan government to act, according to one top official.[8]

Facing stiff resistance from customs personnel, the case was handed off to a small military intelligence taskforce, which worked covertly to investigate the anomalies and identify their source.[9] Even the prosecutors who eventually took over the investigation were unaware it existed until right before Moreno's capture. As one prosecutor recalled, "Just a day before the raid on Moreno's residence, I went to the Attorney General's Office and standing there were military intelligence agents who had participated in identifying the Moreno structure. Perhaps not from a juridical standpoint, but they knew there was a network causing serious damage to the state and that it was necessary to move in."[10]

Though the exposure of such a powerful criminal structure was unprecedented, knowledge of Moreno's illicit dealings and his ties with top military brass was nothing new. The Moreno Network was, in the words of President Arzú, *"un secreto a voces"* ["an open secret"]. Previous leaders admitted their awareness of the scheme but felt there was little they could do to dismantle it. Former president Vinicio Cerezo (1986–1991) confessed that despite rumors of criminal activity by military officers formally under his command, "in reality they operate with a lot of independence," leaving him little recourse.[11] Similarly, ex-president Ramiro de León Carpio (1993–1996) revealed that he "had knowledge of the *contrabandista* Alfredo Moreno Molina but his capture was never

---

[4] Ramírez Espada 1996.   [5] Juárez 1997.
[6] Interview with author, October 21, 2016.   [7] DIA 1991.
[8] Interview with author, May 30, 2017.   [9] Interview with author, June 12, 2017.
[10] Interview with author, November 9, 2016.   [11] Shetemul 1996b.

ordered because no one, not even military intelligence, could provide proof of the accusations."[12]

A week before the raid on Moreno's home, customs director Luis Pedro Toledo submitted his resignation, citing death threats that began even before his nomination and had reached an "unbearable level." "Everyone knows about corruption within customs," affirmed Toledo in a parting interview with the Guatemalan daily *La República*. "It's not new, which indicates that, for [criminal] actions of this magnitude, there have to be well-organized mafias both within and outside of customs."[13]

But where did these well-organized mafias come from? How had they managed to impose their will within Guatemala's customs administration for nearly two decades, diverting millions from state coffers and systematically undermining state revenue extraction? In this chapter,[14] I chronicle the genesis and evolution of the criminal structure operating within Guatemala's customs apparatus, which, while bearing Alfredo Moreno's name, never belonged to him alone. Instead, the Moreno Network was forged by an elite clique of military intelligence officers, who were granted extraordinary discretion while infiltrating the state apparatus to combat Guatemala's insurgent groups in the 1970s and 1980s. Amid the heightened sense of threat triggered by the mid-1970s insurgent expansion, the counterinsurgent elite became further insulated from broader state and military structures, allowing it to introduce a series of predatory institutional arrangements that crystallized into undermining rules. These new rules structured a series of illicit customs procedures to systematically siphon off revenue destined for state coffers. They were strictly enforced through coercion – violent and nonviolent – as military intelligence possessed total control over day-to-day decision-making within the central government. Overall, this process, mapped out in Figure 4.1, mirrors the causal sequence theorized in Chapter 2.

These findings diverge from previous research on the effects of conflict and militarization on the state's extractive capacity, which focus on the role of public mistrust and resulting tax evasion or the negative economic effects of conflict-related instability, which hinders investment.[15] Yet, this bottom-up focus obscures the direct role of state and military leaders in structuring fraud and evasion, particularly where economic elites

---

[12] *Prensa Libre* 1996a.   [13] De León Polanco 1996.
[14] See Schwartz 2020, the article on which this chapter is based.
[15] See Cárdenas et al. 2014; Flores-Macías 2018: 5.

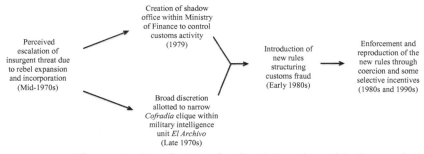

FIGURE 4.1 The wartime introduction of undermining rules within Guatemala's customs apparatus

maintain close linkages to the wartime regime. My approach to extractive "weakness" and systematic customs fraud in Guatemala resonates with a distinct explanation, which focuses on institutional co-optation and distortion.[16] I posit that the institutionalization of customs fraud was driven both by the interests and preferences of those military intelligence elites empowered to seize control of the tax administration, as well as their ability to circumvent countervailing political forces and mechanisms of accountability. Overall, the emergence and evolution of the Moreno Network illustrates how the wartime escalation of insurgent threat facilitates the development of new rules and procedures that distort official state functions such as revenue extraction.

Importantly, it is not this chapter's claim that customs fraud originated during the armed conflict period. Indeed, customs fraud and contraband smuggling are not new phenomena in Guatemala, or Central America generally. Illicit commerce in Central America dates back to the colonial period and is rooted in the Spanish Crown's fragile hold on trade in the Americas. However, there are two features of this prewar history that suggest that patterns of contraband and customs fraud, while widespread, did not constitute rules and procedures that were enforced from above. The first is that political authority in Guatemala prior to the mid-twentieth century was organized regionally and based on *caudillo* or "strong man" rule. The central state was neither sufficiently powerful nor legitimate to coordinate a territorially comprehensive customs regime, predatory or not. In the words of historian Matilde González-Izás, "for over a century and a half, Guatemala was a fragmented nation. The central government was never capable of controlling national territory

---

[16] Ch et al. 2018.

directly; for this reason, it was obligated to select *caciques* [local political bosses] or a segment of provincial elites to act in its name."[17] In other words, the type of centrally managed scheme reflected by the Moreno Network would not have been thinkable given the prewar structure of political power.

Second, and relatedly, the formation of a strong central state did not occur until the 1931 rise of dictator Jorge Ubico, who, according to historical accounts, did more than any other leader to crack down on illicit activity within customs. In 1935, Ubico oversaw the creation of the General Directorate of Customs and the Customs Code, which remained in place until the late 1990s when the Moreno Network revelations prompted the creation of the Superintendent of Tax Administration (SAT) (Chapter 8).[18] Ubico strengthened border security to stem the flow of illegal arms from Mexico and Belize and enacted a *mano dura* [heavy-handed] policy to combat corruption among customs personnel, "who were known to receive bribes for the passage of alcohol and tobacco."[19] Though Ubico also oversaw significant trade liberalization, in bolstering territorial control and administration, the government was able to "reclaim its auditing role" and crack down on contraband.[20] In short, the rules and procedures implemented by the central state under Ubico sought to eradicate customs fraud rather than institutionalize it.

Despite the involvement of members of the economic and political class in smuggling and customs fraud throughout history, there is thus no evidence that these tendencies rose to level of rules rooted in shared expectations and external enforcement. It was the centralization of political authority and militarization of the state following the 1954 coup and counterrevolution that would change this. In the words of one former Ministry of Finance official, once the military was firmly in control of customs, "they began to realize that commerce brings in a ton of money [...] And they began to see that it's not just contraband related to military equipment and supplies for the guerrillas, but that there are people with lots of money evading taxes too."[21]

To illustrate these claims, this chapter proceeds as follows: Picking up where Chapter 3 left off, I first examine how the escalation of the insurgent threat within Guatemala's armed conflict, particularly the second moment of insurgent resurgence in the mid-1970s, led to the infiltration of the customs apparatus. Insulated from broader military structures, *El Archivo*, the

---

[17] González-Izás 2014: 193.    [18] Cordova Noguera 2014: 3.    [19] ASIES 2013: 31.
[20] Ibid.    [21] Interview with author, June 12, 2017.

EMP's intelligence outfit, established a shadow office known as the "Office Special Ministerial Services" (SEM) under the pretext of stemming the flow of arms, cash, and recruits to the insurgency. In the next section, I examine how these developments gave rise to a new rules-making elite: the exclusive clique of high-level intelligence officers, known as the *Cofradía*, which took advantage of their growing mandate to infiltrate government agencies and introduce new rules within customs.

The next two sections examine the intricacies of the undermining rules that evolved within the customs apparatus thereafter. First, I detail the emergence of the Moreno Network and the alternative procedures it crafted, specifically the adjustment of customs duties, the falsification of import quantities, and the "theft" of shipping containers. The next section discusses how the rules associated with these illicit procedures were enforced through the use of coercion and through the co-optation of security forces. The chapter concludes by returning to the causal process articulated in Chapter 2 and elaborating how the escalation of the insurgent threat and the increased decision-making discretion of a narrow military intelligence elite spurred the evolution of undermining rules within Guatemala's customs apparatus.

## MILITARY INTELLIGENCE AND THE INFILTRATION OF CUSTOMS

As described in Chapter 3, the perceived escalation of the insurgent threat in the mid-1970s – a moment of insurgent resurgence and greater popular incorporation – reshaped wartime political structures. Specifically, it triggered the empowerment and insulation of military intelligence elites from the Presidential Military Staff's intelligence outfit, *El Archivo*. By the end of the 1970s, *El Archivo* operatives had been allotted high levels of decision-making discretion and infiltrated a range of defense and non-defense-related ministries. In state agencies as diverse as the postal service, the National Civil Service Office, immigration, the Ministry of Finance, the Public Prosecutor's Office, and the court system,[22] *El Archivo* operatives came to control routine communications and day-to-day decision-making.

The historical archives of the EMP shed light on this high degree of penetration, which included control of personnel transfers and communications. The 1982 year-end report published by the Secretary of the EMP,

[22] CEH 1999, Vol. 2: 100–101.

for example, cites the "coordination between EMP leadership, the Ministry of Communications, the National Civil Service Office, and the National Postal and Telegraph Service for the processing of new appointments."[23] In the same year, the "Special Services" division of the EMP "collaborated extensively for the implementation of the communications systems of the Ministry of Finance, the National Police, and the Treasury Police [*Guardia de Hacienda*]."[24] EMP intelligence officers thus actively participated in staffing decisions and oversaw ministerial communications. As one former intelligence officer told me, "With the new technologies, all state entities had been infiltrated by the end of the 1970s."[25]

The penetration of these government agencies by specialized intelligence operatives was, of course, seen as a very necessary counterinsurgent measure as insurgent groups such as the EGP expanded their base of support among popular organizations and indigenous communities in the mid-1970s. Various security and justice experts explained that the state offices infiltrated at the height of the conflict were viewed as strategic sites "theoretically related to national security," or essential "to monitor the guerrilla movement."[26] The insurgency's reliance on the movement of people, information, money, and arms required the development of new intelligence capacities throughout the state apparatus. Interviews with former intelligence agents and officers suggest that it was specifically the threat of overland weapons smuggling that prompted the tightening of control in border outposts. "Really, it was the increase in the threat of arms entering via land," a former intelligence official remarked. "The entry of arms by sea was easier to control. But the way of impeding [entry via land] was infiltrating the ministries."[27]

Within the Ministry of Finance, which included the General Directorate of Internal Revenue and the General Directorate of Customs, this "infiltration" took the form of a new section called the "Office of Special Ministerial Services" or SEM (*Oficina de Servicios Especiales Ministeriales*),[28] created

---

[23] Secretaría del Estado Mayor Presidencial, División de Comunicaciones. 1982. *Memoria de Labores*. Doc. C.2.1.6.2-5-S042–0003.
[24] Secretaría del Estado Mayor Presidencial, División de Comunicaciones. 1982. *Memoria de Labores*. Doc. C.2.1.6.2-5-S042–0005.
[25] Interview with author, November 7, 2016.
[26] Interviews with author, June 18 and July 1 and 3, 2015; see also, Peacock and Beltrán 2003: 20.
[27] Interview with author, November 7, 2016.
[28] This office is, at times, referred to as *El Archivo*, further illustrating its links to EMP intelligence.

in 1979. The SEM office occupied the eighteenth floor – the top level – of the Ministry of Finance building located in the heart of downtown Guatemala City.[29] The placement of the office on the top floor was strategic. In addition to providing an unparalleled view over Guatemala City's historic center, it granted SEM personnel privileged access to the radio communications system anchored by an antenna atop the building.[30] The communications system allowed SEM officers to correspond with customs agents at territorial entry points and receive information about suspicious activities. Indeed, EMP documents from 1983 cite a "radio laboratory section" operating in the Ministry of Finance, which, among other activities, installed, de-installed, and repaired "base stations" at "different administrative and customs sites."[31]

Though the vast majority of the civilian personnel were not privy to the inner workings of the SEM, many were aware that it existed and was staffed by military officers "on loan" to the Ministry.[32] Though rumors were rampant, Ministry of Finance employees preferred not to pry, especially when it came to military-related matters.[33] The triangulation of archival documentation, however, confirms that the SEM office was directed not just by any military officers, but by members of the EMP inner circle. Communications between the Ministry of Finance and National Police leadership, as well as court documents, name four "chiefs" of the SEM during the late 1970s into the 1980s.[34] EMP personnel registries, while incomplete, confirm that the first three were on the EMP payroll during the precise periods for which they served as SEM chief. Wartime documentation thus corroborates firsthand accounts citing the small, eighteenth-floor SEM office as an EMP intelligence

---

[29] Interviews with author, October 21, November 7 and 9, 2016; CEH 1999, Vol. 2: 101; Moreno declaration, September 19, 1996 (Organism Judicial 2003).

[30] Field notes, October 13, 2016.

[31] Secretaría del Estado Mayor Presidencial, Sistema de Comunicaciones. 1983. Doc. C.2.1.6.2-5-S042–0011.

[32] Author correspondence with Ministry of Finance official, October 26, 2016.

[33] Field notes, October 13, 2016.

[34] These directors of the SEM office are Major Francisco Ortega Menaldo (1979 to March 1982), Colonel Carlos Eliseo Gálvez Miranda (per police correspondence in February and July 1983), Major Roberto Letona Hora (per police correspondence in January 1984), and Major Hugo Francisco Morán Carranza (per police correspondence in January 1986); see AHPN 1983, GT PN 30-01 S009 [Reference No. 5114058]; AHPN 1984, GT PN 30-01 S009 [Reference No. 5113696]; AHPN 1986, GT 50 S028 [Reference No. 4248230]; Secretaría del Estado Mayor Presidencial 1979–1982 [Doc. C.2.1.6.2-5-S001–0040; C.2.1.6.2-5-S001–0042], 1983 [Doc. C.2.1.6.2-5-S001–0049, p. 374], 1984 [Doc. C.2.1.6.2.-5-S005–0013, p. 70].

outpost, established under the pretext of capturing "explosives, weapons, things like that."[35]

The professionalization of Guatemalan military intelligence, which culminated in the infiltration of government ministries by *El Archivo* operatives, illustrates how the counterinsurgent context created a climate propitious for institutional change within state agencies. Under an aggressive US-backed national security mentality, political leadership granted intelligence officers a high degree of operational latitude. This *carte blanche* extended well beyond the use of violence and included control of the communications, personnel decisions, and routine activities within state agencies, notably the Ministry of Finance and its General Directorate of Customs. Combined, these dynamics fostered deep "gaps" between the existing rules and their enforcement.[36] At the height of the Guatemalan armed conflict, the rules of the game were ripe for change.

### THE RISE OF A NEW COUNTERINSURGENT ELITE: THE *COFRADÍA*

As the intelligence apparatus was vested with greater autonomy, narrow groupings of officers within it forged strong personal loyalties. These loyalties solidified into tight intra-military factions that sought political power and state resources through control of *El Archivo*. According to one former intelligence agent, these elite cliques based on "informal affinities" represented an "old boys' club [*amiguismo*],"[37] with members using their positions of influence to favor others in the group. These informal affinities shaped which officers were named to important intelligence posts and the distribution of resources accrued through control of the state apparatus. In addition, the fragmented nature of Guatemala's military structure fostered an environment of persistent intra-military competition for power, influence, and resources.

In the late 1970s and early 1980s, the most powerful of these intra-military cliques came to be known as the "*Cofradía*," a word alluding to the traditional "brotherhood" groups in Mayan communities. At first, the term "*Cofradía*" was used in a more general sense and in response to the intelligence-speak used by CIA advisors working in Guatemala in the 1970s. As a former Guatemalan intelligence officer explained, "When you work for Intelligence, you are part of 'the community.' That's what they'd

---

[35] Interview with author, October 27, 2016.   [36] Mahoney and Thelen 2010.
[37] Interview with author, November 7, 2016.

say in the United States, and so it's the name the advisors used here. But when they came and started using it, our officers said, 'We're not from the community, we're from the *cofradía*,' to make it more Guatemalan [*chapín*]."

Though a more generic term initially, the *Cofradía* came to represent an exclusive clique of military officers that ascended to power with General Fernando Romeo Lucas García (1978–1982), who presided over the bloodiest period of the Guatemalan armed conflict. According to a 1991 US Department of Defense cable, the formation of the *Cofradía* is explicitly linked to intelligence-strengthening efforts as the insurgent threat escalated:

By the late 1970's, it became obvious that at both the tactical and strategic levels, the best of the officers at ranks from captains to colonels, had to be put into positions where their talents could be best used to influence a favorable outcome against the guerrillas. Thus, many of the 'best and brightest' of the officer corps of the Guatemalan army were brought into intelligence work and tactical operations planning. ... But while doing so, the Intelligence Directorate became an 'elite club' within the officer corps, retaining the very best of officers for consecutive intelligence assignments.[38]

Importantly, as the analysis further notes, the *Cofradía*, was "vertical" in nature – a quality that sets Guatemala's intra-military dynamics apart from the rest of Central America. Rather than replicating the "tanda"[39] structure of horizontal loyalties seen within the Salvadoran and Honduran armies, Guatemala's internal military intelligence cliques were mostly based on "leader-subordinate" allegiances.[40] The *Cofradía* was a "vertical column" integrated by officers of various ranks. One of the most prominent *Cofradía* leaders was General Manuel Antonio Callejas y Callejas, the Director of Intelligence during the Lucas García regime.[41] According to US intelligence reports, Callejas y Callejas is variously referred to as the "godfather" of army intelligence and the "bishop" of the *Cofradía*.[42] Before ascending to the top intelligence post, he served as sub-director of the Army's operations division (G-3) and as second in

---

[38] US Department of Defense 1991: 3–4.
[39] *Tandas* are "tightly knit graduating classes from the military academy," which, in twentieth-century El Salvador in particular, "[dominated] the government (and the spoils that went with it) until they were displaced by another *tanda*"; see Goodwin 2001: 157.
[40] US Department of Defense 1991.
[41] Callejas y Callejas was convicted of crimes against humanity for the forced disappearance of fourteen-year-old Marco Antonio Molina Theissen in October 1981.
[42] US Department of Defense 1991; US Department of Defense 1988.

command of the Mobile Military Police [*Policía Militar Ambulante*] and of troops stationed at the Cobán military base in the northern province of Alta Verapaz.[43] He went on to serve as chief of the Army National Defense Staff [*Estado Mayor de la Defensa Nacional*] under President Vinicio Cerezo (1986–1991) and as director of customs under President Jorge Serrano Elías (1991–1993), who was ousted following an attempted self-coup in 1993.

Alongside Callejas y Callejas, the other central figure within the *Cofradía* was Luis Francisco Ortega Menaldo, who was a young major on the EMP payroll during the Lucas García years. Despite his youth, Ortega Menaldo enjoyed significant political influence as the son-in-law of former president Arana Osorio, who oversaw the dramatic increase in counterinsurgent activities following the first moment of perceived threat escalation in the late 1960s, as described in Chapter 3. During his father-in-law's presidency, Ortega Menaldo, known for his elegant dress and command of English, Italian, and French, was a mere adjutant within the EMP; however, by 1978, he was brought on by then-Minister of Finance Hugo Tulio Búcaro to "help control tax collection."[44] Once within the Ministry of Finance, he installed the SEM office and served as its first chief until the coup that ousted Lucas García in March 1982.[45] Even after the 1986 return to civilian rule, Ortega Menaldo occupied prominent political positions, including head of the EMP from 1991 to 1993.

According to US intelligence reports and Guatemalan police documents, other prominent *Cofradía* members included Jorge Roberto Perussina, an infantry major who served as the head of *El Archivo* during Lucas García's tenure;[46] Brigadier General Edgar Augusto Godoy Gaitán, an assistant within the EMP during the late 1970s who would go on to serve as EMP chief in 1990;[47] and Marco Antonio González Taracena, minister of defense in 1995 and 1996. Later in the 1980s, the power of the *Cofradía* was reportedly offset by another faction comprised of field officers – a group known as the *Sindicato* or the "Operators."[48] Among the top *Sindicato* leaders cited by US intelligence reports is Roberto

---

[43] Peacock and Beltrán 2003: 20.    [44] Brenes and Shetemul 1992.

[45] From Moreno's declaration, September 19, 1996 (Organismo Judicial 2003).

[46] AHPN 1982.    [47] Dirección de los Archivos de Paz 2011.

[48] The structure of the *Sindicato* is much closer to the *tanda* phenomenon, in that it is based on class loyalties from Guatemala's military academy (*Escuela Politécnica*). *Sindicato* members were primarily comprised of those from Promotion 73.

Letona Hora, the chief of the SEM office within the Ministry of Finance following the 1983 coup that ousted Efraín Ríos Montt (1982–1983), and Otto Pérez Molina, the former president arrested for his involvement in the customs fraud structure uncovered in 2015, *La Línea*.[49]

As the group controlling the intelligence apparatus at the height of the conflict, the *Cofradía* had a distinct advantage, enjoying broad discretion, sophisticated surveillance technologies, and greater autonomy. Combined, these resources allowed the group to mount new structures to control state activities, which were ultimately appropriated for private benefit.[50] But importantly, the corrupt activities spearheaded and sustained by the *Cofradía* were also underpinned by a hardline counterinsurgent vision used to justify illicit activities. The *Cofradía* was more than an exclusive club grounded in personal affinities; it was also an "ideological group."[51] According to Peacock and Beltrán, the members of the *Cofradía* "adopted a national security strategy that 'framed the conflict within the total polarization [...] of the population.' Civilians were not considered neutral, but potential opposition. The officials that formed part of the *Cofradía* sympathized with the line of thinking of the Taiwanese military, implementing repressive systems of social control and using intelligence information to commit brutal acts of violence."[52]

To the extent that the *Cofradía* used its autonomy and influence to operate on the margins of the law and engage in corruption, such actions formed part of the broader counterinsurgent imperative and were permissible given the group's sacrifices on behalf of the Guatemalan state. As one former military intelligence agent told me, the *Cofradía* "had a lot of power and tremendous influence, but really they overreached [...] They thought they had done good in combatting the guerrillas and so they felt they had a right to do such [corrupt] things."[53] A combination of personal enrichment and ideological orientations motivated the consolidation of the illicit customs procedures. But beyond these specific motivations, the *structure* of this new counterinsurgent elite – its narrow configuration and insulation from countervailing political forces – shaped the nature of subsequent institutional changes.

[49] US Department of Defense 1991.
[50] Peacock and Beltrán 2003: 19; see also, Zamora 2002; Schirmer 1998a: 155; interviews with author, June 25, 2015, July 13, 2015, September 27, 2016, and June 12, 2017.
[51] Interview with author, June 25, 2015.    [52] Peacock and Beltrán 2003: 19.
[53] Interview with author, May 30, 2017.

## THE WARTIME EVOLUTION OF UNDERMINING RULES
## IN CUSTOMS

By the late 1970s, Guatemala's military structures had undergone two critical changes. First, with close US collaboration and economic assistance, the military intelligence apparatus had been overhauled in response to the second moment of perceived insurgent threat escalation in the mid-1970s. Technological inputs and enhanced training elevated the role of military intelligence in rooting out the "internal enemy." Specialized intelligence units with broad discretion successfully infiltrated the entire state apparatus, overseeing day-to-day operations in agencies like the Ministry of Finance. Second, and relatedly, vesting elite intelligence personnel with greater autonomy translated into the formation of exclusive clubs of intelligence officers like the *Cofradía*, which coalesced around deep personal loyalties and a shared, hardline counterinsurgent vision. *Cofradía* members subsequently drew on these affinities and their "conflict capital" to retain political power and access to state resources.

Both developments led to the emergence of predatory activities within Guatemala's customs administration – activities governed by undermining rules that directly contravened formal state revenue extraction. To implement these procedures, the *Cofradía* leadership forged ties with military special agent Alfredo Moreno, who had perfected customs fraud through previous bureaucratic posts. The modalities of customs fraud developed amid conflict were more than corrupt behaviors by customs administrators and inspectors; they were governed by externally enforced rules overseen by the Moreno Network. The failure to abide by the rules – deviating from the procedures for siphoning off customs revenue – resulted in violent and nonviolent punishment, as I will illustrate in the next section. Here, however, I elaborate on how Moreno came to direct the *Cofradía*'s customs fraud activities and the types of illicit procedures that developed.

Alfredo Moreno Molina was born on February 20, 1947 in El Salvador and moved to Guatemala City in his teens. According to early police records, Moreno variously served as an "office clerk [*oficinista*]" and a "driver [*piloto automovilista*]."[54] Yet, by the beginning of the 1970s, Moreno had developed extensive personal and professional ties with top military officials – ties that granted him different positions within the state and ample opportunities to engage in contraband smuggling and

[54] AHPN 1971.

theft. According to PN records, by February 1971, Moreno served as a "special agent" [*confidencial*] for Colonel Manuel Aceituno Arreola, then-chief of the Army Commissary. The Army Commissary imported and sold goods at deeply discounted prices for military members and received significant tax exemptions. In this role, Moreno reportedly carried out "operations of an investigative character" in coordination with military counterparts.[55] By mid-1974, Moreno's boss in the Army Commissary, Enrique Gálvez Sobral, was promoted to director of customs, where he retained Moreno as a special agent on his staff.[56]

From his posts within the Army Commissary and the customs administration, Moreno became well versed in methods of passing contraband and stealing imported goods. He "learned, applied, and perfected" techniques not only to allow unregistered shipments to enter Guatemala, but to "alter legal documents" and undervalue merchandise.[57] Given Moreno's experience and contacts, there was no one better equipped to coordinate fraudulent customs activities as intelligence officers infiltrated the Ministry of Finance following Lucas García's rise to power in July 1978.

At this time, Moreno was brought on board as an "investigator" in the SEM office, the EMP intelligence outpost located on the eighteenth floor of the Ministry of Finance building. There he worked with then-Major Ortega Menaldo, one of the primary *Cofradía* leaders. According to police documentation, Moreno eventually ascended to the post of deputy director of the SEM, just below Ortega Menaldo, who served as director until the coup that ousted Lucas García and brought Ríos Montt to power on March 23, 1982.[58] At this time, Ortega Menaldo was dismissed from his post, while Moreno remained within *El Archivo*.[59]

Officially, Moreno maintained that his role within military intelligence was confined to investigating contraband and that he collaborated closely with the US Embassy to track and seize stolen cars.[60] Yet others with knowledge of the case suggest that underneath his investigative work, Moreno, with the support of top intelligence officers, mounted a well-organized criminal structure within the customs administration, drawing on his extensive contacts inside and outside of the state. While not the head of the scheme, Moreno served as "the manager"; his "bosses were

---

[55] AHPN 1973.    [56] AHPN 1974.    [57] *Siglo Veintiuno* 1996c.    [58] AHPN n.d.

[59] From Moreno declaration, September 19, 1996 (Organismo Judicial 2003).

[60] AHPN 1981; see also, Moreno declaration, September 19, 1996 (Organismo Judicial 2003).

the generals."[61] As one former Ministry of Finance official remarked, with military intelligence's "total control" of customs and Moreno's expertise, together "they took advantage and charged for all of the merchandise that entered [Guatemala]. There was not a single importer who didn't pass through [Moreno] first."[62]

From the SEM office, the Moreno Network devised and implemented a series of customs procedures to capture revenues destined for state coffers. Customs fraud and contraband were no longer just deviant activities on the part of customs personnel at territorial entry points. They instead responded to well-specified and communicated rules coordinated from above and enforced from without; in other words, fraudulent customs *practices* crystallized into a series of *rules* structuring behavior in ways that directly undermined the state's official extractive aims.

The evidence gathered by prosecutors following Moreno's arrest – and especially the testimony of Francisco Javier Ortiz Arriaga, Moreno's right hand known as "Lieutenant Jerez"[63] – revealed two primary procedures developed by the criminal structure to siphon off customs revenues. The first involved the adjustment of customs declarations to underreport the amount of taxes actually paid or to misrepresent the value, quantity, or type of goods entering the country. These adjustments exploited different aspects of the customs declaration process, sometimes with the complicity of importers and sometimes without. Under this broad category, however, the distinct forms of fraud shared a central feature: they relied on the fabrication of forms related to imports and/or customs duties.

One such method involved the falsification of receipts recording the amount of customs duties legally paid by importers. Here, importers would receive a receipt noting the actual amount paid to customs authorities; however, the inspectors verifying the payment [*vistas aduaneros*] would record a significantly lower amount on the copy of the receipt that was then passed on to the Comptroller General's Office and the Ministry of Finance. The Moreno Network pocketed the difference between the actual amount recorded on the original receipt and the falsified, reduced amount on the copy.

---

[61] Interviews with author, November 2 and 9, 2016.

[62] Interview with author, May 30, 2017.

[63] Ortiz Arriaga was the treasurer of *Grupo Salvavidas*, ensuring that the different customs posts provided the amount stipulated by Moreno, which he then delivered to the different network participants (Chapter 7). He received political asylum in Canada following the trial, but returned to Guatemala, serving as a key figure in *La Línea* in 2015.

These kinds of customs duty alterations relied primarily on a form known as the 63-A. According to Ortiz's account,

The 63-A form is a receipt that includes an original and a copy ... and so two forms were created ... one was legal and the other fictitious, but with the same identification number. The original was given to the client, the importer. ... And the copy was made with the false form, which included a much smaller amount than what they paid. ... To give you an example, there would be a form saying they paid 50,000 quetzales, but according to the fictitious form, they paid 1,000, so the state was defrauded 49,000 quetzales.[64]

In other words, this modality of customs fraud took place behind the backs of importers, with falsified documents allowing customs employees to siphon off a large chunk of legally paid taxes. In his declaration, Ortiz suggested that by the mid-1980s, all customs agents engaged in this form of fraud for amounts exceeding 5,000 quetzales ($1,700), on Moreno's orders. There were an estimated 100–150 adjustments per customs house on a weekly basis.[65]

Other falsifications to defraud the state did require the complicity of commercial actors. One, for example, involved reusing old import licenses for new shipments to simulate payment. This method relied on a form referred to as the DC-32, a license emitted following the payment of taxes to the Bank of Guatemala. According to Ortiz, "Per Mr. Moreno Molina's orders, with one of these DC-32 forms given by the Bank of Guatemala, up to ten imports could pass through. ... The exporters just retained and turned them in again when bringing another shipment up to eight or ten days later, all while paying off customs anomalously because it was the law that each shipment required its own DC-32."[66] Here, commercial interests, in coordination with the Moreno Network, played a more active role, benefitting from the use of false documents while paying customs officials and inspectors under the table.

Another mode of fraudulent alterations involved the misrepresentation of the kind or quantity of goods entering the country. Through prior arrangements, customs employees were instructed to underreport the quantity of merchandise or misreport the tariff category to give importers a break. For instance, importers would arrange to

Put a weight that wasn't true because at this time there were mixed tariffs. ... When merchandise came from Panama, ... [an importer] would have 150,000

---

[64] From Ortiz Arriaga testimony, May 25, 1999 (Organismo Judicial 2003).
[65] From Ortiz Henry testimony, May 27, 1999 (Organismo Judicial 2003).      [66] Ibid.

kilos to declare, but 100,000 would be omitted, which is what Mr. Moreno Molina ordered and so that's how they would create the 'consignee guide' [record of merchandise from point of origin]. Mr. Moreno Molina already had the contacts at the warehouses of the *Aduana Central* [Guatemala City customs house], so [the client] would go there to pay the taxes noted on the guide.[67]

Aside from adjustments to misreport the nature of imports or to falsify the amount paid by importers, the second primary method of fraud was the "disappearance" or "theft" of shipping containers. In these cases, customs declarations and receipts "would be stamped as received by the General Directorate of Customs, but taxes were never paid" and the shipment would vanish.[68] Oftentimes, the shipping containers were off-loaded and directed to clandestine fields off of major highways, where they were emptied of merchandise. The contraband would then appear in warehouses or on stores shelves days or weeks later.

Two witnesses that testified at the Moreno trial, former customs inspectors José Mariano Ortiz Henry and Erik de los Ríos, explained in detail how these shipping container "thefts" unfolded. According to De los Ríos, in some cases, shipments would be recorded as transiting through Guatemala from elsewhere in Central America to Mexico; however, the customs administrator at the Tecún Uman customs outpost on the Mexican border "would stamp the form as if the merchandise had left for Mexico when in reality it stayed in Guatemala."[69] A similar procedure was used for merchandise that was destined for Guatemala, with officials at the Guatemala City customs branch signing off on the arrival of shipping containers when they had, in fact, skipped official processing. According to Ortiz Henry, the Moreno Network would charge 8,000 quetzales ($2,700) to arrange the "theft" of forty-foot shipping containers and 4,000 quetzales ($1,400) for twenty-foot ones.[70]

Evidence gathered in the Moreno case further confirms that fraudulent operations were coordinated from the SEM office of the Ministry of Finance. In his role as intermediary between customs personnel and Moreno, Francisco Javier Ortiz recalled that he was often "sent to the Ministry of Finance, the 18th floor, to personally hand over money to Mr. Moreno Molina."[71] Further, the Moreno Network utilized the Ministry's same radio communications system that connected the central customs office to

[67] Ibid.  [68] Ibid.
[69] From De los Ríos testimony, May 26, 1999 (Organismo Judicial 2003).
[70] From Ortiz Henry testimony, May 27, 1999 (Organismo Judicial 2003).
[71] From Ortiz Arriaga testimony, May 25, 1999 (Organismo Judicial 2003).

outlying border locations to communicate about fraudulent operations. As one former Ministry of Finance official described, "The General Directorate of Customs had its radio antennas up on the roof to receive information on customs revenues from all of the ports and other customs locations. They [the Moreno Network] used the same thing. They had radio devices to communicate, but just used a different channel. There was the official channel and their channel."[72]

The illicit earnings were first channeled into different "funds" but were then used to meet a series of quotas assigned to each customs branch. Ortiz Arriaga noted that in the 1980s when he first began as a low-level customs inspector, there was the "major fund" ["*fondo mayor*"], which consisted of the money received for arranging shipping container "thefts" and adjusting the 63-A forms, and the "minor fund" ["*fondo menor*"], which consisted of the bribes accrued by customs agents on the ground when they misreported the value, quantity, or type of merchandise. By the 1990s, however, the two funds were eliminated, and Moreno instead demanded that customs administrators meet a weekly quota of 50,000 quetzales ($16,700), which he then doled out to his associates.[73] Even the accumulation and management of Moreno Network funds was strictly organized and "rule-bound," creating shared expectations among customs personnel.

## ENFORCING THE UNDERMINING RULES

Throughout the 1980s and 1990s, Moreno implemented a series of well-defined procedures governing customs activities – procedures that were then disseminated within the customs apparatus. But the mere existence

---

[72] Interview with author, October 21, 2016. Evidence gathered by the military intelligence-led task force along with documents recovered from Moreno's personal files indicate that the network utilized coded language to communicate about customs adjustments and the status of shipping containers. The system of codes was based on an elaborate soccer metaphor to disguise the fraudulent operations with what seemed to be routine communications about the soccer team allegedly owned by Moreno. For example, the Santo Tomás port was referred to as "*portería del lado norte*" ["the goal on the north side"], while Puerto Quetzal was called "*portería del lado sur*" ["the goal on the south side"]. Shipping containers were referred to as "*jugadores*" or "players" – a "20-year-old player" was a twenty-foot shipping container, while a "40-year-old player" was a forty-foot shipping container. Mention of a "hurt player" ["*jugador lesionado*"] indicated that a shipping container had been captured by authorities, and that network operatives should communicate with the "hospital," the code for the central customs office; see Moreno declaration, September 19, 1996 (Organismo Judicial 2003).

[73] From Ortiz Arriaga testimony, May 25, 1999 (Organismo Judicial 2003).

of the alternative procedures within customs did not guarantee their effective implementation. How did the Moreno Network enforce these new rules and garner compliance?

Within the General Directorate of Customs, the directives issued by the Moreno Network were enforced mostly through coercion – violent and nonviolent. Operating under the thumb of military intelligence elites, the Moreno Network possessed total control over the naming and transfer of customs personnel, recruiting and maintaining participants with threats of layoffs. Francisco Javier Ortiz, for example, only became part of the network when his position as a customs inspector was in jeopardy due to an upcoming round of cuts: "I was on a list of customs inspectors [*vistas aduaneros*] that were going to be let go by the General Directorate of Customs and came to learn that the only way I wouldn't be fired was if I worked for Alfredo Moreno Molina."[74] Once he was involved, Ortiz Arriaga found it impossible to leave "because [Moreno] had all of the information on what we did in customs, he had all of the information on the anomalous operations that effectively took place."[75]

Beyond the possibility of losing one's job or falling victim to blackmail, Moreno also enforced the undermining rules within customs through the threat of violence. According to Ortiz Arriaga, "Moreno made it known that whoever got in his way, he would kill him. He told us that, 'the one who betrays me dies.'"[76] He, along with the other customs operators who testified in 1999, intimated this was the fate of several network associates who died mysteriously in the early 1990s, including lawyer Vicente González, who was believed to have developed discord with Moreno.[77] In another instance, former police officer Carlos Reyes, who worked for Moreno and Salvadoran importer Santos Hipólito Reyes in the "theft" of shipping containers, turned up dead with 38 bullet wounds. According to the testimony of Reyes' associate Ovidio Mancilla Aguilar, the brutal murder occurred when "the money was no longer reaching Mr. Moreno's pocket."[78]

The use of violence to garner compliance with the illicit customs procedures perhaps comes as no surprise given the conflict context and the involvement of high-level military actors. The military intelligence elites that sat atop the Moreno Network structure enjoyed extraordinary "conflict capital" – deep wartime social and political connections and extensive coercive capacities that were widely understood and feared.[79]

---

[74] Ibid.    [75] Ibid.    [76] Ibid.    [77] Ibid.
[78] From Mancilla Aguilar testimony, May 28, 1999 (Organismo Judicial 2003).
[79] Cheng 2018.

Though the case files point to a few murders linked to the violation of the
undermining rules within customs, the testimonies indicate that potential
physical attacks were a powerful driver of behavior among individuals
enmeshed in Moreno Network activities. The latent threat of violence
served as a powerful external sanction for those subject to the criminal
structure's influence.

Beyond the use of coercion, the Moreno Network co-opted personnel
within the state security and judicial sectors to uphold the undermining
rules within customs. As Ortiz Arriaga noted, Moreno's illicit maneuver-
ings within customs were possible because he managed to garner "all of
the support within ... the Comptroller General's Office, the Treasury
Police [*Guardia de Hacienda*], the Public Prosecutor's Office, and the
tribunals, and he had completely closed the loop within the General
Directorate of Customs."[80] Perhaps the most important agency for ensuring the safe passage of contraband was the Treasury Police [*Guardia de
Hacienda*] whose institutional function was "to prevent and pursue
crimes related to contraband and fraud."[81] After the customs personnel
inspecting incoming shipments, the Treasury Police was the next line of
defense against smuggling. Knowing this, Moreno and military intelligence effectively co-opted the Treasury Police, ensuring that it allowed
shipping containers to pass uninspected or, at times, even acted as the
custodians of "stolen" imports.[82]

When the Treasury Police prevented Moreno Network shipments from
entering Guatemala or captured contraband from Moreno associates, key
contacts within the agency worked to get operations back on track.
Within the Moreno case files, former custom inspector Erik de los Ríos
describes one such instance at the Agua Caliente customs point on the
border with Honduras. The regional Treasury Police force had received
information about contraband and prevented it from entering. According
to De los Ríos, Ortiz Arriaga, on Moreno's orders, contacted the Treasury
Police's regional chief, Baudilio Hichos,[83] offering 5,000 quetzales

---

[80] From Ortiz Arriaga testimony, May 25, 1999 (Organismo Judicial 2003).
[81] AHPN 2010: 264.
[82] From Mancilla Aguilar testimony, May 28, 1999 (Organismo Judicial 2003).
[83] Baudilio Hichos served as a member of Congress for twenty-five years, from 1991 to
2016, jumping between five different political parties during this time. In 2016, he was
arrested for a money-laundering scheme involving Guatemala's Social Security Institute
(IGSS) in his home department of Chiquimula. He is also linked to the disappearances of
several student leaders during his time serving in the Treasury Police during the mid- to
late 1980s.

($1,700) for each shipping container he allowed to pass uninspected. After striking the deal, the Moreno Network no longer faced interference in this part of the country.

On the operational front, upholding and enforcing the alternative rules within the customs administration thus required a mix of strategies. Within the General Directorate of Customs, coercion was the mechanism of choice. Operating under the thumb of Moreno and the military intelligence officers running the SEM, customs employees knew that their jobs depended on abiding by the predatory arrangements coordinated by the criminal structure. Once involved, there was little they could do to extricate themselves from the illegal activities given the threat of criminal prosecution. Within key security agencies, however, co-optation was the strategy of choice. By sharing the spoils of fraudulent activities, the Moreno Network garnered the cooperation of security forces, which were critical in shepherding contraband, or at least ensuring that it faced minimal interference in bypassing customs.

CONCLUSION

This chapter illustrated how the narrow counterinsurgent coalition empowered at the height of the Guatemalan armed conflict channeled institutional changes into a series of new undermining rules that systematically distorted customs revenue extraction. Led by an elite military intelligence clique that had infiltrated every corner of the state apparatus by the late 1970s, the Moreno Network not only worked with customs inspectors and administrators to extract bribes from importers, but crafted, implemented, and enforced an entire series of procedures to siphon off customs revenues on a massive scale. These rules systematically subverted the Guatemalan state's extractive activities. In this sense, they constitute what I call undermining rules.

In Chapters 7 and 8, I will examine how the Moreno Network also drew together a high-powered group of lawyers, politicians, and security officials, known as *Grupo Salvavidas*, to buy impunity and guarantee the longevity of the undermining rules within customs. But zooming out to the causal process elaborated theoretically in Chapter 2, the key wartime development that spurred the introduction of undermining rules within Guatemala's customs administration was the perceived escalation of the insurgent threat following the reorientation of rebel strategy and subsequent territorial gains in the mid-1970s. As a result, discretionary power was centralized in an increasingly insulated military intelligence elite, which had thoroughly penetrated the entire state apparatus by the end of the 1970s. This elite political-military bloc then introduced new rules that provided distributional benefits to them narrowly.

The military intelligence, Ministry of Finance, and legal authorities who worked on the case are unequivocal in linking the undermining rules that developed within customs to changes at the height of the Guatemalan state's counterinsurgent campaign. According to one former prosecutor, the intelligence elites operating within the Ministry of Finance "definitely took advantage of the internal armed conflict, and in a way, it gave them a certain amount of impunity to carry out illicit activities. ... Basically, contraband was very attractive because it left them with millions and millions. And the military was the organization protecting it."[84] Given their sophisticated surveillance tools and mandate to infiltrate and control key government ministries, "there was no other group as capable of creating such ordered disorder," in the words of a former customs official.[85]

---

[84] Interview with author, November 9, 2016.     [85] Interview with author, June 2, 2017.

# 5

## Ordering Police Violence

### *Extrajudicial Killing in Wartime Guatemala*

On the morning of September 25, 2006, masked special forces from Guatemala's National Civilian Police (PNC) charged into the notorious Pavón penitentiary to reclaim the facility from the clutches of organized criminal groups within. According to testimonies, the raid, dubbed "Operation *Pavo Real* [Peacock]," began with the gathering of prisoners in Pavón's "civic plaza" and the isolation of some twenty-five to thirty individuals on a list compiled by the Ministry of the Interior and prison officials. Once separated and taken to an isolated part of the detention center, the prisoners were forced to undress, bound, and beaten by state agents.

By the end of the operation, seven prisoners had been killed, many showing signs of torture and execution at point-blank range. Among the dead were detainees deemed leaders of the numerous illicit activities that flourished within Pavón, including Gustavo Adolfo Correa, who controlled the sale of liquor; Erick Estuardo Mayorga Guerra, who controlled the sale of crack cocaine; and Luis Alfonso Zepeda, the president of Pavón's Committee of Order and Discipline (COD), the "political-criminal" power that extorted detainee families. The most prominent prisoner executed was Jorge Batres, a Colombian sentenced to twelve years for drug trafficking. Batres was said to be the primary target of the operation.[1]

The Pavón raid was not the only prison bloodbath recorded during the period. A very similar scene unfolded eleven months earlier following the

---

[1] This narrative is reconstructed from the investigation of the Human Rights Ombudsman (PDH); see PDH 2006a.

escape of nineteen high-risk prisoners in the southern province of Escuintla. On October 22, 2005, the detainees, most of whom were sentenced for violent crimes like murder and kidnapping, utilized a man-made underground tunnel to flee the El Infiernito prison. In response, top security officials devised *"Plan Gavilán"* to track down the fugitives, deploying sixty-eight police agents from the elite Criminal Investigations Service (SIC).[2] Once located, the escaped prisoners were not charged and returned to El Infiernito, but instead tortured or executed on the spot. Investigations implicated the SIC agents in three killings and four cases of torture in late 2005.[3]

According to domestic and international observers, the prisoner killings and abuses in both the Pavón and El Infiernito cases were not excesses carried out by overzealous police agents but formed part of internal plans crafted by senior security officials within the center-right government of Óscar Berger (2004–2008), a member of Guatemala's traditional business elite. Those officials included Carlos Vielmann, then-Minister of the Interior; Víctor Rivera, Vielmann's top security advisor; Erwin Sperisen, head of the PNC; Víctor Hugo Soto Diéguez, chief of the PNC's Criminal Investigations Division (DINC); and Javier Figueroa, the DINC's second-in-command.[4]

According to investigations by the UN International Commission Against Impunity in Guatemala (CICIG), both operations amounted to campaigns of "extrajudicial killing [that] followed a pattern of systematic conduct":[5] conduct surveillance on targeted criminals through a network of informants; deploy elite police groups to eliminate them, usually by firearm and at close range; alter the scene of the crime to create the mirage of an armed confrontation; and manipulate subsequent investigations to ensure impunity for the responsible agents. The upper echelons of Berger's security cabinet were not executing their formal duties, but instead "acted as an organized criminal group that, under the protection of their official ranks, legitimized their illicit actions," in the words of one CICIG document.[6]

---

[2] Fernández 2011: 138.    [3] CICIG 2018.

[4] Carlos Vielmann was acquitted by a Spanish tribunal for the Pavón case, but was facing trial in Guatemala for torture in the El Infiernito case. Víctor Rivera was murdered in April 2008 at the behest of a drug trafficker with whom he had alleged links. Erwin Sperisen was convicted for the Pavón case in a Swiss court in April 2018 and sentenced to fifteen years in prison. Víctor Hugo Soto Diéguez was sentenced to thirty-three years in prison by a Guatemalan court for the Pavón killings in 2013. Finally, Javier Figueroa was acquitted in an Austrian court for the Pavón case in 2011.

[5] Qtd. in Fernández 2011: 459.    [6] Ibid., 361.

The broader pattern of extrajudicial killing during the mid-2000s drew the attention of international officials. Phillip Alston, then-UN Special Rapporteur on Extrajudicial, Summary, or Arbitrary Executions, concluded after his own fact-finding mission that while such actions "have not reached the category of official policy, [due to] their frequency and systematic character, [. . .] they suggest institutional responsibility."[7] Indeed, Guatemala's homicide rate skyrocketed after Vielmann and his team assumed the Ministry of the Interior in July 2004. It stood at roughly thirty-four homicides per 100,000 people when he took office and had climbed to forty-six per 100,000 people by the time he was forced to step down.[8] Though it is impossible to discern precise figures, local NGOs estimated that some eight to 10 percent of murders at the time were carried out "with the purpose of 'eliminating' supposed members of gangs and other criminals."[9] In addition to extrajudicial killings, such incidents represented acts of social cleansing, defined as "executions of gang members, criminal suspects, or other 'undesirables.'"[10]

Extrajudicial killing and the more specific variant, social cleansing, are, of course, not unique to Guatemala, but an unsettling feature of the post-transition landscape in many Latin American countries and throughout the developing world. Across the globe, scholars, journalists, and policy experts have shed light on the deployment of death squads: "clandestine and usually irregular organizations, often paramilitary in nature, which carry out extrajudicial executions and other violent acts against clearly defined individuals or groups of people."[11] Rather than operating independently, such groups most often enjoy "the overt support, complicity, or acquiescence of government," whose agents may participate in death squad activities directly.[12] Death squads have been recorded in El

---

[7] Alston 2007: 11.

[8] Homicide rates collected from PNC data. Many thanks to Carlos Mendoza for sharing these data.

[9] Alston 2009: 8.

[10] Alston 2007: 2. According to conventional definitions, social cleansing is a subset of extrajudicial executions, targeted at social groups considered "undesirable" (i.e., gangs). In this chapter, I use the term "social cleansing" to refer to the summary executions of alleged gang members and criminals, while "extrajudicial" or "extralegal" killing is used to refer to such executions that targeted other individuals more broadly (i.e., political opponents and suspected insurgents). As I will illustrate, the rules governing wartime extrajudicial executions were applied to both categories of "internal enemy" – alleged criminals and alleged insurgents.

[11] Campbell 2000: 1–2.    [12] Ibid.

Salvador[13] and pre-Revolution Nicaragua[14] as a means of securing landed elite interests and within the Brazilian police[15] to combat gang dominance in favela communities. They have further served as quasi-state forms of social control in countries as varied as Uganda, Indonesia, and India.[16]

It might be easy to think of death squad activity as the product of rogue state agents wielding their military capacities on the basis of private interests and amid a climate of limited central control. Indeed, some scholars approach wartime killing through a principal–agent framework in which agents with preferences for violence are more difficult to control, engendering greater brutality.[17] Whether control is a product of ideology, political education to socialize armed actors, or both,[18] the idea is that lower-level combatants are prone to engaging in violence and must be restrained by organizational leadership.

The findings of this chapter, however, speak to an alternative understanding of extrajudicial killing – one that sees this repertoire of violence as a function of structure and regulation from the top of the organizational hierarchy rather than recklessness and a lack of discipline at the bottom. Extrajudicial killings often abide by entrenched rules and procedures, which are routinized and clearly communicated among those implementing and enforcing them. As Daniel Brinks demonstrates in his research on police killings in Buenos Aires, São Paulo, and Salvador de Bahia, such violence constitutes an informal institution – "an informal rule of behavior that goes far beyond what the formal rules contemplate as the proper use of deadly force; this rule broadly condones killing, as long as it occurs in the course of routine policing."[19] In such cases, the alternative rule is enforced by the judiciary, which fails to convict police agents even with evidence of excessive force or crime scene manipulation.[20] Further, such rules *compete* with the formal rules of the game within the security and judicial apparatus – they "[short-circuit] due process and [show] no regard for the physical integrity of those who come into contact with the police."[21]

But where do such rules come from? How does extrajudicial killing by police agents, acts that systematically subvert the rule of law, come to constitute institutionalized procedures that are known and enforced

---

[13] Mason and Krane 1989; Silvia Ávalos 2014; Moncada 2022.      [14] Schroeder 2000.
[15] Huggins 2000.      [16] Kannyo 2000; Cribb 2000; Gossman 2000.
[17] Mitchell 2004; Weinstein 2007.      [18] See Hoover Green 2018.      [19] Brinks 2003: 2.
[20] Ibid., 10–11.      [21] Brinks 2006: 225–226.

within the state apparatus? In this chapter, I seek to answer these questions through the Guatemalan case, examining the origins of present-day undermining rules governing extrajudicial killing by the National Civilian Police. The wartime rules within the PN structured how extrajudicial killings were executed and framed (targeted acts framed as armed confrontations), who carried them out (sanctioned PN agents, *rebajados*, whose employment depended on such activities), and how targets were selected (by the upper echelons of military intelligence and top security cabinet officials).

This chapter argues that the development of such procedures is rooted in the specialization of the police force and the broad discretion granted to concentrated groups of police elites amid the late 1960s period of perceived threat escalation during the armed conflict – the first moment of threat intensification due to high-profile urban guerrilla violence. Specifically, with the creation of highly insulated, elite investigative units like the Detective Corps [*Cuerpo de Detectives*], previous extralegal violence waged by right-wing death squads was incorporated into and institutionalized as routine state activity. The new rules were sanctioned by top military intelligence officials, who devised clear procedures for how to frame the resulting killings to the public. Moreover, they were initially enforced through coercion as low-level police agents facing disciplinary sanctions were integrated into hit squads and forced to uphold the rules to maintain their positions on the force. Overall, the chapter illustrates how, as with Guatemala's customs apparatus, conflict dynamics led to the introduction and consolidation of alternative rules and procedures, which, in this case, systematically distorted the provision of public security and subverted the rule of law (see Figure 5.1).

Importantly, the wartime institutionalization of extrajudicial killing by police forces cannot be readily explained by prewar institutions. While Guatemala's wartime public security force, the PN, is rooted in the urban policing institutions developed for crime prevention following Guatemala's 1821 independence, the link between policing institutions and *public* political authority was never fully cemented in the prewar period. The earliest postindependence effort to formalize policing power occurred in 1825, when the Constituent Assembly issued a decree placing tasks related to the preservation of social order in the hands of "political bosses, municipal councilors, [and] auxiliary neighborhood leaders."[22]

---

[22] AVANCSO 2013: 13.

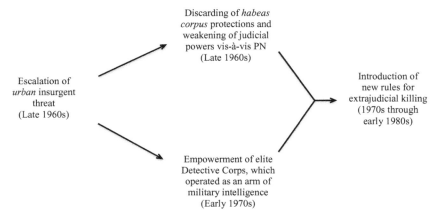

FIGURE 5.1 The wartime introduction of undermining rules within Guatemala's policing institutions

The decree, which crystallized into the 1826 "Police Ordinances," had national coverage, but the police forces created by the measure merely consisted of individuals from the municipality who would conduct routine patrols under the authority of local political bosses. This model prevailed throughout Guatemala's first fifty years of independence and changed only slightly during the Liberal Reform period (1871–1931), which witnessed the fusion of landed elite and state interests due to the country's economic reorientation toward large-scale commercial coffee production.[23] The institutional function of Guatemala's nascent police forces was increasingly directed toward the suppression and control of labor to meet agricultural production needs.[24]

Even after its renaming as the "National Police" in 1925, the institution largely retained its function of "social control" during the dictatorship of Jorge Ubico (1931–1944).[25] This trend would continue even after the October 1944 Revolution, which gave way to ten years of "Democratic Spring" and a host of social, political, and economic reforms. As a study by the Mutual Support Group (GAM) notes, even during this transformative period, Guatemalan police forces were "a nonfunctional police that ... did not develop sufficient size and weight, and, wherever it was sought, projected itself as deficient, weak in technical

[23] Mahoney 2002; Handy 1994; McCreery 1983.    [24] Reeves 2006: 93.
[25] AHPN 2010: 32.

infrastructure, unprofessional, and incapable of guaranteeing the social, economic, and political order."[26]

In sum, the pre-civil war history of Guatemala's police apparatus does not provide a picture of a coherent coercive force rooted in an autonomous or even public source of political authority. Instead, the genesis of the police and its operations throughout the nineteenth and early twentieth centuries was deeply intertwined with the power exercised by groups of economic elites, primarily the country's rural landowning class. These linkages rendered police power diffuse and personalistic. Due to the nature of prewar police authority and institutions, there is little evidence that extrajudicial killings were systematic or abided by a set of shared and coordinated rules prior to the armed conflict. It is only when the PN's structure becomes more centralized and bound to military intelligence following conflict onset that the regulation of extralegal executions occurs.

To illustrate these claims, this chapter builds on the previous discussion of the growing urban insurgent threat in the late 1960s and the creation of the Detective Corps, as described in Chapter 3. The first section examines how these dynamics exacerbated institutional ambiguity by leading to the removal of judicial checks on police activity. Drawing on death squad activities carried out by right-wing paramilitary groups in the 1960s and 1970s, I then demonstrate how the intelligence elites controlling the Detective Corps introduced new rules structuring extrajudicial violence and social cleansing. Planned from above and disguised as the work of the feared *Escuadrón de la Muerte* (EM, Death Squad) and the Secret Anti-communist Army (ESA), the new institutional arrangements involved the use of previously demoted agents known as *rebajados*, who worked with the Detective Corps to collect intelligence on targeted individuals, eliminate them in brutal fashion, and manipulate the crime scene to construct a veneer of right-wing vigilante justice. The concluding section examines how the evolution of the undermining rules structuring extrajudicial violence mirror the broader causal process demonstrated within Guatemala's customs apparatus.

## GROWING INSTITUTIONAL AMBIGUITY: REMOVING JUDICIAL CHECKS ON POLICE POWER

Two critical phenomena laid the foundations for wartime undermining rules governing extrajudicial killings in Guatemala: (1) the perceived

---

[26] GAM 2010: 96.

escalation of the urban guerrilla threat after the vestiges of the first failed rebel uprising regrouped and increased targeted violence against prominent public figures in the late 1960s, and (2) the empowerment of narrow, elite police investigative units like the Detective Corps whose operational discretion far exceeded their formal duties (Chapter 3). Amid the heightened counterinsurgent imperative, the insulated cliques of police elites perceived new opportunities to change the rules of the game as they waged targeted operations to safeguard the state.

These opportunities grew in the late 1960s and early 1970s as Guatemala's political leadership also took steps to dismantle the judicial checks on police power, fomenting even greater institutional ambiguity. This loosening of regulations within the country's security and justice apparatus was driven by an overwhelming sense that, by scrutinizing police evidence against suspected subversives and unconditionally guaranteeing individual liberties, the country's criminal tribunals were direct obstacles to waging counterinsurgency. But in suspending the formal legal framework, political and military leaders also facilitated a growing institutional gray zone, which would permit the evolution of undermining rules that, in turn, distorted the rule of law.

As the threat posed by the FAR insurgency intensified, state security agents increasingly came to see Guatemala's court system as an impediment to counterinsurgent activities. This was largely because the formal legal guarantees built into the Criminal Code – especially those underwriting *habeas corpus* – provided cover for suspected guerrilla operatives, whose clandestine activities could not be sufficiently proven to win convictions. According to the CEH, writs of *habeas corpus* [*recursos de exhibición personal*] were, in fact, effective legal tools to ensure due process and put a stop to inhumane treatment in the early years of the armed conflict. For example, such petitions successfully stopped the torture of political prisoners from the November 1960 military uprising and initiated proceedings against a group of labor leaders being detained illegally.[27] Despite the wartime environment, constitutional guarantees counteracted police abuses, at least initially.

Yet, by the late 1960s, the growing frustrations with these judicial checks on power, amid the perceived escalation of the urban insurgent threat, had altered the institutional landscape. More and more, police forces decried that their efforts were squandered because criminal

---

[27] CEH 1999, Vol. 2: 121.

tribunals would let suspected insurgents walk free due to insufficient evidence. One newspaper article from the time reported that, "we've heard incessant complaints from police elements that it serves no purpose to capture criminals if, just a few days later because of a lack of evidence, they are as free as the trees in La Aurora [a zone of Guatemala City]."[28] A similar sentiment was expressed by members of the Guatemalan armed forces, who saw no use in bringing suspected rebels to trial. According to one ex-soldier testimony,

The Army felt that it was alone in carrying out the battle against the guerrillas. The thinking—this was our feeling—was why am I going to capture a guerrilla fighter if I can't bring him to trial, if there is no one who is going to oppose him? It is better to have him dead than alive because perhaps the tribunal is going to set him free in 15 days. ... The idea of capturing them and bringing them to trial never occurred to us, we never thought about it.[29]

For state security agents, recurring to formal judicial channels not only became undesirable, but completely unviable amid counterinsurgent imperatives.

The mounting mistrust of the court system crystallized into new measures to defang judicial power. In 1966, at the behest of military leaders, the Guatemalan Congress passed amendments to the Criminal Code, which suspended *habeas corpus* protections for those accused of "subversive" or "terrorist" acts.[30] It also freed police agents from the threat of detention while being investigated for abuses. On their face, the measures permitted greater police discretion in a subset of cases and sought to ameliorate the contradiction between waging counterinsurgency and upholding legal norms. In the words of a US government cable emitted at the time, "the net result of the new law is to arrogate the police judgments and functions which once were considered within the domain of the judiciary" in order to respond "to the ever perplexing dilemma of adequate prosecution of criminals without the abuse of police power."[31] A less generous reading of the measure, however, is that political leadership sought to dismantle the formal legal architecture to wrest prosecutorial power from the judiciary and empower police forces with broad operational discretion.

Indeed, the early 1970s witnessed the growing use of state repression to substitute for criminal tribunals, which had been deemed "ineffective in trying the subversives put before them."[32] This period also saw the

---

[28] Qtd. in AVANCSO 2013: 321.  [29] CEH 1999, Vol. 2: 115.
[30] US Embassy in Guatemala 1966: 1.  [31] Ibid.  [32] AVANCSO 2013: 325.

increasing use of "states of exception" to suspend all constitutional guarantees and facilitate heavy-handed counterinsurgent actions. According to a study by the Guatemalan research institute AVANCSO, the repeated state of exception decrees "granted the police legal cover to carry out repressive actions. Further, through the [state of exception], constitutional life was placed outside of the judicial realm and substituted for exception. This political ruse gave significant backing to political [over judicial] power during many years."[33]

In sum, the specialization of the PN and the creation of small, elite investigative units was not the only condition favorable for the development of the undermining rules that would come to structure extrajudicial killing. Successful efforts to diminish formal legal checks on police power generated a pronounced zone of institutional ambiguity – a breach between the prevailing rules of the game that governed criminal prosecution until the late 1960s and the ways in which they were enforced thereafter. This development would also prove crucial as new institutional arrangements within the PN emerged.

### RIGHT-WING DEATH SQUADS AND EXTRALEGAL VIOLENCE

As the escalation of the urban insurgent threat prompted police specialization and facilitated a growing legal and institutional gray zone, the newly empowered police elites of the Detective Corps implemented a series of alternative procedures to eliminate the rebel threat – rules that routinized the extrajudicial killing of those deemed "subversives" and "criminals." These police procedures provided for the identification of targeted individuals through sophisticated intelligence gathering, their elimination by suspended police agents acting as Detective Corps henchmen, and the manipulation of the crime scene to create the mirage of vigilante violence. These activities were regulated and enforced at the highest levels of the Guatemalan government. PN and military leadership oversaw the creation of hit squads, comprised of low-level police agents demoted for disciplinary infractions, which they coerced into carrying out the extrajudicial executions. Further, testimonial evidence suggests that the upper echelons of military intelligence and the Ministry of the Interior had a direct hand in devising the lists of targeted individuals and framing killings as a product of right-wing extremism. In this section, I elaborate

---

[33] Ibid., 324.

how the *practices* of extrajudicial killing became *institutionalized* as the conflict escalated, thereby systematically undermining the rule of law.

The proliferation of right-wing death squads in Guatemala began in the mid-1960s, after the November 1960 uprising at the Zacapa military base, which marked the official onset of the internal armed conflict. Shortly thereafter, clandestine paramilitary organizations began to take shape, sprouting numerous groups including the Organized National Anti-communist Movement (MANO), Eye for an Eye [*Ojo por Ojo*], Righteous Jaguar [*El Jaguar Justiciero*], the New Anti-communist Organization (NOA), and the Anti-communist Council of Guatemala (CADEG).[34] Their primary goal was the eradication of the burgeoning guerrilla cells forming in the country's eastern provinces. For example, the Organized National Anti-communist Movement, also known as "*Mano Blanca*" [White Hand], identified itself with the insignia of a white hand atop a red circle and the motto, "this is the hand that will eradicate the renegades of the nation and the traitors to the homeland."[35] In one of its earliest manifestos, *Mano Blanca* declared that "the gangrene requires amputation of the infected elements, the cancer requires removal at its roots. ... We will impose order, organization, discipline, sense of duty, honesty, and work. No country can survive when anarchy, wearing the mask of democracy, dominates."[36]

Death squads like *Mano Blanca* thus envisioned the complete elimination of those perceived as communist "traitors" through whatever means necessary. Through the end of the 1960s, their mission was made manifest through the circulation of hit lists and the brutal killings that followed. In 1967 alone, more than 500 names appeared on the death lists prepared by the right-wing groups.[37] And by the early 1970s, hundreds of individuals had been brutally murdered, their bodies often strewn on roadsides and in public places.[38]

The brutal repression waged by the right-wing death squads was, in large part, facilitated by its links to soldiers and military officials, who played varying roles in paramilitary activity over time. For the most part, the groups were led by civilians, having been established by large land-owners in northeastern and eastern provinces like Jalapa, Chiquimula, Zacapa, and Izabal. For example, the *Mano Blanca* "command" was comprised of five civilians, among them ranchers Raúl Lorenzana and Orantes Alfaro.[39] Increasingly, death squad operations drew significant

[34] González-Izás 2014: 232.    [35] Ibid., 233.    [36] Ibid.    [37] Ibid., 234.
[38] Bureau of Intelligence and Research 1970: 1.    [39] González-Izás 2014: 233.

financial support from members of Guatemala's traditional oligarchy and business owners in other parts of the country, including Guatemala City, Antigua, and the southern coast.[40]

While initially organized in small groups under local civilian "chiefs," the paramilitary forces became increasingly tied to military commandos in the region. They received formal military training from the Zacapa Military Brigade. Members were also provided armaments directly from army caches. Within some military circles, the civilian-led death squads "were conceived of as the operational arms of [military] intelligence, above all to threaten and carry out executions against political opposition figures."[41] In the case of some death squad organizations, the Guatemalan military had more direct strategic and operational control. According to US government cables, groups like NOA, CADEG, and *Ojo por Ojo* were

...essentially fictional 'organizations,' allegedly composed of violently anti-communist 'patriots' who issue death lists, carry out executions, and, according to their own propaganda fly-sheets, claim credit for such terrorism. Actually, the acronyms and the 'organizations' they represent are psychological warfare devices of [Guatemalan government] clandestine forces – for the most part, the units never did exist except on paper, and the operations they threatened were actually performed by [government] clandestine units.[42]

In other words, the paramilitary organizations were fronts for special forces of the Guatemalan military, who sought to frame the brutal killings as a product of right-wing extremist activity. Given "the apparent inability of [the] judiciary [to] handle the insurgency problem within legal norms,"[43] autonomous military units in the eastern provinces sought to conjure the image of vigilante action to justify selective killings.

It is precisely this model that would become the prevailing method of eliminating suspected "subversives" and "criminals" as the urban insurgent threat mounted and the PN's Detective Corps developed a higher degree of specialization and discretion. Following from this chapter's core claim, the *practices* of extrajudicial violence waged by large landowners and paramilitary units in the late 1960s became *institutionalized* by the early and mid-1970s, constituting a series of new rules and procedures implemented and enforced at the highest levels of Guatemala's military dictatorship. In the remainder of the chapter, I illustrate the nature of these undermining rules, how they were enforced, how they came to regulate urban police action, and their institutional and human toll.

---

[40] Ibid.    [41] Ibid., 233–234.    [42] US Embassy in Guatemala 1968: 3.
[43] US Embassy in Guatemala 1967: 2.

## THE NEW RULES OF THE GAME: STRUCTURING
## EXTRAJUDICIAL KILLING WITHIN THE STATE

After its initial rise and fall at the end of the 1960s, the paramilitary violence that stoked fear in the eastern parts of Guatemala witnessed a swift resurgence in and around Guatemala City following the election – widely labeled fraudulent – of General Kjell Eugenio Laugerud in 1974. The patterns of extrajudicial killing intensified throughout the decade, coming to a head during the regime of General Lucas García (1978–1982). During the first ten months of 1979 alone, there were a reported 3,250 men and women executed in clandestine death squad killings.[44]

Importantly, the death squad murders targeted both suspected insurgent operatives and collaborators, often referred to as "subversive delinquents," as well as those deemed "common delinquents" due to a history of other, seemingly nonpolitical criminal offenses. As a 1981 Amnesty International report noted, the executions involved "people generally considered leaders of public opinion: members of the clergy, educators and students, lawyers, doctors, trade unionists, journalists and community workers. But the vast majority of victims … had little or no social status: they came from the urban poor and the peasantry and their personal political activities were either insignificant or wholly imagined by their captors."[45] The mix of individuals targeted by security forces for extrajudicial execution illustrates that the objectives of police elites extended beyond eliminating high-profile regime opponents to cleansing society of any perceived threats to the political or social order broadly construed. Though the categories of "subversive" versus "common" delinquent were far from clear-cut, both were included in a larger pool of "undesirables" that threatened to disrupt the status quo and were thus subject to the same rules structuring extrajudicial killing.

Primary evidence from former Guatemalan government officials and US government reports, as well as secondary historical accounts, further demonstrate the patterned nature of such extrajudicial killings and how they were enforced from above. The extrajudicial killing procedures began with intelligence gathering on the targeted "criminal" or "subversive" by Detective Corps agents, drawing on the sophisticated techniques and extensive network of informants developed throughout the decade. In many cases, the informants themselves were "common criminals"

[44] *Diario Impacto* 1979.    [45] Amnesty International 1981: 6.

blackmailed into supplying intelligence agents with information.[46] Most often dressed as civilians, detectives would maintain meticulous notes on the daily habits and movements of eventual victims based on this intelligence.[47]

Once identified and tracked, the targeted individuals were murdered in brutal fashion, often by firearm, stabbing, or strangulation. In many cases, the cadavers exhibited skull fractures consistent with execution-style killings at point-blank range. Often the bodies also showed signs of torture and were left in public places. These occurrences were especially frequent with common criminals in Guatemala City's poorer shantytowns and recidivist prisoners captured in or outside of facilities like Pavón[48] – the precise site of the 2006 prison massacre that began this chapter. According to Michael McClintock, "the appearance of bodies of executed 'criminals' on the streets ... was seen as a salutary lesson on the implacable and irresistible power of the state; those who stepped out of line did so at their peril."[49]

But another prominent feature of these routinized police killings was the attribution of responsibility to right-wing "death squads" by affixing justifying notes to the bodies of the dead. For example, in cases of suspected insurgent sympathizers, the cadavers were tagged with labels that read, "For communists, this will befall all of you."[50] In other cases, the victims' bodies were pinned with notes justifying their deaths as justice for common crimes: "For being an attacker and a thief,"[51] and "For being an extortionist"[52] or with typical refrains like "One less"[53] or "Executed."[54] The notes were then signed by one of two groups, which had come to replace the earlier paramilitary organizations of the late 1960s: the *Escuadrón de la Muerte* (EM, the Death Squad) or the *Ejército Secreto Anticomunista* (ESA, the Secret Anti-communist Army).

The attribution of responsibility to these death squad organizations effectively painted the executions as vigilante justice by right-wing extremists frustrated with the ineffectiveness of the state and the judicial system. Indeed, top Ministry of the Interior and military officials repeatedly denied any connections between the Guatemalan state and the EM and ESA. For example, Minister of the Interior Donaldo Álvarez Ruiz admitted that while "the death squads are helping clean out the

[46] CEH 1999, Vol. 2: 44.    [47] CEH 1999, Vol. 3: 91.
[48] McClintock 1985: 179–180.    [49] Ibid.    [50] Barahona 1980.
[51] *Imparcial* 1974a.    [52] *Imparcial* 1974b.    [53] *El Gráfico* 1976.
[54] *La Tarde* 1980.

criminals," they have no links to state security forces.[55] The US State Department monthly reports on violence and human rights in 1979 and 1980 registered a separate category of killings for "rightist activity" or "right-wing terrorism," further bolstering the notion that autonomous anti-communist forces existed in the country and carried out targeted extralegal executions.

However, accounts from those within government and the truth commission reports indicate that this image obscured the reality of extrajudicial killings in Guatemala's urban zones. Instead, the 'death squad' killings were carried out by police forces and coordinated from above by those within the upper echelons of the military and the Ministry of the Interior. On the ground, the "hit squads" responsible for the executions were drawn from the pool of "patrolmen demoted for criminal or disciplinary offenses," which were known as *"rebajados."*[56] As McClintock describes, to maintain their PN affiliation, the *rebajados* "must atone [for their previous infractions] by taking on particularly hazardous or dirty work." They thus constituted a pool of personnel at the bottom of the police hierarchy "available to carry out any task assigned to them."[57] The Detective Corps would coordinate small teams of *rebajados* to carry out the extrajudicial killings, using so-called confidential funds to pay off the executioners.[58] In this sense, much like the modes of enforcement by the Moreno Network in Chapter 4, leaders garnered compliance with the undermining rules within the police through coercion. Facing disciplinary sanction, the desire to retain one's position or ascend the police hierarchy ensured that *rebajado* agents did not deviate from the prevailing rules of the game.

But who devised the list of targets for the Detective Corps, with their *rebajdo* hit squads, to pursue? How were these procedures governing extralegal killings regulated? Both the list of targeted "subversives" and "delinquents" as well the public efforts to frame the extrajudicial violence as right-wing vigilante justice were controlled and executed from the highest levels of government, including the president, the EMP, and the Minister of the Interior. According to former Ministry press secretary Elías Barahona (1976–1980), an insurgent infiltrator, the manufactured death squad activity formed part of the government's plan to eliminate thousands of rebel operatives and sympathizers, while propagating the image of a regime that continued to "seek dialogue and peace."[59]

---

[55] Calderón S. 1978.    [56] McClintock 1985: 185.    [57] Ibid.
[58] See ODHAG 1998.    [59] Barahona 1980.

According to Barahona, the EM and ESA were part of an "official cover-up plan that consists of attributing all of the kidnappings and assassinations to a struggle between political extremes that want to violently achieve power" and sought to portray the government as "trapped between two fires."[60] To lend further credence to this theory, the list of Guatemalans "sentenced to death by the ESA and EM" included the names of top government officials like Álvarez Ruiz, Lucas García, and Minister of Defense Aníbal Guevara.[61] Yet, in reality, the registry of future victims was prepared by military intelligence and Ministry of the Interior officials, who transmitted them to the Detective Corps leaders tasked with coordinating the operational follow-through.

Additional firsthand accounts from within government corroborate these rules and procedures governing extrajudicial executions. In February 1979, Vice President Francisco Villagrán referred to the death squad killings "in such a way as to give rise to [the] interpretation that government security forces were responsible," and further attributed them to "police frustration in seeing released criminals walking the streets."[62] And in equally damning statements, former chief of the Detective Corps Manuel de Jesús Valiente Téllez, who fled the country after persecution by police rivals, "confirmed that the regular security forces were responsible for murders attributed to 'death squads,' and declared that 'as head of the detective corps he had himself been involved in similar murder and 'disappearance' operations ordered by higher authorities."[63]

Rather than excesses of rogue state security forces or "justice" imposed by anti-communist paramilitary groups, the "death squad" killings were instead highly routinized and regulated procedures for eliminating suspected insurgents and criminals. The PN's increasingly sophisticated Detective Corps, which operated with high levels of discretion and autonomy from the PN command, stood at the center of the implementation of these alternative rules, coordinating *rebajado* groups to carry out the selective murders that were overseen and enforced from above. In this sense, the enforcement of the rules, at least initially, occurred primarily through coercion, as the threat of further demotions or the possibility of regaining one's previous post ensured agent compliance in carrying out the extrajudicial killings. Such rule-bound behavior systematically undermined the rule of law and state security provision.

[60] Ibid.    [61] Ibid.    [62] US Embassy in Guatemala 1979a: 1–2.
[63] McClintock 1985: 159; see also, *Prensa Libre* 1981; Schirmer 1998a: 159.

## CONCLUSION

In sum, this chapter illustrated that the police procedures authorizing extrajudicial killing in Guatemala were neither a product of rogue police action nor weak central control. To the contrary, they reflected systematic rules enforced from the top-down. As with the rules governing customs fraud, the pernicious institutional arrangements within Guatemala's National Police emerged out of a dynamic wartime context and the interplay of two factors: (1) the insulation and empowerment of a narrow counterinsurgent elite, and (2) the loosening of the prevailing "rules of the game" – growing institutional ambiguity.

As the urban insurgent threat mounted, police specialization and autonomy became the primary strategy to detect insurgent sympathizers. Moreover, the dismantling of judicial checks on police power created an institutional gray zone and facilitated the introduction of new police procedures. The alternative rules that emerged, which were sanctioned and regulated by the upper echelons of military intelligence, institutionalized extrajudicial killing and framed it as right-wing extremist activity to absolve state forces. Moreover, the use of coercion – threats to job security for *rebajados* already relegated to the bottom of the PN hierarchy – ensured the enforcement of the undermining rules. The inner workings of Guatemala's wartime PN thus illustrate how similar threat environments and coalitional configurations can produce similar *kinds* of institutional changes within distinct state sectors; they can introduce undermining rules that subvert core state functions.

Chapter 9 extends this analysis by examining the factors contributing to the persistence of these new rules within and beyond the wartime period. It traces how the dominant counterinsurgent coalition circumvented security sector reforms spurred by the peace process and explains how we get from the counterinsurgent period to the high-profile prison massacres that began this chapter. But first, I turn to a distinct context in which wartime undermining rules emerged – Nicaragua's land tenure institutions amid the Contra War – as a means of examining the key alternative explanations outlined in Chapter 2.

# 6

## Land and Counterinsurgency

### *Rewriting the Rules of Agrarian Reform in Nicaragua*

On June 25, 1991, Nicaragua's Minister of Agrarian Reform Gustavo Tablada sent shockwaves through Nicaraguan society when he claimed that seventy-four high-ranking officials from the Sandinista National Liberation Front (FSLN) had received legal titles for massive extensions of land in the months after the FSLN's 1990 electoral defeat.[1] In addition to the hasty legalizations, the outgoing government had provided luxury homes expropriated by the state to Sandinista party leaders at deeply discounted prices.[2] Based on inventories from the Ministry of Agricultural Development and Agrarian Reform (MIDINRA), Tablada further claimed that, of the 9,363 titles issued between the FSLN's February 25 loss at the polls and the April 25 transfer of power, only a quarter had gone to the country's rural peasantry – the class that FSLN leaders had, for over a decade, claimed were the protagonists of their revolutionary movement. The morning the story broke, the alleged property abuses earned a label that would become synonymous with Sandinista malfeasance and corruption for years to come: "*La Piñata.*"

For many, the *Piñata* revelations reflected the ultimate distortion of the FSLN's landmark agrarian reform, initiated just after the 1979 revolution that toppled the Somoza dynasty (1936–1979). Despite the significance of reform efforts for many previously landless peasants,[3] the Sandinista's last act stung nonetheless. After over a decade of bloodshed, first during the Sandinista Revolution and then during the civil war between the state

---

[1] Navarrete 1991.     [2] Larson 1993.

[3] It is estimated that by the mid-1990s, some 35 percent of rural families had received land under the Agrarian Reform Law (IRAM 2000: 121).

and the US-backed Contra insurgency, the Sandinista's program of social and economic transformation had ended with regime insiders using their power and influence for personal gain. The parallels with the Somoza-led oligarchy were not lost on the Sandinista's fiercest critics. "This is what thousands of Nicaraguans died for?" asked conservative politician Alberto Saborío the day after the *Piñata* details emerged. "They criticized Somoza for privileging large estates [*latifundismo*], meanwhile they fell into the same thing. How morally bankrupt."[4]

While the *Piñata* scandal drew societal outcry as a striking display of Sandinista hypocrisy, it is best read as a symptom of a much deeper problem that festered during Sandinista rule: land insecurity. The abrupt legalizations carried out on behalf of top Sandinista cadre – authorized through post-electoral legislation – were made possible by the state's inability to regulate land ownership. One study found that, by the end of FSLN rule, some 78 percent of redistributed properties remained formally registered under their pre-Revolution owners.[5] Sandinista rule thus concluded not only with a series of brazen land grabs by political elites, but with land tenure in shambles and countless conflicts flaring up throughout Nicaraguan territory.

Why did the Sandinista's transformative agrarian reform program end in heightened levels of insecurity, corruption, and the overall inability of the state to regulate property rights? In this chapter, I argue that the key to answering this question can be found in how Nicaragua's Contra War (1980–1990) remade the rules of land redistribution and titling.[6] As the perceived threat posed by the Contra insurgency deepened and large numbers of peasant producers defected to the rebel's side, the increasingly narrow and highly centralized FSLN coalition in power implemented a series of alternative rules structuring land provision and administration – rules crafted with the counterinsurgent objective of recovering peasant support and preserving Sandinista political power. The introduction of these new rules, which permitted the individual and provisional titling of unregistered parcels, subverted the state's ability to regulate land owner-ship. They thus constitute undermining rules, or procedures that structure behavior in ways that contravene core state functions.

The Nicaraguan experience is a classic example of the "property rights gap" that has plagued countries throughout the developing world. As Michael Albertus has shown, the under-provision property rights is the

---

[4] Navarrete 1991.    [5] IRAM 2000: 36.
[6] See Schwartz 2022, the article on which this chapter is based.

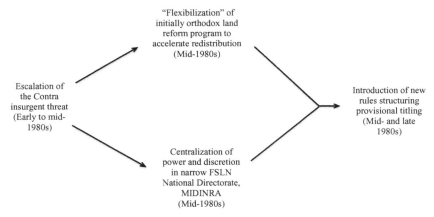

FIGURE 6.1 The wartime introduction of undermining rules within Nicaragua's land tenure institutions

norm rather than the exception following episodes of large-scale land redistribution, contributing to economic inequality and stunted agricultural productivity.[7] While civil war is by no means the only driver, withholding or providing partial and tenuous legal title gives counterinsurgent leaders "an opportunity to build peasant dependencies and manipulate beneficiaries in an effort to ease the pacification of the countryside and create a politically pliable and dispersed support base."[8] Far from "an oversight or political blunder" due to wrongheaded policies or state weakness, it is "one of the most politically valuable policies that land redistribution makes possible."[9]

Building on these claims, this chapter goes one step further in arguing that the FSLN's shifting agrarian approach not only reflected new policies but crystallized into new rules – forged in the crucible of counterinsurgency – that undermined one of the state's core administrative functions for decades. The case demonstrates how the evolving nature of Nicaragua's dominant political coalition shaped the kinds of institutional arrangements that came to characterize the decade of Sandinista rule. The controlled pluralism and corporate linkages that defined early FSLN governance "collapsed under the strains of war and economic stress."[10] By the mid-1980s, the perceived intensification of the insurgent threat and the narrow, insulated nature of the counterinsurgent elite generated new rules of the game with perverse effects on state performance (see Figure 6.1).

[7] Albertus 2021: 169–175.    [8] Ibid., 88.    [9] Ibid.    [10] Chisholm 1991: 40.

More broadly, this chapter contributes to another important issue within conflict scholarship: the connections between insurgency, counter-insurgency, and land redistribution. Prevailing approaches to rebellion premised on rural grievances see land reform as a potentially effective means of diminishing support for insurgency by ameliorating disparities between new beneficiaries and previous landholders, thereby increasing the opportunity costs of joining armed conflict.[11] Early theories thus posited a broad negative relationship between land redistribution and civil conflict through a decline in insurgent support and mobilizing capacity.[12]

Subsequent empirical research on how land redistribution shapes violence and insurgency, however, finds that the effects are not so straightforward. They are instead conditioned on prevailing social structures, namely the ability of wealthy landowners to block redistributive efforts and thus aggravate existing grievances. Notably, Albertus and Kaplan find that in Colombia only the areas that achieved the most extensive land redistribution saw reduced conflict; by contrast, where large landowners managed to block deeper reforms, guerrilla activity endured.[13] Similarly, Finkel, Gehlbach, and Olsen find that Russia's 1861 Emancipation Reform exacerbated peasant disturbances because of how the landed elite effectively co-opted reforms and distorted policy design and implementation.[14] There is thus an emerging scholarly consensus that the effectiveness of wartime land reform as a tool to counter rebellion depends on whether powerful social and economic actors can distort or obstruct such efforts altogether.

This chapter, however, puts forward a distinct explanation for the ultimate erosion of Nicaragua's land reform and administration. Rather than intransigence and co-optation by large landowners, the distortion of Nicaragua's wartime land reform program resulted from the introduction of new rules and procedures by *state actors* seeking to combat the insurgent threat. Rather than the machinations of powerful non-state actors, the new rules of the game were crafted and enforced from within.

Nicaragua's land and property sector also serves an important function within this book by allowing me to probe the three alternative explanations for the wartime emergence of undermining rules posited in Chapter 2 and discussed further in Chapter 3. Relative to Guatemala's wartime context, Nicaragua's Contra War reflected stark differences in regime war-making

---

[11] Albertus 2020: 257.    [12] See Huntington 1968; Paige 1975; Wood 2003.
[13] Albertus and Kaplan 2013.    [14] Finkel et al. 2015.

strategies, regime ideological orientations, and the nature of foreign involvement and support, particularly that of the United States. The mass mobilization that stood at the heart of the FSLN's counterinsurgent campaign, as well as the regime's Marxist-inspired ideology might predict the emergence of new rules and procedures that bolster or reinforce state institutions along the lines of classic war-centered theories of state formation. Yet, the ultimate emergence of undermining rules within land tenure institutions in Nicaragua contradicts these expectations and casts doubt on these alternative theories. Instead, the comparable narrowing and insulation of the dominant counterinsurgent coalition best accounts for the development of similar kinds of institutional logics within wartime contexts that otherwise diverge significantly.

To trace the wartime introduction of undermining rules within land tenure in Nicaragua, this chapter proceeds as follows: first, I discuss the early years of the FSLN's agrarian reform program, which maintained an orthodox, fully collectivized approach and ultimately had limited redistributive effects. I further analyze how Sandinista economic and agrarian policies misread the social structures and practices of Nicaragua's land-owning small and medium peasant producers and increasingly alienated them from the revolutionary project, fanning the flames of insurgency. The subsequent section examines how the perceived escalation of the Contra threat in the early to mid-1980s, as described in Chapter 3, restructured power and decision-making within Nicaragua's land reform and administration. Much in line with the narrowing and insulation of FSLN leadership more broadly, MIDINRA's once decentralized structure became entirely subordinate to central authorities, laying the groundwork for the implementation of undermining rules shielded from potential countervailing forces.

The chapter then turns to the implementation of the alternative institutional arrangements themselves, tracing how the perceived deepening of the Contra threat remade the rules of the Sandinista's agrarian reform program in ways that distorted the state's ability to regulate land tenure. It chronicles how, as the peasant bases of the Contra rebellion grew, land came to be viewed as a counterinsurgent tool on the part of the narrow FSLN leadership, who "flexibilized" the rules of reform to stave off insurgent defection within highland peasant communities. I lay out in greater detail the undermining rules that emerged and came to structure land tenure amid the wartime climate of institutional ambiguity. The new rules entailed (1) the increased provision of land on an *individual* basis, and (2) "legalization" through the *provisional* titling of lands, many of which were not yet formally under state ownership. The new land redistribution procedures were enforced through the FSLN's strict command structure, which, by the mid-1980s, did not tolerate noncompliance with central directives. Finally, the chapter concludes by examining how, despite the "coercion-intensive" nature of the Sandinista's counterinsurgent strategy, the narrow, insulated character of its political decision-making corps still produced undermining rules with pernicious consequences for state administrative activities.

## EARLY AGRARIAN REFORM AND THE ESTRANGEMENT OF THE PEASANTRY (1979–1983)

Following the FSLN's historic victory, the new revolutionary government enacted a series of transformative social and economic policies, none more dramatic than the agrarian reform program. On paper, the agrarian reform program was one of the pillars of the Sandinistas' broader agenda, which was premised on the growth of the public sector and the expanded role of the state in production and development. However, the expansion of the public sector did not translate into another of the Sandinistas' revolutionary promises: the redistribution of land to peasants and agricultural workers. In clinging to a more orthodox, fully collectivized model, FSLN leaders were slow to place productive lands into the hands of those working them. In this section, I describe Nicaragua's agrarian reform institutions during the early phase of Sandinista rule to establish the baseline from which subsequent institutional arrangements would eventually diverge. I also examine how the sluggish pace of redistribution, declines in production, and the estrangement of the rural peasantry put the FSLN's agrarian program on its heels as the Contra War entered its most intense period in the mid-1980s.

Following the 1979 revolution, the FSLN-led unity government inherited an economic situation marked by staggering land inequality and a paltry state sector. Under the Somozas, Nicaragua's productive lands were heavily concentrated in the hands of traditional agroexport elites, who also enjoyed privileged access to public credit at the expense of small peasant producers. Though peasants represented 75 percent of Nicaragua's producing class, they possessed only 13.4 percent of farmlands, with the 25 percent of large commercial producers owning the remaining 86.6 percent.[15] Further, 24 percent of producers with landholdings over

---

[15] MIDINRA 1980, Cuaderno No. 11.

eighty-six acres received a staggering 90 percent of public agricultural credits.[16] To consolidate its personalist rule, the Somoza dynasty had also sold off national assets to members of the Nicaraguan oligarchy and foreign, primarily US capitalists.[17] By the time the FSLN seized power, only nineteen public entities remained, accounting for 15 percent of GDP.[18]

The first Sandinista attempt to bolster the state sector came through Decree #3 issued by the JGRN shortly after proclaiming victory. The decree authorized the confiscation of all property belonging to the Somoza family, members of the National Guard, and Somoza government officials. The first year of confiscations (1979–1980) added 1.6 million *manzanas* (2.8 million acres) of farmland to state coffers – between 20 and 25 percent of the country's total farmland.[19] Additionally, the confiscations "recovered" some 1,200 large estates and a number of key agroindustrial firms.[20] As a result, public sector production rose from 15 to 36 percent of GDP in just one year.[21] By the second year, the confiscations expanded through Decree #782 to lands deemed "idle, underutilized, or rented" on estates larger than 875 acres in the Pacific zone and 1,750 acres elsewhere.[22]

The state's newly acquired lands and businesses formed the Area of the People's Property (APP), which was to be the core of the country's national development model. Though always envisioned as coexisting with private property, APP-driven economic activities were to become "hegemonic," in the words of Minister of Agriculture Jaime Wheelock, in order to "favor changes in the distribution of national income to benefit the popular majorities."[23] The APP was managed by the National Institute of Agrarian Reform (INRA), which was eventually restructured as the Ministry of Agricultural Development and Agrarian Reform (MIDINRA) in April 1981.

But even with the new expropriations, early FSLN agrarian policies hit a series of roadblocks by 1982, including widespread inefficiencies, a lack of labor discipline, mounting indebtedness, a decline in agricultural exports, and the plummeting purchasing power of wages.[24] The early troubles did, however, lend some legitimacy to another strand of MIDINRA policy: that promoting greater land redistribution. MIDINRA had envisioned the creation of two kinds of cooperatives: fully collectivized cooperatives dedicated to agricultural production, known as the Sandinista Agricultural

[16] CIERA 1980: 6.    [17] Vilas 1984: 111–112.    [18] Colburn 1990: 39.
[19] Spalding 1994: 66; Colburn 1990: 42.    [20] Spalding 1994: 66.    [21] Ibid.
[22] Ibid., 70.    [23] Qtd. in Vilas 1984: 212, 216–217.
[24] Ibid., 217; Spalding 1994: 76; Biondi-Morra 1993: 49–54.

Cooperatives (CAS), and Credit and Service Cooperatives (CCS), which would organize the provision of agricultural assistance as an intermediate step toward full collectivization. Following the early troubles, MIDINRA planners came to view rural collectivization as "the principal pathway for the forward progress of revolutionary transformation in agriculture during the coming years."[25]

The cooperatives developed during this phase mostly sprang from the breakup of large, nationalized estates and firms. While the cooperative sector represented only 5.6 percent of the total APP lands at the end of 1980, its share had grown to 26.2 percent by 1983.[26] Slight gains can also be seen in the productive share of cooperatives and small farmers over the same period. With respect to cotton harvests, for example, cooperatives came to account for 25 percent in 1983/84, up from a mere 9 percent in 1980/81.[27]

But even as cooperative development increased, the Sandinista's staunch state-centered and fully collectivized approach reflected deep misunderstandings of the structure of rural society – misunderstandings that would contribute to the increase in insurgent participation among Nicaragua's peasant classes in the mid-1980s. In particular, the FSLN miscalculated the social and political weight of the country's small and medium landowning peasants (those holding less than 865 acres), whose lives and livelihoods were premised on individual landownership. These sectors accounted for half of agricultural production in 1980.[28] Yet, during its first four years, FSLN agrarian and macroeconomic policies advanced with little regard for small and medium peasant producers, stoking resentment and alienating these groups in unforeseen, yet consequential ways.

An important feature that sets Nicaragua apart from Central America's other two Cold War-era conflict countries is its rural class structure and in particular its sizable portion of smaller landowning peasants. According to Eduardo Baumeister, small and medium family-based producers, known as the *chapiolla* bourgeoisie, were the most important coffee-producing class in Nicaragua, in contrast to Guatemala and El Salvador, where coffee production was dominated by large commercial elites.[29] Nicaragua's more

[25] DGFCRA 1982: 3–4.    [26] Baumeister 1998: 185.    [27] Vilas 1984: 240.
[28] Bendaña 1991: 43.
[29] Baumeister 1998. The disparities become clear when one examines the share of land held by these peasant sectors in Nicaragua and Guatemala. In pre-Revolution Nicaragua, nearly half of coffee lands, some 47 percent, were in the hands of sub-family, family, and small employer units, while large estates and producers accounted for the remaining 53 percent. In Guatemala, smaller producers possessed only 16.2 percent of coffee lands,

significant strata of small and medium peasant producers, which mostly resided in the north-central regions of Matagalpa, Jinotega, and Nueva Segovia, possessed strong attachments to individual conceptions of land-ownership and resisted collective agricultural practices. As José Boanerges, a CDS-turned-resistance leader, indicates, "[T]he peasant is very individualistic and very self-concerned [*personalista*], in that he is very resistant to working collectively and opts for a parcel, for his 30 or 50 *manzanas* or whatever, but under a personal title."[30] These sectors held an abiding "mercantile identity," in which a "close, familial, local connection to commercial production" is central.[31] Peasant families were involved in every step of economic activity; "if they sell [what they produce] it is to be able to increase and multiply their production."[32]

The fierce attachment to individual landownership within these peasant sectors brought them into direct conflict with the FSLN's two-pronged agrarian reform strategy, which, on the one hand, centered on state-run farms and agribusinesses, and, on the other hand, privileged an orthodox, fully collectivized model of redistribution.[33] The mere existence of a small and medium peasantry was anathema to the FSLN's political project, which envisioned a robust rural proletariat as the engine of revolutionary progress. An explicit aim of the land reform program was to "de-peasantize [*descampenizar*]" the Nicaraguan countryside by creating a class of wage laborers employed on state farms.[34] As David Kaimowitz writes, "the government thought the sector of small and medium commercial producers was small and of little importance. ... The peasantry as a social category was considered incompatible with socialism for many mid-level officials in key ministries."[35] At the top, similar attitudes about the peasantry prevailed. One MIDINRA top official remarked that, "the peasant population was an isolated population, with little cultural development and which could easily be manipulated."[36] The cultural and economic significance of individual property for many poor peasants was not perceived as genuine, but reflected the folly of "a salaried worker

---

and large agricultural and agroexport elites held the remaining 83.8 percent. Beyond constituting a smaller share of the landholding population, Nicaragua's large commercial producers remained deeply fragmented along Liberal and Conservative lines through the nineteenth and early twentieth centuries, further weakening their political position vis-à-vis smaller landowners. By contrast, Guatemala's Liberal coffee elite maintained a tight grip on political power; see Paige 1997: 60; Mahoney 2002: 106.

[30] Bendaña 1991: 251.    [31] Núñez Soto 1991: 368.    [32] Ibid.
[33] Baumeister 1998: 94.    [34] Ibid.    [35] Kaimowitz 1988: 58.
[36] Interview with author, March 1, 2017.

trapped in a subsistence economy, backward and incapable of under-standing, as a producer, the nature of the transformations sown by the fall of *somocismo* and the ascent of a new popular power."[37]

The Sandinistas' misunderstanding of Nicaragua's small and medium peasant producers and the goal of transforming them into a class of rural wage workers translated into a series of agrarian and macroeconomic policies that stoked deep resentment across the north-central highlands. Notably, landowning peasants who resisted collectivization received scant attention in the form of land redistribution or credit and assistance. From 1981 to 1984, 82 percent of redistributed lands went to the fully collectivized cooperatives (CAS), while only 18 percent went to the par-tially collectivized credit and service cooperatives (CCS) or individual peasants.[38] The rural peasantry, however, was much more inclined to form CCS. According to the National Cooperative Census carried out in 1982, peasants were 80 percent of CCS members, while salaried workers were the remaining 20 percent; conversely, 53 percent of CAS member-ship were salaried workers, with peasants representing 47 percent.[39]

In addition to the prejudicial provision of land and credit, peasants with small landholdings were also hit hard by FSLN market controls, including the strict regulation of "internal commerce, prices, warehous-ing, the supply of goods, and domestic channels of commercialization."[40] Given the importance of smaller-scale agricultural production for peasant "survival and reproduction," in the eyes of individual peasant producers, FSLN surveillance and confiscations amounted to "asphyxiating them or alienating them completely."[41] In the words of Francisco García Rivera, a peasant who eventually joined the Nicaraguan Resistance (RN), "the treatment on the part of the authorities was terrible, everyone was living in uncertainty. They didn't let us work peacefully because at every moment they were on the finca seeing what we had, how many *manzanas*, how many cattle, to take note. It was an absolute control and you no longer felt secure in what you possessed."[42]

As the economic detriments of early FSLN policies disproportionately accrued to small and medium peasant landholders, more and more began to adopt the oppositional attitudes of large *latifundistas*, viewing the cooperative movement and state firms as the enemy:

---

[37] Ortega 1988: 201–202.  [38] Gutiérrez 1988: 119.  [39] Núñez Soto 1991: 319.
[40] Ibid., 368.  [41] Ibid.  [42] Bendaña 1991: 168.

[Small peasant landowners] echoed the propaganda of the large landowners, in suggesting that the provision of land, credit, and goods to cooperatives contributed to 'making people lazy' [*hacer haragana a la gente*]. State enterprises and cooperatives, also perceived as Sandinista thus came to represent, for small property owners, a kind of 'new landowner' with substantial resources and high levels of technology.[43]

Though the Sandinista political platform, on its face, would have facilitated a more organic alliance with the rural peasantry, the reality could not have been farther from the truth. By the mid-1980s, Sandinista policies had unwittingly created fertile terrain for Contra recruitment.

## MIDINRA AND THE CENTRALIZATION OF LAND ADMINISTRATION

Peasant alienation, in combination with the US-backed mobilization of Contra forces, intensified the sense of threat posed by the insurgency. As described in Chapter 3, heightened fears of FSLN vulnerability in the early to mid-1980s corresponded to key changes in the composition of insurgent forces, which shifted the locus of the threat from US-coordinated Somoza allies outside of national territory to peasant-led insurgent forces with deep attachments in Nicaraguan highland communities. Under the pretext of ramping up efforts to eliminate Contra forces and safeguard the revolutionary project, the dominant wartime decision-making coalition became narrower and more insulated, perceiving any dissenting voices as potential counterrevolutionary opposition that could jeopardize FSLN rule. As the nine commanders of the Sandinista National Directorate (DN) sidelined other social, political, and economic sectors, they further concentrated decision-making discretion in their own hands, ultimately introducing new rules within land reform aimed at peeling off rebel support.

This conflict-induced centralization was particularly pronounced within Nicaragua's newly inaugurated land reform and administration agency, known as MIDINRA. Under the FSLN, "centralism spurred a return to the tendency to acquire property rights based on the initiative of rulers."[44] Observers, in fact, speculate that this centralizing tendency and "MIDINRA's power played a real role in leaving unresolved the updating of the land registry." [45] In other words, existing state institutions were unenforced and shielded from societal pressures to make room for alternative rules to take root.

---

[43] Ibid., 44.    [44] IRAM 2000: 36.    [45] Ibid., 37.

In principle, MIDINRA was organized to foster broad participation and consultation. Underneath the minister of MIDINRA, there was a vice minister of agrarian reform, who coordinated all activities related to cooperative development, land reassignment, and titling.[46] The minister and vice minister were advised by a diverse group of experts and civil society leaders, known as the National Agrarian Reform Council. The Council's members included the secretary general of the Rural Workers' Association (ATC), the president of the National Union of Agricultural Workers and Cattle Ranchers (UNAG) – both FSLN-affiliated mass organizations – the director of CIERA (MIDINRA's research arm), the director of the Nicaraguan Finance Corporation, and a delegate from the Ministry of Planning.[47] Similar kinds of organizational entities were replicated at the regional level through the Regional Agrarian Reform Councils, which provided recommendations to the MIDINRA delegates overseeing activities in the country's six regions and three special zones.[48]

Though MIDINRA's national and local structures, in theory, facilitated input from societal groups outside of FSLN circles, the reality of decision-making within the agrarian reform program was much different. MIDINRA's strict, vertical organization ensured that regional delegates operated as faithful surrogates of top party authorities. As the Ministry's 1983 work plan indicates, "the Regional Directorates and Special Zone Directorates of MIDINRA – as small-scale, comprehensive expressions of the central level – encompass organs that guarantee compliance with the functions of the Ministry."[49] The latitude allotted to local cadre to implement agrarian reform policies more tailored to community needs was thus limited. Dissatisfaction with MIDINRA's strict hierarchical procedures became pervasive at the local level, particularly among resettled peasant communities. As one 1986 CIERA report admonished, "We consider that the style of centralized, vertical, and non-participatory conduct has produced [. . .] an unnecessary erosion of the [Sandinista] Front and the State in terms of resources and prestige."[50]

Insulated from outside political pressures and operating in a strict, vertical fashion, MIDINRA officials often substituted "political criteria" for formal selection procedures when it came to land reassignment.[51] Numerous land titling acts issued in 1983, 1984, and 1985 provide extensive histories of the cooperatives and individual peasants slated to receive legal titles, revealing that they most often had deep ties to the

---

[46] MIDINRA 1983b: 39.    [47] MIDINRA 1983a: 30.    [48] Ibid.    [49] Ibid., 9.
[50] DGFCRA 1986b: 7.    [51] Interview with author, January 23, 2017.

FSLN dating back to the insurrection.[52] Though coordinated by local party officials, such partisan decisions were also very much guided and sanctioned by those at the top. A high-level MIDINRA official described this process: The redistribution orders ascended to Minister Wheelock's office in Managua after receiving approval from the Regional Agrarian Reform Council, which included delegates from the presidency, military, Ministry of the Interior, and Sandinista party. Wheelock would approve the number and kinds of titles that would be granted in a given zone.[53] Further, the nine FSLN commanders who formed the DN were often present at titling ceremonies, infusing them with a revolutionary spirit. Titling was not merely the product of local decision-making, but a set of institutionalized procedures sanctioned at the top. As the escalation of the Contra threat prompted FSLN leadership to rethink the prevailing rules within agrarian reform, the structure of the rules-making coalition would ensure that the changes to come would not be subject to broad input but would instead be devised by a narrow coalition of party leaders who possessed total political control.

### LAND AS A TOOL OF COUNTERINSURGENCY: THE INTRODUCTION OF NEW UNDERMINING RULES

The growing insurgent territorial presence and perceived military threat led to a dramatic reorientation of the land reform program to gain back lost ground. Rather than primarily a means of social and economic transformation, by 1984, agrarian reform became a tool of counterinsurgency.[54] It would "now be used to confront the Contra threat" both by satisfying the land demands of potential insurgent recruits and arming the peasantry for military defense.[55] In this moment, the procedures governing land redistribution and titling were altered, generating undermining rules that came to distort the Nicaraguan state's ability to regulate landownership and opening up a "property rights gap." With the drastic shift in the bases of Contra support and the heightened sense of insurgent military threat, the reorientation of FSLN counterinsurgent priorities and actions – including the use of land redistribution to reassert state

---

[52] See, for example, DGFCRA 1983a; DGFCRA 1983b; DGFCRA 1983c; DGFCRA 1983d; DGFCRA 1984c.
[53] Interview with author, March 1, 2017.
[54] Ortega 1988: 203; Marti i Puig 1997: 84; Spalding 1994: 83.
[55] US Embassy in Managua 1983.

control – created space between previous land reform procedures and their enforcement. Amid this institutional gray zone, FSLN elites introduced alternative arrangements for redistributing and titling lands on a provisional basis, which subverted state administrative functions while allowing Sandinista leaders to maintain peasant dependence and rural control. Rather than constituting an ill-informed or poorly executed policy, the new redistributive procedures became a series of rules governing how land was titled.

Though the early years of FSLN rule brought important socioeconomic benefits to Nicaragua's urban and rural poor, the escalation of rebel activity began to erode revolutionary advances toward the end of 1983. From its inception, the US-backed Contra insurgency saw economic destabilization as a means of bringing down the Sandinista regime, targeting state-owned agribusinesses and farms as early as 1981.[56] However, the economic costs of the counterrevolution increased dramatically a few years later as peasants flocked to the Contra cause and deepened the insurgency's foothold within Nicaragua, as discussed in Chapter 3. By the beginning of 1984, Contra forces launched attacks against ten cooperatives per month on average.[57] Between 1984 and 1987, the war-induced damages – both the destruction of goods and lost production – amounted to an estimated 40 percent of potential annual exports.[58]

The damages wrought by the armed conflict were not only economic, but political. With the 1981 dissolution of the unity government and the tightening political grip of the nine-man National Directorate (DN), the FSLN was now solely to blame for the country's economic woes – an attitude that emerged quite clearly in the November 1984 general elections. Though the opposition coalition refused to participate and the FSLN won handily, the abstention levels were significant in regions heavily battered by conflict, as well as zones where small and medium peasant producers represented a sizable share of the population.[59] Despite the victory, the results signaled to Sandinista leadership that the future of the revolutionary project was at risk due to eroding political support.

By 1984, the DN determined that the deteriorating military, economic, and political conditions warranted the "flexibilization" of agrarian policies to accelerate redistribution and meet local demands in peasant communities vulnerable to Contra recruitment. According to Baumeister, this "flexibilization" involved four key components: (1) "an increase in the

---

[56] Fitzgerald 1988: 36–37.   [57] Invernizzi et al. 1986: 214.   [58] Fitzgerald 1988: 37.
[59] MIDINRA 1985b: 2.

pace of reform"; (2) an increase in the provision of lands that were "not strictly collective," such as individual titles and credit and service cooperatives (CCS); (3) the development of titling procedures for lands occupied by landless peasants and those on APP properties; and (4) the liberalization of price controls put in places during the early years of Sandinista rule.[60] Per MIDINRA plans and reports, the rationale for this institutional "flexibilization" was rather straightforward: to "strengthen the alliance with the peasantry"[61] as a bulwark against counterrevolution and "to recover its social base in the countryside ... via concessions."[62] In particular, efforts to "massify" land titling were seen as "a means of re-establishing [peasant] trust and security in the possession of their lands."[63]

The shifts in agrarian policies were primarily targeted at the central and northern highland regions, which, in the subnational scheme devised by the FSLN, included Regions I (Estelí, Nueva Segovia, and Madriz), V (Boaco and Chontales), and VI (Jinotega and Matagalpa). These, along with the indigenous communities on the Atlantic coast,[64] were the zones most vulnerable to rebel incursion. Moreover, these regions contained tens of thousands of displaced families demanding land for resettlement. In 1985 and 1986 alone, some 300 properties were purchased or expropriated by the government to resettle communities forced to flee war zones.[65]

The new procedures to reassign lands on a massive scale were a part of "the contingency plans and immediate actions" to facilitate "grand mobilizations of the people in arms and decisive military victories against the counterrevolution."[66] "Part of the war was the deployment of agrarian reform actions" in these regions.[67] In 1984, for example, MIDINRA, Ministry of Defense, and Ministry of the Interior officials formulated and implemented a unified plan for Regions I and VI, which included measures ranging from land provision to the mass import of arms and foodstuffs to "influence all aspects affecting the will of the peasantry toward the Revolution."[68]

As a result of the FSLN program of "flexibilization," the pace of redistribution changed rapidly. In the first ten months of 1984 alone,

---

[60] Baumeister 1998: 166–167.     [61] CIERA 1988: 6.     [62] MIDINRA 1984: 36.
[63] DGFCRA 1984b: 21.
[64] In 1987, the FSLN government passed a statute granting autonomy to indigenous communities in the northern and southern Caribbean coast zones and recognizing traditional, communal forms of property.
[65] IRAM 2000: 35.     [66] MIDINRA 1984: 14.
[67] Interview with author, March 1, 2017.     [68] Ibid.

the government titled 2.15 million acres of land that it distributed to 35,000 families.[69] In 1985, an additional 890,000 acres were redistributed to some 19,070 families.[70] Overall, the land area titled to cooperatives, indigenous communities, and individual peasants between 1984 and 1986 was nearly three-and-a-half times that titled between 1981 and 1983 and benefitted over twice as many families.[71]

But as important as the acceleration in the pace of titling, the new rules of redistribution dramatically tilted the collective–individual balance of land provision. Recognizing the clash between orthodox forms of collectivized agriculture and the individual-based structures that prevailed among the rural peasantry, FSLN leaders made much greater allowances for individual and semi-collective titling to shore up military and productive activities. Between 1981 and 1984, individual and semi-collective lands represented only 18 percent of all redistributed area; however, they had grown to 47 percent during the 1985–1987 period.[72] In the years following the 1984 shift, the trend toward individual titling only became more pronounced. According to MIDINRA figures, there was a relatively even mix of individual and semi-collective titles issued in 1985; yet, the following year, individual parcels represented a clear majority, some 73 percent of lands and 86 percent of titles handed over.[73] Nicaragua's pre- and post-1984 land reform efforts thus bear little resemblance. While not wiping out collective agricultural institutions completely, the FSLN's initially strict vision of agrarian reform had largely been brushed side due to military and economic necessities. This reorientation thus created a "gap" propitious for the introduction new rules.

But as peasant pressures mounted and displacement increased, FSLN leadership was left with a critical dilemma: Where would the land for new peasant beneficiaries come from? While Sandinista cadres had previously resisted the breakup of state-run farms and productive enterprises, such measures now became unavoidable to meet peasant demands. Further, the dismantling of APP farms and enterprises was of political import; for many individual peasant producers, APP properties, which enjoyed disproportionate public credit and technical assistance, had become "the symbol of the betrayal" of the revolutionary process.[74] Much of the redistributed land post-1984 thus came from the breakup of already acquired APP properties. According to a 1985 MIDINRA year-end report, roughly half of the redistributed land under the "*Plan*

---

[69] Invernizzi et al. 1986: 225.    [70] MIDINRA 1986: 5.    [71] CIERA 1989: 41.
[72] Gutiérrez 1988: 119.    [73] MIDINRA 1987a: 152.    [74] MIDINRA 1985c: 9.

*Extraordinario"* ["Extraordinary Plan"] that year came from the nationalized properties due to "the increasing necessities of land for thousands
of peasant families without land or directly affected by the aggression."[75]
By the end of the war, only 35 percent of land was concentrated in state-
run firms, while 65 percent had been assigned to cooperatives and
individuals.[76]

Yet, it quickly became clear that ceding APP lands would not be
enough to meet peasant demands. As a result, the government passed
more legislation in 1986 to expand the criteria of expropriation to idle
lands regardless of size and to cover land claimed in the name of "national
development." Following the passage of the 1986 Agrarian Reform Law,
the land reform movement "exploded," and in 1986 alone, the FSLN
carried out 30 percent of all expropriations.[77] Oftentimes, the expropriated lands were a result of voluntary sales by Sandinista-allied commercial elites or negotiations with landowners, who put up little resistance
when offered cash payments. Yet, other times, and especially as conflict
violence exacerbated financial strains, land negotiations and promises of
compensation were less credible and heavily politicized. In principle,
MIDINRA officials intended for the expropriations to be "carefully
planned, to distinguish the cases that should undergo a process of negoti-
ation, those that should be oriented toward striking a blow to the
counterrevolution ... from those owned by [individuals] who have fled
the country and whose properties are required for the urgent need of
peasant resettlement."[78] In practice, the confiscations became more reck-
less and increasingly flouted formal legal channels.

Combined, the accelerated pace of reform, more individually oriented
nature of redistribution, and hasty expropriations to meet the overwhelming demand prompted another key institutional change: It altered the
rules of legalization and titling, privileging the doling out of provisional
titles that ultimately exacerbated property insecurity. With the peasant
demand for land outpacing the FSLN's ability to formally nationalize it,
many of the parcels titled to peasant families beginning in 1984 had not
technically passed into state hands. Though it is difficult to discern the
precise number, one study found that 78 percent of redistributed properties investigated remained under the names of their pre-Revolution
owners.[79]

[75] MIDINRA 1986: 6.   [76] Baumeister 1998: 184.   [77] Spalding 1994: 83–84.
[78] DGFCRA 1985: 10.   [79] IRAM 2000: 36.

The failure to formally incorporate expropriated lands into the state sector, however, did not prevent local Sandinista officials from issuing provisional titles as a means of maintaining social control and rendering the population "legible" amid heightened fears of insurgent defection.[80] Though the titles looked like those established by the Agrarian Reform Law, they "lacked any registered record."[81] According to a study by the Institute for Investigation and Application of Development Methods (IRAM), this was the case for 70 percent of titles issued before the end of FSLN rule in 1990 – "they were provisional titles that could not be entered into the public registries because they did not contain previous ownership records and were granted with the intention of being temporary."[82]

Evidence suggests that top FSLN leadership including members of the party vanguard, which possessed increasingly centralized control over political and economic policy, implemented the more informal mechanisms of titling as an instrument of rural control. The provisional titles were in part a means of preventing land reform beneficiaries from immediately selling their plots, thereby jeopardizing the Sandinistas' leverage in the countryside. As one former MIDINRA official articulated, "had the [agrarian reform properties] formed part of a market, very quickly people would have sold [what they received] and then they would have come back wanting us to give them more land."[83] In other words, the strategic dependence cultivated by the new FSLN approach would have been undercut by the extension of full marketable titles. Then-vice president of Nicaragua Sergio Ramírez similarly acknowledged that "to take away the Contras' support base, we changed course and decided to transfer individual property titles to the peasants" – a move that he deems "insufficient" due to its informal nature, because "those titles could neither be sold nor transferred."[84]

Reports from field visits to the areas most affected by post-1984 redistribution efforts suggest the precarious nature of the titles was not a political blunder or a function of state weakness, but a deliberate wartime political strategy meant to strengthen the FSLN's rural control. Local FSLN officials, who were the eyes and ears of national leadership on the ground, similarly recognized that land redistribution on an individual basis was critical to "securing and tightening ... the alliance with the most advanced sectors of the peasantry."[85] According to local reports,

[80] Albertus 2021.    [81] IRAM 2000: 39.    [82] Ibid.
[83] Interview with author, March 1, 2017.    [84] Ramírez 2011: Loc 2976–2977.
[85] MIDINRA 1987b: 19–20.

efforts to resettle families and provide "greater access to land, credit, [and] technical and material assistance" were an effective strategy to "demystify [...] the propaganda of the Contras" and generate "a strong dependence on state attention."[86]

The new top-down strategy for cultivating peasant dependence through informal, provisional titling was by many accounts widespread. In interviews with local officials and residents throughout the country, CIERA researchers found that "the better part of the titles handed out have been provisional titles" and that "there has not been a follow-up process for affected areas and titling."[87] The failure to "follow up" the provisional titles with full formalization speak to the ways in which the FSLN wielded tenuous property rights as a counterinsurgent tool to maintain and strengthen peasant allegiances. This strategic aspect is also underscored by the locations in which provisional titling was most prevalent. In Region VI, the coffee-growing zones of Jinotega and Matagalpa, which were hotbeds of Contra recruitment, researchers reported as the most significant challenges "the lack of legalization of lands captured by the State [and] the excess of provisional titles."[88]

Even according to the accounts of FSLN officials themselves, provisional titling was carried out as a means of addressing the deepening problem of displacement and resettlement in conflict zones – albeit one that abided by a distinctly political logic. For example, a MIDINRA evaluation of the land reform program from the first trimester of 1985 notes how during this period, "formal titling was minimal; however, [we] did achieve the relocation of displaced peasants in war zones affected by the aggression, effectively handing over the properties physically but leaving the formal titling pending for the second trimester."[89] Though the official FSLN directive was to "flexibilize" the agrarian reform program, leaders wielded the withholding of full titles to control local productive and defense activities. As one MIDINRA report urged, "The policy of assigning titles to cooperatives should remain until after a certain amount of time in which they have demonstrated some level of organizational stability. During this period, the beneficiaries should be assured of and provided provisional legal backing."[90]

Much in line with the logic of the property rights gap described above, it is unlikely that the withholding of full property rights in favor of granting tenuous provisional titles was simply a policy error, a product

[86] Ibid., 22.    [87] DGFCRA 1984a: 1.    [88] Ibid., 32.    [89] DGFCRA 1985: 13.
[90] DGFCRA 1986a: 22.

of state weakness, or a function of FSLN ideology. After all, the revolutionary regime had proven itself capable of not only implementing countrywide mass literacy and vaccination campaigns, but it also mobilized the Nicaraguan population for defense on a scale unprecedented in Central America. Moreover, the strict adherence to a fully collectivized agricultural model was far from static, illustrating that the FSLN's ideological orientation cannot fully explain the wartime developments within the land reform program. Because of the dramatic shifts in the pace and modalities of redistribution, there is little reason to believe that ideology proscribed parallel transformations in the provision of property rights. Moreover, there is little evidence that FSLN leadership planned to revert to collective titling once the Contra threat abated – another possible reason for the tenuous and informal nature of mid-1980s titling efforts. Instead, in 1987 as violence diminished and the Contra were in retreat, the regime continued its strategy of "reducing private property confiscations and putting an end to the Agrarian Reform firms," according to Wheelock.[91] Likewise, it sought to "fulfill its pending commitments to private property owners, such as payments and indemnities . . . in the case of confiscations that exhibited inconsistencies."[92] Far from reimposing its previous orthodox model, FSLN leadership doubled-down on individual titling – a move consistent with the strategic nature of the mid-1980s agrarian reform policies.

The FSLN's increased control through programs like agrarian reform allowed it to recover territory and overpower insurgent efforts, yet at a tremendous cost to secure land tenure for the regime's base. The reorientation of the land reform program to appeal to small and medium peasant landholders coincided with successful FSLN efforts to beat back the Contra insurgency. For example, one former agrarian reform architect notes that the unified plan for Regions I and VI cited earlier facilitated "a turning of the tide in the defensive capacity of the [Sandinista] Army, such that in 1986 and 1987, the Contra was stopped and militarily . . . placed in a state of defeat."[93] According to top Sandinista commander General Humberto Ortega, the revolutionary forces achieved significant Contra defeats by "striking the Contra and taking its territory and military capacity away; sticking to the issue of territory, organizing a broad mechanism of popular defense; and appealing to the people, in particular the peasantry through agrarian reform."[94] Top FSLN leadership thus

---

[91] Wheelock 1991: 7.    [92] Ibid.    [93] Interview with author, March 1, 2017.
[94] "Los contra" 1987.

attributes the decisive military gains, in part, to the strategic reorientation of titling procedures.

Relatedly, there is some evidence that the new rules of titling were effective in binding peasants to the regime. Some peasant accounts indicate that the prospect of individual land did diminish the possibilities of rural defection to the Contra. For example, as Cornelius Herrera, a peasant in the contested community of Pantasma, described in 1985, "now I wouldn't say that I'm resentful of [the FSLN]; they wanted to negotiate a *finca* for me but they couldn't find a way. But I've now spent a year working with them."[95] Indeed, the new policies "re-created dependent relationships with [the FSLN's] peasant supporters"[96] in ways that appear to have furthered counterinsurgent efforts.

But following the FSLN's 1990 electoral loss, which brought to power center-right UNO opposition leader and former JGRN member Violeta Barrios de Chamorro (see Chapter 10), it became clear that the vast majority of agrarian reform titles issued during the decade of Sandinista rule lacked formal and permanent legal backing.[97] In his treatise attempting to debunk the *Piñata* allegations, Minister Wheelock admits that as much as 80 percent of the titles issued before the electoral loss were provisional.[98] Lacking firm legal backing, peasant families and agricultural workers lived in fear that their parcels would be reclassified as state lands and returned to their pre-Revolution owners.[99]

## CONCLUSION

Nicaragua emerged from the decade-long Contra War with staggering levels of land insecurity and conflict, which facilitated brazen land grabs on the part of top political elites. At first glance, these phenomena might be construed as outcomes of wartime institutional degradation, as the strains of armed conflict decimated the state's capacity to regulate land tenure and property ownership. But upon closer inspection, wartime institutional changes within the Sandinista's landmark agrarian reform program reveal something else: the institutionalization of undermining rules that systematically contravened the state's administrative functions. The undermining rules, which consisted of hasty confiscations and precarious provisional titling, were devised by a narrow, highly centralized, and vertically structured FSLN ruling party, which became more

---

[95] CIERA 1986: 122.    [96] Horton 1999: 239–240.    [97] IRAM 2000: 36.
[98] Wheelock 1991: 10.    [99] Ibid., 167.

insulated and employed greater discretionary authority as the insurgent threat mounted.

Overall, the introduction of undermining rules within land tenure institutions during the Nicaraguan conflict casts doubt on a primary explanation for variation in wartime institutional development, as well as classic theories of how war "builds" the state. Beginning in the early 1980s, the FSLN-led state, which had already implemented several transformative social programs, mobilized the Nicaraguan population for defense on a scale unprecedented in Central America (Chapter 3). According to prominent approaches to war and statebuilding, this type of wartime extraction from mass actors induces societal bargaining and bolsters administrative institutions.[100] FSLN leaders "squeezed the means of war from their own populations."[101] This mode of waging war embodies the classic explanation for how war induces statebuilding: With such "coercion-intensive" strategies, rulers sought access to "the resources [citizens] controlled through household taxation, mass conscription, censuses, police systems, and many other invasions of small-scale social life," implying "penetration and bargaining [that] laid down new state structures."[102]

Yet, this chapter's analysis reveals that, somewhat surprisingly, undermining institutional logics emerged within Nicaragua's land reform program instead. The narrow and insulated nature of the FSLN governing coalition and the escalation of the Contra threat resulted in the introduction of new rules that, while seeking to recover peasant support for the Sandinista-led state, also subverted land and property administration to strengthen rural social control. These findings challenge conventional war-centered explanations of state formation premised on the social sectors from which wartime resources are marshalled. Instead, this case illuminates the central role of wartime political structures and coalitional configurations in mediating institutional change within the state apparatus. Having elaborated processes of wartime institutional evolution within the three Central American cases, I now turn to Part II, which evaluates when and how the undermining rules developed in armed conflict persist beyond it.

---

[100] Tilly 1990: 30–31.    [101] Ibid.    [102] Ibid., 25.

PART III

INSTITUTIONAL PERSISTENCE

# 7

## Transition, Peace, and Postwar Power
## in Central America

Though Central America's armed conflicts were not unique during the Cold War era, the region's ability to dodge the "conflict trap" – to avoid civil war relapse – sets it apart from a majority of postwar settings. But overcoming a return to conflict is merely the first peacetime hurdle; within fragile, transitional settings, wartime elites often find new opportunities to secure and strengthen the institutional status quo.[1] Under what conditions do the perverse and predatory rules devised in war persist within and beyond it?

This book posits that the persistence or disruption of the undermining rules, much like wartime institutional change itself, is a question of political coalitions. To reproduce the undermining rules, the counterinsurgent elite must broaden the distributional coalition – the web of sectoral interests with a vested stake in the conflict-era institutional landscape. As this broader array of political and economic blocs continues to garner benefits through the implementation of the undermining rules, they become self-enforcing. Further, when this distributional coalition effectively adapts to the postwar environment and continues to control political and economic power and resources, the undermining rules can survive state reforms. By contrast, the undermining rules face chronic instability when there are frequent realignments among elite stakeholders beyond the conflict period. Overall, the ability of the dominant counterinsurgent coalition to adapt to regime transition and peace while co-opting new arenas of political and economic influence can overcome

---

[1] See Lake 2017; Barma 2017.

institutional overhaul, new norms and attitudes toward appropriate bureaucratic behavior, and even the ouster of wartime perpetrators of corruption and human rights abuses.

Before examining the Guatemalan and Nicaraguan cases in-depth, this chapter first lays the foundations for the second half of the book by discussing each country's respective road from armed conflict to political transition and peace. The second half of the chapter examines the foundations of institutional persistence (or chronic instability) within the three institution-level cases discussed in Chapters 4, 5, and 6: Guatemala's customs apparatus, Guatemala's policing institutions, and Nicaragua's land administration. Specifically, it traces how in the first two cases, the dominant counterinsurgent coalition made a concerted effort to knit together a wider array of sectoral interests with a stake in the undermining rules in customs and the security sector – it sought to broaden the respective distributional coalitions. By contrast, the FSLN failed to engage in such efforts within the land reform sector, paving the way for coalitional volatility and elite realignments which disrupted the wartime institutional status quo. These critical differences explain why similar processes of wartime institutional evolution ultimately diverge, producing distinct long-run outcomes.

## THE ROAD TO TRANSITION AND PEACE

The push for political liberalization and peace on a regionwide scale in Central America began in the early and mid-1980s with the formation of the Contadora Group to forge a path to regional stability. Amid continuing violence and US opposition, the Contadora Group quickly fizzled; however, it laid the groundwork for a second, more significant initiative known as the Esquipulas Accords, spearheaded by Costa Rican president Óscar Arias in 1987.

Despite these unified, regional initiatives, the pathways to transition look rather distinct in Guatemala and Nicaragua. Guatemala experienced a gradual turn toward political liberalization, which, in 1986, culminated in the inauguration of the first elected civilian administration in twenty years; however, the formal end of armed conflict did not occur until a decade later, after the continuation of low-intensity violence and a protracted peace process in the early 1990s. By contrast, amid the mounting economic and human toll, Nicaragua's Contra War came to a more abrupt end after the FSLN's electoral defeat forced Sandinista elites into compromise to secure revolutionary gains. This section lays out these distinct trajectories, which had important implications for power structures and coalitional configurations in the cases at the heart of this book.

## Guatemala: The Protracted Peace and the Entrenchment of Wartime Interests

As the longest of Central America's three Cold War-era armed conflicts, Guatemala also experienced the most drawn-out process of democratic transition and civil war termination. The seeds of transition were sown following the 1983 coup that ousted General Efraín Ríos Montt, the military dictator who oversaw mass violence, including "acts of genocide," against rural Mayan communities, according to the UN-sponsored Historical Clarification Commission (CEH). Despite his mere 16 months at the helm of the Guatemalan state, Ríos Montt's rule brought increasing international condemnation and exacerbated intra-elite divisions, which ultimately triggered greater political liberalization.[2]

The first steps toward realizing reforms emerged during the subsequent regime of General Óscar Humberto Mejía Víctores (1983–1986), who replaced Ríos Montt following a military coup led by younger field officers, including the eventual president and alleged *La Línea* architect Otto Pérez Molina. The rise of Mejía Víctores brought to power a more moderate, institutionalist wing of the Guatemalan military, which "recognized that a façade of constitutional democracy was needed to overcome the contradictions of direct military dictatorship."[3] Though rural warfare and military social control continued, violence declined significantly. The new regime also permitted the formation of a constituent assembly, which rewrote the constitution in 1985. That same year Guatemalans went to the polls to elect Christian Democrat Vinicio Cerezo, who assumed power in January 1986 as the first civilian president in nearly twenty years.

While bringing greater political opening, the transition also served to safeguard core military interests and preserve military political power. Though violence remained relatively low, the Guatemalan military's post-1983 guiding doctrine, the "Thesis of National Stability" justified continued repression against political opposition.[4] The preservation of military interests was even more pronounced behind-the-scenes.

---

[2] See Isaacs and Schwartz 2020 for a discussion of these international and domestic dynamics.
[3] Jonas 2000: 26.    [4] Schirmer 1998a: 235–257.

The Cerezo government forged a *de facto* "power-sharing agreement" with the top military brass, led by institutionalist general Héctor Alejandro Gramajo, minister of defense from 1987 to 1990. The civilian administration and leading military officials found common cause in support for liberalization and in their shared interest to fend off the radical right-wing military factions, which launched numerous coup attempts in the late 1980s.[5] Yet, the relationship between Cerezo and the top military leadership was nowhere near a genuine and equal partnership. Through elite military units like the EMP, military leaders maintained tight control over politics and policy, generating a post-transition environment of "supervised democracy"[6] and "the civilian continuation of the counterinsurgency state."[7]

The preservation of military political influence, in part, explains the eight-year gap between Guatemala's return to civilian rule and the initiation of the peace process. Though military leaders like Gramajo recognized their role "as actors in the democratization process," they continued to see the armed forces as "guarantor of the survival of the State" in neutralizing armed opposition.[8] This vision prompted sustained, though lower-intensity state-sponsored violence and further hampered negotiations. Demands by the umbrella insurgent organization, the URNG, for "wholesale demilitarization, the restructuring of the armed forces, and purges of the worst human rights abusers within the military" as preconditions for peace talks were non-starters given the military's abiding political grip.[9] Yet, as the Cold War finally came to a close and the insurgency, though depleted, remained a thorn in the military's side, both camps moved toward the negotiating table.

Initial progress was briefly derailed when President Jorge Serrano (1991–1993), Cerezo's successor, attempted to dissolve Congress and suspend the constitutional order – an event known as the *Serranazo*. Yet international outcry alongside Guatemalan military leaders' refusal to back Serrano's self-coup was ultimately a boon for negotiations, convincing the organized business sector – the Coordinating Committee of Agricultural, Commercial, Industrial, and Financial Associations (CACIF) – of the need to "abandon the pro-*golpe* forces" that stood as an obstacle to peace.[10] Human rights ombudsman Ramiro de León Carpio (1993–1996), who replaced Serrano, resumed talks, and by

---

[5] Wilkinson 2002: 319; Rosada-Granados 1999: 194–205.     [6] ODHAG 1998: 251.
[7] Jonas 1991: 171.     [8] Schirmer 1991: 11.     [9] Isaacs and Schwartz 2020: 16.
[10] Jonas 2000: 42.

January 1994, government, military, and URNG leaders had agreed to the "Framework Accord for the Resumption of the Negotiating Process."

The subsequent negotiations generated six substantive accords, covering topics like human rights; the resettlement of displaced populations; the creation of a truth commission (the CEH); recognition of the identity and rights of indigenous peoples; social, economic, and agrarian issues; and civilian control of the armed forces (see Table 7.1). On December 26, 1996, at the National Palace in Guatemala City's historic center, recently elected president Álvaro Arzú (1996–2000) led the signing ceremony for the "Accord for a Firm and Lasting Peace," officially ending Central America's longest and bloodiest Cold War-era conflict.

However, while laying the foundations for an enduring peace, the transition and negotiations also facilitated the entrenchment of Guatemala's dominant wartime political coalition – the key factor explaining the persistence of undermining rules in customs and the security sector. Despite the striking breadth of the final agreements, there were several moments that underscore how Guatemalan political, economic, and military elites consolidated their own power through the transition and peace process. The most reactionary elements of Guatemala's organized business community and military officer corps saw the state as "giving away too much" and, alongside their civilian political allies, resisted many of the core proposals to promote accountability and to address the deep social and economic inequalities that contributed to conflict. At their behest, the successful negotiations set off, in Jonas' words, "a process of deterioration"[11] that would culminate in the rejection of constitutional reforms to enshrine Accord provisions into law and the co-optation of peace by wartime elites.

Guatemala's organized business sector through its primary representative body, CACIF, allied with the Arzú government to limit the scope of changes through the Accord on Social and Economic Issues and the Agrarian Situation. CACIF also ensured that the agreements left the country's regressive tax system untouched and did not commit future governments to specific fiscal reforms.[12] Reactionary elements of Guatemala's military elite also threatened to throw the peace process off course through resistance to accountability for human rights abuses and the strengthening of civilian authority. Though the Arzú government empowered members of the moderate, institutionalist wing of the military

---

[11] Jonas 2000: 10.   [12] Ibid., 13; see also, Rettberg 2007.

TABLE 7.1 *Guatemalan peace accords and core provisions*[13]

| Peace accord | Date signed | Notable provisions |
| --- | --- | --- |
| Framework Accord for the Resumption of the Negotiating Process | January 1994 | - United Nations elevated from observer to moderator<br>- Civil society participation involves making nonbinding consensus proposals<br>- Timetable for completing negotiations (initially by end of 1994) |
| Comprehensive Accord on Human Rights | March 1994 | - Respect for international human rights and humanitarian law<br>- Respect for independence of institutions protecting human rights like Public Prosecutor's Office (MP) and Human Rights Ombudsman (PDH)<br>- Elimination of illegal security organizations responsible for human rights abuses<br>- Establishment of UN peace verification mission (MINUGUA) |
| Accord on the Resettlement of Population Groups Uprooted by Armed Conflict | June 1994 | - Guarantee of conditions for voluntary return of displaced persons<br>- Recognition of land and land tenure as a basic factor in reintegration of the displaced<br>- Creation of technical commission to identify needs of the displaced |
| Accord on the Identity and Rights of Indigenous Peoples | March 1995 | - Formal recognition of Guatemala as a multiethnic, multicultural, and multilingual nation<br>- Protection of cultural rights and institutions like language, names, dress, ceremonial sites, and sacred places<br>- Creation of laws to criminalize ethnic discrimination<br>- Education reforms to promote multilingual and multicultural education<br>- Incorporation of customary law in municipal code |

[13] See Jonas 2000: 69–92 for a comprehensive look at the different peace agreements.

| Peace accord | Date signed | Notable provisions |
|---|---|---|
| | | - Proposed ratification of international laws protecting against discrimination and facilitating community consultation in decision-making |
| Accord on Social and Economic Issues and the Agrarian Situation | May 1996 | - Decentralization of development planning<br>- Increased social spending on education, healthcare, social security, and housing<br>- Market-assisted land redistribution<br>- Creation of national survey and land registry<br>- Increasing tax ratio by 50 percent by year 2000 |
| Accord on the Strengthening of Civilian Power and the Role of the Armed Forces in a Democratic Society | September 1996 | - Establishment of National Civilian Police (PNC) as entity responsible for internal security<br>- Redefinition of military's mission as confined to external defense<br>- Replacement of intelligence and presidential security units with civilian-run entities under Interior Ministry<br>- Demobilization of civilian self-defense patrols (PACs) and Mobile Military Police<br>- 33 percent reduction in military troop levels and budget<br>- Professionalization of civil service<br>- Professionalization of judicial system |
| Operational Accords | December 1996 | - Cease-fire<br>- Proposal of constitutional reforms to enshrine Accords into law<br>- Creation of Electoral Reform Commission<br>- Legal integration of the URNG<br>- Timetable for Accord implementation from 1997 to 2000 |

during peace negotiations,[14] influential hardliners opposed ceding any
ground to the URNG and the domestic and international organizations
they deemed leftist sympathizers. Military negotiators successfully diluted
agreements related to truth-seeking and accountability for human rights
violations.[15] Economic elite and military-led efforts to hollow out core
peace provisions were only exacerbated by the weakness of the UN's role
through its peace verification mission, MINUGUA, which lacked the
political clout and enforcement capacity to overcome the peace resisters.[16]

The contempt and cynicism of traditional political, business, and military sectors and the weakness of international enforcement culminated in
the resounding failure of efforts to formally codify Peace Accord provisions
into law through the May 1999 constitutional referendum, due in large
part to a vicious opposition campaign mobilized by groups like CACIF, the
Association of Military Veterans of Guatemala (AVEMILGUA), and the
Evangelical Church.[17] The failed referendum signaled "a decisive tendency
toward reduced political participation,"[18] consolidating power in the
hands of long-privileged political, economic, and military leaders. Amid
this elite intransigence and entrenchment, the dominant wartime coalition
expanded its reach and brought other key sectors into the fold – setting the
stage for the persistence of the undermining rules governing customs fraud
and extrajudicial killing.

### Nicaragua: Stalled Talks, Sandinista Defeat, and Coalitional Volatility

In contrast to Guatemala's lengthy journey to political transition and
peace, conflict termination in Nicaragua unfolded much more rapidly.
The FSLN's negotiations with Contra forces and electoral defeat at the
hands of the National Opposition Union (UNO) occurred within the span
of two years. Moreover, Nicaragua's postwar political landscape faced
pronounced elite realignments due to the FSLN's loss of power in April
1990 – another marked difference relative to the Guatemalan context.

---

[14] Holiday 1997: 72.
[15] Though military representatives eventually agreed to the establishment of the Historical
Clarification Commission (CEH), they guaranteed that it would refrain from naming
perpetrators of human rights abuses and that its findings could not spur further criminal
prosecutions. The passage of the National Reconciliation Law in 1996 further neutralized
any judicial implications of truth commission findings by providing a blanket amnesty for
conflict-era abuses, except for crimes of torture, forced disappearance, and genocide. See
Isaacs 2010: 5–6.
[16] Stanley 2013.     [17] Cojtí Cuxil 1999: 23.     [18] Brett and Delgado 2005: 45.

Despite deepening fragmentation, the Sandinistas never completely departed the political scene. Instead, former president and party secretary-general Daniel Ortega adopted an increasingly personalist leadership style and pursued a series of strategic adaptations, which generated persistent volatility within the dominant political coalition.

Developments in the mid-1980s facilitated conflict termination in Nicaragua. These included the mounting human and economic toll of the US-backed Contra onslaught, waning domestic support for the FSLN's political and economic program, and the increasingly strained relationship between the Sandinistas and their Soviet backers. Economic devastation in Nicaragua mounted as the US-backed Contra campaign advanced throughout the 1980s. Resistance forces, under the direction of CIA advisors, deliberately targeted sites of economic production, including cooperatives and state-owned enterprises.[19] Moreover, the US trade embargo imposed in 1984, combined with *de facto* sanctions imposed by international financial institutions like the World Bank and Inter-American Development Bank (IDB), ratcheted up the economic pain.[20] According to some estimates, by 1987 "property destruction totaled $221.6 million; production losses $984.5 million. Nicaraguan economists estimated monetary losses due to the trade embargo at $254 million and the loss of development potential from war at $2.5 billion,"[21] though others have put the latter figure at $4 billion.[22] By the beginning of 1990, executive officials reported a wartime death toll of 30,865, including state personnel, Contra fighters, and civilians.[23]

Economic ruin and inflation also triggered the erosion of FSLN political support – the first signs of which became evident with the 1984 elections. As mentioned in Chapter 6, the November 1984 general elections took place after lengthy negotiations with opposition political parties, which ultimately decided to boycott the contest.[24] The FSLN won 67 percent of the vote, including 60 percent of seats in the newly formed National Assembly.[25] Despite robust support for continued Sandinista political rule at the national level, internal FSLN reports painted a more pessimistic picture. In rural areas battered by violence – including those in which more than 40 percent of peasant families had benefitted from land redistribution – abstention rates in some cases approached 50 percent with "potential FSLN opposition" calculated at nearly two-thirds in Regions

---

[19] Invernizzi et al. 1986: 214.    [20] Kruijt 2011: 73; Kornbluh 1991: 327.
[21] Kornbluh 1991: 345.    [22] Martí i Puig 1997: 117.    [23] Kornbluh 1991: 344.
[24] Williams 1994: 177–178.
[25] Martí i Puig 2010: 82–83; Weaver and Barnes 1991: 127–128.

V (Chontales and Boaco) and VI (Matagalpa and Jinotega).[26] The signs of growing discontent with FSLN governance in areas targeted for social and economic benefits, while not enough to displace incumbent leadership, were cause for concern among many Sandinista elites.

A final development that prompted Nicaraguan leaders to seek a way out of armed conflict was the waning economic, military, and political support of the Soviet Union as the Cold War fizzled. Though Soviet support for the FSLN never matched that provided to the Cuban regime nor paralleled the extent of US assistance to the Contra, arms procurement, oil deliveries, and technical support did play a role in the FSLN war effort. By 1985, the Soviet bloc accounted for 20 percent of Nicaragua's total trade.[27] But the Soviet government denied the FSLN the hard currency required to overcome mounting economic crisis and refused military support in the event of a direct US invasion. By 1986, oil shipments had declined by 40 percent and overall Soviet aid was cut by two-thirds.[28]

In response to these challenges, FSLN leadership turned to the negotiating table through a series of regional efforts that, while well-intentioned, were repeatedly hindered by the United States' virulent anti-Sandinista stance. The initial steps toward peace negotiations in Nicaragua took shape through the Contadora process.[29] Though the Ortega regime was amenable to the initial negotiations, the United States refused to dismantle its military bases and exercises in Honduras in exchange for the FSLN's dismissal of Soviet and Cuban advisors. Nicaragua finally withdrew from the process when Guatemala, El Salvador, and Honduras failed to denounce the Contras.[30]

Following a similar failure of the first Esquipulas talks, the dialogue was revived by Costa Rican president Óscar Arias, who brokered a historic deal signed by all five Central American countries, which agreed:

(1) to decree amnesty for irregular forces (who would also be obligated to release their prisoners); (2) to vehemently call for a cease-fire in countries where armed conflicts were underway; (3) to promote a pluralistic, participatory democracy, without outside interference, guaranteeing complete press freedom, and assuring access of all political parties . . . ; (4) to call on the governments within and without the region to cease all aid, whether military, logistical, financial, or even propagandistic, to all irregular forces or insurrectional movements, with the exception of aid for repatriation or relocation; and (5) to prevent irregular forces from using the territory of any Central American state . . . as bases of supply.[31]

[26] MIDINRA 1985b: 64–65.    [27] Walker 2003: 187.    [28] Ibid., 187–188.
[29] Goodfellow and Morrell 1991: 371, 374.    [30] Ibid., 373–374.    [31] Ibid., 379.

In the aftermath of the agreement, the Ortega administration established the National Reconciliation Commission (CNR), appointing regime opponent Cardinal Miguel Obando y Bravo as head. It also opened its doors to the United Nations Observation Mission to Central America (ONUCA).[32] Meanwhile, in February 1988, the US Congress, in opposition to the Reagan administration, voted to deny critical financial assistance to the Contra.

With new spaces for dialogue and the new posture toward peace within the US Congress, the FSLN, led by General Humberto Ortega, and the Nicaraguan Resistance (RN) concluded a first set of cease-fire agreements at Sapoá in March 1988. They later negotiated additional demobilization accords in 1989 after agreeing to modify the electoral regime and set national and municipal elections for February 25, 1990, eight months ahead of schedule.[33] With agreements by the Central American presidents to demobilize Contra forces in their territory, the new US administration of George H.W. Bush had little option but to abandon Reagan's previous campaign.[34]

Negotiations in the late 1980s laid the groundwork for formal peace; however, it was the shocking FSLN defeat in the 1990 elections that played the decisive role in ending conflict. Following FSLN-backed political reforms, the National Opposition Union (UNO), an anti-Sandinista coalition forged by groups from across the political spectrum, decided to participate and put forward as its presidential candidate Violeta Barrios de Chamorro, a member of the short-lived governing junta established after the 1979 revolution. With 86 percent turnout, Chamorro won 54.7 percent of the vote, while President Daniel Ortega won only 40.8 percent.

With the FSLN's impending loss of executive power, state and insurgent forces, urged by former US president Jimmy Carter, sat down at the negotiating table to craft a definitive end to the fighting.[35] Just prior to Chamorro's inauguration on April 25, 1990, the Sandinista Popular Army (EPS), Contra forces, and representatives of the president-elect signed three peace accords that established a cease-fire, the UN-managed disarmament of RN fighters, and the withdrawal of state forces from five rural zones.[36] Viewing the electoral outcome, peace process, and impending political transition as clear signs that democratization and economic reform were on the horizon, the Bush administration lifted the Reagan-era economic embargo and immediately asked Congress to

[32] Kruijt 2008: 136.    [33] Ibid.; Goodfellow and Morrell 1991: 386.
[34] Goodfellow and Morrell 1991: 386–387.    [35] Kruijt 2008: 137.    [36] Speck 1990.

provide $300 million in financial assistance to the new government.[37] From the US government perspective, the election had empowered a political and ideological ally in its struggle to dismantle the FSLN-led transformations of the previous decade, now through peaceful, institutional means.

These developments, however, set the stage for repeated elite realignments and coalitional volatility, in contrast to the elite consolidation and entrenchment witnessed in Guatemala. Importantly, the election of Chamorro only constituted a "partial loss of the power apparatus"[38] for the Sandinistas, first because the UNO exhibited all the fragmentation and discord that one might expect of a blanket opposition coalition. The UNO was an agglomeration of fourteen political parties ranging from the far left to the far right.[39] Beyond discontent with Sandinista policies, there was little programmatic consensus holding the UNO governing coalition together. The right-wing, ex-Contra bloc, represented by the figure of new vice president Virgilio Godoy, a representative of the most reactionary landed and private sector elites, made it particularly difficult for the Chamorro government to advance politically and negotiate with the FSLN.[40] In addition, despite losing the presidential election and legislative majority, the Sandinistas retained thirty-nine of the ninety-three seats in Nicaragua's National Assembly[41] and had loyal civil servants across the state apparatus, including within social and economic policymaking agencies and the judiciary.[42]

Amid the fractures within the opposition, Chamorro and her moderate advisors had no choice but to strike a series of compromises with the FSLN to move political transition forward and placate popular demands. Within the 1990 Protocol of Transition, the Chamorro administration ceded continued Sandinista control within several arenas. The incumbent FSLN leadership recognized Chamorro as the electoral victor and legitimate president of Nicaragua with the power to name new ministers, while Chamorro permitted lower-level bureaucrats named under the Sandinistas to retain their posts. Importantly, the UNO government pledged "to respect the current Army's and Police Force's command structures" and, per an informal accord, leave revolutionary commander Humberto Ortega as head of the armed forces, in exchange for FSLN commitments to depoliticize the military and reduce its size by 85 percent.[43]

---

[37] Leogrande 1996: 343; Prevost 1996.      [38] Núñez Soto et al. 1998: 540.
[39] Merrill 1994: 105.      [40] Núñez Soto et al. 1998: 548.      [41] Leogrande 1996: 343.
[42] Dille 2012: 95.      [43] Ibid., 88; see also, Yashar 2018: 290–291; Ruhl 2003.

These compromises also left in place the redistributive gains made under the FSLN's agrarian reform, which I will examine in Chapter 10.

But despite remaining a significant force, the FSLN's 1990 electoral defeat upended the narrow, vertical structure of power that had governed Nicaragua, generating years of instability and reaccomodation. The circumscribed, tightly knit party leadership, which had assumed total control over the state apparatus through the DN, became subordinate to other party organs like the National Congress and Sandinista Assembly, which sought to chart a new course for the FSLN as a party in opposition.[44] As Martí i Puig writes, "[O]n the organizational level, the FSLN's loss of control of government meant that the party-state structure that had been established over a decade was destroyed. ... Party structures that overlapped with state administration also collapsed, creating considerable organic crisis that affected the DN's leadership capacity."[45]

In the early 1990s, the FSLN party apparatus fell victim to a tug-of-war between two rival factions – the so-called renovation movement (MRS) headed by former vice president Sergio Ramírez and former minister of health Dora María Téllez and the "Democratic Left" (ID) led by former Interior Minister Tomás Borge and Daniel Ortega.[46] After the triumph of Ortega's clique by the mid-1990s, only three of the original commanders of the DN – Ortega, Borge, and former FSLN Political Commission coordinator Bayardo Arce – remained atop the party structure, with the latter two subordinate to Ortega as party secretary-general.[47]

In addition to the fractures within the FSLN, the coalitional bases of the Chamorro administration itself disrupted the wartime status quo. Chamorro's rise ushered in an internationally backed liberal democratic regime, which sought to lay the groundwork for a new constitutional order. Closely aligned with the Bush administration, the government paired political reforms with Washington Consensus stabilization programs, which empowered a corps of US-aligned technocrats that sought to swiftly remake the Nicaraguan economy. Led by Chamorro's Minister of the Presidency Antonio Lacayo, the "neophyte advisers had an unshakeable, though untested belief in the efficacy of the free market" and were quick to apply "the rigorous laissez-faire strategies proposed by the IMF, the U.S. Agency for International Development (USAID), and the World Bank."[48]

---

[44] Martí i Puig 2010: 86.    [45] Ibid.    [46] Ibid., 88.    [47] Ibid., 89.
[48] Close 1999: 64.

The international community, and the United States in particular, secured neoliberal orthodoxy and cemented its place within Nicaragua's dominant postwar governing coalition by ramping up economic aid. During the Chamorro years, Nicaragua received the highest levels of US foreign aid per capita of any developing country in the world.[49] This assistance also spawned new civil society groups not affiliated with the mass organizations of the FSLN, further altering the political landscape. As Nilsson notes, "[A]mply financed by the donor community, the early 1990s witnessed an explosion of civil society organizations. ... Ex-combatants formed short-lived associations in order to strengthen their negotiating position toward the government [...and] an ever increasing host of newly created NGOs engaged in reconciliation programs."[50] Notably, conservative trade unions and organized business interests, represented by the Higher Council of Private Enterprise (COSEP), came to play a more significant role in political and economic policymaking.[51]

The US-promoted neoliberal program that prevailed during the Chamorro years reflected the disruption of the Sandinista political project and the narrow, vertical, and insulated FSLN coalition that dominated decision-making in the 1980s. During the Chamorro administration, the FSLN behaved as a party in opposition, developing an adversarial strategy premised on "[staging] contentious, disruptive, extraparliamentary movement politics (protest, at times accompanied by violence) while making deals with the government."[52] In the latter part of the chapter, I explore what this meant for coalitional configurations within Nicaragua's land administration and how it facilitated repeated disruptions in the undermining institutional arrangements implemented during conflict.

## THE SEEDS OF INSTITUTIONAL PERSISTENCE VERSUS CHRONIC INSTABILITY

While both the Guatemalan and Nicaraguan armed conflicts ended in the early and mid-1990s, there are key differences in the two countries' political trajectories in the latter stages of conflict and its aftermath, particularly when it comes to coalitional dynamics. For Guatemala's narrow military intelligence elite that seized control of the state in the late 1970s, conflict decline provided an impetus to draw together a more robust, multi-sectoral coalition of private sector elites, organized criminal

[49] Prevost 1996: 311.      [50] Nilsson 2018: 144.      [51] Prevost 1996: 311.
[52] Close and Martí i Puig 2011: 9.

operatives, and political officials to shore up the wartime rules. Meanwhile, the Sandinistas' 1990 electoral defeat disrupted the prevailing political coalition and set the stage for repeated realignments and persistent volatility throughout the 1990s and 2000s.

The remainder of this chapter demonstrates these political divergences within the three institution-level cases examined in the first half of this book: Guatemala's customs apparatus, Guatemala's policing institutions, and Nicaragua's land reform sector. First, with respect to Guatemala's customs administration, I examine how the Moreno Network laid the foundations of institutional survival by broadening the distributional coalition – the web of interest groups with a stake in the fraudulent customs procedures. The next section details how similar dynamics unfolded within Guatemala's police apparatus as the counterinsurgent elite expanded extrajudicial killing procedures to security agencies beyond the Detective Corps and garnered the continued buy-in of landed elites. Lastly, I assess how transition and reform in Nicaragua, while generating compromise with FSLN organizations initially, allowed a new constellation of political and economic forces to emerge within the land and property sector, disrupting the dominant wartime coalition.

## Guatemala: Broadening the Distributional Coalition within Customs

As Guatemala's internal armed conflict died down in the late 1980s and political transition approached, the Moreno Network sought to institutionalize the new rules governing customs fraud. While the use of coercion ensured the day-to-day compliance with the illicit customs procedures in a short-term sense (Chapter 4), the military intelligence officers pulling the strings also sought to secure the survival of the undermining rules into the future, particularly as the perceived insurgent threat faded. This required a longer-term vision for consolidating impunity and a robust client base to render the new wartime rules self-enforcing. As a result, the Moreno Network forged a broader distributional coalition of state and non-state actors who reproduced the undermining rules within customs. This coalition included two key sets of actors: (1) an association of lawyers, politicians, judges, and military officers known as *Grupo Salvavidas*, which bribed state officials to guarantee impunity for illicit activities; and (2) importers and commercial elites who recurred to the Moreno Network's services. By knitting together these two core interest groups, the narrow counterinsurgent elite laid the foundations for preserving the undermining rules within customs in the longer term.

On the political front, the Moreno Network developed a robust organizational body, which used the resources accrued through customs fraud to buy impunity within the Public Prosecutor's Office (MP) and court system, as well as finance electoral campaigns. The pressure group became known as *Grupo Salvavidas* ["life preserver" group], a name alluding to its function of rescuing those facing prosecution for human rights and corruption-related crimes.[53] *Grupo Salvavidas* was reportedly created by Moreno, his deputy Francisco Javier Ortiz Arriaga, and Salvadoran smuggler Santos Hipólito Reyes and came into being in 1989. Though it became a formal legal entity, the group, comprised of lawyers, judges, and high-ranking public officials, was created to serve as "a powerful influence-peddling [*tráfico de influencias*] network within all spheres of political power in the country."[54] In the words of one informant, "the name '*Salvavidas*' had its significance. On the one hand, to cover the backs of the members of the group and, on the other hand, to be able to save anyone involved in actions related to contraband, drug trafficking, and tax evasion from the application of justice in the most sound and immediate way."[55] Through strategically managing and distributing the resources accrued through contraband smuggling and customs fraud, *Grupo Salvavidas* fulfilled its primary function: to foster silence and complicity, ensuring the continued enrichment and political survival of its members and associates.

According to Ortiz Arriaga's testimony, *Grupo Salvavidas* consisted of "a support committee, an ad hoc committee, a board of directors, and branches."[56] The ad hoc committee, comprised of Moreno, Ortiz Arriaga, lawyers Elio Sánchez and Vicente González, and Col. Augusto Catalán, served as the intermediary between *Grupo Salvavidas* and the customs administration, issuing personnel transfers and disciplinary sanctions for noncompliance. It also decided how to respond when the network's allies faced legal consequences.

The board of directors coordinated *Grupo Salvavidas'* strategy and oversaw the distribution of resources to its members. Alfredo Moreno was the board's president, Elio Sánchez was the vice president, judge Osmundo Villatoro was the secretary, and Ortiz Arriaga was the treasurer. Former dictator Efraín Ríos Montt was in charge of judicial affairs, and his party's presidential candidate, Alfonso Portillo, who served as

[53] See Robles Montoya 2002; Peacock and Beltrán 2003.    [54] *La República* 1996a.
[55] Ibid.    [56] From Ortiz Arriaga testimony, May 25, 1999 (Organismo Judicial 2003).

president from 2000 to 2004, was in charge of political affairs.[57] In fact, Portillo received biweekly campaign contributions from the group – funds raised directly from customs fraud operations at the Valle Nuevo and Pedro de Alvarado customs houses – which he admitted to following Moreno's arrest.[58] The "branches" were *Grupo Salvavidas* members who were not on the board of directors but operated within distinct state agencies, offering bribes and exerting influence to impede investigations and judicial proceedings.

Finally, "all of the military officials" formed the "support committee." Among those integrating this group, according to the Moreno Network case files, were Generals Ortega Menaldo and Callejas y Callejas, the most prominent *Cofradía* leaders, as well General Roberto Letona Hora and Col. Hugo Morán Carranza, both former chiefs of the eighteenth-floor SEM office within the Ministry of Finance. According to Ortiz Arriaga, the support committee "opened up the influence peddling" by drawing on its vast knowledge and control of the state apparatus.

The modus operandi of *Grupo Salvavidas* was to target key actors participating in the investigations and trials of members or associates, offering bribes in exchange for information, silence, or favorable outcomes. Though it often channeled resources toward the obstruction of investigations into conflict-era human rights violations,[59] *Grupo Salvavidas* largely interfered in cases related to the very contraband and customs fraud activities coordinated by the Moreno Network. According to a prosecutor in the Moreno case, "*Grupo Salvavidas* was created precisely to settle the judicial cases related to contraband. ... [They] would give money to those who would clean up their tracks so that everyone remained silent."[60] One such case occurred in the southern department of Jutiapa, along the border with El Salvador. Authorities had detected "anomalies in the 63-A forms at customs locations in San Cristóbal, Valle Nuevo, and Pedro de Alvarado."[61] Local prosecutors took charge of the investigations, compiling a long list of customs inspectors and administrators reportedly involved in illegal activities. With the help of *Grupo Salvavidas*, the customs personnel amassed 250,000

---

[57] *La República* 1996b.
[58] From Ortiz Arriaga testimony, May 25, 1999 (Organismo Judicial 2003); *Siglo Veintiuno* 1996b; Shetemul 1996a.
[59] These cases included the murder of Guatemalan forensic anthropologist Myrna Mack and American innkeeper Michael DeVine.
[60] Interview with author, November 9, 2016.
[61] From Ortiz Arriaga testimony, May 25, 1999 (Organismo Judicial 2003).

quetzales ($83,000), which *Salvavidas* member Vicente González then handed off to the MP investigators assigned to the case. They promptly shelved the investigation before any charges were filed.[62]

Beyond the *Grupo Salvavidas* legal apparatus, the long-term viability of the Moreno Network also depended on a solid client base demanding the criminal structure's services. This client base was cultivated among a wide range of foreign and domestic business elites and importers, who grew accustomed to the savings they accrued by arranging customs duty adjustments and shipment "thefts" in exchange for off-the-books payments. As discussed in Chapter 4, not all the fraudulent procedures developed within the customs administration depended on the complicity, or even knowledge, of importers. But while some private sector actors remained in the dark or were coerced, many sought out the criminal structure regularly to conduct business. The case files from the Moreno investigation and trial highlight ongoing relationships between Alfredo Moreno and several foreign and domestic importers, who were critical to upholding the prevailing rules of the game within customs. One prominent example is the import-export company Bonanza, S.A., which dealt primarily with electronic equipment and household appliances. During raids on Moreno's residence and Bonanza's Guatemala City warehouse, investigators recovered receipts for large expenditures made by Moreno himself.[63] In addition, there are letters from Moreno to Bonanza owner Armando Cabané informing him that "various planned changes to general directors, including the director of customs and various ministers are ready" – moves that would presumably facilitate the fraudulent operations within customs.[64]

Another private sector actor that surfaces in the Moreno investigations is German importer Peter Stolz, the owner of the Guatemala City-based "Lup" warehouses. According to Ortiz Arriaga, Stolz imported "boxes with clothing, electronics, ceramics, fruit, and whiskey" and relied on the falsification of customs forms to misreport the nature and quantity of the merchandise.[65] But according to prosecutors, Stolz developed a seven million-quetzal ($2.3 million) debt with Moreno, leading to tensions that

[62] Ibid.; De los Ríos testimony, May 26, 1999 (Organismo Judicial 2003).
[63] *La República* 1996c.
[64] Letter to "Bonanza, S.A., Armando Cabane," December 22, 1991 (Organismo Judicial 2003) [Internal record: 2437].
[65] From Ortiz Arriaga testimony, May 25, 1999 (Organismo Judicial 2003).

were eased by the mediation of *Grupo Salvavidas* members Alfonso Portillo and Roberto Letona Hora.[66]

In addition to Guatemala City-based importers, the Moreno Network developed commercial relations with US businesses as well. For example, an important client was the Miami-based Interamerica, Inc., which shipped US goods to Guatemala. Based on a series of faxes, investigators came to believe that Interamerica representatives "organized the distribution of contraband coming from the United States to all of the retailers that sold it [in Guatemala]."[67] On different occasions, Moreno, under the nickname *"El Colocho"* [the curly-haired one], advised Interamerica of changes within the ministerial posts that favored the criminal structure. When Otto Leal Rembert[68] was named deputy administrator of the central customs location in Guatemala City, Moreno told Interamerica's owner that their "objective" had been "reached."[69] In another communication, Moreno relayed that an individual referred to as the *"Procurador Fiscal* ... has command in customs and knows the 'values,' he will be involved in the unloading of shipping containers."[70]

Communications recovered from Moreno's properties not only illustrate the assurances he provided to clients regarding personnel arrangements within different state entities. He also reported on the state of operations within customs. For example, Moreno sent urgent communications to Interamerica officials about a shipping container held up at the Quetzal Port because of a change in customs inspectors, which brought in new personnel unaware of previous under-the-table arrangements. These new inspectors had added significant fines and taxes due to the misreporting of merchandise. With the help of customs employees under the direction of Moreno associate Óscar Rolando Chávez, Moreno indicates that, "the only thing I can do is go to the computer and erase all the information on the authorization to not leave a footprint. ... No one, not even the director [of customs] himself is permitted to annul a fiscal stamp already authorized with a designated number in the computer. But we had to erase the number everywhere the fiscal stamp passed," otherwise

---

[66] Hernández S. 1996b.    [67] *El Periódico* 1996.
[68] Otto Leal is the brother-in-law of former director of military intelligence and president Otto Pérez Molina, who was accused of orchestrating the 2015 customs fraud scandal known as *La Línea*; see US Department of Defense 1993.
[69] Letter to "Interamerica, Inc.," October 18, 1992 (Organismo Judicial 2003) [Internal record: 2276].
[70] Letter to Interamerica, Inc. owner, February 9, 1996 (Organismo Judicial 2003) [Internal record: 2270–2271].

the shipping container would not be able to leave customs without paying the additional fines and taxes. Moreno also wrote to Interamerica that the preferential treatment illustrates "there's an interest that things always turn out well for you" and that without erasing all traces of the container, it "would not have been able to leave for anywhere. But thanks to the astuteness of [Óscar] Rolando [Chávez] and *El Colocho* it will be brought to a warehouse in the capital."[71] The incident thus illustrates how the Moreno Network mobilized its vast resources and contacts within the customs apparatus to keep its "customers" satisfied and to garner their continued buy-in to the alternative rules within the customs apparatus.

These importers reflected legal businesses that dealt in licit merchandise, yet through unlawful means. However, there is some evidence that the Moreno Network was also a conduit for *illicit* goods, such as narcotics. According to investigators, Moreno's connection to the drug trade was through Salvadoran importer Santos Hipólito Reyes, who worked with businessmen to transport drug shipments disguised as containers of licit merchandise. According to prosecutor Óscar Contreras, with the raids on Moreno's and Reyes' properties, "there was sufficient evidence to affirm that there existed narco-contraband within the activities carried out by these two bosses. They utilized the network to traffic cocaine, primarily through their connections to international drug trafficking."[72] According to the 1999 testimony of Ovidio Mancilla Aguilar, who served as Reyes' personal security, the Salvadoran importer also smuggled arms from his home country.[73] Thus, while the network developed a solid client base among legal businesses, Moreno also appropriated the customs structure to gain a foothold in nascent, highly profitable illicit trades as well. These stakeholders, both licit and illicit, would play a critical role in upholding the undermining rules, particularly with peace and the disarticulation of the Moreno Network on the horizon.

### Guatemala: Broadening the Distributional Coalition within the Security Sector

Similar dynamics of coalitional broadening developed within Guatemala's policing agencies. The introduction and implementation of the new

[71] Letter to "Interamerica, Inc.," No date (Organismo Judicial 2003) [Internal record: 2263–2266].
[72] Hernández S. 1996c.
[73] From Mancilla Aguilar testimony, May 28, 1999 (Organismo Judicial 2003).

undermining rules structuring police extrajudicial killings emerged with the removal of judicial checks on police activity and the creation of the elite Detective Corps, which operated under the thumb of Guatemalan military intelligence (Chapter 5). But, in line with this book's broader theory, these new institutional arrangements became an entrenched feature of state action because a much broader set of public and private interests stood to gain through their enforcement. The coalition underwriting the extrajudicial execution procedures was broadened to further institutionalize them in two ways: (1) by diffusing the alternative rules to other parts of the state security apparatus, and (2) by garnering the buy-in of economic elites.

First, the alternative rules governing extralegal killings did not remain confined to the Detective Corps but were implemented by other branches of Guatemala's police force. Though the Detective Corps was primarily responsible for coordinating small groups of *rebajados* [demoted police agents] to carry out death squad killings, historical evidence suggests that, eventually, each PN division came "[to maintain] 'dirty squads' charged with picking up and killing suspected criminals and assisting the army's political murder operations."[74] Further, US government cables detail conversations between Embassy officials and President Vinicio Cerezo (1986–1991), who acknowledged the role of state security forces in 'death squad' activity throughout 1986 and 1987 after the transition to civilian rule.[75] At the beginning of 1989, US officials reported that, "selected individuals within the PN had been responsible for the death of numerous criminals in Guatemala. Former PN members who had left the PN for a variety of reasons were rehired into the Department of Criminal Investigations (DIC) of the PN [the agency that the replaced the Detective Corps] for the specific purpose of capturing and killing individuals with long criminal records."[76] The extrajudicial killing procedures thus became institutionalized not only within the Detective Corps, but among its successors and the police apparatus writ large.

But the undermining rules also took root within other parts of the state security apparatus, such as the Treasury Police – the force tasked with combatting contraband and customs fraud. In early 1988, investigators discovered that Treasury Police leaders and agents were behind the

---

[74] McClintock 1985: 160.
[75] US Embassy in Guatemala 1986a; US Department of State 1986; US Embassy in Guatemala 1986b; US Embassy in Guatemala 1987a; US Embassy in Guatemala 1987b; US Embassy in Guatemala 1987c: 4.
[76] [Former Members of Guatemala National Police] 1989.

notorious *"pánel blanca"* ["white van"] kidnappings and killings, which stoked terror throughout Guatemala City and hearkened back to similar crimes committed by the Detective Corps in the late 1970s. Within a few weeks, eight individuals, many of whom were popular organizers and affiliates of the University of San Carlos (USAC), were picked up by armed assailants driving a white van. Six of the eight later turned up mutilated and murdered.[77] The *modus operandi* was virtually identical to previous extrajudicial killing procedures: "[T]hey were committed by armed persons in military or police clothing, with some dressed as civilians; they used light colored vans with polarized windows and without license plates, or plates belonging to individuals; the material authors of the crimes acted with complete freedom and impunity; they did not hide their faces nor act with secrecy, but the apprehensions were conducted in the light of day and in the public's eye."[78] Following the removal of the Treasury Police's chief and six agents implicated in the scheme, Minister of the Interior Juan José Rodil and PN chief Julio Enrique Caballeros admitted that the killings were not only carried out by one white van but by several.[79]

According to subsequent police proceedings, the Treasury Police agents claimed that they were "only complying with orders from above" and were operating "to detect contraband liquor" and other illegal goods.[80] But in reality, the acts of torture and extrajudicial killing reflected the extension of the undermining rules within the police to another branch of the state security apparatus – one that had also fallen under the tight control of Guatemala's military intelligence elites, developed its own network of informants for intelligence-gathering purposes, and executed "death squad"-style killings to take out political opposition.[81] According to the CEH, recurring to such procedures shored up the institutional and financial interests of the Treasury Police, who did the bidding of both military intelligence officials and private actors.[82]

In addition to the array of state security agencies, another critical set of actors that developed a stake in the undermining rules was Guatemala's traditional private sector elite, particularly the landed oligarchy, which remained threatened by popular unrest even after the fighting died down in the late 1980s. While ranchers and commercial agricultural producers in Guatemala's eastern provinces initiated paramilitary activities, these same actors bought in to the state-regulated practices of extrajudicial

---

[77] El Gráfico 1988a, 1988b.    [78] CIDH 1998: 59.    [79] El Gráfico 1988c, 1988d.
[80] AHPN 1988: 1.    [81] CEH 1999, Vol. 2: 87–88.    [82] Ibid., 93–98.

killing when they became centralized under military intelligence and the Detective Corps in the 1970s. In fact, the testimony of Elías Barahona, Ministry of the Interior press secretary, revealed that the names that appeared on Death Squad (EM) and Secret Anti-communist Army (ESA) 'death lists' during the Lucas García regime were often provided by "a sector of private enterprise," especially in cases of labor leaders who were agitating for workers' and land rights.[83] Indeed, US government officials posited that, by 1979, most of the 'death squad' killings in its monthly records "are probably the victims of business interests, often local landowners operating with greater or lesser impunity."[84] No longer needing to wage their own anti-communist campaigns, private sector elites developed a stake in the institutionalized procedures for eliminating political and economic threats.

The interest of the landed class in death squad killings persisted even after the de-escalation of political conflict. In the view of rural landowners, the continued implementation of the undermining rules was a necessary means of keeping the peasantry at bay as democratic transition gave way to increasing calls for land reform. In fact, in early 1987, renewed signs of ESA activity emerged along Guatemala's southern coast as the threat of peasant-led land invasions mounted. According to US Embassy advisors, coastal ranchers were "scared and angered" by potential land seizures and were likely behind the continued paramilitary threats.[85] Guatemala's economic elites thus had an abiding stake in extralegal killing procedures even after the conflict died down and in the face of a changing political landscape.

### Nicaragua: Disruption and Elite Realignment in the Land Administration

While the dominant counterinsurgent coalition within Guatemala's customs and policing institutions knitted together a broader set of interests with a stake in the new undermining rules, Nicaragua's land and property sector, by contrast, saw the disruption of the narrow, insulated FSLN elite previously in control, generating volatility. This divergent trajectory was due in large part to the stunning UNO electoral triumph in February 1990, which forced the Sandinistas to transform from the party in power to the country's major opposition bloc. Initially, the FSLN

---

[83] Amnesty International 1981: 8.    [84] US Embassy in Guatemala 1979b: 6.
[85] US Embassy in Guatemala 1987b.

remained a formidable political force through its loyal bureaucratic cadre and hold on legislative power. As a result, the Chamorro administration allowed the FSLN to maintain control of the military and police. Yet, this was not the case with land reform and tenure institutions, where a series of compromises ultimately allowed a new set of interests to transform the prevailing order.

The overhaul of land tenure institutions and the displacement of the undermining rules governing land distribution and titling were a result of the distinct elite coalition that came to dominate Nicaragua's political and economic landscape at war's end. As discussed above, the Chamorro administration was ultimately comprised of "a group of technocrats educated in US universities, well-versed in theories of monetarism and neoliberal ideology" who "[shared] the business sector's faith in the market's invisible hand" and sought to "[dismantle] state controls, [privatize] state-owned land, and [lower] taxes."[86] In addition to the UNO technocrats who oversaw institutional restructuring, the new post-war coalition was driven by US government and civil society leaders, as well as representatives of international financial institutions, who applied pressure and provided technical assistance to spur reform.

This new neoliberal coalition took shape within the land and property sector during the transition between the Ortega and Chamorro administrations. The UNO factions that initially sought to direct the course of the land reform program consisted of two broad forces: reactionary oligarchic sectors linked to Somoza rule and the more moderate "democratic bourgeoisie," which "controlled executive power [and] imposed a democratic-business project that would gradually denature the Revolution."[87] While the former group sought to completely overturn the redistributive gains of the previous decade, the latter bloc, comprised of Chamorro's closest allies like son-in-law and Minister of the Presidency Antonio Lacayo, recognized the need for compromise with FSLN producer and mass organizations.

After a series of strikes in May and June 1990 by state workers, Lacayo spearheaded a more consultative middle course – at least in appearance – beginning with the land issue. In October 1990, the government established the National Agrarian Commission (CNA), a deliberative body tied to the Presidency that would "study the problems and tensions that are generally present within Nicaraguan agriculture, especially those which are threats to the peace and stability of the nation."[88] In a break from the

---

[86] Rocha 2019: 115.    [87] Núñez Soto et al. 1998: 539.
[88] Presidencia de la República de Nicaragua 1990.

vertical, FSLN-dominated land administration of the mid- and late 1990s, the CNA, presided over by Lacayo, incorporated a wide swath of government, popular, and producer representatives including the Minister of Agriculture, the Minister of the Interior, the head of the Sandinista Army, the director of National Institute of Agrarian Reform (INRA), a representative of the National Union of Agricultural Workers and Cattle Ranchers (UNAG), a representative of the demobilized RN combatants, and a representative of the Rural Workers' Association (ATC), among others.[89]

Yet despite this pragmatic and deliberative orientation at the outset, the combination of domestic and international neoliberal interests that dominated Nicaragua's post-transition landscape eventually transformed structures of political power within the land and property administration. Ultimately, post-transition arrangements were crafted by Nicaraguan technocrats and business elites, the US government, international financial institutions, and international civil society organizations – groups committed to neoliberal principles and that saw "the primary challenge facing the Chamorro regime as one of market modernization."[90]

The US government was a driving force within this new neoliberal coalition. In partnership with new Minister of Agriculture Roberto Rondón Sacasa, himself a large landowner,[91] US government officials sought the creation of a land restitution and compensation system and leveraged recently renewed economic assistance to press their demands. Of course, the primary concern of US representatives was the US citizens who had been affected by property seizures under the Sandinistas in the 1980s; however, "a secondary, more charitable result of the American role [was] advanced: clarification of property ownership rights, improvement of the property registration system, and improved administrative and judicial processes [that] all improve the rule of law and the economic foundation of Nicaragua."[92]

US government assistance for remaking the rules within land tenure was accompanied by the backing of US civil society groups and international financial institutions, which became key members of the dominant postwar political coalition within the land administration. A team of experts and mediators from the Carter Center, the American Bar Association, and the UW–Madison Land Tenure Center advised the Nicaraguan judiciary as it developed formal procedures to resolve land disputes and created five courts to address property issues.[93] This same

[89] Ibid.    [90] Everingham 1998: 250.    [91] Spoor 1994: fn 14.    [92] Dille 2012: 256.
[93] Ibid., 129.

US civil society team also crafted mechanisms "to improve the ability of government administrative agencies in reviewing nearly 16,000 claims by former owners and the 112,000 petitions for formal titles by current occupants." The project was carried out with $3.7 million in United Nations Development Program (UNDP) funds beginning in early 1995.[94] Other internationally funded projects provided support to register legal titles. The World Bank, for example, financed investigations into and collections of existing land registries, which provided the foundation of the regularization process.[95]

This transformation in Nicaragua's dominant political coalition was also facilitated by the shrinking of the country's public sector and departure of leading Sandinista cadre as the neoliberal reforms of the early 1990s progressed. The international financial institution- and US government-imposed structural adjustment program that conditioned economic assistance entailed rapid and extensive privatization measures that dismantled state-owned agricultural enterprises and slashed government posts. According to Spalding, "of the 351 [state-owned] firms that were set to disappear through privatization, the government had privatized, liquidated, or transferred 233 by 1992."[96] The fully collectivized CAS cooperatives, which already began to disappear under the FSLN due to wartime imperatives, were parceled at an even faster pace.[97] And Sandinista officials increasingly departed government agencies, either due to state compression or the pursuit of private sector ventures or NGO work.[98] In short, though the Chamorro administration initially pursued compromise with FSLN leaders and organizations on the land issue, the course of neoliberal reforms ultimately undid many of these concessions, further reshuffling the dominant political coalition that emerged following transition.

## LOOKING AHEAD

The run-up to and years following transition in Guatemala and Nicaragua exhibit clear contrasts, which laid the groundwork for divergent longer-term institutional trajectories. Guatemala's protracted transition and peace process facilitated the deepening of the wartime elite consensus that restricted the scope of peacebuilding and shaped the contours of the post-war political order to serve long-standing political, military, business, and

---

[94] Ibid.    [95] IRAM 2000: 44; Deininger and Chamorro 2002: 5.
[96] Spalding 2017: 158.    [97] Jonakin 1996: 1180.    [98] Spoor 1994: 192–193.

criminal interests. Meanwhile, the FSLN's surprising 1990 electoral defeat brought to power a corps of Washington-backed technocrats committed to political and economic liberalism. The UNO government of Violeta Chamorro thus disrupted the dominant FSLN coalition. By examining these coalitional dynamics at a more fine-grained institutional level, we see that the dominant counterinsurgent coalition in Guatemala's customs and public security sectors knit together a broader set of interests with a stake in the wartime status quo, facilitating coalitional stability and entrenchment; meanwhile, Nicaragua's transition-era dynamics generated upheaval and volatility within the land and property sector, producing coalitional disruption and realignment.

But what do these differences mean for the wartime undermining rules analyzed in Chapters 4, 5, and 6? To what extent did conflict-induced institutional arrangements endure beyond periods of state reform? And what are the precise mechanisms of institutional resilience and survival? The latter half of the book provides an in-depth examination of these questions by telling the story of what happened within Guatemala's customs and policing institutions and Nicaragua's land administration as new regimes took root. Chapter 8 chronicles the persistence of wartime customs fraud following the disarticulation of the Moreno Network, focusing on how the narrow counterinsurgent elite and its public and private sector allies co-opted new political and economic spaces. Chapter 9 illustrates a similar dynamic within Guatemala's newly minted National Civilian Police (PNC), which continued to uphold the rules governing extrajudicial executions. Finally, Chapter 10 illustrates how frequent elite realignments in postwar Nicaragua fomented chronic instability for the undermining rules governing land redistribution and titling. The comparison between Guatemala and Nicaragua demonstrates that the longer-term endurance of the institutional arrangements devised in conflict depends on the stability of the coalitions invested in them.

# 8

# Guatemala

## *The Persistence of Customs Fraud*

Alfredo Moreno's arrest and the exposure of the powerful customs fraud scheme that took his name unfolded just months before the signing of the "Accord for a Firm and Lasting Peace," which brought Guatemala's peace process – and the thirty-six-year internal armed conflict – to a close. The September 1996 revelations, which signaled the involvement of top military intelligence officials, demonstrated that the costs of the Guatemalan armed conflict went well beyond the lives lost and the human rights violations inflicted. Efforts to defeat the rebels provided counter-insurgent elites the justification and the operational latitude to forge alternative institutional arrangements to siphon off state resources on an extraordinary scale.

Given the timing and nature of the case, tax and customs administration reforms became a centerpiece of Guatemala's peacebuilding agenda. Government officials not only sought to implement more traditional post-authoritarian measures, such as the subordination of the military and police to civilian rule, but they also treated bureaucratic reforms within the country's fiscal apparatus as critical to sustaining peace and improving governance long term. While analyses of Central America note the vast deficiencies of institutional reforms in the late 1990s and early 2000s,[1] the transformations to Guatemala's tax administration were quite sweeping. They encompassed the successful expulsion of military, police, and judicial officials linked to the Moreno Network,

---

[1] Cruz 2011; Bowen 2019; Wade 2016; Lehoucq 2012; Schneider 2012.

purges and restructuring within the port system, and the creation of an entirely new fiscal apparatus.

These changes, however, failed to dislodge the undermining rules that distorted customs activities and subverted formal revenue extraction – a reality not only made clear by the 2015 *La Línea* case, but which also plagued peacetime administrations from the late 1990s on.[2] How did the customs fraud procedures institutionalized at the height of civil war endure for nearly two decades despite reform efforts?

It is conceivable that the customs fraud operations in Guatemala survived due to geopolitical and economic dynamics unrelated to wartime processes. For example, they may have been sustained due to the increase in drug trafficking and contraband smuggling through Central America, particularly as US-backed counter-narcotics campaigns cracked down on trafficking routes through the Caribbean in the 1980s and 1990s. Yet, this explanation cannot fully account for the wide range of licit goods funneled through the criminal scheme, or the precise modalities of customs fraud, which abided by nearly identical procedures relative to the Moreno Network period. Alternatively, the preservation of the fraudulent arrangements may have been driven by greater deregulation and free trade with the United States through agreements like the Central American Free Trade Agreement (CAFTA) established in 2006. But this explanation is also incomplete, failing to account for the role of US authorities in pressuring to dismantle schemes like *La Línea*. It also falls short in explaining precisely how trade liberalization might foment the rule-bound predatory procedures within customs.

In examining the nearly twenty-year trajectory between the Moreno Network and *La Línea*, this analysis instead demonstrates that the persistence of the undermining rules within Guatemala's tax administration is best attributed to the endurance of the broad distributional coalition forged by the Moreno Network in the late 1980s and 1990s (Chapter 7), specifically the adaptive abilities of those with a stake in the fraudulent customs procedures.[3] Despite their displacement from the formal state sphere, the military intelligence elites that oversaw the illicit customs scheme managed to exercise coercive power through political party

---

[2] Though the type of evidence from the Moreno Network and *La Línea* cases is not available for the intervening governments, particularly those of Óscar Berger (2004–2008) and Álvaro Colom (2008–2012), interviewees suggested that the undermining rules persisted, though they were not likely coordinated from the highest levels of the executive branch as with *La Línea*.

[3] See Schwartz 2021a, the article on which this chapter is based.

channels, placing strategic allies within government and ensuring continued impunity for the fraudulent customs operations. Moreover, measures to further privatize the port system allowed conflict-era elites to occupy new, extra-state spaces critical to upholding the undermining rules. In sum, the survival of the undermining rules does not simply reflect the inability to disrupt the dominant wartime coalition within government circles; rather, it illustrates the failure to guard against that coalition's reconstitution and continued influence after its initial displacement from the state sphere.

To elaborate these claims, this chapter proceeds as follows. The first section discusses the series of reforms implemented by the Arzú government in the aftermath of the Moreno Network revelations, including (1) the expulsions of high-ranking military officials, police leaders, and other state personnel implicated in the scheme; (2) the intervention and restructuring of Guatemala's port system; and (3) the creation of a new fiscal framework and tax and customs institutions in the form of the Superintendent of Tax Administration (SAT).

The next section evaluates how the undermining rules in customs outlasted these sweeping reforms, illustrating how the wartime distributional coalition, while largely displaced from the state sphere, managed to penetrate new semi- and extra-state spaces like political party channels and private port concessions, particularly during the administration of Alfonso Portillo (2000–2004). This part also illustrates how *La Línea* represents another moment of postwar adaptation, as the sectoral interests with a stake in the undermining rules gained a greater foothold within the executive branch. The final section evaluates the two other possible mechanisms laid out in Chapter 2: (1) the manipulation of formal institutional reforms, and (2) the endurance of collective beliefs legitimizing the undermining rules.

## REFORM IN THE AFTERMATH OF THE MORENO NETWORK REVELATIONS

The first step in exposing the Moreno Network came with the September 1996 arrest of Alfredo Moreno and the raid on his home and other properties. However, with the trove of information seized in the ensuing days and weeks, the investigation quickly metastasized, revealing a wide range of collaborators within Guatemala's military and security sector, tax administration, judiciary, and port system. As new evidence shed light on the breadth of the coalition with a stake in the undermining rules, the conservative government of Álvaro Arzú (1996–2000) implemented a series of measures intended to disarticulate the Moreno Network and the customs fraud scheme it had mounted. In this section, I describe the three core components of this reform agenda: the expulsion of officials implicated in illicit customs operations, the intervention of Guatemala's port system, and the establishment of a new fiscal framework and bureaucracy, the Superintendent of Tax Administration (SAT).

## Expulsions of High-Level Officials

Following Moreno's arrest, investigations by the MP and military leadership shed light on the broad array of state actors that formed part of the coalition underwriting the fraudulent customs procedures coordinated by the Moreno Network. Though very few of the individuals faced criminal prosecution, a substantial number – even those once thought untouchable – were dismissed from their positions and prevented from exercising formal state power. For government reformers who sought to dismantle the broader distributional coalition with a stake in the alternative rules, the expulsions were a critical step toward reconfiguring political power to disrupt the institutional status quo.

Early assessments by the MP estimated that the Moreno Network was made up of some 250 individuals from agencies across the Guatemalan state.[4] The initial round of expulsions, however, focused on Guatemala's security and customs apparatus. On September 17, just three days after Moreno's arrest, executive officials announced the dismissals of nine high-ranking military officers, four National Police (PN) chiefs, the head of the Treasury Police [*Guardia de Hacienda*], and four customs administrators.

The list of military leaders, which was based on internal Army investigations,[5] had perhaps the most profound public impact, revealing the tight grip that elite intelligence cliques had on routine customs operations. The most notorious of the officers expelled was Luis Francisco Ortega Menaldo, the EMP officer who was the architect and first chief of the SEM, the shadow office established on the eighteenth floor of the Ministry of Finance building (see Chapter 4). Though Ortega Menaldo – a leading member of the *Cofradía* intelligence faction – never faced justice for this or other alleged abuses, in March 2002, his US visa was revoked due to his purported involvement in drug trafficking.[6]

---

[4] *La República* 1996d.    [5] Hernández S. 1996d.    [6] Font 2002.

Alongside Ortega Menaldo, the initial list of military officials forced into retirement included then-Vice Minister of Defense César Augusto García González; Colonels Mario Roberto García Catalán, Rolando Augusto Díaz Barrios, Jacobo Esdras Salán Sánchez, Juan Guillermo Oliva Carrera, and Napoleón Rojas Méndez; Major Luis Arturo Alvarado Batres; and Navy Captain Romeo Guevara Reyes.[7] Many of the military officials separated from their positions had sustained communications with and received gifts from Moreno, according to files recovered during the investigation.

It quickly became clear, however, that some on the list were even more deeply entrenched in illicit activities. For example, Salán Sánchez was a reported member of the influence-peddling association *Grupo Salvavidas* alongside Ortega Menaldo, using coercion and bribery to guarantee impunity for wartime abuses.[8] Others were not only linked to predatory activities within customs, but also to high-profile human rights violations. Juan Guillermo Oliva Carrera, for instance, was the accused intellectual author in the 1990 murder of Guatemalan anthropologist Myrna Mack, though he was absolved in 2002. Similarly, Mario Roberto García Catalán was believed to have orchestrated the murder of US innkeeper Michael DeVine, a crime for which he never stood trial.[9] The profiles of those dismissed in the days after Moreno's capture illustrate how human rights abuses and customs fraud were not separate wartime phenomena but were perpetrated by the same military intelligence actors empowered at the height of the counterinsurgent campaign.

As the Moreno Network investigation continued, another prominent military leader was discharged: General Roberto Letona Hora who, at the time of his expulsion, was a military attaché at the Guatemalan Embassy in the United States.[10] Letona Hora served as SEM chief under the military government of General Óscar Mejía Víctores beginning in 1983, during which time he allegedly developed strong ties with Moreno.[11] Even after ceding the post, Letona Hora was a primary liaison between the Moreno Network and international commercial interests seeking to arrange customs duty adjustments.[12]

Beyond military circles, the Arzú administration also sought to dismantle the vast coalition surrounding the Moreno Network by taking aim

---

[7] Robles Montoya 2002: 126; Ramírez Espada 1996; Hernández S. 1996e.
[8] Peacock and Beltrán 2003: 37.    [9] Perera 1993: 262.
[10] Bautista and Hernández S. 1996; *La República* 1996e.    [11] *Crónica* 1996.
[12] Zamora 2002.

at top police leadership, which, according to sources within the PN, "collaborated with Moreno, informing him of the locations of raids and checkpoints, so that his contacts could pass without incident. When one of Moreno's vehicles was detained, they called any one of the [police] chiefs and its release was ordered immediately."[13] Investigators soon discovered that police complicity extended well beyond the initial expulsions, leading to the removal of twelve more implicated PN chiefs a week later.[14] Eventually, the dismissals within the civilian security apparatus moved even farther up the chain of command, leading to the separation of sitting Vice Minister of the Interior Mario René Cifuentes Echeverría, who "took advantage of his post as vice minister to prevent the action of security forces against the Moreno Network."[15] And while top security officials formed the core of the wartime distributional coalition with a stake in the fraudulent customs procedures, Moreno Network allies also operated from civilian posts within the customs administration, judiciary, Comptroller General's Office, and immigration services, leading to a spate of dismissals in these agencies.

Despite fears of reprisals,[16] government reformers took swift action to remove those implicated in the illicit customs activities. In the words of one former finance official, "the structure most linked to Ortega Menaldo was hit hard."[17] Despite the reach and scope of the illicit customs fraud scheme, the campaign to dismantle the coalition underwriting the predatory rules of the game did not shy away from reaching into the highest levels of Guatemalan political and military power.

### Port Intervention

Another key reform measure meant to shift the balance of power and dismantle the wartime distributional coalition was the intervention of Guatemala's port system to extricate it from the control of military elites. Guatemala's national port system consisted of two main ports: the Quetzal Port on the Pacific Ocean, and the Santo Tomás de Castilla Port on the Atlantic Ocean. Both were administered by their own port companies, which, while state-owned, were highly decentralized. Though overseen by boards of directors named by distinct government and business organizations, the administration of day-to-day port operations was

---

[13] *Prensa Libre* 1996b.    [14] *El Gráfico* 1996b; Montenegro Lima 1996.
[15] González Moraga 1996.    [16] *Siglo Veintiuno* 1996f.
[17] Interview with author, June 12, 2017.

largely contracted out to private companies, which constructed port infrastructure and, in some cases, maintained their own terminals to offload and process shipping containers.[18]

As highlighted in Chapter 4, the perceived increase in insurgent capacity and support in the 1970s provided the pretext to install a robust military presence at all territorial entry points, including the country's major ports – a move that gave rise to some of the earliest drug-trafficking organizations based in Guatemalan territory.[19] Military control of the ports not only included ramping up the presence of soldiers on the ground, but also extended to the leadership of the port companies. Successive governments in the 1970s, 1980s, and 1990s placed port leadership in the hands of high-level military officials linked to elite intelligence units, much like the customs apparatus. Even as the armed conflict wound down and the peace process began, the most important ports remained sites of near-total military control. As the CEH notes, "the naming of retired [military] officials as directors of the Santo Tomás de Castilla Port Company established the Army's links with the system of maritime import and export, which was of significant impact to the national economy."[20]

The port system thus became another target of government-led efforts to disarticulate the web of state contacts that the Moreno Network had woven. Less than a month after the exposure of the criminal structure, President Arzú designated auditors to identify sources of corruption and propose remedies. At the Santo Tomás de Castilla Port, the Arzú government named Ángel González García, deputy director of the Civil Aeronautical Agency, tasking him with uncovering "the acts of corruption ... that have led to lost merchandise and the deterioration of the National Port Company."[21] Meanwhile, for the intervention of the Quetzal Port, officials named Luis Fernando Paiz Rodas, director of the Latin American Association of Port Authorities, to take the lead in overhauling port practices.[22] With the intervention, government reformers hoped to "eliminate the daily theft of shipping containers that results from the suspected infiltration of Moreno Network affiliates in the ports."[23]

---

[18] Carcamo Miranda 2018: 75–85.
[19] See González-Izás 2014: 288. One of the organizations that emerged in the eastern part of the country and came to control trafficking corridors along the Atlantic Ocean, the border with El Salvador, and the border with Honduras was known as the Zacapa Cartel, which was led by former military commissioner and death squad member Arnoldo Vargas.
[20] CEH 1999, Vol. 3: 80.    [21] *El Gráfico* 1996c.    [22] López and Hernández S. 1996.
[23] Ibid.

Indeed, the early auditing efforts confirmed that port officials had played a key role in "the falsification of documents, which served to alter the declared merchandise or note lesser quantities" to defraud the tax administration.[24] Beyond improving controls to detect fraudulent activities, the special auditors also pushed government officials to dismiss top port authorities and the members of the board of directors for each of the port companies. Removing port company leadership largely targeted the high-ranking active and retired military officers that had come to occupy key posts within the port system as the counterinsurgent campaign escalated.[25] For example, the head of the Quetzal Port Company was top navy commander Captain Mario Enrique García Regás, while, at the Santo Tomás de Castilla Port, the head of the board of directors was Marco Antonio González Taracena, the former minister of defense. Both were removed following the intervention decree.

Beyond dismissing top port officials, other port reforms included eliminating the tremendous excess of port employees at Santo Tomás de Castilla,[26] reconfiguring auditing procedures at both ports to combat corruption, and enhancing security for shipping containers entering and leaving port installations.[27] Wresting control of the port system from Moreno Network associates and establishing streamlined auditing and security systems was thus the second part of the Arzú administration's three-pronged approach to disrupting the institutional status quo.

## The Creation of the SAT

The final and most significant structural change undertaken to eliminate the wartime customs fraud procedures was the remaking of the tax and customs administration itself. Beginning on the heels of the peace process, Ministry of Finance leaders took to implementing a new vision for an independent and expert-led tax collection agency, staffed by personnel without links to previous administrations. In the late 1990s, and with significant international assistance, Guatemala witnessed the dissolution of the conflict-era General Directorates of Customs and Internal Revenue,

---

[24] *Siglo Veintiuno* 1996e.    [25] López and Hernández S. 1996.
[26] According to investigators, the Santo Tomás de Castilla Port employed 1,800 individuals, compared to the 675 employees at the similarly sized Quetzal Port; see Arana and Castañaza 1996.
[27] Colindres 1996.

the dismissal or retirement of thousands of employees, and the creation of the Superintendent of Tax Administration (SAT).

The bases of these reforms were established in the "Accord on Socioeconomic Issues and the Agrarian Situation," which was signed on May 6, 1996. Within the Accord, the Guatemalan state pledged to increase its tax burden by 50 percent between 1995 and 2000 – a commitment that would set the goal at 12 percent of GDP. The Accord further stipulated a series of policy measures to help tax authorities achieve this objective, which included "promoting a reform to the Tax Code to establish heavier sanctions for evasion," "strictly regulating tax exemptions with the view of eliminating abuses," "strengthening the existing mechanisms of investigation," and "simplifying and automating fiscal administration."[28]

Though the Accord did not explicitly mandate the creation of an entirely new fiscal apparatus, top Ministry of Finance officials were convinced that there was no rescuing the two existing entities responsible for tax collection. In the words of one high-ranking Ministry of Finance official, "when we went in to see what was going on with the General Directorates of Customs and Internal Revenue, we saw that there was corruption on all sides."[29] In November 1996, then-Minister of Finance José Alejandro Arévalo announced the dissolution of both branches, whose activities would be subsumed by the new tax collection agency known as the Superintendent of Tax Administration (SAT).[30]

The SAT, designed by Arévalo and other experts with the support of international financial institutions like the World Bank, was created through legislation passed in January 1998 "as an institutional response to corruption."[31] Decree 1–98, which established the legal foundation of the SAT, accorded it a variety of institutional functions, including "the collection, control, and auditing of all taxes, except those collected by the municipalities, the administration of the customs system, [and] carrying out judicial actions to collect taxes."[32]

The establishment of the SAT reflected the culmination of a yearlong, technocratic process to clean up and modernize Guatemala's public finances and fiscal framework to "recover society's confidence in public authority."[33] An institutional aspect crucial to bolstering public trust in the country's fiscal apparatus was enhanced autonomy, which was built into the SAT's design. Whereas the Ministry of Finance was led by

---

[28] Government of Guatemala 1996a.       [29] Interview with author, May 30, 2017.
[30] *Siglo Veintiuno* 1996d; Ajanel Soberanis 1997.       [31] Arévalo 2014.
[32] ICEFI 2007: 220.       [33] Arévalo 2014: 5.

executive appointees who controlled internal and customs revenue collection, the SAT was headed by a board of directors, which consisted of the Minister of Finance as president, as well as the superintendent named by the executive branch and three additional members named by the legislative branch, the courts, and the country's universities, respectively.[34] Moreover, unlike the Ministry of Finance, the SAT was not subject to previous civil service laws restricting its ability to hire new employees, thus allowing it to pursue more independent processes for vetting and training personnel.[35] The SAT would also maintain its own budget. Despite some political wrangling, in the end President of Congress Arabella Castro Quiñones hailed the approval of the SAT as "consolidating a change to the legal structure that permits future authorities to modernize the General Directorates of Customs and Internal Revenue, which, for years, have been dens of corruption due to the discretional power of their officials."[36]

Beyond creating a more modern, autonomous tax collection entity, the creation of the SAT was accompanied by another key transition-era reform measure: the expulsion of civil servants associated with past administrations and corrupt activities. Given the thorough penetration of the customs and internal revenue services by organized criminal interests, the team of experts and authorities leading the SAT's design was adamant on starting fresh with new employees that met more rigorous educational standards. The purge of customs employees thus deepened the earlier Arzú administration efforts that removed high-ranking Moreno Network affiliates by targeting those responsible for implementing the undermining procedures on the ground.

In a very small number of cases, inspectors, auditors, and administrators from the General Directorates of Customs and Internal Revenue were absorbed by the SAT or funneled into administrative posts within the now-separate Ministry of Finance. However, the dissolution of the previous tax administration resulted primarily in the dismissal or voluntary retirement of existing personnel, some of which had been in their posts for decades.[37] This was especially the case for customs personnel, most of which, in the words of eventual SAT Superintendent Carolina Roca, "did not even pass primary school and thus [had] to leave their posts to provide space to those who meet the requirements."[38] Prior to the initiation of SAT operations in January 1999, the team of reformers

[34] *El Gráfico* 1997.    [35] Guerra 1997.    [36] Larra and Dardón 1998.
[37] Interviews with author, May 30, June 12, and November 15, 2017.    [38] Guerra 1997.

arrived at an agreement with the unions to create a voluntary retirement program. In the end, there was an exodus of some 2,000 customs employees. Just 1.25 percent of prior personnel remained in their posts.[39] The creation of the SAT not only established a new fiscal framework, but also introduced a fresh bureaucratic corps that met more rigorous professional and educational standards.

## POST-REFORM INSTITUTIONAL SURVIVAL

Despite the promise of transition-era reform measures to purge, modernize, and strengthen Guatemala's tax administration and port system, the country's fiscal apparatus became overwhelmed by corruption, fraud, and illicit activity once again. Evasion remained rampant. Only on one occasion in the subsequent two decades did the SAT manage to meet the 12 percent tax burden established in the Peace Accords, reaching 12.1 percent in 2016.[40] The outcomes were far from the image projected by the team of experts and officials who conceived of the SAT and oversaw its establishment. As one the SAT's early champions described to me, the agency "started as a dream and turned into a nightmare."[41] How did the undermining rules within Guatemala's customs service survive despite the reforms undertaken to remake the state's fiscal framework and efforts to redistribute political power away from counterinsurgent elites?

This analysis reveals that the survival of the fraudulent customs procedures is best attributed to the ability of the wartime distributional coalition with a stake in the undermining rules to reconstitute itself on the margins of state power. In the remainder of this chapter, I illustrate how this postwar adaptation occurred through the capture of new political party and port spaces and evaluate two alternative mechanisms – the manipulation of reforms and the endurance of collective beliefs about the legitimacy of the old rules of the game.

## The Adaptation of the Wartime Distributional Coalition

Efforts to restructure political power within the tax administration and to purge the Guatemalan state of those groups that formed the dominant

---

[39] Interviews with author, May 30 and November 15, 2017.
[40] SAT 2016; see Sánchez (2009) for a comprehensive analysis of the failures of postwar tax reform.
[41] Interview with author, May 30, 2017.

wartime distributional coalition ultimately had a limited effect on the survival of the undermining rules within customs. Instead, the military, political, and economic actors that coalesced around the fraudulent customs activities – namely, *Grupo Salvavidas* and the domestic and international business elites examined in Chapter 7 – seized new channels on the margins of the formal state sphere. These spaces were, in large part, facilitated by Guatemala's nascent political party system and by greater economic liberalization. The array of sectoral interests knit together by the Moreno Network thus adapted to the new post-transition environment by straddling the public and private, formal and informal spheres. This allowed them to maintain impunity for the illicit customs activities, locate strategic allies within government, and adjust the fraudulent procedures within the post-reform landscape.

First, Guatemala's return to elected, civilian rule and political liberalization offered new avenues of influence through the party system. The previously dominant counterinsurgent elite that devised and enforced the customs fraud procedures quickly occupied these new semi-state spaces, allowing them to uphold the undermining rules from without. We see this dynamic through one political party in particular, the right-wing, populist Guatemalan Republican Front [*Frente Republicano Guatemaltecto*, FRG]. The FRG, which became the electoral vehicle of former dictator Ríos Montt, rose to prominence in the late 1990s. When the Constitutional Court barred Ríos Montt from seeking the presidency due to his participation in the 1982 coup, Alfonso Portillo, a Congressional deputy from Guatemala's Christian Democratic Party, became the FRG's candidate in 1999. Garnering wide support across Guatemala's countryside, Portillo won and assumed office in January 2000, with the FRG forming the largest legislative bloc. In the words of Peacock and Beltrán, the FRG was "an important vehicle for the consolidation of the authority of the 'hidden powers' ... that exercised an enormous influence, ... further weakening the government's capacity to fight against corruption and impunity."[42] Having consolidated its hold on political power, the FRG constituted a new avenue through which the architects of the Moreno Network adapted to and preserved the wartime distributional coalition and the undermining rules governing customs fraud.

Among the past figures that again ascended with Portillo and the FRG were three military intelligence officials discharged from the armed forces

---

[42] Peacock and Beltrán 2003: 41.

in late 1996 due to their links with the Moreno Network: the architect of the SEM and its first chief, Retired General Luis Francisco Ortega Menaldo, and former colonels Jacobo Salán Sánchez and Napoleón Rojas Méndez. Though Ortega Menaldo never formally occupied a government position during the Portillo administration, experts indicate that he was one of Portillo's top advisors.[43] Similarly, Salán Sánchez served as the *de facto* head of the EMP – a unit Portillo had vowed to dismantle upon taking office. Rojas Méndez was a campaign security advisor to Portillo and then second-in-command of presidential security during Portillo's presidency.[44]

Thus, while the FRG allowed the displaced military blocs to eventually regain access and dominance within the state sphere, they utilized new extra-governmental political channels to do so. In the words of one former military intelligence officer, actors like Ortega Menaldo, Salán Sánchez, and Rojas Méndez "left the Army but when Portillo returned, they entered again, but now as part of an external structure."[45] As another former official put it, the ex-intelligence elites "returned to the orbits of influence surrounding presidential power and customs."[46] Despite the primarily informal roles played by the former intelligence officers, unofficial access to state power ensured their influence in naming personnel and moving state funds, which were disproportionately funneled to the EMP.[47]

Importantly, the former military intelligence elites sought to shore up the predatory customs procedures by naming SAT officials who would do their bidding – by placing criminal operators on the "inside." Though initial SAT appointees reportedly refused to bow to political pressures,[48] in 2002, Portillo named Marco Tulio Abadío as SAT superintendent, a move that led to the "destruction of [the institution] as we knew it," in the words of one economist.[49] Abadío, who served as head of the Comptroller General's Office during the Arzú government, became superintendent of the SAT through an apparent accord with the retired military elites seeking to control the customs administration once again.[50] In March 2004, he was indicted for the embezzlement of over $5.5 million through a series of shell companies, which he had transposed from the Comptroller General's Office.[51] Even with the reconfiguration of political

[43] Ibid., 23; Font 2002.     [44] Reyes 2004a.     [45] Interview with author, May 30, 2017.
[46] Interview with author, June 12, 2017.     [47] Peacock and Beltrán 2003: 50.
[48] Trejo 2001.     [49] Interview with author, June 13, 2017.
[50] Interview with author, June 12, 2017.     [51] Palma 2004.

power within the state, the ex-military elites who oversaw the Moreno Network preserved the wartime distributional coalition by maneuvering on the outside to locate strategic allies inside.

Beyond co-opting new spaces within Guatemala's more competitive political landscape, the wartime distributional coalition also sought alternative economic spaces afforded through market reforms. This was particularly the case with Guatemala's port system, which, alongside numerous state-owned enterprises, experienced rapid privatization during the Arzú government.[52] While Guatemala's major ports had consisted of both public and private features since their inception, the intervention and auditing processes undertaken after the Moreno Network revelations generated a host of new private concessions related to port infrastructure and services. These concessions provided new avenues for previously dominant actors to maintain the undermining rules governing customs fraud by adjusting fraudulent procedures and keeping state authorities out of customs processing. For instance, following the October 1996 intervention of the Santo Tomás de Castilla Port, the government awarded some $8 million in new contracts to *Equipos del Puerto*, a private firm created by former employees of the state-owned port company's Department of Containers, which received the concessions without a competitive bidding process.[53] The new, privatized mechanisms of moving imports were thus in the hands of the same actors once controlling them from within the state.

These new post-conflict economic spaces also provided economic elites with a stake in the customs fraud procedures new avenues to uphold the wartime rules of the game. Portillo's presidency signaled the increasing political power and involvement of an "emerging" economic elite class, comprised of new-moneyed importers and commercial interests who served as a counterweight to the traditional oligarchic sectors that had long dominated Guatemala's political landscape. Emblematic of this private sector faction was Julio Girón, a chemicals importer, who was a close friend of Portillo's and became his private secretary in the early 2000s.[54] Not only did importers like Girón have Portillo's ear politically, they also came to occupy important posts in Guatemala's ports and customs system, allowing them to revive and reconsolidate the fraudulent procedures. Immediately after Portillo took office, Girón was named president of the Quetzal Port Company, where he also owned multiple businesses

[52] Interview with author, May 30, 2017; see also, Bull 2008: 61–116.
[53] *El Periódico* 2000a.    [54] González 2002.

responsible for the offloading and transport of shipping containers. From this position outside of the official state sphere, Girón allegedly coordinated the same kinds of fraud and contraband smuggling implemented by the Moreno Network in the 1980s and 1990s. He stepped down in July 2002, after accusations by US officials that the port company was not doing enough to stop the flow of drugs and chemical precursors.[55] Economic elites within the import–export sector like Girón thus represent a key component of the wartime distributional coalition, which achieved new access through transition-era reforms.

The transformations within the port system also had other pernicious consequences conducive to the reconsolidation of wartime sectoral interests. For example, while the package of post-transition reforms sought to vest authority in a modernized, independent tax administration, the increasing privatization of port services led to new autonomous pockets that were beyond the tax authority's control. As one customs inspector remarked, "the different firms within the port were in agreement to not give all of the information on shipping containers to the SAT. And so there were a lot of containers that they would refer to as 'fly' ... in that there never existed any register of the container. ... It was as if it never entered the country."[56] The method described here as "fly" is virtually identical to the shipping container "disappearances" that occurred during the Moreno Network era, illustrating how similar rules were upheld via new channels of influence.

Another example of the reconstitution of the wartime distributional coalition following reforms can be seen in new private port infrastructure projects, like the Inter-Oceanic Corridor or "dry canal," which sought to connect the Atlantic-based Santo Tomás de Castilla and Pacific-based Quetzal Ports. Among those spearheading the project was ex-colonel Mario Roberto García Catalán, one of nine military officials discharged following the Moreno Network investigations.[57] In a 2011 interview, García Catalán's cousin and partner in the project, former Lieutenant Guillermo Catalán, indicated that the duo's military ties facilitated the concession.[58] Though the Inter-Oceanic Corridor remains under development, it illustrates how well-connected former military elites seized new economic spaces from without to maintain their influence.

[55] Guoz 2002; *El Periódico* 2002.     [56] Interview with author, November 15, 2017.
[57] *El Gráfico* 1996a.     [58] Arce 2011.

## *New Players, Same Game:* La Línea

Evidence from the period following the Moreno Network revelations suggests that the wartime procedures governing customs fraud largely endured because of the continued influence of the *Cofradía* military intelligence clique and its state and private sector allies. However, with the 2015 *La Línea* revelations, the MP and CICIG signaled that the reconstitution of the coalition underwriting the illicit customs procedures during the Portillo presidency was not confined to the group most closely linked to the Moreno Network, but extended to rival military factions. In many ways, the 2011 election of Retired General Otto Pérez Molina represented the ascendance of a military elite alliance that had bitterly opposed Ríos Montt, Portillo, and the former intelligence elites brought to power with the FRG. Instead, Pérez Molina, the top military representative during the peace negotiations, belonged to the more institutionalist faction of the armed forces. Though this wing of the army, known as the "Operators" ["*Sindicato*"], remained peripheral when the illicit customs activities were first devised in the late 1970s, one of its affiliates, Roberto Letona Hora, became chief of the eighteenth-floor SEM office controlling customs operations following the 1983 coup.[59] While the precise military elites overseeing the illicit customs operations were reshuffled, the broader web of sectoral interests remained unchanged.

*La Línea* thus reflects a state-based criminal network very similar to the Moreno Network, yet one that exercised much more direct control through the executive branch. It utilized methods of customs fraud and contraband smuggling that mirror those conceived at the height of the counterinsurgent period. But per MP and CICIG investigations, *La Línea*'s hierarchy consisted of a "top level" comprised of the president, vice president, and their representatives who oversaw the necessary personnel transfers and benefitted financially from the scheme; a "mid-level" of intermediaries outside of and within the SAT who coordinated the customs duty adjustments; and a "low level" of customs inspectors and auditors who ensured the illegal adjustments were carried out on the ground.[60]

External mid-level intermediaries corresponded with internal network members within the upper echelons of the SAT to transmit information on

[59] Peacock and Beltrán 2003: 25–26.    [60] CICIG and MP 2015.

the importers that coordinated with *La Línea*, thereby ensuring they were assigned to offloading ramps with customs inspectors who would allow shipments to pass with the falsified tax values and payments. Spreadsheets recovered by investigators illustrate how *La Línea* members organized the operations, listing the name of the enterprise, the shipping container registration number, the name of the customs inspector controlling the ramp to which the container was directed, the type of merchandise, the declared value, and the "charge" levied by the criminal structure, which ranged from 30 to 40 percent of the declared value.[61]

In addition, the coalition underwriting *La Línea*'s illicit customs activities mirrored the wartime alliance between retired military officials, tax authorities, importers and private sector elites, and organized criminal elements. Within the structure, the president's and vice president's interests were represented by Baldetti's private secretary Juan Carlos Monzón, a retired army captain who was discharged in 1996 after suspected involvement in a car theft ring run by several of Alfredo Moreno's relatives.[62] From outside of government, Salvador Estuardo González, president of one of Guatemala's major publishing companies, coordinated the administrative and financial dimensions of the illicit customs operations, overseeing the distribution of profits.[63] González's relationship with Pérez Molina extends back decades to when his father served as Pérez Molina's boss within the EMP during the 1990s. Finally, within the SAT, top officials, such as Superintendents Carlos Muñoz and Omar Chacón and customs head Claudia Méndez, ensured that the placement of inspectors and auditors allowed the illicit customs duty adjustments to proceed unimpeded.

In sum, the composition of *La Línea* underscores the notion that similar kinds of undermining rules persisted within Guatemala's customs administration despite two decades of political turnover. They were not epiphenomenal to the precise individuals in power, but instead a product of the multi-sectoral coalition that stood to gain politically and financially through the implementation of the alternative institutional arrangements. Though the players were distinct, the broader constellation of public and private sector interests endured and facilitated the survival of the wartime procedures that expressly contravened the state's extractive functions.

---

[61] Ibid., 22.   [62] Barreto 2015; *El Periódico* 2013.   [63] Barreto 2016.

### EVALUATING OTHER MECHANISMS OF
### INSTITUTIONAL PERSISTENCE

Overall, this analysis finds the greatest support for the proposition that institutional persistence is driven by the adaptation of the conflict-era distributional coalition on the margins of state power. Though previously dominant military and political blocs were displaced from the state sphere and structural reforms remade Guatemala's customs apparatus, new extra-state channels allowed wartime sectoral interests to wield continued influence by adapting the undermining rules, securing impunity, and locating strategic allies on the inside. This study, however, is also attentive to two other mechanisms: (1) the manipulation of formal institutional reforms, and (2) the endurance of collective understandings that render the undermining rules "appropriate" or "legitimate."

Observably, the first alternative mechanism – incumbent manipulation of the timing or enforcement of institutional reforms – would result in Arzú administration attempts to stall reform efforts or impede the enforcement of new SAT provisions, which my analysis does not bear out. After the revelations, the sitting government acted swiftly to remove implicated political and military officials and undertook a robust, internationally backed process to build a new tax entity, which exceeded Peace Accord provisions. Instead of waiting for the completion of the investigations, the Arzú government decided to dismantle the criminal structure. As then-Minister of Foreign Affairs Eduardo Stein confirmed, "The decision of President Arzú was to proceed immediately to prevent [the accused] from destroying evidence and maintaining access to these levels of power."[64]

Of course, an important critique of the Arzú administration's approach was that, following the expulsions, criminal prosecutions for those involved never came to fruition, weakening the potential deterrent effect of judicial sanctions, as one executive official noted.[65] Beyond Moreno himself, very few individuals stood trial for customs fraud and contraband, and the small pool of those who were tried did not include the high-level military and government officials expelled following the Moreno Network revelations. Instead, investigators focused their energies on individuals like Salvadoran smuggler Santos Hipólito Reyes, who was accused of coordinating drug, weapons, and contraband smuggling with

---

[64] Presidencia de la República de Guatemala 1997: 315.
[65] Interview with author, June 12, 2017.

the Moreno structure.[66] Outside of Reyes, the commercial "clients" of the Moreno Network were barely even investigated, according to an ex-intelligence agent, both because of the narrow national security focus and Arzú's close ties with Guatemala's traditional economic elite.[67]

Just as importantly, while discharged, the military intelligence elites that designed the alternative rules to siphon off customs revenue evaded criminal prosecutions. Though leading *Cofradía* members were dismissed from the military, authorities never managed to file charges against them for wartime corruption. In late 2002, during Portillo's tenure, Attorney General Carlos de León Argueta announced investigations into five powerful ex-military intelligence actors: Francisco Ortega Menaldo, Napoleón Rojas Méndez, Jacobo Esdras Salán Sánchez, Mario Roberto García Catalán, and Manuel Callejas y Callejas. The cases eventually led to the seizure of documents and declarations before the MP, but they were shelved a year and a half later.[68] Salán Sánchez, Rojas, and Portillo were eventually convicted for corruption and embezzlement carried out in the early 2000s, while Callejas y Callejas was convicted of forced disappearance in 2018; however, this was well after their ties to the Moreno Network came to light and they reconstituted the wartime distributional coalition.[69]

The second hypothesized mechanism – collective understandings of the undermining rules as "appropriate" – also finds less support here. If this mechanism plausibly accounted for institutional persistence, we would expect to see the continuation of wartime views that military elites "had the right to do these [corrupt] things" because of their heroic acts in defense of the country or that such behavior was socially permissible among customs inspectors and administrators.[70] Instead, the wartime justification for the customs fraud scheme fell away with the end of the armed conflict. Moreover, SAT reforms sought to combat collective understandings of the undermining rules as "normal" or "legitimate" by purging the bureaucracy and vetting new personnel, as discussed above. According to executive officials, the government's only option was "to remove this function from Public Finance employees ... since, to date, the authorities have not been able to locate the employees that engage in acts

---

[66] According to a 2015 report by *El Periódico*, Reyes remained a fugitive for two years following the Moreno Network revelations and then remained free after paying 15,000 quetzales as bail. He was allegedly murdered in 2014. See Santos 2015.

[67] Interview with author, May 30, 2017.      [68] Dávila and Palma 2002; Reyes 2004b.

[69] See Peacock and Beltrán 2003.      [70] Interview with author, May 30, 2017.

of corruption given the sophisticated mechanisms that they utilize." As detailed above, this view resulted in the exodus of nearly 99 percent of prior customs personnel.

To fill the void, the SAT contracted and trained a new bureaucratic corps that met more rigorous educational standards. Conversations with those involved in the process as well as members of the first cohort of new customs inspectors suggest that these vetting procedures instilled a new sense of public duty – a new collective understanding of how tax administration personnel ought to behave. In the words of one former customs inspector hired with the creation of the SAT, those entering the new bureaucratic posts "were very good, they had principles.[71]" As a result, the corrupt agents within the tax administration were now "in the minority." The training and resources for new personnel, of course, were modest. According to one former inspector, "we were only given very basic training, and so, above all, we were learning as we went. But the intention to do things correctly was there." In spite of the challenges as the SAT remained "in diapers," those within the new agency "were more transparent ... so the SAT began to advance little by little.[72]"

Though new SAT personnel faced clear obstacles, there is little evidence that the normative acceptance of the undermining rules drove their survival. With the pretext of counterinsurgency no longer a viable defense of military intelligence's total control of customs, previous justifications for the alternative institutional arrangements within customs faded. Moreover, new SAT personnel entered their posts with distinct understandings of appropriate bureaucratic conduct. As a result, the ideational underpinnings of the wartime rules within customs do not appear to be the primary driver of institutional persistence in this case.

## CONCLUSION

An in-depth examination of the twenty-year period between the exposure of the Moreno Network and the discovery of *La Línea* illustrates that the modalities of customs fraud – the rules and procedures that subverted customs revenue extraction – survived multiple governments and robust reform efforts primarily because the broader distributional coalition with a vested stake in the previous institutional order successfully adapted to and exerted influence from new political and economic spaces.

---

[71] Interview with author, November 15, 2017.    [72] Ibid.

The decades-long distortion of Guatemala's customs administration was not necessarily the result of insufficient institutional reforms, but inattention to where the targets of reforms would go and what they would do in the aftermath. In the words of one former political official, "it's that these people [previously powerful wartime figures] are there, and they have time, they have space … and they are more creative than the rest. They persist, they live in the shadows, and they wait for an opportunity to return, for someone to open the door."[73]

Though the ex-military intelligence, state, and private sector actors remained "in the shadows" because authorities failed to bring them to justice, efforts to redistribute power and resources away from the wartime elites that oversaw the fraudulent customs procedures were quite extensive in the context of the fragile postwar landscape. Instead, institutional persistence was primarily a question of coalitional endurance and the co-optation of new political and economic spaces. This case thus illustrates how undermining rules can outlast conventional peacebuilding and bureaucratic reforms, however well-resourced and well-intentioned, because they fail to account for how the remnants of conflict-era coalitions find new venues beyond the formal state sphere through which to piece themselves back together.

[73] Interview with author, June 12, 2017.

# 9

## Guatemala

### *The Persistence of Extrajudicial Killing*

Guatemala's tax administration was not the only agency in which the undermining rules implemented amid conflict continued to subvert routine activities long after armed conflict had ended. Within the public security sector, particularly the new National Civilian Police (PNC), wartime procedures governing extrajudicial killing continued to structure police behavior, at times enforced from the highest levels of the president's security cabinet. As the Pavón and El Infiernito prison killings in the mid-2000s illustrate (Chapter 5), small, elite cliques of investigative police continued to operate autonomously from broader police structures, acting as hit squads on behalf of top political leadership. Officials then sought to frame the abuses as armed confrontations between criminals and state forces. How did the undermining rules governing extrajudicial killings endure well into Guatemala's period of formal peace and democratic transition? Do the mechanisms of postwar institutional persistence in this case coincide with those found in Guatemala's tax and customs apparatus?

It is plausible that the undermining rules structuring extrajudicial killing had less to do with wartime factors and more to do with contemporary social and political dynamics. As scholars like Yanilda González note, police forces in Latin America often remain "authoritarian enclaves" in new democracies due to fragmented societal preferences for reform and related electoral incentives.[1] Indeed, *mano dura* [heavy-handed] public security policies have become the prevailing approach to

---

[1] González 2020.

tackling the rise in organized crime and gang activity, not only in Guatemala, but in other Central American countries like El Salvador and Honduras as well. These campaigns largely involve criminalizing gang membership or designating gangs as "terrorist" organizations, imposing lengthy prison sentences for suspected gang members, and deploying police and military to the streets to carry out raids and round-ups. Such policies have not only failed to reduce levels of violence but have also been linked to "credible reports [of] extrajudicial killings by vigilante groups,"[2] much like those perpetrated during Guatemala's conflict period.

Despite their inefficacy, such *mano dura* campaigns have been incredibly popular among the Guatemalan public. According to survey data from the Latin American Public Opinion Project (LAPOP), some two-thirds of Guatemalans supported *mano dura* government policies in 1999, a figure that has diminished since, but remained at 42 percent in 2012.[3] Throughout the 2000s, a large proportion of Guatemalan citizens also approved of the use of vigilante justice, a figure that peaked in 2010 at 43.2 percent.[4] Popular opinion in favor of extrajudicial killing has been further fueled by media pressures for "the government [to] 'do something' about an escalation in gang-related crime."[5] Disparate societal preferences then may plausibly drive the persistence of "authoritarian coercion" in the Guatemalan case.[6]

While this chapter does not deny that popular demands, electoral incentives, and media influence allow extrajudicial killing to endure, such an explanation cannot necessarily account for the precise *structure* of such acts – their rule-bound nature and the routinized procedures that govern them. As the Pavón prison killings that opened Chapter 5 illustrate, post-conflict policing in countries like Guatemala deploy similar scripts and procedures for extrajudicial killing. Moreover, focusing in on these precise scripts and procedures reveals that they are upheld not just by police agents and leaders, but by a range of other actors and interest groups – investigative and prosecutorial entities, the judicial system, and business elites. Shifting our focus from outcome (police violence) to process (the procedures governing extrajudicial killing) not only uncovers how "democratic processes often sustain and uphold authoritarian police," but how an array of wartime elites appropriate new democratic spaces to maintain the previous rules of the game.[7]

---

[2] Seelke 2007: 4.    [3] Azpuru 2013: 231.    [4] Ibid., 229.    [5] Seelke 2007: 3.
[6] See González 2020.    [7] Ibid., 25.

Overall, this chapter argues that the persistence of undermining rules governing extrajudicial killings in this institutional context was driven by the survival of the broader wartime distributional coalition with a stake in them – namely, the political, military, and economic elites that sought to cleanse society of "undesirables" and eliminate criminal competitors to their illicit enrichment schemes (Chapter 7). However, the channels through which these diverse sectoral interests continued to uphold the alternative institutional arrangements were somewhat distinct. While the customs administration witnessed the near-total expulsion of wartime personnel, the same cannot be said for the police. Facing high violent crime rates, the government of conservative president Álvaro Arzú feared a lapse in security with the complete purge of wartime PN personnel. The government instead opted to "recycle" previous officers through limited training courses – moves that coincide with another of the potential mechanisms of postwar institutional persistence, incumbent manipulation of reform implementation. In addition, the incorporation of old PN agents within the new police force may have contributed to the survival of collective beliefs and attitudes that rendered the undermining rules "normal" and thus socially permissible, another of the alternative mechanisms discussed earlier.

Yet importantly, this chapter posits that the failure to expel previous police agents interacted with the peacetime reconsolidation of the state-military-private sector alliance that upheld the rules governing extrajudicial killing, which ensured that behavior by low-level police agents was, in fact, communicated and enforced from above. A close examination of the case further reveals that the continued influence of previously dominant counterinsurgent elites drove the Guatemalan government's foot-dragging and manipulation when it came to transformations within the new civilian police force. In contrast to Guatemala's customs apparatus, this case is thus one in which multiple mechanisms of institutional persistence are present, illustrating the distinct pathways through which the wartime undermining rules survive transition and peace. Yet, the preservation and adaptation of the wartime distributional coalition stands at the center of my analysis, fueling the other post-conflict security sector processes that occurred.

To elaborate these claims, the rest of the chapter proceeds as follows. In the next section, I describe the impetus for and nature of police reforms in the context of Guatemala's peacebuilding moment, including the creation of the new National Civilian Police (PNC) in 1997. Next, I analyze how the dominant wartime distributional coalition comprised of political, security sector, and economic elites managed to survive peacebuilding reforms and uphold the undermining rules governing extrajudicial executions to eliminate "undesirables." In an important contrast with Guatemala's customs administration, the PNC saw the direct reentry of these groups into the upper echelons of the security cabinet, highlighting a somewhat different pathway of postwar institutional persistence.

Finally, I evaluate the two other mechanisms of institutional persistence – incumbent manipulation of peacebuilding and governance reforms and the endurance of collective beliefs about "appropriate" police conduct – finding more evidence for these approaches here relative to the preceding case. Yet, at the same time, I suggest that the manipulation and limited enforcement of police reforms set out in the Peace Accords was partially driven by the reconsolidation of the wartime distributional coalition rather than the other way around. Moreover, even if shared understandings of police killings as "legitimate" persisted within the PNC, my analysis shows that the ordering and organization of extrajudicial violence was carried out by the political, economic, and security sector elites that comprised the wartime distributional coalition. I conclude by reflecting on how this case illustrates the varied dynamics of postwar institutional persistence, but also how it is similarly grounded in the adaptation and survival of conflict-era constellations of political power.

## POST-CONFLICT REFORMS

Following the 1983 coup that ousted General Ríos Montt, Guatemala's internal armed conflict witnessed a period of marked de-escalation. This de-escalation was a product of the significant blow the military struck to the insurgency and its support base through the scorched earth campaign of the late 1970s and early 1980s, as well as Guatemala's increasingly tarnished international image due to grave human rights violations.[8] The push toward negotiated settlement, however, coincided with persistently high levels of police violence in the late 1980s and early 1990s.[9] This paradox, and the subsequent police reform it brought about, is the subject of this section. Here, I evaluate efforts to remake the police apparatus, remove it from the clutches of military intelligence control, and dismantle the wartime rules governing extrajudicial killings.

---

[8] For more on the process of de-escalation, see Isaacs and Schwartz 2020.
[9] See Yashar 2018: 149–207.

## Peace Process, Continued Police Violence, and the Impetus for Reform

Despite Guatemala's transition to civilian rule and the de-escalation of rural violence, extrajudicial killings by state security personnel continued unabated. The ascent of former human rights ombudsman Ramiro de León Carpio to the presidency in 1993 brought renewed hope that state abuses would be restrained; however, violence only accelerated. In the first six months of 1993, the Mutual Support Group (GAM) recorded ninety-one extrajudicial executions, which it largely attributed to eight new paramilitary commands that sought to "attack in the darkness, create division, and not allow a new Guatemala to flourish."[10] In the first half of 1994, Amnesty International reported some 160 extrajudicial killings.[11] Beyond sheer numbers, this period also witnessed several high-profile killings that disrupted the visions of peace and democratization on the horizon. These included the murders of the President of the Constitutional Court Eduardo Epaminondas González Dubón and politician and journalist Jorge Carpio Nicolle, owner of the daily *El Gráfico*.[12]

Though PN forces were not the only state security entities involved in such acts, news reports from the period corroborate their central role in upholding the wartime institutional arrangements governing extrajudicial executions.[13] For example, just before the inauguration of the PNC, a former chief of the Anti-Kidnapping Command and a police agent from the criminal investigation division stood trial for torture and kidnapping.[14] A spate of extrajudicial killings in the Pavón prison also signaled the endurance of social cleansing procedures, which were linked to private criminal and economic groups.[15] Speaking to *La República* in late 1993, GAM activist-turned-Congresswoman Nineth Montenegro argued that the continuation of extrajudicial violence was driven by "a small group (the agro-export sector) with the support of the security groups [that] have control in order to maintain the status quo."[16]

Archival evidence and other firsthand accounts indicate that the continuing subordination of Guatemalan police forces to military intelligence units facilitated the persistence of the PN-perpetrated extrajudicial killings. Despite efforts to remake the Detective Corps' successor, the Division of Technical Investigations (DIT), the grasp of intelligence officers on the PN's investigative personnel and functions remained firm.

---

[10] *La República* 1993.     [11] Amnesty International 1994: 3.     [12] Ibid.
[13] Palacios 2000; *El Periódico* 1998.     [14] *Prensa Libre* 1997; Najarro 1997.
[15] Trejo 1994; *Prensa Libre* 1997.     [16] *La República* 1993.

As Marie-Louise Glebbeek writes, the police chiefs in Guatemala City were directly under the control of the military's Directorate of Intelligence, and "even ordinary personnel such as police officers and agents often had double functions and worked at the same time for military intelligence units and for the National Police. A considerable number of individuals were mentioned in both personnel registries. ... The same person wore a military uniform in the military registry and a police uniform in the registry of the National Police."[17] At both the strategic and operational levels, there was virtually no separation between the PN and military intelligence.

A more specific way in which military intelligence continued to enforce extrajudicial killing procedures within the police was through conducting parallel investigations that supplanted those of the Division of Criminal Investigations (DINC), the entity that substituted the DIT following the 1986 return to civilian rule. Given the linkages between military intelligence elites and the officers who oversaw the DINC, Intelligence Directorate (G-2) agents were deployed to the scene of extrajudicial killings to tamper with evidence and whitewash the acts to ensure impunity. As one PN detective stated in 1992:

The G-2 always shows up at a crime scene. They have a [police] radio. They are always there. You can recognize which of them is G-2 because they always carry either a .45 mm or a .9 mm [pistol]. They often wear sunglasses and dress in tennis clothes, but you can pick out their weapon under their belts. And they usually arrive on a bicycle or a motorbike.

Q: Is it possible they were responsible for these crimes?

It is more than just possible. Since the G-2 uses only two calibers of weapon—a .45 or .9 mm—there is a lot of speculation within the National Police about this. Publicly, the spokesperson says we are not related to the army and that we are in charge of criminal investigations in Guatemala. But there are always two investigations going on simultaneously: that of the police and that of the G-2 watching the police.[18]

By conducting unofficial investigations and cover-ups, Guatemalan military intelligence served to enforce the alternative rules governing extrajudicial killing by ensuring that the acts went unpunished.[19]

Efforts to establish a police command and investigative unit that operated independently from intelligence agencies and to curtail parallel activities were consistently thwarted by military leaders. Just after De

---

[17] Glebbeek 2001: 433–434.    [18] Qtd. in Schirmer 1998a: 179–180.
[19] See Brinks 2006: 216–218.

León Carpio assumed the presidency, he named a new civilian police chief, Mario René Cifuentes Echeverría,[20] who sought the removal of military officers from the upper echelons of the PN. According to conversations between US political advisors and Cifuentes in 1993, the police director lamented the continuing presence of six military "advisors" who were really "spies [*orejas*] for the military." Cifuentes further reported that the spies were "responsible to the interim police director Lt. Colonel Fernández Ligorría[21] . . . [who] enriched himself at the police and doesn't want to give up control or risk being exposed. To buttress his position, he has successfully sold the idea to the military high command that it cannot completely remove itself from the police."[22]

The continuing infiltration of the police by military intelligence was thus fueled by the desire of high-ranking officials to maintain their institutional privileges and secure the alternative rules governing police activities. Despite the de-escalation of armed conflict, the security sector hierarchies that implemented and enforced the alternative procedures remained intact well into the 1990s, ensuring that PN-led extrajudicial killings continued unabated.

## Remaking the Police: The Creation of the PNC

Efforts to diminish military influence in public security affairs began with the peace process, which laid the groundwork for the reformed National Civilian Police (PNC). The Guatemalan government, military, and guerrilla representatives signed the "Agreement on the Strengthening of Civilian Power and on the Role of the Armed Forces in a Democratic Society" in September 1996. The Agreement laid out the bases of the PNC, which would be "the only armed police force competent at the national level whose function is to protect and guarantee the exercise of the rights and freedoms of the individual; prevent, investigate, and combat crime; and maintain public order and internal security."[23]

In addition to these basic institutional functions, the Agreement put forward several other principles and objectives that would guide the formation of the PNC. For one, it included a dramatic increase in the size

[20] In November 1996, Cifuentes was removed for his suspected ties to the Moreno Network, as detailed in Chapter 8.
[21] Lt. Colonel Julio Fernández Ligorría was also one of the military officers linked to the Moreno Network. See Peacock and Beltrán 2003.
[22] US Embassy in Guatemala 1993.    [23] Government of Guatemala 1996b, Article 23.

of the police force from 12,000 to at least 20,000 members by late 1999, as well as the expansion of police coverage throughout national territory. It further committed to the reform of public security laws; the establishment of formal hiring and promotions procedures, which included a six-month training course for recruits at the new Police Academy; an increase in the public security budget and police salaries; and targeted recruitment efforts within rural indigenous communities so that the makeup of the police force reflected the population it would serve.[24]

As importantly, the strengthening of the new police force would be accompanied by stipulations to remove the military from internal security functions and reduce its institutional strength vis-à-vis the police. The PNC was to be placed under the control of the Ministry of the Interior – which also administered immigration services and the prison system – and "under the direction of civil authorities."[25] Further, both the size of the Guatemalan armed forces and military spending as a percentage of GDP was to be reduced by 33 percent in the years immediately following the signing of the Accords.[26]

The Agreement on the Strengthening of Civilian Power envisioned a rather sweeping transformation of the Guatemalan public security apparatus; yet, to enshrine the Accord into law, the reforms would have to be passed by a constitutional referendum, which failed in May 1999 (Chapter 7). In spite of this blow to the peace process, the PNC, which was formally created in July 1997, made significant strides during its initial years. By October 1999, it had grown to 17,330 members[27] – short of the 20,000-member goal laid out in the Accord, but still a 60-percent increase. Further, the PNC managed to extend its presence to all twenty-two departments of the country. At the outset of reforms, top military officials also made good on the Accord's central objective of disrupting the hardline corps of intelligence officers that had maintained a firm grip on police power and operations. Under the leadership of its more moderate, institutionalist faction, the armed forces not only conceded some *de jure* political and economic power, but even undertook efforts to purge their ranks of the most extreme antidemocratic officers accused of coup plotting in the lead-up to the peace process.[28]

There were also important gains made with respect to public perceptions of and trust in the police, as well as institutional morale and performance. In the words of Marie-Louise Glebbeek, "the new force

---

[24] See Glebbeek 2001.   [25] Government of Guatemala 1996b.   [26] Ibid., Article 63.
[27] Glebbeek 2001: 438.   [28] Schirmer 1998a: 269–274.

has a more service-oriented spirit and was received well by the majority of the population. They are better paid, better trained and seem to be more effective than their predecessors: the arrest rates are up and violent death and kidnapping rates are down."[29] According to a report from the Washington Office on Latin America (WOLA), in those early years, "the government had approved new laws, raised police salaries, and provided equipment, weapons, and vehicles; the majority of these measures were undertaken with little financing from the international community, showing a willingness on the part of the PNC to invest its own resources. In general, the institution was well received by the population, at least compared to the old force."[30]

But a critical limitation with respect to the construction of the new police was the recycling of officers and agents from the previous force.[31] Fearing a lapse in security provision amid high levels of crime, President Arzú and government officials opted to reincorporate police personnel from the PN into the newly minted PNC.[32] Though the estimates vary, somewhere between one-half and two-thirds of the PNC was comprised of previously serving members.[33] In principle, new recruits were supposed to partake in a six-month training course through the Police Academy, which included new protocols related to human rights protections. But in reality, recruits from the old force went through an expedited three-month version.[34] Despite the improvements that came with the renovation of the police force, there is a broad consensus among experts that the recycling of personnel from the "old guard" seriously "undermined, the quality, efficiency, and professionalism of the PNC, ... limiting the impact of the reforms."[35]

The reforms that brought about Guatemala's new civilian police force thus exhibited important contrasts with the remaking of the country's tax and customs apparatus. In the latter case, Arzú administration officials carried out rather successful bureaucratic purges and vetting programs, which allowed the SAT and its customs division to start anew with better trained personnel that, according to firsthand accounts, shared a greater sense of public duty and integrity. The same cannot be said for the PNC. Instead, the failure to ensure police turnover and to implement the stipulated training for old recruits, speak to the two other mechanisms of institutional persistence put forward in Chapter 2: incumbent

---

[29] Glebbeek 2001: 438.    [30] WOLA 2009: 4–5.    [31] See Yashar 2018: 157.
[32] Gavigan 2009: 66.    [33] Glebbeek 2001: 438; WOLA 2009: 4.
[34] Gleebeek 2001: 438.    [35] WOLA 2009: 5.

manipulation of the timing and implementation of peacebuilding reforms and the endurance of collective beliefs about "appropriate" or "legitimate" behavior. I further evaluate these two approaches toward the end of the chapter; but first, I turn to the period following the PNC's creation to examine how the adaptation and survival of the wartime distributional coalition allowed for the endurance of the undermining rules governing extrajudicial killings.

### POST-REFORM INSTITUTIONAL SURVIVAL

Because such a significant share of the wartime PN force was reincorporated into the new civilian-led police institution, the pathway of institutional persistence here is somewhat distinct from Guatemala's customs apparatus. Yet, in line with the analysis in the preceding chapter, I find that the reconstitution and persistence of the dominant wartime distributional coalition played a central role in the survival of the undermining rules within policing institutions. While it is possible (if not likely) that agents from the old PN would engage in similar extrajudicial *practices* characteristic of the counterinsurgent period, their coordinated enforcement as a series of *rules* continued, I argue, because of the elite coalition with a vested stake in them. As discussed in Chapter 7, this coalition included former military intelligence officials, members of elite investigative units within the PNC, and right-wing private sector leaders seeking to eliminate social "undesirables" like gang members, both to remove the threat they posed to Guatemalan society and to their own criminal enterprises.

The reconstitution of this wartime distributional coalition was achieved during the government of Alfonso Portillo and his FRG party, which effectively "took the police corps back to the years prior to the signing of the Peace Accords"[36] and constituted "the watershed moment in the perversion of the PNC."[37] According to one security and justice expert, there was a slight decline in social cleansing and extrajudicial executions in the immediate years following the peace process, "but the FRG enters and the escalation of violence begins again. Before, [crime] prevention and criminal investigation were privileged. But the FRG arrived, and they had another project in mind."[38]

The Portillo administration's alternative police "project" subverted early PNC progress on numerous fronts. On a more technical level, in

---

[36] GAM 2010: 191.    [37] Interview with author, October 31, 2017.
[38] Interview with author, November 22, 2017.

the words of one former military officer, the Portillo period "destroyed" the new Police Academy created in the late 1990s with the assistance of Spain's Civil Guard.[39] Since its inception, the Academy had overseen a training program to prepare recruits for policing tasks within the new, democratic framework, as well as more rigorous standards for hiring and promotion; however, the arrival of Portillo witnessed the jettisoning of these new procedures to promote those closest to the regime.

Just days after Portillo took office in 2000, he named a series of police chiefs who did not meet the requirements of the 1997 National Police Law, which stipulated that PNC officials "must have been police commissioners and have passed the training course in order to access the institutional hierarchy."[40] Though the newly named Director of the PNC Baudilio Portillo Merlos claimed that the officials in question had completed the required courses, the Police Academy had no record of their participation. In the words of security expert Carmen Rosa de León, "this attitude [was] a backward step in the professionalization of the PNC and there's no way a police career exists if later the chiefs are named at the convenience of the sitting authorities."[41]

But beyond demolishing the new standards, the Portillo administration continued the *de facto* subordination of police forces, particularly the Criminal Investigation Service (SIC), to military intelligence. According to new SIC agents, the military intelligence officers from the elite EMP unit remained in charge of registering and providing identification for new investigative agents graduating from the Police Academy.[42] The wartime parallel investigations of extrajudicial killings conducted by military intelligence to cover up or manipulate evidence also continued well into Portillo's tenure.[43]

By placing the SIC and other police entities under the control of military intelligence structures, the Portillo administration marshaled the reconstruction of the wartime distributional coalition that had devised and enforced the rules governing extrajudicial killings. It further entrenched that political-military coalition by promoting hardline military officials linked to the wartime *Cofradía* clique to top security posts like Minister of the Interior. In August 2000, Portillo named Byron

[39] Interview with author, May 30, 2017. It is important to note, as some have argued, that Spanish government support may have led to an unsustainable and inappropriate policing model within the Guatemalan context. See Gavigan 2009: 69.
[40] *El Periódico* 2000b.    [41] Qtd. in Zelada 2000.    [42] *El Periódico* 2000c.
[43] Méndez Arriaza 2001.

Barrientos, former military intelligence officer, as Minister of the Interior. Former colleagues of Barrientos indicated that "he was an unconditional collaborator of retired generals Francisco Ortega Menaldo and [Manuel Antonio] Callejas y Callejas," the two godfathers of the *Cofradía* intelligence clique.[44] In November 2001, General Eduardo Arévalo Lacs was transferred from his position as Minister of Defense to Minister of the Interior in direct contravention of the Peace Accord provision mandating civilian control of the Ministry.[45] Arévalo Lacs' naming similarly signaled the "consolidation of the influence of retired general Francisco Ortega Menaldo over President Alfonso Portillo on military and public security matters."[46]

On the one hand, this reconsolidation of the wartime distributional coalition reinstated many of the corrupt, predatory activities that the *Cofradía* spearheaded at the height of the counterinsurgent campaign in the late 1970s and early 1980s. In the words of one human rights defender, "the police and military were converted into [sites of] plunder" with the arrival of the new Ministry chiefs.[47] Indeed, in 2011 Portillo and Arévalo Lacs were indicted for embezzling some $15 million from the Ministry of the Defense a decade earlier.[48]

But just as importantly, there was a dramatic increase in extrajudicial executions recorded during Portillo's presidency, hearkening back to the peak period of wartime violence and the undermining rules governing targeted killings disguised as right-wing paramilitary attacks. As the most hardline, repressive military intelligence clique consolidated its dominance, the wartime institutional arrangements it had created were revived as well. During the first five months of 2002, the number of extrajudicial killings surpassed all of those registered the previous year, leading human rights defenders to posit the return of large-scale social cleansing campaigns.[49] By the middle of Portillo's tenure, the threats and attacks against human rights defenders swelled to 374, including 49 killings – many of which exhibited the same *modus operandi* of the conflict period and motivated the creation of the UN International Commission against Impunity in Guatemala (CICIG).[50]

The efforts to scrap Peace Accord commitments that impeded the reconstitution of the wartime distributional coalition carried through from the Portillo administration to the government of Óscar Berger,

---

[44] Guerra 2000; see also, Peacock and Beltrán 2003.    [45] Del Cid 2001.    [46] Ibid.
[47] Interview with author, October 31, 2017.    [48] CICIG 2011.    [49] Castillo 2002.
[50] See Open Society Justice Initiative 2016: 29.

during which time the undermining rules within the public security apparatus persisted as well. Berger, a scion of Guatemala's traditional oligarchy, preserved the modification of the National Police Law introduced during Portillo's government to continue permitting non-career officers to ascend to PNC leadership, thereby "breaking the hierarchical structure."[51] Erwin Sperisen, a former member of President Álvaro Arzú's security team with no police experience, was named chief of the PNC and brought on board several military advisors.[52] The appointments ensured that PNC investigations continued to function under the thumb of military intelligence.[53]

But beyond the endurance of military intelligence influence, Berger, a member of the traditional oligarchy, reintroduced another key player from the counterinsurgent coalition: the reactionary private sector elite linked to previous death squad structures. The top emissary of this group within the upper echelons of the public security apparatus was Carlos Vielmann, named Minister of the Interior in July 2004.[54] In his youth, Vielmann was affiliated with the right-wing, anti-communist National Liberation Movement (MLN), seen by many as the political arm of paramilitary groups operating at the height of the war.[55] He would later serve as president of the Guatemalan Industrial Chamber, the conglomeration of the country's major business sectors, thus demonstrating the persistent influence of right-wing business leaders. Intent on reducing Guatemala's escalating violent crime rate, particularly extortion and kidnapping directed at business leaders, Vielmann brought on board security advisor Víctor Rivera, a Venezuelan linked to El Salvador's right-wing party ARENA, which was involved in paramilitary activity in the early 1990s.[56]

Mirroring the Guatemalan armed conflict period, Ministry of the Interior leadership coordinated small, elite teams of PNC investigative agents to carry out extrajudicial killings against suspected delinquents, as well as competitors within Guatemala's criminal underworld. As one former CICIG investigator told me, on Vielmann's watch, Rivera "created a killing machine." It began as a "social cleansing structure but later came to be seen as a means of generating income."[57] In the prison massacre and executions discussed in Chapter 5, the rules and

---

[51] WOLA and Fundación Mack 2019: 18.     [52] Ibid.; Castillo and Guoz 2005.
[53] Sas 2005.     [54] Guoz 2004.     [55] Llorca 2004; Hernández Batres 2014: 9.
[56] Interview with author, January 4, 2017; Fernández 2011.
[57] Interview with author, January 4, 2017.

procedures structuring extrajudicial executions were virtually identical to their wartime counterparts: crime scenes were tainted and investigations manipulated in acts coordinated from above to guarantee impunity.

During Vielmann's first year as minister, there was a 230-percent increase in total violent homicides, including a 2000-percent increase in killings with signs of strangulation and a 3000-percent increase in execution-style murders at point-blank range.[58] Though it is impossible to discern what proportion of those extrajudicial killings were committed by the elite PNC investigative cliques under the direction of Vielmann and Rivera, the staggering increases suggest a revival of the wartime rules governing extrajudicial killings.

In sum, the period following the creation of the PNC illustrates how the survival and reconsolidation of the wartime alliance of political, military, and private sector elites contributed to the endurance of the rules governing extrajudicial killings targeted at those deemed "delinquents." According to investigations, the motivations underlying the alternative police procedures were likely varied – ranging from the desire to cleanse Guatemalan society of gangs to the elimination of criminal competition to state and private actors enmeshed in illicit activities.[59] Despite differences in both the motives and the precise players, the broad set of sectoral interests that, in concert, exerted influence through state channels allowed the undermining rules to persist, despite the postwar efforts to dismantle them.

## EVALUATING OTHER MECHANISMS OF INSTITUTIONAL PERSISTENCE

Though the reconsolidation and continued influence of the wartime distributional coalition facilitated institutional persistence in the context of Guatemala's police apparatus, the failure of police purges reflect other mechanisms highlighted in Chapter 2: (1) incumbent manipulation of the timing and enforcement of reforms, and (2) abiding collective ideas that deemed the undermining rules and procedures "normal" or "appropriate."

A potentially important alternative mechanism driving postwar institutional persistence in this case is that the Guatemalan government manipulated the timing, implementation, and/or enforcement of peace-building and governance reforms until domestic and international

---

[58] PDH 2006b: 10–11.    [59] See Fernández 2011.

pressures died down, allowing the old rules of the game to survive untouched. The observable implications of this alternative in the case of Guatemala's police apparatus would be Arzú administration attempts to stall police reforms. In other words, incumbents use their "agenda-setting power" to overcome demands for change and thus preserve the status quo.[60]

Throughout Arzú's tenure, we observe the manipulation of police reform timing and implementation in several respects due to Guatemala's post-peace crime wave. Most notably, the Arzú government opted to forgo the relatively thorough purging and vetting of police agents stipulated in the Accords, instead "recycling" old PN agents – over half of the new force.[61] These "recycled" agents were subject to limited training to instill democratic, prevention-oriented practices. In addition, the PNC, while formally tasked with preserving internal order and preventing crime, was in practice often passed over for domestic security-related tasks in favor of the military,[62] which, per Accord provisions, was to return to the barracks. Given the PNC's fragile institutional framework and capacities, military leadership kept its forces "on the front line … because necessity obliges us to be there," in the words of then-Defense Minister Héctor Barrios Celada.[63] Whether under the weight of continuing military influence or popular pressure to stem rising crime, the Arzú administration authorized military involvement in internal security activities, even tasking army intelligence with overseeing a new anti-kidnapping command.[64]

Despite the manipulation and non-enforcement of some dimensions of the police reforms in the late 1990s, others were carried out rather effectively. In the span of just a few years, the Arzú government oversaw the expansion of the PNC in size, territorial coverage, and ethnic representation. And while the military still played a central role in domestic security in contravention of the Accords, under the sitting regime, military officers were removed from civilian leadership posts within the upper echelons of the Ministry of the Interior and the PNC. Despite the clear limitations, the Arzú government did not wield its institutional power to completely stall and sideline reforms, instead selectively carrying out some while limiting others.

---

[60] Capoccia 2016: 1111.
[61] According to Spence (2004), PN agents formed 60 percent of the new PNC, while, according to Hernández Batres (2014: 7) the figure was 52 percent.
[62] See Yashar 2018: 164–169.    [63] Schirmer 1998b: 30.    [64] Ibid., 28.

Compared to the case of Guatemala's tax and customs administration discussed in Chapter 8, there is much more evidence that incumbent "agenda-setting power" and the manipulation of reforms may have contributed to the postwar persistence of the rules governing extrajudicial killings by police agents. However, it is also important to recognize that the collapse of key aspects of the PNC reforms occurred not under Arzú, but following the rise of Portillo, who ushered in the reconsolidation of the wartime distributional coalition. Rather than have an independent effect on the survival of the conflict-era status quo, the manipulation of peacebuilding reforms and the reconstitution of the wartime distributional coalition worked in tandem.

This dynamic, for example, can be seen with the violation of peace provisions that the PNC and Ministry of the Interior be led by civilians – clauses violated with Portillo's naming of Barrientos in 2000 and Arévalo Lacs in 2001. Existing accounts indicate that the re-ascendance of the *Cofradía* military intelligence clique through formal and informal channels during Portillo's tenure led to the promotion of Barrientos and Arévalo Lacs, key members of the counterinsurgent elite, within the purportedly civilian security cabinet. This shift was thus driven by the reconsolidation of the wartime distributional coalition rather than the other way around. Though this sequencing does not diminish the salience of the alternative mechanisms under examination, it does illustrate how reform manipulation was deeply intertwined with the constellation of political and economic forces that again came to dominate in the early 2000s.

Similarly, my analysis of the postwar persistence of the extrajudicial killing procedures within the police illustrates that the second alternative mechanism – the persistence of collective beliefs that render the wartime rules legitimate – also finds some support. Perhaps the most salient observable implication of this alternative is the continuation of agents from the militarized, wartime PN within the ranks of the new PNC, which we find in this case. By staffing the new force with old agents, PN officers who may have come to understand extrajudicial violence as an appropriate means of defending the Guatemalan state from subversion and crime, "merely changed from military to civilian police uniforms, transferring their old tactics, doctrine, and institutional culture to the new institution."[65] In other words, the "recycling" of PN agents also facilitated the

---

[65] Cruz 2011: 15.

recycling of wartime cultural scripts and shared beliefs that deemed the undermining rules permissible.

While this may be the case, it is important to recognize how the extrajudicial killing procedures made manifest during and after the armed conflict were also more than the collective "common sense"; they were enforced externally by members of the security cabinet, who represented the different sectoral interests that comprised the wartime distributional coalition. For example, in the case of police killings in the mid-2000s during the Berger government, internal CICIG documentation indicates that the rules and procedures governing extrajudicial executions were enforced by what investigators deemed "a criminal organization."[66] Informants and witnesses allowed CICIG authorities to "establish the form in which the criminal structure operates and how Vielmann, Spiresen [sic], Soto Diéguez, Figueroa, and Victor Rivera managed the 'operations' and how they gave money in exchange for detaining and exterminating people" in cases like Pavón, El Infiernito, and the assassination of three Salvador members of the Central American Parliament in 2007.[67] Rather than simply the actions of lower-level PNC agents engaging in routine policing, the pattern of extrajudicial killings adhered to established rules and procedures that were communicated and implemented from above by political and security sector elites.

The persistence of cultural scripts authorizing the undermining rules does not preclude the central role played by the old counterinsurgent elite in structuring the extrajudicial killing procedures. If the PN officers that formed the new PNC were predisposed to abide by such rules because of shared beliefs of their "appropriateness," the reconsolidation of the wartime distributional coalition was also critical to ensuring they were implemented on the ground and were subsequently met with impunity.

CONCLUSION

In contrast to the preceding chapter, multiple modes of postwar institutional persistence played out within Guatemala's police apparatus. While the reconsolidation of the wartime distributional coalition under the Portillo government played a central role, the manipulation of reforms under Arzú – namely the "recycling" of PN agents into the new force – allowed for the militarization of domestic security and may have

---

[66] Qtd. in Fernández 2011: 382, 392.    [67] Ibid., 99.

sustained collective beliefs that extrajudicial violence constitutes "legitimate" police behavior. In this sense, the three mechanisms of institutional persistence interact, together contributing to the endurance of the alternative rules and procedures long after conflict's end.

Guatemala's police institutions also offer another important contrast with the customs apparatus discussed in Chapter 8. In the latter case, the wartime distributional coalition upheld the undermining rules largely by adapting to new semi- and extra-state spaces – political party channels and port concessions – created through tax and customs administration reforms. However, with respect to Guatemala's policing institutions, the reconsolidation of the wartime distributional coalition happened in a much more direct way, with members of the counterinsurgent elite occupying leadership posts within the security cabinet and the upper echelons of the PNC. This case thus speaks to a slightly varied pathway of postwar institutional persistence in which the sectoral interests with a stake in the wartime institutional landscape again ascend to positions of formal state power.

# 10

# Nicaragua

## *Chronic Instability in Postwar Institutions*

While the preceding chapters illustrate the conditions under which the undermining rules that develop in civil war persist beyond it, Nicaragua's land tenure institutions provide a stark contrast. Alternative procedures governing provisional titling, which had a dramatic effect on land insecurity, conflict, and corruption, became the prevailing institutional arrangements as FSLN leadership sought to peel peasant support away from the Contra insurgency (Chapter 6). Yet these procedures did not endure following the FSLN's 1990 electoral loss and the subsequent end of the Contra War. Though the redistributive gains were largely left intact, the wartime rules of the game were dismantled by the regularization campaign that took place at war's end under the center-right National Opposition Union (UNO), led by President Violeta Barrios de Chamorro (1990–1997). Despite persistent challenges, the new procedures for determining land and property ownership – in line with the administration's neoliberal orientation – legalized previously tenuous claims and provided restitution to previous owners. However, these new postwar institutional arrangements were again disrupted with the pact between subsequent Liberal president Arnoldo Alemán (1997–2002) and Daniel Ortega, eventually giving way to the second period of FSLN rule which saw pro-poor rural policies and large-scale land reconcentration in the hands of private developers.[1]

When it comes to the rules governing land tenure, postwar Nicaragua is best characterized as a case of chronic instability, "multiple, frequent,

---

[1] Ripoll 2018; Rocha 2019.

and connected episodes of disjunctive change."[2] Though chronic instability may be triggered by a number of factors, in this context, the "uncertain and rapidly shifting" distribution of political power in Nicaragua in the 1990s and mid-2000s prevented the wartime rules and procedures of land titling from taking root, instead fomenting "serial replacement."[3] These dynamics illuminate the post-conflict divergences between the Guatemalan cases elaborated in Chapters 8 and 9 and Nicaragua's contemporary institutional landscape. While the Guatemalan context witnessed the expansion and adaptation of the wartime distributional coalition, Nicaragua instead saw the repeated reconfiguration of political power, even within Ortega's second tenure (2007–present). The comparison thus illustrates that the postwar survival of the undermining rules is not inevitable, but instead a result of how wartime elites navigate transition.

This chapter traces how the disruption of the dominant wartime distributional coalition and subsequent elite political realignments upended the undermining rules governing land titling (see Table 10.1). After losing executive power in the 1990 elections, the FSLN retained considerable influence and successfully pressured the UNO government into compromise on key political issues, including securing redistributive gains; however, within the land and property sectors, a new decision-making coalition came to dominate – one comprised of UNO technocrats, US government agencies, and international civil society groups, as described in Chapter 7. As a result, new procedures to secure and formalize land acquisitions emerged. Though overlapping claims and conflicts persisted in the 1990s and 2000s, the old rules of the game structuring provisional titling were, in large part, dismantled. However, this US-aligned neoliberal coalition was again unsettled with the return of the FSLN to the political scene through a series of bargains with the ruling Liberal Party in the early 2000s. While championing the social and economic project of the revolutionary period, the second moment of FSLN governance beginning in 2007 ushered in distinct institutional arrangements – furthering both the reconcentration of land for large-scale extractive projects and targeted pro-poor rural policies.

The findings of this chapter are consistent with theoretical claims that property rights gaps are most likely to close with democratic transition and under foreign pressure.[4] Indeed, the Chamorro administration's

---

[2] Bernhard 2015: 977.    [3] Levitsky and Murillo 2013: 100.    [4] Albertus 2021.

TABLE 10.1 *Elite realignments in post-transition Nicaragua*

| Government | Dominant political coalition | Changes in land and property administration |
|---|---|---|
| Violeta Barrios de Chamorro – UNO (1990–1997) | Domestic and international neoliberal elite comprised of government technocrats, US government, US civil society organizations, IFIs | - Revision and formalization of agrarian reform titles issued previously<br>- Mechanisms to secure restitution for private property owners affected by agrarian reform<br>- Privatization of state-owned farms and enterprises |
| Arnoldo Alemán – PLC (1997–2002) | 1997–1998: Liberal elites and *confiscados* [landowners affected by FSLN-era confiscations]<br>1999–2001: Alemán-Ortega pact leads to realignment that privileges PLC and FSLN political elites | 1997–1998:<br>- Continuation of formalization campaign<br><br>1999–2001:<br>- Freezing of existing property cases; new tribunal that uses discretion to favor FSLN- and Alemán-allied property owners<br>- Cancellation of some agrarian reform titles in Managua<br>- Increased evictions |
| Enrique Bolaños – PLC (2002–2007) | PLC-FSLN elite alliance, despite attempts to diminish FSLN influence | - Continuation of policies under PLC-FSLN pact |
| Daniel Ortega – FSLN (2007-present) | 2007–2018: New FSLN-led coalition, with strategic alliances with business elite, Catholic Church, and mass organizations; co-optation of other political parties<br>2018–present: Narrowing of dominant coalition around personalist Ortega-Murillo regime and family | 2007–2018:<br>- Agrarian populist approach, with some social programs<br>- Titling of indigenous lands<br>- Re-concentration of land in hands of large landowners and commercial interests<br><br>2018–present:<br>- Land invasions and takeovers targeted at political opponents<br>- Government discretion over property seizures |

sweeping formalization campaign responded to outcry among insecure urban and rural land reform beneficiaries and economic elites. Moreover, the US government and international financial institutions tied critical postwar economic assistance to the implementation of a robust structural adjustment program that placed private property rights at the center (Chapter 7). But treating these titling and dispute resolution efforts as successful also obscures how subsequent elite realignments fomented continued instability. While the wartime rules of incomplete, provisional titling succumbed to foreign and democratic pressures, repeated shifts in the dominant political coalition beginning in the late 1990s generated significant volatility, as this chapter will show.

To demonstrate these claims, the chapter proceeds as follows. The next section examines postwar land conflict and insecurity in Nicaragua, illustrating the high levels of overlapping claims and the violence and restitution demands that accompanied them. Subsequently, the chapter assesses the immediate postwar reforms implemented by the new constellation of political and economic forces that emerged within the land and property sector, which were detailed in Chapter 7.

The next section explores how political realignments again upended land tenure institutions in the early 2000s, particularly as Daniel Ortega's FSLN brokered deals with Liberal leaders. Before concluding, the next section examines current land insecurity and conflict due to new institutional arrangements forged since Ortega's successful re-ascendance to the presidency in 2007. Here, I posit that Ortega's reconsolidation of power was, in part, driven by his efforts to broaden the coalition of sectoral interests with a stake in his political and institutional project, reflecting an important contrast relative to the first decade FSLN rule in the 1980s. Yet, these dynamics again disrupted land and property administration in ways that have fomented insecurity.

## POSTWAR LAND INSECURITY

As the decade-long Contra War drew to a close at the end of the 1980s, Nicaragua's land and property sector was in shambles. As the insurgent threat escalated, the Sandinista-led government took to remaking the land reform program by introducing alternatives rules governing the hasty reassignment and provisional titling of often unregistered lands (Chapter 6). Following the FSLN's 1990 electoral loss, which brought to power center-right UNO opposition leader and former JGRN member Violeta Barrios de Chamorro, it became clear that the vast majority of agrarian reform titles issued during the decade of Sandinista rule lacked formal and permanent legal backing.[5] But in addition to the hasty titling procedures, the undermining rules within land tenure had produced heightened land insecurity and costly restitution demands.

The proliferation of provisional titles, the failure to update regional and national land registries, and claims of property theft by previous occupants (who were often still listed as the legal landowners), generated high levels of tenure insecurity. Lacking firm legal backing, peasant families and agricultural workers lived in fear that their parcels would be reclassified as state lands and returned to their pre-Revolution owners.[6] These anxieties not only affected provisional titleholders, but tens of thousands of cooperative members and individual peasants with definitive titles that included errors or had no documentation at all. According to Stanfield, over 100,000 titles issued before 1990 contained a defect of some kind.[7] Even with Law 88, passed by the FSLN in 1990 to automatically formalize temporary titles, competing land claims persisted and exacerbated the already precarious situation of countless families. Over a decade after the transition, 83 percent of rural land claims were still pending or under appeal.[8]

Not surprisingly, land insecurity often erupted into violence. Arguing that "the state's acquisition of the rights to their land had happened under duress," previous landowners sought to forcibly reoccupy lands, while agrarian reform beneficiaries "reacted angrily to the threat of eviction."[9] When prior property owners did not stage takeovers, they often took advantage of the chaos and uncertainty to demand state compensation they said was never provided. By the mid-1990s, prior owners had filed some 16,000 claims related to contested properties.[10]

In the case of reassigned cooperative lands, conflicts often took the form of collective land seizures, which peaked in the early years of the UNO government with 220 occurring in 1991 and 162 in 1992, per

---

[5] IRAM 2000: 36.   [6] Ibid., 167.   [7] Stanfield 1995: 13.
[8] Broegaard 2005: 852.   [9] Stanfield 1995: 4–5.   [10] Dille 2012: 129.

police statistics.[11] Unfulfilled promises regarding the provision of land to ex-combatants, both former Contra and Sandinista fighters, only increased the violence associated with land conflicts in the early 1990s, particularly among those who resisted demobilization and transformed into criminal groups.[12] Additionally, at times, "farm invasions" by ex-combatants were "staged by indebted large farmers wanting to avoid foreclosure."[13]

In sum, though political violence had largely died down with the 1990 cessation of civil war,[14] conflict related to land claims and property ownership continued to wreak havoc throughout Nicaraguan territory, as regional and national land registries remained in shambles and restitution claims threatened to plunge the country into deeper economic crisis. Amid this volatile political landscape, how would the newly installed UNO government address the wartime institutional arrangements that had sown confusion and conflict? And to what extent would the new procedures within the land and property administration remain stable? The remainder of the chapter examines these questions.

### THE NEW RULES OF LAND ADMINISTRATION UNDER CHAMORRO

The 1990 electoral defeat of the FSLN at the hands of one-time JGRN member Violeta Barrios de Chamorro shocked both Nicaraguan society and the international community, ending a decade-long revolutionary period that had deteriorated under the strains of war and economic crisis. The UNO victory stirred hopes among the FSLN's most virulent domestic and international opponents that a new liberal democratic order might

---

[11] Cuadra Lira and Saldomando 2000: 26.    [12] Ibid., 17–24.

[13] Deininger and Chamorro 2002: 4.

[14] Despite the disarmament that took place, dissatisfied ex-combatants on both sides, who continued to live in poverty and did not receive the land and other benefits that were promised, again took up arms and waged protracted conflict between 1993 and 1997. The ex-Sandinista groups were known as *"re-compas"* and the ex-Contra groups were known as *"re-Contras."* See Kruijt 2011: 79; Cuadra Lira and Saldomando 2000; Williams 1994: 181–182. In some cases, it appears as though UNO coalition members and representatives of the organized business sector, through the Superior Council for Private Enterprise (COSEP), distributed arms to ex-Contra forces. See Williams 1994: 181.

emerge and that the confusion and conflict sown by the hasty, often politically motivated, redistribution of land might be resolved. Yet, the Chamorro government did not completely erode FSLN political influence, nor did it wholly erase the redistributive gains of the revolutionary period. However, the first postrevolutionary government did prompt a marked realignment of political forces and usher in a new decision-making coalition rooted in neoliberal orthodoxy, as described in Chapter 7. As a result, the previous undermining rules within land reform – the procedures governing provisional titling – were largely dismantled in favor of a new arrangements to formalize land ownership.

Following the UNO electoral victory, the incoming Chamorro government and outgoing FSLN leadership brokered a series of deals to secure the transition given the FSLN's continued political clout (Chapter 7). The compromise that perhaps had the widest effect within Nicaraguan society related to agrarian reform. While addressing the property dilemma was a top government priority, the Chamorro administration never envisioned undoing the redistributive gains made during the decade of Sandinista rule. Instead, as a means of maintaining peace and stability, the government primarily sought to resolve land disputes by offering compensation to pre-Revolution landowners when full restitution could not be achieved.

Within the UNO policy agenda issued before the election, Chamorro committed "to guarantee land for … a) those who have received titles for the use of land under the Sandinista agrarian reform and are in possession of land, [and] b) for those who have occupied lands, who will be converted into subjects of the agrarian reform, regardless of judicial decisions and the right to indemnity of the affected."[15] This approach was again echoed within the Protocol of Transition following UNO's electoral victory:

> We agree on the necessity of providing tranquility and juridical security to the Nicaraguan families that have benefitted from urban and rural properties by virtue of the assignations made by the state before February 25, 1990, harmonizing them with the legitimate rights that the Nicaraguans whose properties were affected have before the law … Forms of adequate compensation will be established for those who may be affected [*perjudicados*].

As part of this compromise, the UNO government permitted the *Piñata* laws – those hastily passed in the lame duck period between the 1990 election and the subsequent transition – to stand, providing legal backing to

---

[15] Lacayo 2005: 299.

the FSLN cadre accused of seizing properties for private benefit.[16] Though the failure to return lands to their pre-Revolution owners certainly generated conflict, the Chamorro administration calculated that, with roughly one-third of Nicaraguan territory affected by redistribution,[17] the risks posed by stripping peasant beneficiaries of newly acquired lands were far greater.

With the end of the Contra conflict, the new administration also sought to placate the tens of thousands of ex-combatants – RN fighters and EPS soldiers – whose demobilization was conditioned, in part, on promises of land. Though the provisions were left somewhat vague, the May 1990 Managua Declaration called for "giving priority to ex-Contras in the return of confiscated properties and for establishing 'development-poles' – that is, 'units of production defined for the benefit of the community and the country' – to satisfy the ex-Contras' material needs."[18] The government also vowed to recognize the land rights of a smaller group of former EPS officials that agreed to step down as part of transition-era agreements to reduce the size of the Nicaraguan military.[19]

Given the political weight of the various interest groups emerging from the revolutionary and conflict period, Chamorro-era land policies came to focus on four groups: (1) pre-Revolution owners whose lands had been confiscated improperly; (2) workers within state-owned enterprises that were soon to be privatized; (3) demobilized Contra combatants; and (4) demobilized soldiers from the EPS.[20] With such a wide variety of claims and claimants, the Chamorro administration faced enormous challenges in displacing the undermining rules in favor of a more streamlined and formalized series of institutional arrangements.

But even within this constrained policy space, the UNO government dramatically remade land tenure institutions – that is, the rules and procedures by which land ownership was validated and legalized – because of the new neoliberal interests that emerged dominant, as described in Chapter 7. The wartime undermining rules that governed the granting of provisional land titles were scrapped almost immediately in favor of new internationally backed procedures for regularizing property rights and resolving the disputes that dotted the Nicaraguan countryside. The institutional changes revolved around: (1) the revision and

---

[16] President Chamorro even vetoed legislation passed by the National Assembly to overturn Laws 85, 86, and 88, known collectively as the "*Piñata* laws." See Dille 2012: 125.
[17] Broegaard 2005: 852.    [18] Abu-Lughod 2000: 36.    [19] Ibid., 34, 48.
[20] Martí i Puig and Baumeister 2017: 386.

formalization of agrarian reform titles issued during the transition period; (2) the establishment of mechanisms to secure restitution for private property owners affected by the agrarian reform; and (3) the privatization of state-owned farms and enterprises, in line with the administration's orthodox neoliberal agenda and to compensate ex-RN and EPS combatants.[21]

To initiate the new titling procedures, the Chamorro administration issued Decree No. 35-91 to create the Office of Territorial Ordering (*Oficina de Ordenamiento Territorial*, OOT), whose primary purpose was to review the lands claimed under the *Piñata* laws passed in early 1990 and issue formal titles, or *solvencias*, to those who followed the rules for lodging land claims.[22] In order to do so, the OOT relied on provincial, inter-institutional commissions to investigate how the property in question was acquired and any denunciations lodged against those in possession of it. After collecting the documentation, the OOT then submitted it to a national commission to make the final determination about the granting of formal titles. If the national commission denied the formal title to the landholder on the basis of abuses discovered in the investigation process, the case would be remitted to the Attorney General's Office to pursue restitution through legal channels.[23] The approved *solvencias* would then be inscribed in the formal registries of the Nicaraguan Institute of Agrarian Reform (INRA), created in May 1990 as the overarching body tasked with "the direction and application of agrarian reform and rural development policy."[24] With the persistence of overlapping claims, the Chamorro government passed Law 209, the Law of Property Stability, in 1995 to expedite the resolution of disputes by strengthening recognition of land reform titles granted under the FSLN.[25]

Another set of new institutional procedures established soon after the transition facilitated the compensation of landowners who claimed their properties had been unjustly seized during FSLN rule. In September 1992, the Chamorro administration issued Decree No. 51-92 to launch the Office for the Quantification of Indemnities (OCI) "to determine the fair value of properties that could not be returned to their original owners for the purpose of compensation."[26] In conjunction with the National Review Commission (CNRC), the OCI established the process for

---

[21] IRAM 2000: 42–43.     [22] Dille 2012: 126.
[23] IRAM 2000: 47. According to research by Benjamin Dille (2012: 126), *solvencia*, or formal title, applications were denied in roughly half of the cases lodged.
[24] IRAM 2000: 48.     [25] Ibid.; Roche 2006: 598–599.     [26] Dille 2012: 127.

determining who was due compensation for previously seized lands and what they were owed.[27]

Finally, to provide a mechanism for privatizing state-owned enterprises and compensating ex-combatants, the Chamorro administration also created the General Board of National Public Sector Corporations (CORNAP) in May 1990. CORNAP was responsible for identifying the properties to be privatized, the beneficiaries of privatization, and the rental or purchase value of previous state-owned properties. The primary beneficiary groups of the privatization campaign were: (1) retired EPS officials who had been promised land to reduce the size of the army; (2) workers and officials in state-owned enterprises; (3) demobilized RN fighters; (4) the pre-Revolution property owners; and (5) private individuals and corporations who wished to purchase the property.[28]

The new titling procedures evolved significantly over the period of Chamorro administration reforms in the early and mid-1990s and went a long way toward closing the property rights gap opened during Sandinista rule. As economists Klaus Deininger and Juan Sebastián Chamorro describe, "while initially beneficiaries received only a title certificate which fell short of full legal proof of ownership, realization of the fact that these were deficient in many respects led subsequently to official instructions to give out only titles that had also been properly registered."[29] While implementation of these new postwar procedures faced clear limitations due to reduced personnel and resource shortages, they laid the groundwork for new institutional arrangements to take root within Nicaragua's land and property sector. As Trackman et al. noted in the late 1990s, "the real property registry in Nicaragua, after years of disuse, is now part of a much larger system of institutions dedicated to the regularization of land holdings, resolution of disputes relating to land, and inscription of property rights."[30]

According to various NGO and research institute reports, the new titling procedures made important progress in resolving land claims and regularizing tenure, particularly for the marginalized communities benefitted by the FSLN-led redistribution program in the 1980s. In the early 1990s, through executive intervention, the Chamorro government began the process of distributing some 268,000 *manzanas* (nearly 500,000 acres) grouped into 686 fincas, per IRAM.[31] According to Deininger and Chamorro, between 1992 and 2002, the Nicaraguan government

---

[27] Ibid.     [28] IRAM 2000: 43.     [29] Deininger and Chamorro 2002: 5.
[30] Trackman et al. 1999.     [31] IRAM 2000: 125.

had awarded over 40,000 legal titles, nearly completing the titling of the "reform sector."[32] Importantly, according to a 2000 survey conducted by the World Bank, the University of Wisconsin, and a local NGO, land regularization had a dramatic effect on investment and land values. The receipt of registered land titles increased land values by 30 percent, roughly equal to the value of appreciation over 20 years of continuous ownership.[33] Purchasing a plot under the new institutional order led to a 28-percent increase in land values, likely due to receipt of the necessary documentation to prove ownership.[34] Moreover, with tenure security came a roughly 9-percent increase in the propensity to make land-related investments.[35]

The new procedures, however, were not without serious limitations and shortcomings. The pressures for redistribution and formal titling created a situation in which "the land assignations and regularization of land tenure that continued in the 1990s often ... involved a mix of politically motivated decisions and decisions more in line with the long-term objectives of the ordering of property ownership."[36] Amid the privatization campaign of the early 1990s, several elite families successfully reasserted control over Nicaragua's export sector,[37] while, at the local level, municipal officials and politically connected residents engaged in land grabs similar to the *Piñata* tactics deployed by FSLN cadre prior to ceding power.[38] In other words, the new procedures were not immune from discretionary decision-making that favored regime insiders. In addition, a substantial number of overlapping land claims persisted even though the Chamorro government had spent $650 million on bond compensation for pre-Revolution landowners demanding restitution.[39] These disputes moved through the CNRC and court system at a crawl due to the weak judicial capacity and the backlog of cases.

Significant problems also remained for those beneficiaries of the 1980s land reform program seeking to secure their property claims. Despite the dent made in legalizing provisional titles, inconsistencies in titling and inscription for post-1990 land market transactions persisted, especially for poorer, small-scale farmers who lacked the funds to regularize their lands.[40] Even with legal title, many small producers continued to perceive that their claims remained tenuous, especially beneficiaries of collective

[32] Deininger and Chamorro 2002: 5.    [33] Ibid., 18.    [34] Ibid.    [35] Ibid., 15.
[36] IRAM 2000: 125.    [37] Everingham 2001: 71.    [38] Broegaard 2009: 161–165.
[39] Everingham 2001: 69; see also, Broegaard 2009: 156; IRAM 2000.
[40] Broegaard 2009: 159; Broegaard 2005.

land reform titles.[41] Due to this insecurity, "many peasant producers, agrarian reform beneficiaries, and demobilized people began to sell their lands at inordinately low prices," with large landholders in possession of capital and credit benefitting from the sales.[42] These dynamics, which were congruent with the Chamorro government's orthodox market-based approach, spurred a significant reconcentration of lands. By 1995, the "reformed sector" – properties still in the hands of their agrarian reform beneficiaries – had been reduced by some 22 percent.[43] For this reason, the first postwar decade is often referred to as the period of "counterreform."

Postwar changes to land tenure and administration under the Chamorro government faced the dual imperative of securing redistributive gains for agrarian reform beneficiaries and guaranteeing private property rights and compensation for pre-Revolution landowners, at the behest of the US government and international financial institutions. What emerged was a new neoliberal institutional order that displaced the hasty, tenuous titling of the wartime period. However, this disruption of the prevailing constellation of political and economic forces would not be the last. As the next section illustrates, the postwar political coalition would again be reshuffled during the subsequent administration of Arnoldo Alemán, who, in alliance with Daniel Ortega and the FSLN, pursued short-term gain at the expense of consolidating the new property regime.

### POLITICAL REALIGNMENT AND INSTABILITY UNDER THE ALEMÁN-ORTEGA PACT

The 1996 electoral contest to determine Chamorro's successor pitted the FSLN's Daniel Ortega against Managua mayor Arnoldo Alemán of the center-right Liberal Constitutionalist Party (PLC), which led an alliance of anti-Sandinista liberal parties. Amid the deep polarization left over from the 1980s, Ortega was a heavy underdog going into the October 1996 election. Despite Alemán's ultimate triumph with 51 percent of the vote, the FSLN managed to significantly close the gap, winning 36 National Assembly seats and demonstrating its continued political weight.[44]

In many ways, the Alemán administration promised the endurance of the political and economic project initiated under Chamorro. Alemán continued the agricultural modernization and formalization campaign

---

[41] Broegaard 2005: 860.    [42] Nygren 2004: 133.
[43] Pérez and Fréguin-Gresh 2014: 244.    [44] Walker 2003: 62.

began under his predecessor, expanding titling efforts to shore up the new private property regime.[45] He also maintained the Chamorro government's neoliberal view that "rural development is to be achieved through clarified property rights and increased productivity,"[46] spurring efforts to update land registries and formalize claims. At the same time, the new administration similarly recognized the need to maintain the FSLN's redistributive achievements, vowing to protect smallholders that benefitted under the agrarian reform of the 1980s.[47]

However, the Alemán administration also generated renewed hopes among those pre-Revolution landowners [*confiscados*] seeking the return of their confiscated properties, leading to an explosion of new claims and disputes. Disappointed by the accommodationist approach of Chamorro, *confiscados* saw the new government, particularly new vice president Enrique Bolaños (himself a victim of the FSLN expropriation campaign), as "a clear signal that past injustices would soon be corrected."[48] Miami-based Nicaraguans and US citizens were reinvigorated by Liberal indications that they would pursue complete compensation or full return for previously confiscated lands, triggering an organized legal campaign against the formalization of agrarian reform claims.[49]

On its face, the Alemán government's approach to the property question appeared as though it would continue stably down the course charted by Chamorro's technocratic team. Yet another moment of elite political realignment – the Alemán-Ortega pact – instead unsettled the post-conflict institutional order and ensured that "persistent conflict became embedded in official efforts to design a robust property regime."[50] As part of Ortega's efforts to acquire a greater FSLN foothold within state agencies and change constitutional provisions to improve his future electoral prospects, new rules and procedures within the land and property sectors exacerbated tenure insecurity among small landholders and stacked the deck against those seeking restitution for previous expropriations. As a result, the Alemán years, which again reshuffled the dominant decision-making coalition, further fueled chronic instability in the rules governing land titling.

As *confiscado* pressure ramped up, Alemán sought to negotiate a new property law to expedite the resolution of disputes, resulting in Law 278. Through further modification of the new legislation, the PLC government

---

[45] Boucher et al. 2005: 110; Nygren 2004: 133; Chamorro and Deininger 2002: 5.
[46] Nygren 2004: 133.    [47] Roche 2006: 599; Boucher et al. 2005: 110.
[48] Everingham 2001: 77.    [49] Ibid.    [50] Everingham 2001: 61–62.

sought to tighten conditions on FSLN beneficiaries that did not live up to the terms of their property acquisitions. While continuing to recognize agrarian reform titles,[51] the government's proposal would impose a more stringent timetable on debt payments and lease compliance, mandating that property owners in violation forfeit their titles.[52] These stipulations were largely "designed to honor [Alemán's] campaign promise to protect the poor while making those receiving larger properties pay."[53]

Yet the FSLN did not accede to the new demands without political concessions. Leveraging the property dilemma, Ortega and Alemán engaged in a series of informal negotiations, which would come to be known as "*el Pacto*" ["the Pact"]. In exchange for placating the *confiscado* backers of Alemán, Ortega brokered constitutional reforms that "modified legislative powers over the selection of magistrates, changed the eligibility criteria for the national and municipal elections of 2000, and required only 35 percent of the vote to win the presidential election of 2001."[54] The Pact further cemented FSLN-PLC control by granting "representation quotas" within three key institutions: the Comptroller General's Office, the Supreme Court, and Supreme Electoral Council.[55] The negotiations further altered the administration of justice to insulate both *caudillo* leaders from potential sanction for malfeasance, although once out of office Alemán was convicted for money laundering and embezzlement.[56]

The elite political realignment and the constitutional and legislative effects of the Pact upended the nascent postwar property regime, demonstrating how shifting coalitional configurations contributed to chronic instability. First, the increasingly politicized judiciary that emerged from the Pact exacerbated discretionary decision-making when it came to *confiscado* claims. Under Alemán's Law 278, existing property cases within the court system were frozen as the Supreme Court sought to establish new specialized property tribunals under the Office for Peaceful Settlement of Disputes (DIRAC).[57] Beyond exacerbating the backlog in cases, FSLN leadership, as part of the informal accord with the PLC,

[51] IRAM 2000: 51. It is important to note, however, that only those agrarian reform titles registered by INRA would be recognized, posing a challenge for small, poor beneficiaries who lacked the funds to see this formalization process through.
[52] Everingham 2001: 81; Roche 2006: 599–600.     [53] Dille 2012: 134.
[54] Everingham 2001: 81.     [55] Martí i Puig 2008: 83.
[56] The Supreme Court, stacked with FSLN loyalists, acquitted Alemán in 2009 under the second period of Ortega rule.
[57] Dille 2012: 145.

pushed for the inclusion of its affiliates as the arbitrators and judges within the new tribunals, ensuring that decisions would "favor entrenched interests," including FSLN and Alemán-allied property owners.[58] Rather than improve upon the Chamorro-era efforts to devise new dispute resolution mechanisms, the Ortega-Alemán alliance entrenched discretionary decision-making.

Amid the negotiations to protect regime insiders and FSLN elites, Law 278 also unsettled previous guarantees made to agrarian reform beneficiaries. For example, provisions within the legislation canceled agrarian reform titles within Managua's urban limits, even those that had been formalized within the property registry, making INRA responsible for resident resettlement.[59] The law also allowed for more recently settled urban poor to be evicted from their properties to facilitate city development.[60] In other words, institutional changes under Alemán not only disrupted avenues for resolving land disputes but made vulnerable the claims of those agrarian reform beneficiaries that had been subjects of the postwar regularization campaign.

In sum, while the Alemán administration pursued an ideological project very similar to the neoliberal consensus advanced under Chamorro, it also reshuffled the dominant political coalition in a way that disrupted the nascent institutional order within the land and property sector. Facing robust FSLN opposition and plagued by corruption, the Liberal government acceded to "rampant legal ambiguity" that fueled chronic instability.[61] As Everingham notes, "the willingness of the Liberal administration and the FSLN to use property rights as bargaining chips in the late 1990s indicates that the resolution of legitimate ownership hinged on short-term electoral advantage rather than on the long-term objective of institutional durability."[62]

## CAUDILLO RULE AND LAND INSECURITY DURING ORTEGA'S SECOND REIGN

The elite realignment that characterized the Pact not only disrupted the new property regime crafted in the early and mid-1990s, but also laid the legal, political, and institutional groundwork for Daniel Ortega's return to the presidency – and his sixteen-year second reign, which endures as of this writing. Following unsuccessful attempts to return to formal political

---

[58] Ibid.  [59] Castillo Martínez 1997.  [60] Ibid.  [61] Everingham 2001: 62.
[62] Ibid., 83.

power in 1996 and 2001, Ortega's deals with Alemán, which included
reducing the vote threshold to win the presidency, allowed him to reclaim
the executive branch, beating out Nicaraguan Liberal Alliance (ALN)
candidate Eduardo Montealegre with 38 percent of the vote in 2006.
Since his inauguration in early 2007, Ortega has maintained an increasingly authoritarian grip on the presidency through the incremental dismantling of institutional checks on executive power and a personalist
governance style reminiscent of the Somoza dynasty.[63]

The decision-making coalition Ortega marshaled in the lead-up to and
since the 2006 election stands as a stark contrast to his earlier alliance
during the Contra War. On the one hand, Ortega and the FSLN have
pursued pro-poor policies aimed at strengthening the social safety net for
Nicaragua's most vulnerable sectors. Yet, on the other hand, Ortega has
deliberately sought to forge the broader, elite-based distributional coalition the FSLN lacked in the 1980s. In addition to courting historic
enemies within the leadership of the Catholic Church and former
Contra forces, Ortega built strong ties with Nicaragua's traditional business class, perhaps some of the greatest antagonists to the prior revolutionary project.[64] In doing so, Ortega continued the export-led, neoliberal
policies of his predecessors, fomenting insecurity among urban residents
and rural peasants whose lands are coveted for large-scale development
projects. Moreover, since the administration's brutal crackdown on political dissent and the subsequent defection of the private sector in mid-
2018, politically motivated land takeovers have further disrupted the
institutional order within the land and property administration. Despite
Ortega's stranglehold on political power, his second tenure has spurred
continued chronic instability even three decades since the end of the
Contra War.

Upon his return to the presidency, Ortega, often invoking the revolutionary project of the 1980s, promoted a pro-rural, pro-poor policy
discourse, "claiming a general support for agricultural and food related
livelihoods."[65] Indeed, as Ripoll notes, government-drafted national production plans have championed small-scale, family-based agricultural
producers and sought to combat poverty in the Nicaraguan countryside.[66] Among the pro-poor policies implemented in the early years of
Ortega's second rule was the *Hambre Cero* [Zero Hunger] program,
which distributed domestic animals to rural families on small plots of

---

[63] See Thaler 2017.     [64] See Martí i Puig and Baumeister 2017; Spalding 2017.
[65] Ripoll 2018: 9.     [66] Ibid.

land and provided technical assistance to diversify agricultural production.[67] Other programs such as *Usura Cero* [Zero Usury] have provided
microcredit to support small businessowners, largely women. Many of
these social and agricultural programs are administered by local community organizations first known as the Citizens' Power Councils (CPC) and
later the Family Offices (GF) – organs controlled by Ortega's wife and
current vice president Rosario Murillo, who is accused of utilizing them
for partisan purposes.[68] Despite the clientelist nature of the regime's
"assistentialist" initiatives, pro-poor social and economic policies have
had a measurable effect on rural livelihoods, reducing rural poverty from
76 to 59 percent between 1993 and 2015.[69]

Renewed efforts to secure and formalize land titles for indigenous
communities on the Caribbean coast also emerged during the early years
of Ortega's return. With the 2003 passage of a new Demarcation Law (Law
445) under Ortega's predecessor Enrique Bolaños, the newly created
National Demarcation and Titling Commission (CONADETI) was tasked
with securing collective land titles for more than 20 Indigenous Territorial
Governments (GTIs) and thus making good on the Autonomy Statute
passed under the first period of FSLN rule in 1987.[70] Despite its slow start,
the initial years of Ortega's second tenure witnessed "the titling of 15 indigenous and ethnic territories covering 22,000 square kilometers."[71]
Though the resource-strapped CONADETI failed to resolve the numerous
conflicts in the Caribbean Coast Autonomous Region (RAAN), significant
headway was made through collaboration with communal authorities and
local villages.[72]

But despite this approach, the second Ortega government undercut
many of the social and economic benefits of its pro-poor policies by
pursuing a robust alliance with Nicaragua's private sector elite and maintaining the export-led neoliberal approach of its predecessors. After jettisoning economic elite support in the early 1980s, Ortega's second tenure
again instantiated the corporatist model of the early JGRN, only this time
treating the organized private sector as a *de facto* governing partner.
Perhaps reflecting the process of political learning following the
1990 electoral loss, the post-2006 consolidation of Ortega's rule relied
on forging a broader distributional coalition of economic powerholders
that stood to gain through the prevailing institutional order.

---

[67] Martí i Puig and Baumeister 2017: 392.    [68] Ibid.    [69] Ibid., 393–394.
[70] Finley-Brook 2016: 338.    [71] Finley-Brook 2012: 395.
[72] Finley-Brook 2016: 344–345.

Following the FSLN's return, Nicaragua's wealthiest businessman and first billionaire Carlos Pellas characterized the ties between Ortega and the private sector elite as an "alliance entailing a unity of purpose … in a political effort for development and [creating] confidence in the business sector."[73] Until 2018, the Ortega regime treated the organized business sector, through its main representative entity COSEP, as a "parallel authority and space of dialogue that has substituted formal legal institutions," in the words of one economist.[74] Another interviewee for this project went even further in describing COSEP's president José Adán Aguerri as the "corporatist operator" and the Ortega government's "prime minister" at the time.[75] The second FSLN government has also been characterized by "the weakening of the producer organizations created by the FSLN during the Revolution, and the limited capacity of peasants and wage workers to organize nationally to demand economic measures that are more favorable to them."[76]

Most indications suggest that this distinct constellation of elite interests had an important effect on property rights, eroding both the redistributive gains of the 1980s and the formalization process undertaken in the postwar years. As Kai Thaler notes, the new governing alliance "has worked well both for the preexisting elite and for crony capitalists associated with Ortega: Nicaragua's economic growth has primarily benefited few, with a huge increase in multimillionaires since 2010 in what remains the Americas' second-poorest country."[77] Nicaragua has also continued to see a substantial reconcentration of land into the hands of large agricultural producers. These distributive dynamics have been accompanied by the discriminatory provision of credit and technical assistance in favor of the largest landholders with limited access for medium and small farmers.[78] Moreover, new extractive industries and development projects, such as the Chinese-financed Inter-Oceanic Canal, threaten further displacement of rural communities vulnerable to expropriation or environmental devastation. As researcher José Luis Rocha notes, the continued "counterreform" under the second Ortega administration created "a perverse symmetry with the reform of the 1980s: while in the past the process of granting land was accelerated for military reasons, here the expropriations would be carried out for economic reasons."[79]

---

[73] Qtd. in Thaler 2017: 163.      [74] Interview with author, January 13, 2017.
[75] Interview with author, December 15, 2016.
[76] Martí i Puig and Baumeister 2017: 394.      [77] Thaler 2017: 163.
[78] Ripoll 2018: 9–10.      [79] Rocha 2019: 123.

Similarly, the acceleration of community GTI titling from 2008 to 2010 has been undercut by continued land grabs either tacitly or overtly supported by the Ortega regime. Evidence from Nicaragua's coastal indigenous territories suggests that improvements in the formalization and registration of communal lands have suffered under the second FSLN administration, which has overseen "the domestication of regional autonomy to a neoliberal capitalist accumulation model."[80] Despite continuing the provision of community titles to indigenous and Afro-descendent communities in the RAAN, the process of "clearing" titled territory – registering and demarcating land plots and removing illegal occupants – has languished, provoking continued conflict and insecurity.[81]

Despite the Ortega regime's early efforts to garner the buy-in of Nicaragua's economic elite families, the Spring 2018 government crackdown following protests against a proposed pension reform prompted the defection of the organized private sector from the dominant political coalition, again destabilizing the prevailing constellation of political and economic forces. On May 30, 2018, Pellas publicly declared that the political model that had shaped the country under Ortega in recent years "had been exhausted," while, around the same time, COSEP leader José Adán Aguerri stated that the organized private sector had removed itself from "the spaces it had occupied [within public institutions]."[82]

This latest elite realignment has entailed even greater instability within land tenure. While the Ortega government has yet to make good on its threats to rollback tax cuts and credits in the aftermath of the private sector's defection,[83] there is growing evidence that the dissolution of the previous political coalition and Ortega's waning popular support has triggered a series of politically motivated land takeovers targeting regime opponents. According to the National Union of Nicaraguan Producers (UPANIC),[84] the latter half of 2018 saw the invasion of nearly 11,000 acres of land in seven departments in the country's central highlands and along the Pacific Coast.[85] The targeted nature of the takeovers and the failure of state security forces to respond have signaled to observers that they are retaliatory acts that "are directed and correspond to the

---

[80] González 2018: 78.     [81] Ibid., 79–80.

[82] Conectas 2021. Aguerri was imprisoned by the Ortega-Murillo regime in June 2021 following his vocal opposition to government repression.

[83] Ibid.

[84] UPANIC was also a vocal critic of the first FSLN government beginning in the early 1980s.

[85] Salazar 2018.

government's intention to create chaos."[86] In the words of UPANIC president Michael Healy,[87] "what's being invaded are the best properties, the best lands, the most expensive, and this creates alarm within the productive sector.... This is another direct repression against the private sector because it is united with the people, fighting for democratization and justice."[88] The reconfiguration of the dominant political coalition following the 2018 crackdown has again sown instability within Nicaragua's property sector, as an increasingly personalist authoritarian regime substitutes discretion and politicization for secure property rights.

## CONCLUSION

Through analyzing the postwar transformations within Nicaragua's land tenure institutions, this chapter further illustrates the critical role of coalitional dynamics in facilitating the endurance or instability of undermining rules that evolve in wartime settings. Within Nicaragua's land and property sector, the early 1990s emergence of a new constellation of political and economic elite interests, namely, UNO technocrats, US government agencies, and international financial institutions and development organizations, initially played a critical role in dismantling the provisional titling procedures that subverted land security. Yet, subsequent shifts in elite political alignments fomented the continued disruption of the postwar institutional order, generating chronic instability.

The creation of this new postwar coalition did not simply amount to political turnover following the FSLN's 1990 electoral defeat. The Sandinista's bureaucratic reach and popular support ensured that it retained political influence even while permitting transition. However, following the compromise that allowed the so-called *Piñata* laws to remain on the books, Sandinista influence gave way to a new technocratic alliance that carried out dispute resolution and restitution processes, advanced formal titling, and remade the land registry, effectively undoing the wartime rules that had sown insecurity and conflict during the previous decade.

Yet these transformations did not last into the late 1990s and 2000s, as elite political realignments embedded conflict and instability within land

---

[86] Olivares 2018.

[87] Healy was also arrested by the Ortega-Murillo regime in 2021 and was sentenced to thirteen years in prison in mid-2022 for "damaging national integrity." See Medrano 2022.

[88] Olivares 2018.

tenure institutions and generated new property rights gaps. The Liberal government of Arnoldo Alemán struck a series of informal accords with Ortega that facilitated FSLN political interference in resolving land claims and fomented insecurity for small property owners, including agrarian reform beneficiaries. Ortega's return to the presidency in 2007 brought further contradictions, mixing some pro-poor policies with efforts to court the organized private sector and further private development and natural resource extraction. This approach undercut the tenure security of rural peasants and indigenous communities vulnerable to expropriation and environmental devastation. Moreover, the early 2018 dissolution of the Ortega-COSEP alliance further destabilized property institutions, as politically motivated land invasions escalated.

This analysis of Nicaragua's postwar land tenure institutions helps advance two key claims about the nature of postwar institutional survival. First, when compared with the Guatemalan cases in Chapters 8 and 9, the Nicaraguan context illustrates how the postwar institutional landscape is shaped by the ability of the wartime distributional coalition to adapt to peace and transition and continue to uphold the conflict-era rules of the game. As the 1990 election ushered in a new decision-making coalition, the FSLN, while maintaining its grassroots appeal, was unable to sustain the narrow vanguard that ruled in the 1980s. By contrast, Guatemala's counterinsurgent coalition forged a broader alliance of sectoral interests as a means of surviving transition and postwar reform. It therefore ensured that an array of political and economic blocs with a stake in the undermining rules remained in positions to uphold them.

Second, Nicaragua's post-conflict landscape illustrates that even when the wartime distributional coalition does not remain completely intact, conflict-era political interests can generate significant institutional instability as they jockey to retain influence. At first glance, the Nicaraguan case might be seen as one of institutional breakdown following the FSLN's ouster; however, this assessment misses the chronic instability – the "multiple, frequent, and connected episodes of disjunctive change"[89] – that lasted for decades and continues to characterize Nicaragua's property rights regime. Rather than just the dissolution of the wartime rules of the game, Nicaragua's frequent postwar political realignments have also prevented new rules and procedures from consolidating in their stead.

[89] Bernhard 2015: 977.

# 11

# Conclusion

## *The Institutional Legacies of Civil War*

Across the globe, civil war has taken a tremendous toll, not only on the individuals and communities directly affected by violence but on entire societies living under the scourge of conflict. Armed conflict claims generations of parents, children, siblings, spouses, political leaders, workers, teachers, thinkers, artists, and activists. It can have profound, sometimes intergenerational, traumatic effects for those who experience it. Civil war forces families to cope with the absence of loved ones and the household economic losses that accompany their absence. It can induce mistrust and fragmentation as victims and perpetrators continue to live side by side. It can decimate meaningful religious sites and disrupt long-standing cultural practices. It can set health, education, and human development back decades.

Scholars, policymakers, and activists have dedicated their lives and careers to understanding and illuminating the untold human consequences of internal armed conflict – sometimes at the risk of great personal peril. But while we have learned much about the human costs of civil war, we still only have a limited grasp of what conflict leaves behind in another sense: its institutional toll. The perceived threats, existential fears, and emergency actions that permeate wartime environments not only prompt state security forces to kill, torture, maim, detain, disappear, and massacre; they also spur elites to remake the foundations of the state itself – the very rules and procedures that structure state activities and behavior. Sometimes those institutional innovations reshape the state for the better, strengthening security, welfare, and administrative efficiency. Yet often, the institutional consequences of civil war have perverse effects on the state apparatus, undermining political and economic development goals.

240

This book has illuminated these institutional legacies of civil war in a regional context where they continue to have profound and pernicious consequences: Central America. During the latter half of the twentieth century, Guatemala, El Salvador, and Nicaragua were embroiled in brutal armed conflicts, which, combined, claimed some 350,000 lives and displaced tens of millions more. But beyond the staggering human toll of these Cold War-era conflicts, Central America continues to confront the serious, long-standing consequences of war for state institutions. Today, Central America's institutional landscape is rife with alternative, often predatory, rules of the game that distort the ability of state agencies to perform routine functions like tax collection and public goods provision. Save for a few isolated pockets of institutional effectiveness, corruption and criminality have become the region's "operating system" – the rule rather than the exception.[1] While the drivers of state-based criminality in Central America are manifold and complex, wartime institutional changes played a critical role in shaping the region's dire political reality today.

The first big question this book has tackled is how armed conflict shapes state development. It offered a new theory of how civil war dynamics and processes breed and consolidate pernicious institutional procedures that subvert state functions – what I conceptualize as undermining rules. As the perceived escalation of insurgent threat unsettles the institutional landscape, existing or newly empowered counterinsurgent elites remake the rules governing state activities. Military leaders entrusted to wage counterinsurgency possess greater capacities for coercion due to new combat and surveillance technologies and the militarization of society. Moreover, the specter of a serious internal threat facilitates greater operational latitude and discretion, allowing counterinsurgent leaders to penetrate and control key policy arenas. These dynamics allow political and military elites to devise and enforce new rules developed under the pretext of eradicating the enemy within.

The first half of the book illuminated the causal process underlying the wartime development of undermining rules within different state sectors across two distinct Central American conflict settings: Guatemala and Nicaragua. Amid Guatemala's right-wing military dictatorship, the Moreno Network, a criminal structure forged by military intelligence elites, institutionalized illicit procedures for capturing customs revenues

---

[1] Chayes 2017.

(Chapter 4). Meanwhile, at a prior moment of perceived threat escalation, counterinsurgency led to the enhanced autonomy and specialization of several elite investigative units within the National Police (PN). Through the fusion of these forces and privatized death squads, institutional procedures to eliminate political and social "undesirables" through extralegal means came to distort public security provision (Chapter 5). Similar dynamics of institutional change can also capture wartime developments within land reform, which is sometimes used as a counterinsurgent tool. In wartime Nicaragua, the growing territorial presence of the US-backed Contra insurgency led to a dramatic reorientation of the Sandinista's agrarian reform policies, prompting greater individual and provisional titling and undermining the state's ability to regulate land ownership (Chapter 6).

Placing these diverse cases into conversation with one another allows us to distill similar dynamics and causal processes that account for wartime transformations within state institutions broadly. These in-depth analyses also push us to reorient conversations on state formation away from a focus on war's "strengthening" or "weakening" effects and toward more nuanced approaches that capture the alternative institutional logics that distort state functioning amid the upheaval of conflict.

Beyond elaborating a new explanation for wartime institutional change, this book also extended its theory-building approach to another crucial question: Why do the undermining rules developed in conflict endure within and beyond it, often despite sweeping reforms? Here, I illustrated how institutional persistence also depends on the endurance and power of the political coalition underwriting the alternative rules of the game. By forging a broader array of sectoral interests with a stake in the wartime status quo, the undermining rules become consolidated and continue to systematically distort state activities. In postwar institutional contexts where the counterinsurgent coalition remains intact and continues to wield extraordinary influence (even on the margins of official government power), we can expect the prevailing institutional arrangements to endure as well. By contrast, when the wartime distributional coalition fails to adapt and repeated elite realignments render the distribution of power uncertain, conflict-era institutions experience chronic instability.

The latter half of the book illustrated these diverse postwar possibilities by contrasting the survival of the undermining rules in Guatemala's customs administration (Chapter 8) and policing institutions (Chapter 9) with the chronic instability within Nicaragua's land reform program

(Chapter 10). Though Guatemala's tax and policing institutions faced varying degrees of postwar reform, in both cases, the counterinsurgent coalition, which knitted together a broader set of political and economic allies, effectively adapted to peace and transition, upholding the fraudulent customs procedures and the rules governing extrajudicial killings. Post-conflict Nicaragua, however, faced frequent elite political realignments, which repeatedly upended the rules of the game within property ownership and titling.

Overall, this book offers a novel theory of how civil war subverts state development, focusing on the ways in which wartime institutional evolution and persistence remake the state apparatus during and after conflict. In the remainder of this chapter, I extend these theoretical insights in three ways. First, I explore the extent to which the causal process elaborated here might travel beyond irregular civil war settings and reflect processes of institutional change in other threat-laden environments. Second, I revisit the scope conditions laid out in Chapter 2 and discuss when we might observe the wartime emergence of state-bolstering or "reinforcing" rules, as well as whether different institutional logics can emerge in distinct policy arenas within the same state. Finally, I elaborate the broader theoretical, conceptual, and policy implications of this research. I focus particular attention on what this framework means for state development amid armed conflict, the relationship between the state and organized crime in war, the theory and practice of post-conflict reconstruction, and understandings of "the state" more broadly. My hope is that these insights and implications will enrich future research on the legacies of conflict, postwar reconstruction, and statebuilding.

## INSTITUTIONAL CHANGE BEYOND CIVIL WAR

Overall, this book envisioned the process of wartime institutional change elaborated throughout to apply to a subset of civil wars – irregular armed conflicts in which insurgent forces are perceived or constructed by rulers as a serious threat to the survival of the state. Beyond the nature of conflict itself, this book's claims about the creation of undermining rules are most likely to apply to civil wars waged by authoritarian governments, whether institutionalized military regimes or more traditional or personalist dictatorships. This is because authoritarian contexts often facilitate the bypassing of institutional channels of deliberation and the concentration of decision-making power in a narrow group of ruling elites. Finally, counterinsurgent elites are most likely to devise and implement undermining rules in institutional domains deemed vulnerable to insurgent penetration or critical to eliminating the rebel threat. This is because political and military leaders must use the pretext of curbing insurgent infiltration or eliminating the "internal enemy" to justify unsettling the prevailing order and introducing new wartime procedures. We are more likely to see this justification deployed in areas like police and intelligence services, the justice system, migration, and border and customs control, while policy domains like healthcare, education, and infrastructure are less likely to be sites of institutional innovation (though this will also depend on military interpretations and strategies).

But it is also possible that this book's theory of wartime institutional change generalizes to contexts well beyond irregular civil wars, including other threat-laden scenarios like foreign subversion and criminal conflict, as well as neighboring countries affected by transnational conflict dynamics. First, the processes of institutional change and persistence theorized in this book may travel beyond civil war to threat environments that trigger processes of "securitization." This book has argued that the primary impetus for wartime institutional change is the perceived escalation of the insurgent threat; however, it is plausible that other perceived threats operate in a similar way, creating greater institutional ambiguity and centralizing power and decision-making discretion. The construction of threat, of course, occurs in response to a wide range of situations, including foreign conflict, organized criminal violence, and crises such as climate change and migrant influxes – scenarios that foment securitization, or the "interrelated practices ... that bring threats into being" and necessitate "a customized policy ... to immediately block their development."[2]

Yet, at the same time, there are some non-civil war environments that may be more susceptible to the kinds of institutional changes elaborated in this project than others. The deep internal quality of the threat – its perceived locus within the state apparatus itself – is critical to the militarization of the state and the centralization of power that facilitates undermining rules. While this threat of state infiltration may be less salient amid traditional interstate wars, foreign subversion, or "the empowerment of third-party proxies – local non-state groups – with the aim of degrading the target state's authority over its territory,"[3] may be more prone to the wartime development of undermining rules in accordance with this book's theory. As Melissa Lee illustrates in cases

---

[2] Balzacq 2011: 3.    [3] Lee 2020: 8.

across South and Southeast Asia and the post-Soviet space, foreign subversion "[supports] alternative governing authorities and [erodes] domestic sovereignty," forcing state leaders to dedicate increased resources and devise new strategies to confront the internal proxies of the foreign sponsor.[4] Though such processes breed "weakened" forms of statehood in Lee's analysis, we can also imagine how they might provide justification for so-called states of exception and the unchecked empowerment of a narrow political and military elite, which devises new undermining rules within the state.

Beyond foreign subversion, we can also envision the institutionalization of undermining rules within another non-civil war threat context: state-criminal conflict. Organized criminal actors exert tremendous influence in politics worldwide, as groups ranging from transnational trafficking organizations to local gangs account for an increasing share of homicidal violence, not only in Latin America but in Asia and Europe as well.[5] To preserve an environment of impunity and sustain their illicit profits, such criminal organizations "must gain some level of state protection."[6] This necessitates their infiltration of the state apparatus through arrangements that may take the form of alliances, "cooperation between organized crime and the state for mutual benefit," or integration, when "organized crime gains access to political influence, information, and networks in their efforts to expand their illicit activities and defeat rivals while also avoiding law enforcement."[7]

While these dynamics of state-criminal cooperation have often been viewed as drivers and manifestations of state weakness, we can also imagine how the deep internal quality of organized criminal threats would trigger the centralization of decision-making discretion and operational latitude in a specialized group of security sector elites empowered to prosecute a "war" against criminality. Indeed, in contexts throughout Latin America, governments have forged specialized counter-narcotics and anti-kidnapping units within the police and military that have often been trained, equipped, and vetted by the United States as an antidote to criminal penetration of already compromised security forces.[8] We have seen similar patterns beyond Latin America in places like Nigeria, where the Special Anti-Robbery Squad (SARS) has been accused of torture and

---

[4] Ibid., 49.   [5] Barnes 2017: 969–970.   [6] Trejo and Ley 2020: 38.
[7] Barnes 2017: 976.
[8] Honduras' anti-organized crime response unit known as the TIGRES is one example. See Chayes 2017: 31.

extrajudicial execution,[9] and the Philippines, where President Rodrigo
Duterte (2016–2022) used the scepter of a "drug emergency" to deploy
police and military hit squads against poor, marginalized communities.[10]
In short, because of the perception that illicit groups seek to infiltrate and
co-opt state agencies, state-criminal conflict may well be another non-civil
war setting prone to the evolution of undermining rules.

In addition to these other threat-laden environments, there is also a
possible transnational extension of the theory elaborated in this book:
Can the perceived escalation of the insurgent threat within one civil war
context trigger similar processes of institutional change in a neighboring
country? In other words, can there be cross-border or regional diffusion
of the causal sequence described in this study? Given the growing recognition of the transnational dynamics of civil war,[11] this is a very important avenue for future research. The framework presented here, which
depends on the *construction* of threat or *perceptions* of threat escalation,
would suggest that cross-border spillover is indeed possible. When an
insurgency has developed a territorial base and network of support
beyond state borders, the perception of internal threat within a neighboring state may trigger similar processes of militarization and centralization
that breed undermining rules.

Given the regional scope of this project, one particularly fruitful country context in which to examine these transnational dynamics is
Honduras. Though Honduras did not experience its own civil war, it
was seen as a potential site of insurgent penetration and became an
important staging ground for US-backed counterinsurgent operations in
Central America.[12] In light of the predatory, undermining rules that have
come to define Honduras' political landscape,[13] it is worth examining the
extent to which these alternative institutional arrangements are rooted in
wartime transformations that occurred in the 1970s and 1980s. Such
analysis could illuminate critical transnational extensions of the causal
processes identified in this book.

## THEORIZING THE WARTIME EMERGENCE OF REINFORCING RULES AND STATE DIFFERENTIATION

In addition to whether this book's theoretical insights apply beyond civil
war contexts, this study begs two further questions: First, under what

---

[9] Amnesty International 2016.      [10] Human Rights Watch 2017: 31.
[11] See Checkel 2013.      [12] Schulz and Schulz 2018.      [13] See Chayes 2017.

conditions might we expect the wartime emergence of *reinforcing*, rather than undermining, rules that bolster state aims? And second, is it possible for counterinsurgent coalitions to differ across different policy arenas within the same state, leading to the wartime emergence of distinct institutional logics? In this section, I probe these two extensions of my study theoretically and by invoking brief case illustrations from Colombia's internal armed conflict as well as Nicaragua's Contra War.

As noted in Chapter 2, undermining rules may not be the only kind of institutional logic that emerges in the context of civil war. It is conceivable that processes of institutional creation within conflict can yield rules that are complementary in nature, producing substantive outcomes that converge with and bolster a given state aim. Though this book focuses chiefly on the evolution of undermining rules, what accounts for the introduction of reinforcing rules? The structure of the rules-making elite, I posit, is the key factor that differentiates the wartime emergence of undermining institutional logics from the development of reinforcing ones. The logic underlying this claim is similar to existing theoretical and empirical accounts of statebuilding within internal conflict. Slater, for example, argues that when the threat posed by violent internal contention is perceived by "a wide range of elites" as "endemic and unmanageable," they come together to form "protection pacts," or "broad elite coalitions" that consent to statebuilding.[14]

As with the introduction of undermining rules, I posit that the emergence of reinforcing rules also begins with the perceived escalation of the insurgent threat, which opens up an institutional gray zone and deepens the need to introduce new rules to address the heightened sense of state vulnerability. But rather than empowering a narrow, insulated counterinsurgent elite or further centralizing power in existing rulers, the perceived escalation of threat instead prompts state elites to draw together a broad-based coalition *to create the new rules*. The new rules thus emerge from a more expansive, deliberative process in which the interests of distinct and sometimes competing elites are represented. The broad-based nature of the rules-making coalition reduces the chance that any one faction crafts the rules for its own benefit or in ways that may directly undermine state functions. Having established a broad-based coalition in favor of the rules at the outset, the new reinforcing institutional arrangements are then reproduced through the gains they generate and the ability of coalition members to monitor their implementation.

---

[14] Slater 2010: 5–6; see also, Rodríguez-Franco 2016; Flores-Macías 2014.

We can see these differences play out through a brief examination of a case often cited as illustrative of civil war's statebuilding potential: Colombia's 2002 "Democratic Security Tax." In 2002, the Colombian government managed to do what has most often eluded its counterparts in Latin America and much of the developing world: enact a net wealth tax affecting the top 1 percent of the population.[15] The reform, known as the "Democratic Security Tax," was earmarked for security expenditures and came to represent 20 percent of the defense budget.[16] Though adopted by decree initially, Congressional legislation renewed the tax for three subsequent three-year periods, during which time it represented between 2.5 and 5 percent of government revenue. Additionally, the government undertook significant efforts to revamp the efficiency of the tax administration itself, implementing technological changes to combat evasion and triple the amount of revenue collected by the tax and customs administration (DIAN) between 2002 and 2012.[17]

The adoption of the new tax was driven by the escalation of Colombia's armed conflict, which had become particularly violent in the early 2000s. As Diana Rodríguez-Franco writes, "the wealth tax was introduced in Colombia when the rulers faced dire security conditions but lacked the resources to respond to the financial requirements of warfare."[18] Gustavo Flores-Macías similarly posits that the crisis "[forced] the government to take extraordinary measures to secure resources, including declaring a state of emergency."[19] But the deepening insurgent threat, while contributing to a climate propitious for institutional change, cannot fully explain the *kinds* of wartime institutions adopted. Rather, it is the broader nature of the dominant political coalition that best explains the development of reinforcing rules within the tax administration.

The new rules of the game that contributed to the Colombian state's extractive efforts were devised by a political coalition that went beyond state counterinsurgent elites. President Álvaro Uribe, the right-wing candidate who came to power with the backing of private sector leaders, had maintained robust linkages with the business community throughout his presidency, appointing prominent business leaders to key cabinet posts.[20]

---

[15] Flores-Macías 2014: 477–478.    [16] Ibid., 479.    [17] Rodríguez-Franco 2016: 204.
[18] Ibid., 198.    [19] Flores-Macías 2014: 484.
[20] Ibid., 489. As Rettberg (2007: 47–48) illustrates, these dynamics were quite distinct from the previous government of Andrés Pastrana, which witnessed a deterioration of business support for the attempted peace process.

Security gains following the adoption of the Democratic Security Tax consolidated private sector buy-in and reinforced government-business cohesion, allowing the subsequent renewal of the measure.

Not only did the solidarity of business elites contribute to the emergence of rules and procedures favorable for revenue extraction, but there were also mechanisms of accountability ensuring their participation was more than mere window-dressing. Notably, an "Ethics and Transparency Committee," which included "businessmen, academics, former ministers, the attorney general, and presidents of the main business associations, sought to periodically report on how revenue from the wealth tax was spent" and closely monitored military acquisitions.[21] The committee's oversight, in addition to the more general mechanisms of government-business dialogue and collaboration, ameliorated concerns that resources accrued through the tax were being diverted from efforts to strengthen security and falling into corrupt hands.[22] While acute internal security threats in Colombia provided the impetus for institutional change, rather than empower a narrow clique of military elites, it instead drew together a broader set of sectoral interests conducive to the emergence of reinforcing rules.

The 2002 creation of Colombia's net wealth tax, introduced initially through emergency wartime powers, demonstrates the crucial role of coalitional configurations in shaping the kinds of institutional logics that take root within the state. Unlike the Guatemalan and Nicaraguan cases detailed in Chapters 4 through 6, the Colombian case suggests that when the wartime political coalition empowered to introduce new rules incorporates a broader set of political and economic blocs and interests – when it includes offsetting forces – the resulting institutional arrangements are more likely to bolster, rather than subvert state functions.

Moreover, in focusing on the institutional level, this project also warrants discussion of whether the distinct coalitional structures that generate divergent institutional logics can take shape within the same state. In other words, can we imagine different kinds of wartime coalitions emerging within different state sectors, producing undermining and reinforcing rules in distinct policy arenas simultaneously?

While it is beyond the scope of this book to examine this question systematically, I conclude this section by offering some preliminary insights. In line with scholarly approaches that call for disaggregating

[21] Rodríguez-Franco 2016: 203.     [22] Flores-Macías 2014: 490.

the state, it is my contention that coalitional structures – and their attendant consequences for wartime institutional change – can, in fact, vary across policy arenas and across time within the same civil war context. We see this, for example, with Nicaragua's community- and prevention-oriented policing institutions, which, in contrast to the undermining rules within land tenure, bolstered state security objectives.

Following the 1979 Revolution, FSLN officials introduced new policing procedures that eschewed the excessive use of force and relied on robust community structures to control crime. The impetus for these distinct institutional arrangements was the broader, multi-sectoral rules-making coalition that came to power within the public security sector. This coalition encompassed local community governance associations, rural and urban labor organizations, and even the private sector, knitted together through corporatist linkages to the ruling regime. Of course, by the mid-1980s, the FSLN's National Directorate (DN) had sidelined many of these social and economic blocs and substantially narrowed the dominant political coalition (Chapter 3). Yet, even in the relatively short period of time, we can see how the diverse anti-Somoza coalition responsible for the revolutionary triumph also transformed the rules governing crime control in ways that bolstered the rule of law, at least initially.

The establishment of the Sandinista National Police occurred amid the void in security institutions in the aftermath of the July 1979 revolution. Rather than adapt or reform previous Somoza-era security forces like the National Guard (GN), FSLN leadership effected a clean break by removing GN officials from power and "[eradicating] all vestiges of the security apparatus of the old regime."[23] What emerged in the wake of the previous repressive institutions was a new force created from scratch and formally established as the Sandinista National Police through Decree 485 on August 9, 1980. The first Minister of the Interior overseeing its functions was DN member Tomás Borge. Former guerrilla commander René Vivas Lugo served as the police's first director-general.[24]

Despite their lack of experience, FSLN security officials eventually established new preventive and community-oriented security procedures that, in Deborah Yashar's words, solidified the image of the Sandinista Police as a "revolutionary and popular" institution rather than an institution of "domination."[25] According to those staffing the new force, agents were trained to see themselves as "of the community" rather

---

[23] Cruz 2011: 19.     [24] Sierakowski 2020: 26; McNeish et al. 2019: 9.
[25] Yashar 2018: 286.

than figures of authority that existed on a plane above ordinary Nicaraguans.[26] This institutional culture oriented police activities away from repression and toward the "prevention, neutralization, and solution of criminal acts."[27] Importantly, the preventive and community-oriented mentality not only informed the Sandinista Police's broader institutional culture and spirit – its *mística revolucionaria* [revolutionary mystique] – but the actual policing procedures that were implemented in the early 1980s. As Dammert and Malone explain, "Reformers emphasized the need to elaborate rules (and clearly explain them) to limit the use of violence, develop strategies to deter the excessive use of force, and strengthen preventive mechanisms for controlling crime."[28] In practice, these strategies not only focused on community-level investigation and intelligence-gathering to resolve crime, but encouraged police agents to work hand-in-hand with residents in cleaning streets and participating in community festivities to build trust in the institution.[29] Police corruption, ranging "from petty bribery to large-scale enrichment," was largely wiped out and sanctioned harshly when discovered.[30]

The new institutional arrangements that defined the Sandinista Police effectively bolstered crime prevention and the rule of law because of the tight linkages forged between the officers and local neighborhoods via community governance organs – features indicative of the broader, multi-sectoral alliance underlying Sandinista security institutions in the early revolutionary years. As Dammert and Malone note, "from its inception, the National Police included a network of institutions at the local level that would not only prevent crime but also exercise government presence."[31] Chief among these neighborhood-level institutions were the Sandinista Defense Committees (CDS) and the heads of sector [*jefes de sector*]. In addition to monitoring price controls and implementing mandatory conscription,[32] the CDS' most prominent local function was in the realm of crime prevention and social control. The CDS organized twenty-four-hour neighborhood patrols to prevent criminal activity.[33] They were also responsible for issuing residence cards that were critical to gaining access to services in one's home locality.[34] The so-called heads

---

[26] Van de Velde 2011: 53.   [27] Nuñez de Escorcia 1985: 22.
[28] Dammert and Malone 2020: 82.   [29] Van de Velde 2011: 53; Cruz 2011: 22.
[30] Sierakowski 2020: 27–28.   [31] Dammert and Malone 2020: 84.
[32] MIDINRA 1985a: 16–17.   [33] Sierakowski 2020: 28.
[34] MIDINRA 1985a: 16–17.

of sector were linked even more closely to the state security apparatus as designated "specialists in public neighborhood security."[35]

Combined, the local representatives and governance organizations allowed the Sandinista Police to develop a "social control system of unprecedented effectiveness,"[36] which succeeded in reducing crime and violence in the initial years of FSLN rule. Between 1981 and 1982, total reported criminal acts (homicide, murder, theft, and assault) declined by roughly 54 percent. The following year (1982–1983), the country registered an additional 20 percent drop.[37] During the same period, the proportion of reported crimes that were solved also experienced a steady increase from 44.7 percent in 1980 to 51.6 in 1981, 53.3 in 1982, and 71.5 in 1983.[38] Ex-officials and scholars alike link these changes in large part to the new community-based and prevention-oriented rules of policing and the unique procedures forged through neighborhood governance networks. As McNeish et al. argue, "[T]hrough these structures the national police were able to not only generate a strong contact with the local community but ensure the rapid exchange of information regarding crime and local development concerns. They also enabled the police to proactively identify particular threats at an earlier stage and efficiently intervene to prevent and remove these risks."[39]

How do we explain the contrast between the undermining rules governing provisional land titling and the reinforcing rules that limited the police's excessive use of force and contributed to crime prevention in Nicaragua? Importantly, the neighborhood CDS networks were crosscutting in nature, galvanizing middle- and working-class communities in crime prevention.[40] A continuation of the *Tercerista* faction's more pragmatic approach, these "broad-based fronts" pursued "the further incorporation of the bourgeoisie and middle classes."[41] By contrast, Nicaragua's land and property sector analyzed in Chapter 6 quickly succumbed to a more centralized and vertical structure imposed by DN leaders, which sidelined other sectoral interests. Though the police experienced similar shifts as counterinsurgency progressed, these initial contrasts between the public security and land administrations indicate the importance of recognizing the state apparatus – and the political coalitions that inhabit it – as varied and complex. Further elaborating when and why these coalitional structures vary across policy arenas is an important area of future research.

---

[35] McNeish et al. 2019: 9.    [36] Adam 1988: 9.    [37] Núñez de Escorcia 1985: 11–14.
[38] Ibid., 14.    [39] McNeish et al. 2019: 16–17.    [40] Adam 1988: 12.
[41] Chisholm 1991: 32, 35.

## BROADER IMPLICATIONS

By retraining our analytical lens on how wartime processes of institutional change shape state development in the longer term, this book also invites discussion of several broader takeaways related to war and post-war statebuilding, as well as how we understand, define, and evaluate "the state" more generally. I conclude by elaborating four key implications of this research, which I hope will guide scholars, policymakers, and practitioners moving forward. They include: (1) incorporating the central state into analyses of wartime institutions, (2) focusing renewed attention on the state-organized crime nexus within armed conflict, (3) rethinking conventional approaches to post-conflict reconstruction and reform, and (4) moving beyond "state weakness" to unpack the alternative logics by which states operate.

### Unpacking Wartime Institutional Change within the Central State

Over the past decade, scholars of conflict and post-conflict environments have increasingly brought into focus the institutional consequences of civil war, specifically those institutional innovations devised by rebel and paramilitary actors at the local level.[42] This study, however, illustrates the need to systematically consider the machinery of the central state, as it too is remade amid internal armed conflict. Doing so not only allows us to develop new insights into the effects of civil war on under-explored arenas of state activity, but also assess how wartime institutional changes might emanate from the center out.

Within studies of the micro-dynamics of conflict, divided sovereignty and territorial competition play a critical role in prompting armed actors to create new rules and procedures to control civilians and elicit compliance on the ground. Amid the complexity and fluidity of wartime environments, local institutions can help state, insurgent, and paramilitary actors regulate and channel behavior toward strategic ends. In some cases, such institutional innovations constitute novel mechanisms of political control in un- or under-governed territorial zones, while in others, they compete with already existing institutional structures at the local level. Overall, the upheaval and disruption of civil war can create space for new social and political orders – new rules of the game – to emerge.

[42] Arjona 2014, 2016; Ch et al. 2018.

By pulling back the curtain on the inner workings of the counter-insurgent state, we can identify similar dynamics within a distinct set of political domains: the institutions that structure state activity. Wartime institutional evolution not only occurs on the ground in conflict zones, but also within the central state apparatus itself, thereby reshaping the behavior of state elites – and their non-state allies. While understanding local institutional processes can help us identify the community-level consequences of conflict, civil war also affects a host of centrally administered institutional processes related to taxation, coercion, and public goods provision that take place on a plane above local politics. Moreover, such institutional changes may flow outward and shape the wartime rules of the game introduced at the subnational level. As conflict scholars continue to study the institutional legacies of civil war, we would do well to move beyond the narrow focus on local insurgent orders and retrain our analytical lens on the machinery of the central state as well.

## Rethinking the State-Organized Crime Nexus in War

Relatedly, this book urges scholars and policymakers to rethink the relationship between state institutions and organized criminal activity within armed conflict settings. While a large scholarly and policy literature examines how insurgent and paramilitary actors engage in profitable illicit activities to sustain their military organizations,[43] less attention has been focused on uncovering the nexus of the *state* and organized crime during wartime. In illuminating how armed conflict allows state leaders to devise and implement new predatory rules of the game, this book seeks to start a broader conversation about systematizing our understanding of state-based criminality in conflict zones. Such a research agenda might begin by delineating the different ways in which state actors and activities intersect with organized crime amid armed conflict. Here, I briefly elaborate three possible intersections: (1) state actors as criminal opportunists in conflict; (2) state organizations and symbols as legitimizing wartime criminal enterprises; and (3) state institutions as encompassing new rules and procedures authorizing criminal activities.

First, in the same way that rebel and paramilitary leaders wield their coercive capacities to profit from organized criminal activities, state leaders

---

[43] Collier 2000; Hazen 2013.

also take advantage of illicit wartime opportunities to accrue political and economic benefits – a dynamic we see in numerous conflict settings. For example, Mampilly demonstrates how the Sri Lankan conflict "resulted in new opportunities for corruption by reducing the accountability of the political leadership" and facilitating graft through military expenditures.[44] Similarly, in the Balkans, Serbian leader Slobodan Miloševic "nurtured a symbiotic relationship between the state and organized crime" in which military and government officials became "local war profiteers," controlling smuggling.[45] This wartime opportunism also recalls Will Reno's "shadow state," a model of political authority "constructed behind the façade of laws and government institutions" in which rulers "manipulate external actors' access to markets, both formal and clandestine, in such a way to enhance their power."[46] Overall, globalized conflict settings characterized by informal and fragmented transnational economies can provide state actors new opportunities to garner personal profits – a dynamic further fueled by wartime militarization and coercion.

But the role of powerful state actors in seizing illicit wartime economic opportunities is not the only manifestation of the state-organized crime nexus within conflict contexts. More than an assemblage of actors and organizations, the state is also "an idea, deeply implanted in the minds of its citizens,"[47] a notion that is "projected, purveyed and variously believed in different societies at different times."[48] This ideational aspect lends the state "socio-political cohesion" and legitimacy that other political organizations lack.[49] This approach underlies another way in which the state-organized crime nexus manifests itself within armed conflict settings: states, as recognized actors on the global stage, provide wartime illicit activities a veneer of legality and legitimacy. The symbols of the state not only further organized criminal enterprises linked to state leaders and bureaucrats but provide cover for rebel groups engaged in war profiteering.

Rachel Sweet's analysis of state-rebel dynamics in the Democratic Republic of Congo illustrates how bureaucrats leverage state power to "market" state legitimacy to insurgent groups[50] and how rebels recur to state agencies to manufacture legitimacy and shield wartime transactions from legal scrutiny.[51] This coordinated legal veneer also aids firms engaged in illicit economic activities with armed groups because state certification and licensing provides plausible deniability regarding motive – "to be

---

[44] Mampilly 2011: 187.   [45] Andreas 2004: 44, 48.   [46] Reno 2000b: 434.
[47] Young 1988: 30–31.   [48] Abrams 1988: 82.   [49] Lemay-Hébert 2009: 21.
[50] Sweet 2020: 224.   [51] Sweet 2021.

considered illegitimate, firms must *knowingly* trade with rebels [emphasis included]."[52] Bart Klem illustrates similar dynamics in Sri Lanka, where a variety of actors appropriated "the state's insigne" to conjure "a sense of legitimacy and supremacy."[53] These examples illustrate a second way in which the state and organized crime intersect in armed conflict: the state as an ideational construct confers a veneer of legality on otherwise subterranean and illicit economic activities that flourish amid civil war.

A final way of conceptualizing the state-organized crime relationship in conflict is that laid out in this book: the emergence of new rules and procedures within state institutions that structure and sanction organized criminal activities. Though not all the cases detailed here involve illicit economic activities, a key takeaway from the Guatemalan context in particular is the way in which political and military leaders utilize the pretext of eliminating an internal enemy to remake the rules and procedures governing state activity itself. This dynamic goes beyond opportunism. State actors elevate wartime illicit activities for personal profit into institutional procedures – a process I term the "criminalization of the state."

The criminalization of the state refers to the refashioning of the rules governing state behavior to achieve illicit, often predatory aims.[54] At its core, the criminalization of the state is about institutions, not actors. Rather than the fusion of governmental and organized criminal actors or the penetration of the state by predatory elites to serve particularistic interests, it entails the remaking of the fabric of state governance itself – the development of alternative rules and procedures guided by perverse, often predatory logics. It reflects "the action of legal and illegal organizations, which, through illegal practices, seek modifications within the state to influence, among other things, the creation, interpretation, and application of the rules of the game and public policy ... to obtain lasting benefits."[55] While not solely the product of armed conflict, the criminalization of the state sheds light on the powerful and predatory logics that underlie state (mal)functioning in conflict and post-conflict contexts.

The above insights point to the need for renewed and systematic attention to the intersection of the state and illicit economies in civil

---

[52] Ibid., 1116.    [53] Klem 2013: 695.

[54] Bayart et al. (1999: 13–16; 96–97) defines the "criminalization of the state" as the rise of "parallel" circuits of power that fragment political authority and spread armed conflict. Meanwhile, Schlichte (2017: 112) conceptualizes it as characterized by "close linkages between 'underworlds' and political personnel." My usage here is somewhat distinct.

[55] Garay et al. 2008.

war. It is my hope that this book will contribute to building this research agenda and unpacking the diverse manifestations of the state-organized crime nexus within conflict and post-conflict environments.

### Reimagining Post-Conflict Reconstruction and Reform

Beyond focusing greater attention on wartime institutional changes within the state, this book also holds important implications for approaches to post-conflict reconstruction and reform. At the broadest level, the findings here challenge a fundamental assumption inherent in both scholarly and policy conversations about postwar political imperatives: that the central objective of post-conflict environments is (or ought to be) rebuilding state institutions. As discussed in the Introduction, scholars have treated post-war state reconstruction as a critical antidote to civil war relapse. Once initiated, civil war is thought to drive further institutional deterioration as contestation over territorial control increases and state investment in public goods provision wanes. By constructing robust state institutions following conflict, international and domestic actors can enhance government legitimacy, effectively monopolize the use of force, and ameliorate grievances that threaten to exacerbate violence. Building the state anew has, therefore, become a taken-for-granted policy recommendation for addressing the numerous social, political, and economic challenges found in postwar settings.

This focus on rebuilding state institutions, however, rests on a fundamental, yet flawed assumption: that postwar states are blank slates upon which new institutions can simply be refashioned or built anew. Viewed through the analytical lens put forward in this book, such an assumption overlooks what civil war leaves behind in an institutional sense – the ways in which the postwar political landscape is already populated by myriad institutional formations that continue to shape development and state functioning. Rather than blank slates, the postwar state apparatus reflects a constellation of complex rules and procedures often created or reshaped by conflict processes themselves. Therefore, understanding the varied logics that drive state institutions emerging from conflict ought to precede the one-size-fits-all prescription to "rebuild" the state.

This book instead suggests that postwar policy agendas must focus just as much attention on *unmaking* predatory wartime institutional arrangements as they do on *remaking* the scaffolding of the state. Where alternative rules and procedures that expressly contravene state administration have taken root, the first imperative of the postwar period may be a process of *deconstruction*. Drawing from the explanation of postwar institutional persistence elaborated in Chapter 2, dismantling wartime undermining rules requires dismantling the broader distributional coalition underwriting them – that is, the array of sectoral interests that accrue political and material benefits from their continued implementation and enforcement. Remaking the rules of the game is thus a matter of disrupting the dominant political coalition that maintains a vested interest in the wartime institutional order.

The members of this coalition do not belong exclusively to the formal state sphere, but also include non-state actors as I illustrate most clearly through the postwar persistence of Guatemala's customs fraud procedures (Chapter 8). Thus, in addition to moving away from simplistic, one-size-fits-all policy recommendations, post-conflict research must look beyond the rigid strictures of "the state" to understand why perverse wartime institutional arrangements endure beyond armed conflict. If a variety of private actors also "do well out of war,"[56] our analytical lens must be widened to better capture how these actors continue doing well *after* war too.

This is why, from a policy perspective, a comprehensive and coordinated approach that takes a birds-eye view of the post-conflict political and economic landscape is so critical. Implementing this kind of reform program is no easy feat in fragile, resource-strapped environments where wartime political and economic elites maintain power. Postwar governments would be hard-pressed to carry out this strategy on their own in the absence of international political, economic, and technical support through "shared sovereignty" arrangments or forms of "governance delegation."[57] But recent international experiences provide us some templates for what an integrated rule of law approach might look like.

The landmark UN-backed International Commission against Impunity in Guatemala, whose efforts to uncover the *La Línea* customs fraud scheme in 2015 opened this book, is one such template. Launched at the end of 2007, the CICIG, working hand-in-hand with the Public Prosecutor's Office (MP), investigated and prosecuted the "illegal security forces and clandestine security organizations" [*cuerpos ilegales y aparatos clandestinos de seguridad*, CIACS] that emerged from the armed conflict period and continued to engage in organized crime and human rights violations.[58] Particularly toward the end of the CICIG's decade-long

---

[56] Collier 1999.     [57] Ciorciari 2021; Matanock 2014.     [58] Schwartz 2021b.

period of operation, Commissioner Iván Velásquez (2014–2019) shifted the focus from tackling discrete high-profile corruption cases to illuminating the more complex "political-economic networks" that sought to institutionalize corruption within the Guatemalan state.[59] Though the CICIG's mandate ended under embattled Guatemalan president Jimmy Morales (2016–2020) at the end of 2019,[60] the Commission provides a model for post-conflict rule of law strategies that focus not just on prominent state officials in an isolated fashion, but instead integrate the political and economic spheres and target the broader distributional coalitions upholding the predatory rules of the game.

Guatemala's CICIG is not the only example. In Kosovo, the European Union launched a similar initiative known as EULEX (European Union Rule of Law Mission in Kosovo), whose mandate extends beyond the investigation and prosecution of war crimes to corruption, organized crime, and other financial crimes.[61] Liberia's experience with the Governance and Economic Management Assistance Program (GEMAP) (2005–2010) and the Solomon Islands' Australian-backed Regional Assistance Mission (RAMSI) (2003–2017) are other illustrative examples. In the Liberian case, GEMAP addressed corruption and criminality while simultaneously mitigating financial mismanagement and strengthening institutions.[62] RAMSI, initiated in the wake of civil unrest known as "the Tensions," combined demobilization and disarmament efforts with initiatives to "end government corruption and extortion and stabilize government finance."[63] While these experiments in hybrid governance are far from perfect, they reflect a much-needed turn from a narrow, state-centered approach that overlooks the multisectoral character of the war-time coalitions seeking to preserve the undermining rules into regime transition and peace.

## Rethinking State "Weakness"

Finally, in rethinking how civil war shapes state development, this book challenged the dominant metric used to evaluate and classify states within political science: according to their "weakness" or "strength." Indeed,

---

[59] Ibid., 12.
[60] Morales himself was under investigation for receiving illicit campaign contributions, while his son and brother were under investigation for defrauding the state's property registry. For more on the struggle over the CICIG, see Schwartz 2019.
[61] Chivvis 2010.    [62] Hope 2010.    [63] Whalan 2010: 631.

state weakness (or strength) has come to constitute a core variable of interest in studies on a range of topics including armed conflict,[64] corruption,[65] public goods provision,[66] and democratic consolidation.[67] Yet conventional understandings of state strength and weakness provide a rather reductionist picture of the myriad logics by which state institutions operate. State capacity has, by and large, become synonymous with the concept of infrastructural power, or "the capacity to actually penetrate civil society, and to implement logistically political decisions throughout the realm."[68] In other words, "state weakness exists when a state *does not generally perform the tasks expected of it*" (emphasis included) – tasks like the extraction of tax revenue, the control of violence, and the administration of basic goods and services.[69] States that fail to meet this "neo-Weberian yardstick" are unable to do so because of their supposed "weakness."[70]

But the failure of state actors and organizations to implement and enforce routine policy decisions does not necessarily signal their *inability* to do so. Instead, what often looks like state weakness is the manifestation of alternative logics guiding state activities. For example, political actors may choose not to enforce rules and policies deliberately depending on their own electoral incentives and the broader social policy landscape.[71] Beyond deliberate enforcement decisions, phenomena that appear to be driven by state weakness may in fact represent any number of other institutional logics at work; far from constituting "a harbinger of [state] collapse," such alternative logics provide "a clue to their endurance."[72] For example, the complex, yet often stable relationships between the formal state sphere and "traditional" or "pre-state" political actors like chiefs and warlords may result in apparent deficiencies in state extraction, coercion, and administration, but are not necessarily the manifestation of some latent incapacity.[73] As Rebecca Tapscott describes in the Ugandan context, arbitrary regime decision-making is often "not a by-product of disorganization, ineptitude, poverty, or other shortcomings stereotypically characteristic of 'fragile' or 'low-capacity' states" but a strategic approach to sow unpredictability in the service of authoritarian rule.[74] Relatedly, the "internationalization of the state" – the robust engagement

---

[64] Sobek 2010; Thies 2005, 2006, 2010; Hendrix 2010; Fearon and Laitin 2003.
[65] Bersch et al. 2017; Geddes 1994.    [66] Rotberg 2004.    [67] Linz and Stepan 1996.
[68] Mann 1984: 189.    [69] Soifer 2015; Tilly 1975; Hanson and Sigman 2013.
[70] Beissinger 2017.    [71] Holland 2017.    [72] Heathershaw and Schatz 2017: 21.
[73] Ibid., 17; see also, Klyachkina 2019; Murtazashvili 2016; Mukhopadyay 2014.
[74] Tapscott 2021: 30.

of foreign governments and NGOs – presupposes forms of rule that are not weak, but altogether distinct because of the dynamics of international intervention.[75] Accordingly, this book pushes scholars and policymakers to rethink the core problem of post-civil war environments not as one of weak, absent, or defunct institutions, but of the often stable presence and operation of alternative logics – logics born in war – that distort policy-making and development in the long term.

The manifestations of these undermining logics are often not all that distinct from social, political, and economic outcomes in weak institutional settings in the developing world where corruption stymies the provision of healthcare and infrastructure, state-perpetrated violence claims lives in marginalized communities, wealthy individuals evade taxes unencumbered, and politicians regularly accept kickbacks in exchange for state contracts. What is different, however, is that these routine activities are not the product of absent or deficient controls, regulations, and enforcement mechanisms to prevent them, but instead reflect the presence of a distinct set of rules and procedures facilitating them. They are its "operating system," "built into the functioning of such countries' institutions."[76] In this sense, these undermining institutional logics are not synonymous with state weakness, nor are they an observable implication of the state's inability to carry out those tasks expected of it. They instead may reflect a highly durable reconfiguration of state power to achieve alternative ends often associated with institutional perversion. Moreover, such patterns of institutional development are not epiphenomenal to the individuals that dominate government decision-making in a given moment, instead often outlasting political turnover.

This book has reevaluated conventional approaches to state weakness and illuminated how they obscure the complex logics that underlie state behavior in many conflict and post-conflict contexts. This distinct approach to the wartime roots of state perversion is critical for capturing the numerous woes that plague institutions in the developing world. By digging beneath blunt indicators of state capacity and rote explanations premised on state weakness, we can shed light on the functioning of alternative, often subterranean, rules and procedures that abet state predation and undermine development. We can also rewrite conventional international policy agendas that view state weakness as the driver of instability, violence, and underdevelopment. The roots of these systemic

---

[75] Schlichte 2017.   [76] Chayes 2017: 3–4.

challenges may not necessarily be found in institutional decay and deficiency, but in those perverse and powerful rules of the game devised in the shadows of conflict and beyond. The central problem of the post-war state is not necessarily the feeble institutions most often portrayed by scholars and policymakers, but instead – and in the words of one former Guatemalan official – "rather effective institutions, but for the wrong reasons."[77]

---

[77] Interview with author, June 23, 2015.

# Appendix
# List of Interviews and Archival Collections

## LIST OF INTERVIEWS

| Date | Interviewee | Location |
|------|-------------|----------|
| May 30, 2014 | Human rights activist | Guatemala City |
| June 4, 2014 | Human rights activist | Guatemala City |
| June 5, 2014 | Historian | Guatemala City |
| July 3, 2014 | Researcher and political commentator | Guatemala City |
| June 8, 2015 | Economist | Guatemala City |
| June 12, 2015 | Political consultant | Guatemala City |
| June 15, 2015 | Ministry of Foreign Affairs official | Guatemala City |
| June 15, 2015 | Former Ministry of Finance official | Guatemala City |
| June 15, 2015 | Researcher and political commentator | Guatemala City |
| June 16, 2015 | Historian | Guatemala City |
| June 17, 2015 | Security expert and Ministry of Foreign Affairs official | Guatemala City |
| June 17, 2015 | Journalist and politician | Guatemala City |
| June 18, 2015 | Consultant and political analyst | Guatemala City |
| June 18, 2015 | Academic | Guatemala City |
| June 19, 2015 | Indigenous rights activist | Guatemala City |
| June 23, 2015 | Security expert and former civilian intelligence official | Guatemala City |
| June 23, 2015 | Former Ministry of Foreign Affairs and executive official | Guatemala City |

*(continued)*

*(continued)*

| Date | Interviewee | Location |
|------|-------------|----------|
| June 24, 2015 | Criminal justice expert | Guatemala City |
| June 24, 2015 | Private sector representative | Guatemala City |
| June 25, 2015 | Anti-corruption activist | Guatemala City |
| June 25, 2015 | Human rights activist | Guatemala City |
| June 25, 2015 | Historian | Guatemala City |
| June 26, 2015 | Sociologist | Guatemala City |
| June 30, 2015 | Academic and security expert | Guatemala City |
| July 1, 2015 | Private sector leader | Guatemala City |
| July 1, 2015 | Security expert and human rights activist | Guatemala City |
| July 2, 2015 | Security and justice expert | Guatemala City |
| July 2, 2015 | Former Presidential Commission on Human Rights official | Guatemala City |
| July 2, 2015 | Security expert and academic | Guatemala City |
| July 3, 2015 | Corruption and justice expert | Guatemala City |
| July 6, 2015 | Retired military officer | Guatemala City |
| July 6, 2015 | Academic | Guatemala City |
| July 13, 2015 | Human rights activist | Guatemala City |
| July 15, 2015 | Retired military officer | Guatemala City |
| July 15, 2015 | Retired military intelligence officer | Guatemala City |
| July 16, 2015 | Investigative journalist | Guatemala City |
| July 17, 2015 | Military officer | Guatemala City |
| September 27, 2016 | Investigative journalist | Guatemala City |
| October 13, 2016 | Ministry of Finance employee | Guatemala City |
| October 21, 2016 | Former Ministry of Finance official | Guatemala City |
| October 26, 2016 | Retired military officer | Guatemala City |
| October 26, 2016 | Investigative journalist | Guatemala City |
| October 26, 2016 | Former insurgent leader | Guatemala City |
| October 26, 2016 | CICIG official | Guatemala City |
| October 27, 2016 | Retired military intelligence officer | Guatemala City |
| October 27, 2016 | Retired military intelligence officer | Guatemala City |
| October 27, 2016 | Investigative journalist | Guatemala City |
| November 7, 2016 | Retired military intelligence agent | Guatemala City |
| November 7, 2016 | Retired military officer | Guatemala City |
| November 8, 2016 | SAT official | Guatemala City |
| November 9, 2016 | Former prosecutor and SAT official | Guatemala City |
| December 15, 2016 | Journalist | Managua |
| December 16, 2016 | Former military advisor | Managua |
| January 4, 2017 | Former CICIG investigator | San José, Costa Rica |

| Date | Interviewee | Location |
|------|-------------|----------|
| January 12, 2017 | Lawyer | Managua |
| January 13, 2017 | Economist and private sector representative | Managua |
| January 13, 2017 | Security expert | Managua |
| January 17, 2017 | Economist | Managua |
| January 23, 2017 | Economist and agrarian expert | Managua |
| January 24, 2017 | Constitutional law expert | Managua |
| January 31, 2017 | Journalist and organized crime expert | Managua |
| March 1, 2017 | Former MIDINRA official | Managua |
| March 1, 2017 | Former military advisor | Managua |
| May 24, 2017 | Former Ministry of Finance official | Guatemala City |
| May 30, 2017 | Former Ministry of Finance official | Guatemala City |
| May 30, 2017 | Retired military officer | Guatemala City |
| May 30, 2017 | Retired military intelligence agent | Guatemala City |
| Mary 31, 2017 | Former SAT official | Guatemala City |
| June 2, 2017 | Former SAT and customs official | Guatemala City |
| June 7, 2017 | Security expert and former civilian intelligence official | Guatemala City |
| June 12, 2017 | Researcher and former Secretariat of Planning official | Guatemala City |
| June 12, 2017 | Former Ministry of Finance official | Guatemala City |
| June 13, 2017 | Economist | Guatemala City |
| June 15, 2017 | Economist | Guatemala City |
| June 16, 2017 | Former Ministry of Finance official | Guatemala City |
| June 23, 2017 | Peacebuilding expert and former Ministry of Foreign Affairs official | Guatemala City |
| October 9, 2017 | Human Rights Ombudsman's Office representative | Guatemala City |
| October 9, 2017 | Security expert and academic | Guatemala City |
| October 31, 2017 | Human rights activist | Guatemala City |
| November 3, 2017 | Academic | Guatemala City |
| November 15, 2017 | Former customs inspector | Guatemala City |
| November 15, 2017 | Former customs inspector and shipping company manager | Guatemala City |
| November 22, 2017 | Human rights activist | Guatemala City |

## ARCHIVAL COLLECTIONS

## Guatemala

| Collection | Archive | Location |
|---|---|---|
| Records of the National Police (PN), 1882–1997 | *Archivo Histórico de la Policía Nacional* (AHPN) | Guatemala City |
| Records of the Ministry of Finance, 1970s–1990s | Ministry of Finance | Guatemala City |
| Judicial records from case against Alfredo Moreno Molina, 1996–2010 | Archive of the *Organismo Judicial* (OJ) | Guatemala City |
| Recovery of Historical Memory (REMHI) | Archive of the *Oficina de Derechos Humanos del Arzobispado de Guatemala* (ODHAG) | Guatemala City |
| Archive of the *Estado Mayor Presidencial* (EMP) | *Archivo General de Centroamérica* (AGCA) | Guatemala City |
| Daily newspaper *El Gráfico*, 1980s and 1990s | *Hemeroteca Nacional* | Guatemala City |
| Daily newspaper *Prensa Libre*, 1980, 1993–1999 | *Hemeroteca Nacional* | Guatemala City |
| Daily newspaper *La República*, 1996 | *Hemeroteca Nacional* | Guatemala City |
| Daily newspaper *Siglo XXI*, 1992–1996 | *Hemeroteca Nacional* | Guatemala City |
| Daily newspaper *El Periódico*, 1997–2013 | *Hemeroteca Nacional* | Guatemala City |
| Weekly magazine *Crónica*, 1996 | *Hemeroteca Nacional* | Guatemala City |
| Serie *La Morgue* (newspaper clippings from daily *Imparcial*) | *Centro de Investigaciones Regionales de Mesoamérica* (CIRMA) | Antigua |
| Archive of *Inforpress Centroamericana* | *Centro de Investigaciones Regionales de Mesoamérica* (CIRMA) | Antigua |
| Serie Cartapacios (Finanzas Nacionales, Violencia en Guatemala), 1972–1982 | *Centro de Investigaciones Regionales de Mesoamérica* (CIRMA) | Antigua |
| *Diario Oficial de Guatemala*, 1979–1982 | *Centro de Investigaciones Regionales de Mesoamérica* (CIRMA) | Antigua |

| Collection | Archive | Location |
|---|---|---|
| Serie Diario *El Gráfico* (Ministerio de Defensa, Ministerio de Finanzas, Contrabando y Robos), 1968–1998 | *Centro de Investigaciones Regionales de Mesoamérica* (CIRMA) | Antigua |
| Archive of the *Comité Holandés de Solidaridad con Guatemala*, 1980–1982 | *Centro de Investigaciones Regionales de Mesoamérica* (CIRMA) | Antigua |
| Collection of Amnesty International publications, 1979 | *Centro de Investigaciones Regionales de Mesoamérica* (CIRMA) | Antigua |
| General Documents Collection | *Centro de Investigaciones Regionales de Mesoamérica* (CIRMA) | Antigua |
| Guillermo Paz Cárcomo Collection | *Centro de Investigaciones Regionales de Mesoamérica* (CIRMA) | Antigua |
| Archive of the *Coordinadora Alemana de Solidaridad con Guatemala* (Ayuda Policía Nacional, Contrainsurgencia) | *Centro de Investigaciones Regionales de Mesoamérica* (CIRMA) | Antigua |
| Thelma Porres Collection | *Centro de Investigaciones Regionales de Mesoamérica* (CIRMA) | Antigua |
| Alba Amanda Pedroza Collection | *Centro de Investigaciones Regionales de Mesoamérica* (CIRMA) | Antigua |
| Robert Trudeau Collection | *Centro de Investigaciones Regionales de Mesoamérica* (CIRMA) | Antigua |
| Guatemala and the United States | Digital National Security Archive | Washington, DC and Online |

## Nicaragua

| Collection | Archive | Location |
|---|---|---|
| IHCA Collection | *Instituto de Historia de Nicaragua y Centroamérica* (IHNCA) | Managua |
| IHNCA Collection | *Instituto de Historia de Nicaragua y Centroamérica* (IHNCA) | Managua |
| *Memoria Centroamericana* | *Instituto de Historia de Nicaragua y Centroamérica* (IHNCA) | Managua |
| Archives of the *Centro de Investigaciones y Estudios de la Reforma Agraria* (CIERA), MIDINRA, 1980–1988 | Digital Library "Reforma agraria y transformaciones en el sector agropecuario en Nicaragua, (1979–2015) | Online (no longer available) |
| Archives of the *Dirección General de Fomento Campesino y Reforma Agraria* (DGFCRA), MIDINRA, 1979–1987 | Digital Library "Reforma agraria y transformaciones en el sector agropecuario en Nicaragua, (1979–2015) | Online (no longer available) |
| Collection *Orlando Núñez Soto*, 1978–2015 | Digital Library "Reforma agraria y transformaciones en el sector agropecuario en Nicaragua (1979–2015) | Online (no longer available) |
| Nicaragua | Digital National Security Archive | Washington, DC and Online |
| *Sección especial de investigaciones* miscellaneous records, 1983–1984 | Nicaragua, Hoover Institution Archives | Stanford University |
| Alvaro Jose Baldizon Alvarez miscellaneous papers, 1985–1986 | Nicaragua, Hoover Institution Archives | Stanford University |
| Ministerio de Defensa miscellaneous records, 1985–1987 | Nicaragua, Hoover Institution Archives | Stanford University |
| Antonio Ybarra Rojas depositions, 1993 | Nicaragua, Hoover Institution Archives | Stanford University |
| Enrique Bermúdez Varela papers, 1977–1990 | Nicaragua, Hoover Institution Archives | Stanford University |
| Eden Pastora Gómez interviews, 1992 | Nicaragua, Hoover Institution Archives | Stanford University |

| Collection | Archive | Location |
|---|---|---|
| Leonel Poveda Sediles papers, 1982–1986 | Nicaragua, Hoover Institution Archives | Stanford University |
| Alfonso Robelo C. papers, 1978–1990 | Nicaragua, Hoover Institution Archives | Stanford University |
| *Resistencia Nicaragüense* Records, 1983–1989 | Nicaragua, Hoover Institution Archives | Stanford University |
| *Resistencia Nicaragüense Ejército* Records, 1979–1993 | Nicaragua, Hoover Institution Archives | Stanford University |
| Roger Miranda Collection, Miranda-Ratliff papers, 1987–2000 | Nicaragua, Hoover Institution Archives | Stanford University |

# Bibliography

Abrams, Philip. 1988. "Notes on the Difficulty of Studying the State." *Journal of Historical Sociology* 1(1): 58–89.

Abu-Lughod, Deena I. 2000. "Failed Buyout: Land Rights for Contra Veterans in Postwar Nicaragua." *Latin American Perspectives* 27(3): 32–62.

Acemoglu, Daron, Leopoldo Fergusson, James A. Robinson, Dario Romero, and Juan F. Vargas. 2018. "The Perils of High-Powered Incentives: Evidence from Colombia's False Positives." NBER Working Paper No. 22617. Available at www.nber.org/papers/w22617.

Adam, Barry D. 1988. "Neighborhood Democracy in Nicaragua." *Dialectical Anthropology* 13(1): 5–15.

Agamben, Giorgio. 1998. *Homo Sacer: Sovereign Power and Bare Life.* Translated by D. Heller-Roazen. Stanford, CA: Stanford University Press.

2015. *Stasis: Civil War as a Political Paradigm.* Stanford, CA: Stanford University Press.

AHPN [Historical Archive of the National Police]. 2009. *Departamento de Investigaciones Criminológicas de la Policía Nacional, 1968–1986.* Guatemala City: AHPN.

2010. *La Polícia Nacional y sus Estructuras.* Colección de Informes, vol. 2. Guatemala City: Archivo Histórico de la Policía Nacional.

Ajanel Soberanis, Carlos. 1997. "Ejecutivo propone suprimir direcciones de Rentas Internas y Aduanas en 1998." *Prensa Libre.* April 18: 78.

Albertus, Michael. 2020. "Land Reform and Civil Conflict: Theory and Evidence from Peru." *American Journal of Political Science* 64(2): 256–274.

2021. *Property without Rights: Origins and Consequences of the Property Rights Gap.* New York: Cambridge University Press.

Albertus, Michael and Oliver Kaplan. 2013. "Land Reform and a Counterinsurgency Policy: Evidence from Colombia." *Journal of Conflict Resolution* 57(2): 198–231.

271

Allison, Graham T. and Morton H. Halperin. 1972. "Bureaucratic Politics: A Paradigm and Some Policy Implications." *World Politics* 24 (Spring Supplement): 40–79.

Alston, Philip. 2007. "Los derechos civiles y políticos, en particular las cuestiones relacionados con las desapariciones y ejecuciones sumarias." Report of the Special Rapporteur on Extrajudicial Execution. United Nations Human Rights Council. 4th Period of Sessions. February 19.

2009. "Promotion and Protection of All Human, Civil, Political, Economic, Social, and Cultural Rights, including the Right to Development." Report of the Special Rapporteur on Extrajudicial Execution. United Nations Human Rights Council. 11th Period of Sessions. May 4.

Amnesty International. 1981. "Guatemala: A Government Program of Political Murder." AMR 34/02/81. London: Amnesty International Publications.

1994. "Guatemala: Extrajudicial Executions Persist under Government of Former Human Rights Procurator." July. AMR 34/31/94.

2003. "¿Servicios de inteligencia responsables, o represión reciclada? Disolución del Estado Mayor Presidencial y reforma de los servicios de inteligencia." June 9. AMR 34/031/2003.

2016. "'You Have Signed Your Death Warrant': Torture and Other Ill Treatment by Nigeria's Special Anti-Robbery Squad (SARS)." September 21. AFR 44/4868/2106.

Andreas, Peter. 2004. "The Clandestine Political Economy of War and Peace in Bosnia." *International Studies Quarterly* 48: 29–51.

2008. *Blue Helmets and Black Markets: The Business of Survival in the Siege of Sarajevo.* Ithaca, NY: Cornell University Press.

Arana, Edgar and Carlos Castañaza. 1996. "Destituyen a González Taracena." *Siglo Veintiuno.* October 7: 5.

Arce, Alberto. 2011. "Corredor Interoceánico: el puente privado que atravesará Guatemala." *Plaza Pública*, December 13. Available at www.plazapublica .com.gt/content/corredor-interoceanico-el-puente-privado-que-atravesara-guatemala.

Arévalo, José Alejandro. 2014. "Razones y propósitos de la SAT en el contexto histórico de su creación 1996–1998." Presentation on 18th Anniversary of the SAT. Guatemala City.

Arjona, Ana M. 2014. "Wartime Institutions: A Research Agenda." *Journal of Conflict Resolution* 58(8): 1360–1389.

2016. *Rebelocracy: Social Order in the Colombian Civil War.* New York: Cambridge University Press.

Arjona, Ana, Nelson Kasfir, and Zachariah Mampilly. 2015. *Rebel Governance in Civil War.* New York: Cambridge University Press.

ASIES [Association for Social Investigation and Studies]. 2013. "Análisis de la defraudación aduanera y el contrabando en Guatemala." Guatemala City.

2017. "Fortalecimiento de la recaudación tributaria, transparencia aduanera y reducción del comercio exterior ilícito en Guatemala." Guatemala City.

Associated Press. 1970a. "Guatemala Terrorists Kidnap West German Envoy on Street." *The New York Times.* April 1: 1, 14.

1970b. "Foreign Minister of Guatemala Kidnapped and Held for a Trade." *The New York Times*. February 28: 1.

Autesserre, Séverine. 2014. *Peaceland: Conflict Resolution and the Everyday Politics of International Intervention*. New York: Cambridge University Press.

AVANCSO [Association for the Advancement of the Social Sciences in Guatemala]. 2013. *Ordenar, vigilar, perseguir y castigar: Un acercamiento histórico a la institución policial en Guatemala*. Cuadernos de Investigación No. 27. June. Guatemala City: AVANCSO.

Avelar, Bryan and Juan Martínez d'Aubuisson. 2017. "En la intimidad del escuadrón de la muerte de la policía." *Factum*. August 22. Available at http://revistafactum .com/en-la-intimidad-del-escuadron-de-la-muerte-de-la-policia/.

Azpuru, Dinorah. 2013. *Political Culture of Democracy in Guatemala and the Americas, 2012: Towards Equality of Opportunity*. Tenth Study of Democratic Culture of Guatemalans. Latin American Public Opinion Project (LAPOP). Nashville, TN: Vanderbilt University.

Balcells, Laia. 2012. "The Consequences of Victimization on Political Identities: Evidence from Spain." *Politics & Society* 40(3): 311–347.

Balcells, Laia and Christopher M. Sullivan. 2018. "New Findings from Conflict Archives: An Introduction and Methodological Framework." *Journal of Peace Research* 55(2): 137–146.

Ballentine, Karen and Jake Sherman. 2003. *The Political Economy of Armed Conflict: Beyond Greed and Grievance*. Boulder, CO: Lynne Rienner Publishers.

Balzacq, Thierry. 2011. "A Theory of Securitization: Origins, Core Assumptions, and Variants." In *Understanding Securitisation Theory: How Security Problems Emerge and Dissolve*. Ed. Thierry Balzacq. New York: Routledge. 1–30.

Barahona, Elías. 1980. "Testimonio de un guerrillero infiltrado en el gobierno del general Lucas García." *El Día* [Mexico]. October 9: 14.

Barma, Naazneen H. 2017. *The Peacebuilding Puzzle: Political Order in Post-Conflict States*. New York: Cambridge University Press.

Barnes, Nicholas. 2017. "Criminal Politics: An Integrated Approach to the Study of Organized Crime, Politics, and Violence." *Perspectives on Politics* 15(4): 967–987.

Barnett, Michael, Hunjoon Kim, Madalene O'Donnell, and Laura Sitea. 2007. "Peacebuilding: What is in a Name?" *Global Governance* 13(1): 35–58.

Barreto, Bill. 2015. "De Moreno a La Línea: la huella militar en la defraudación aduanera." *Plaza Pública*. August 22. Available at www.plazapublica.com.gt/ content/de-moreno-la-linea-la-huella-militar-en-la-defraudacion-aduanera-o.

2016. "Eco, el narrador de La Línea." *Plaza Pública*. March 14. Available at www.plazapublica.com.gt/content/eco-el-narrador-de-la-linea.

Bates, Robert. 2001. *Prosperity & Violence: The Political Economy of Development*. London: W.W. Norton.

Bateson, Regina. 2013. "Order and Violence in Postwar Guatemala." Ph.D. diss. New Haven, CT: Yale University.

Baumeister, Eduardo. 1998. *Estructura y reforma agraria en Nicaragua: 1979–1989*. Managua: Ediciones CDR-ULA.

Bautista, Giovanni and Hernández S. Ramón. 1996. "Ejército destituye al general Letona Hora por caso Moreno." *Prensa Libre*. November 11: 4.

Bayart, Jean-François, Stephen Ellis, and Béatrice Hibou. 1999. *The Criminalization of the State in Africa, African Issues*. Oxford: J. Currey.

Beissinger, Mark R. 2017. "Beyond the Neo-Weberian Yardstick? Thinking of the State in Multiple Registers." In *Paradox of Power: The Logics of State Weakness in Eurasia*. Eds. John Heathershaw and Edward Schatz. Pittsburgh, PA: University of Pittsburgh Press. 232–243.

Bellows, John and Edward Miguel. 2009. "War and Local Collective Action in Sierra Leone." *Journal of Public Economics* 93: 1144–1157.

Bendaña, Alejandro. 1991. *Una Tragedia Campesina: testimonios de la resistencia*. Managua: Editora de Arte.

Bennett, Andrew and Jeffrey T. Checkel. 2015. *Process Tracing: From Metaphor to Analytical Tool*. New York: Cambridge University Press.

Bergholz, Max. 2016. *Violence as a Generative Force: Identity, Nationalism, and Memory in a Balkan Community*. Ithaca, NY: Cornell University Press.

Bernhard, Michael. 2015. "Chronic Instability and the Limits of Path Dependence." *Perspectives on Politics* 13(4): 976–991.

Bersch, Katherine, Sérgio Praça, and Matthew M. Taylor. 2017. "State Capacity, Bureaucratic Politicization, and Corruption in the Brazilian State." *Governance* 30(1): 105–124.

Besley, Timothy and Torsten Persson. 2008. "Wars and State Capacity." *Journal of the European Economic Association* 6(2–3): 522–530.

Biondi-Morra, Brizio N. 1993. *Hungry Dreams: The Failure of Food Policy in Revolutionary Nicaragua, 1979–1990*. Ithaca, NY: Cornell University Press.

Blattman, Christopher. 2009. "From Violence to Voting: War and Political Participation in Uganda." *American Political Science Review* 103(2): 231–247.

Boas, Taylor C. 2007. "Conceptualizing Continuity and Change: The Composite-Standard Model of Path Dependence." *Journal of Theoretical Politics* 19(1): 33–54.

Boucher, Stephen R., Bradford L. Barham, and Michael R. Carter. 2005. "The Impact of 'Market-Friendly' Reforms on Credit and Land Markets in Honduras and Nicaragua." *World Development* 33(1): 107–128.

Bowen, Rachel E. 2017. *The Achilles Heel of Democracy: Judicial Autonomy and the Rule of Law in Central America*. New York: Cambridge University Press.
2019. "The Weight of the Continuous Past: Transitional (In)justice and Impunity States in Central America." *Latin American Politics and Society* 61(1): 126–147.

Boyle, Michael J. 2014. *Violence after War: Explaining Instability in Post-conflict States*. Baltimore, MD: Johns Hopkins University Press.

Brenes, Carmen Sofía and Haroldo Shetemul. 1992. "La voz que siempre atiende el Presidente." *Crónica*. September 10: 16, 19. Available at www.cronica.ufm.edu/index.php/DOC271.pdf.

Brenner, Neil, Bob Jessop, Martin Jones, and Gordon Macleod (eds.). 2003. *State/Space: A Reader*. Malden, MA: Wiley-Blackwell.

Brett, Roddy. 2016. *The Origins and Dynamics of Genocide: Political Violence in Guatemala*. London: Palgrave Macmillan.

Brett, Roddy and Antonio Delgado. 2005. *The Role of Constitution-Building Processes in Democratization: Case Study of Guatemala*. Stockholm, Sweden: International IDEA.

Brinks, Daniel M. 2003. "Informal Institutions and the Rule of Law: The Judicial Response to State Killings in Buenos Aires and São Paulo in the 1990s." *Comparative Politics* 36(1): 1–19.

2006. "The Rule of (Non)Law: Prosecuting Police Killings in Brazil and Argentina." In *Informal Institutions and Democracy: Lessons from Latin America*. Eds. Gretchen Helmke and Steven Levitsky. Baltimore, MD: The Johns Hopkins University Press. 201–226.

Brinks, Daniel M., Steven Levitsky, and Maria Victoria Murillo. 2019. *Understanding Institutional Weakness: Power and Design in Latin American Institutions*. Cambridge Elements: Politics and Society in Latin America. New York: Cambridge University Press.

Brockett, Charles D. 2005. *Political Movements and Violence in Central America*. New York: Cambridge University Press.

Broegaard, Rikke J. 2005. "Land Tenure Insecurity and Inequality in Nicaragua." *Development and Change* 36(5): 845–864.

2009. "Land Access and Titling in Nicaragua." *Development and Change* 40 (1): 149–169.

Brown, Timothy C. 2001. *The Real Contra War*. Norman: University of Oklahoma Press.

Bueno de Mesquita, Bruce, Alastair Smith, Randolph M. Siverson, and James D. Morrow. 2003. *The Logic of Political Survival*. Boston, MA: MIT Press.

Bull, Benedicte. 2008. *Globalización, Estado y Privatización: Proceso político de las reformas de telecomunicaciones en Centroamérica*. San José, Costa Rica: FLACSO.

2014. "Towards a Political Economy of Weak Institutions and Strong Elites in Central America." *European Review of Latin American and Caribbean Studies* 97: 117–128.

Cajina, Roberto J. 1997. *Transición política y reconversión militar en Nicaragua, 1990–1995*. Managua: CRIES.

Calderón S., José. 1978. "Admite el Ministro Guatemalteco de Gobernación que en el País Opera un 'Escuadrón de la Muerte.'" *Excelsior* [Mexico]. July 31.

Call, Charles. 2012. *Why Peace Fails: The Causes and Prevention of Civil War Recurrence*. Washington, DC: Georgetown University Press.

Campbell, Bruce B. 2000. "Death Squads: Definition, Problems, and Historical Context." In *Death Squads in Global Perspective: Murder with Deniability*. Eds. Bruce B. Campbell and Arthur D. Brenner. New York: St. Martin's Press. 1–26.

Capoccia, Giovanni. 2016. "When Do Institutions 'Bite'? Historical Instituitonalism and the Politics of Institutional Change." *Comparative Political Studies* 49(8): 1095–1127.

Carcamo Miranda, Jennifer Iliana. 2018. "Régimen Jurídico de Gestión Portuaria y la Situación de los Puertos de Guatemala." Thesis. Facultad de Ciencias Jurídicas y Sociales. Guatemala City: Universidad Rafael Landívar.

Cárdenas, Mauricio, Marcela Eslava, and Santiago Ramírez. 2016. "Why Internal Conflict Deteriorates State Capacity? Evidence from Colombian Municipalities." *Defence and Peace Economics* 27(3): 353–377.

Carey, John M. 2000. "Parchment, Equilibria, and Institutions." *Comparative Political Studies* 33(6–7): 735–761.

Carusi, Annamaria and Marina Jirotka. 2009. "From Data Archive to Ethical Labyrinth." *Qualitative Research* 9(3): 285–298.

Casas-Zamora, Kevin. 2011. *The Travails of Development and Democratic Governance in Central America.* Policy Paper Number 28. Washington, DC: Brookings Institution.

Castillo, Edy. 2002. "Muertes violentas muestran repunte en la capital." *El Periódico.* May 24: 6.

Castillo, E. and A. Guoz. 2005. "Sperisen: 'Los militares tienen mística y saben recibir órdenes." *El Periódico.* January 20: 4.

Castillo Martínez, Ernesto. 1997. "The Problem of Property and Property Owners." *Envío.* No. 196. Available at www.envio.org.ni/articulo/2049.

CEH [Comisión de Esclarecimiento Histórico]. 1999. *Guatemala: Memoria del silencio.* Guatemala: United Nations.

Centeno, Miguel Angel. 2002. *Blood and Debt: War and the Nation-state in Latin America.* University Park, PA: Pennsylvania State University Press.

Centeno, Miguel A., Atul Kohli, and Deborah Yashar (eds.). 2017. *States in the Developing World.* New York: Cambridge University Press.

Ch, Rafael, Jacob Shapiro, Abbey Steele, and Juan F. Vargas. 2018. "Endogenous Taxation in Ongoing Internal Conflict." *American Political Science Review* 112(4): 996–1015.

Charnysh, Volha and Evgeny Finkel. 2017. "The Death Camp Eldorado: Political and Economic Effects of Mass Violence." *American Political Science Review* 111(4): 801–818.

Chayes, Sarah. 2017. *When Corruption is the Operating System: The Case of Honduras.* Washington, DC: Carnegie Endowment for International Peace.

Checkel, Jeffrey T. 2013. *Transnational Dynamics of Civil War.* New York: Cambridge University Press.

Cheng, Christine S. 2018. *Extralegal Groups in Post-Conflict Libera: How Trade Makes the State.* New York: Oxford University Press.

Cheng, Christine S. and Dominik Zaum (eds.). 2011. *Corruption and Post-Conflict Peacebuiding: Selling the Peace?* London: Routledge.

Chisholm, Robert. 1991. "Nicaragua Libre: Pragmatic Corporatism in the Revolution." *Journal of Conflict Studies* 11(1): 27–45.

Chivvis, Christopher S. 2010. *EU Civilian Crisis Management.* Santa Monica, CA: RAND Corporation.

Christian, Shirley. 1986. *Nicaragua: Revolution in the Family.* London: Vintage.

CICIG [International Commission Against Impunity in Guatemala]. 2011. "Ex Presidente Portillo y dos de sus ex ministros integraron una estructura paralela para sustraer fondos del Estado." April 26. Available at www.cicig.org/casos/ex-presidente-portillo-y-dos-ex-ministros-integraron-una-estructura-paralela-para-sustraer-fondos-del-estado/.

2013. "Sentencias condenatorias en proceso que apoya la CICIG." Guatemala City.

2015. "Capturas por fraude a la Policia Nacional Civil." Comunicado de Prensa 027. Guatemala City.

2018. "Extrajudicial Executions and Torture Case." November 22. Available at www.cicig.org/cases/extrajudicial-executions-and-torture-case-2/?lang=en.

CICIG and Ministerio Público (MP). 2015. "La Línea: Máximos Beneficios." Presentation. Guatemala City. August 25.

CIDH [Inter-American Court on Human Rights]. 1998. "Caso de la 'Panel Blanca' vs. Guatemala." Sentence emitted on March 8. San José, Costa Rica.

Ciorciari, John D. 2021. *Shared Sovereignty in Fragile States*. Stanford, CA: Stanford University Press.

Close, David. 1999. *Nicaragua: The Chamorro Years*. Boulder, CO: Lynne Rienner Publishers.

Close, David and Salvador Martí i Puig. 2011. "The Sandinistas and Nicaragua since 1979." In *The Sandinistas and Nicaragua since 1979*. Eds. David Close, Salvador Martí i Puig, and Shelley A. McConnell. Boulder, CO: Lynne Rienner Publishers. 1–20.

Cohen, Mollie J., Noam Lupu, and Elizabeth J. Zechmeister. 2017. *The Political Culture of Democracy in the Americas, 2016/17*. Nashville, TN: Latin American Public Opinion Project (LAPOP), Vanderbilt University.

Cojtí Cuxil, Demetrio. 1999. "The Impact of the Popular Referendum on Compliance with the Indigenous Accord and on Democratization in Guatemala." In *The Popular Referendum (Consulta Popular) and the Future of the Peace Process in Guatemala*. Ed. Cynthia J. Arnson. Washington, DC: Woodrow Wilson International Center for Scholars. 21–26.

Colburn, Forrest. 1990. *Managing the Commanding Heights: Nicaragua's State Enterprises*. Berkeley: University of California Press.

Colindres, Félix. 1996. "Fraude por cielo, mar y tierra." *Crónica*. October 18: 19–20, 23–24.

Collier, Paul. 1999. "Doing Well out of War." Conference on Economic Agendas in Civil War. London: World Bank.

2000. "Rebellion as a Quasi-Criminal Activity." *The Journal of Conflict Resolution* 44(6): 839–853.

Collier, Paul and Anke Hoeffler. 2004. "Greed and Grievance in Civil War." *Oxford Economic Papers* 56(4): 563–595.

Collier, Paul and Nicholas Sambanis. 2002. "Understanding Civil War: A New Agenda." *Journal of Conflict Resolution* 46(1): 3–12.

Collier, Paul, V.L. Elliott, Håvard Hegre, Anke Hoeffler, Marta Reynal-Querol, and Nicholas Sambanis. 2003. *Breaking the Conflict Trap: Civil War and Development Policy*. A World Bank policy research report. Washington, DC: World Bank and Oxford University Press.

Conectas. 2021. "El idilio de Daniel Ortega con el gran capital." *Plaza Pública*. January 27. Available at www.plazapublica.com.gt/content/el-idilio-de-daniel-ortega-con-el-gran-capital.

Cordova Noguera, Ana María. 2014. "La Administración Tributaria." Thesis. Department of Juridical and Social Sciences. Guatemala City: Universidad Rafael Landívar. October.

Cribb, Robert. 2000. "From *Petrus* to Ninja: Death Squads in Indonesia." In *Death Squads in Global Perspective: Murder with Deniability*. Eds. Bruce B. Campbell and Arthur D. Brenner. New York: St. Martin's Press. 181–202.

*Crónica*. 1996. "Otro militar que cae por el caso Moreno." November 15: 23.

Cruz, José Miguel. 2011. "Criminal Violence and Democratization in Central America: The Survival of the Violent State." *Latin American Politics and Society* 53(4): 1–33.

Cuadra Lira, Elvira and Angel Saldomando. 2000. "Conflictos rurales en Nicaragua: Las tierras de la discordia." The North-South Institute. Managua. September.

Dahl, Robert A. 1971. *Polyarchy: Participation and Opposition*. New Haven, CT: Yale University Press.

Daly, Sarah Zukerman. 2014. "The Dark Side of Power-Sharing: Middle Managers and Civil War Recurrence." *Comparative Politics* 46(3): 333–353.

Daly, Sarah Zukerman, Laura Paler, and Cyrus Samii. 2020. "Wartime Ties and the Social Logic of Crime." *Journal of Peace Research* 57(4): 536–550.

Dammert, Lucía and Mary Fran T. Malone. 2020. "From Community Policing to Political Police in Nicaragua." *European Review of Latin American and Caribbean Studies* 110: 79–99.

Darden, Keith. 2008. "The Integrity of Corrupt States: Graft as an Informal State Institution." *Politics & Society* 36(1): 35–60.

Dargent, Eduardo, Andreas E. Feldman, and Juan Pablo Luna. 2017. "Greater State Capacity, Lesser Stateness: Lessons from Peru's Commodity Boom." *Politics & Society* 45(1): 3–34.

Darnton, Christopher. 2022. "The Provenance Problem: Research Methods and Ethics in the Age of Wikileaks." *American Political Science Review*. 116(3): 1110–1125.

Davenport, Christian. 2010. "Data from the Dark Side: Notes on Archiving Political Conflict and Violence." *PS: Political Science & Politics* 43(1): 37–41.

Dávila, Edwin and Claudia Palma. 2002. "Investigarán a Ortega Menaldo y otros militares." *El Periódico*. October 24: 3.

De León, Evelyn. 2015. "Caso La Línea: así se repartían las ganancias por la defraudación." *Soy502*. June 5. Available at www.soy502.com/articulo/casoredsat-asi-repartieron-ganancias-defraudacion.

De León Polanco, Eduardo. 1996. "Luis Pedro Toledo Godoy: Renunció Director General de Aduanas." *La República*. September 6: 2.

Deininger, Klaus and Juan Sebastián Chamorro. 2002. "Investment and Income Effects of Land Regularization: The Case of Nicaragua." World Bank Policy Research Paper 2752. January. Washington, DC: World Bank Development Research Group.

Del Cid, Marvin. 2001. "Con la llegada de Arévalo militarizan Gobernación." *El Periódico*. November 30: 3.

*Diario Impacto*. 1979. "Primeros Diez Meses del año: 3,250 Personas (Hombres y Mujeres) Murieron 'Escuadronados.'" November 14.

Dille, Benjamin B. 2012. "Ill Fares the Land: The Legal Consequences of Land Confiscations by the Sandinista Government of Nicaragua, 1979–1990." Ph. D. diss. London: London School of Economics.

Dirección de los Archivos de Paz. 2011. "El Estado Mayor Presidencial en Guatemala: una aproximación." Secretaría de la Paz. Guatemala City.

Doyle, Michael W. and Nicholas Sambanis. 2006. *Making War & Building Peace.* Princeton, NJ: Princeton University Press.

Eibl, Ferdinand, Steffen Hertog, and Dan Slater. 2021. "War Makes the Regime: Regional Rebellions and Political Militarization Worldwide." *British Journal of Political Science.* 51(3): 1002–1023.

Ejército de, Nicaragua. 2009. *Ejército de Nicaragua: 30 años de vida institucional (1979–1990).* Managua: Government of Nicaragua.

El Gráfico. 1976. "Con 10 balazos aparece una nueva víctima del 'Escuadrón.'" March 26.

    1988a. "¿Y el pánel de la muerte?" March 4: 7.

    1988b. "¿Cayó la pánel blanca?" March 11: 6.

    1988c. "'Son varios los páneles blancos…'" May 5: 4.

    1988d. "Sensacionales revelaciones." June 7: 7.

    1996a. "Inteligencia militar dirige operativo anticrimen." September 15: 16.

    1996b. "Destituidos otros 12 jefes de la Policía Nacional." September 25: 3.

    1996c. "Nombran Interventor del Puerto de Santo Tomás de Castilla." October 7: 3.

    1997. "La SAT permitirá que personal actúe con honradez." November 3: 7.

El Periódico. 1996. "MP investiga a empresario." November 28: 3.

    1998. "Minugua encuentra vicios del pasado en la nueva Policía Nacional Civil." September 16: 2–3.

    2000a. "Santo Tomás de Castilla: Un oscuro negocio." March 6: 2–3.

    2000b. "Jefes de la PNC con problemas." January 19: 3.

    2000c. "Byron Lima Oliva: Un infiltrado en el SIC." May 8: 2–3.

    2002. "Julio Girón: El Montesinos de Guatemala." October 7: 2–3.

    2013. "El oscuro pasado de Juan Carlos Monzón Rojas." November 11: 4–5.

    2015. "Resumen caso La Línea." October 9. Available at https://elperiodico.com.gt/cartas/2015/10/09/resumen-caso-la-linea/.

Engvall, Johan. 2017. "License to Seek Rents: 'Corruption' as a Method of Post-Soviet Governance." In *Paradox of Power: The Logics of State Weakness in Eurasia.* Eds. John Heathershaw and Edward Schatz. Pittsburgh, PA: University of Pittsburgh Press. 73–87.

Everingham, Mark. 1998. "Neoliberalism in a New Democracy: Elite Politics and State Reform in Nicaragua." *The Journal of Developing Areas* 32(2): 237–264.

    2001. "Agricultural Property Rights and Political Change in Nicaragua." *Latin American Politics and Society* 43(3): 61–93.

Falleti, Tulia G. 2016. "Process Tracing of Extensive and Intensive Processes." *New Political Economy* 21(5): 455–462.

Fearon, James D. and David D. Laitin. 2003. "Ethnicity, Insurgency, and Civil War." *American Political Science Review* 97(1): 75–90.

Ferguson, James and Akhil Gupta. 2002. "Spatializing States: Towards an Ethnography of Neoliberal Governmentality." *American Ethnologist* 29(4): 981–1002.

Fernández, Lafitte. 2011. *Crimen de Estado: El caso Parlacen*. Guatemala City: F&G Editores.

Finkel, Evgeny, Scott Gehlbach, and Tricia D. Olsen. 2015. "Does Reform Prevent Rebellion? Evidence from Russia's Emancipation of the Serfs." *Comparative Political Studies* 48(8): 984–1019.

Finley-Brook, Mary. 2012. "Market Citizenship in Eastern Nicaraguan Indigenous Territories." *AlterNative: An International Journal of Indigenous Peoples* 8(4): 393–409.

2016. "Territorial 'Fix'? Tenure Insecurity in Titled Indigenous Territories." *Bulletin of Latin American Research* 35(3): 338–354.

Fitzgerald, E.V.K. 1988. "Estado y Economía en Nicaragua." In *El Debate sobre la Reforma Agraria en Nicaragua: transformación agraria y atención al campesinado en nueve años de reforma agraria (1979–1988)*. Eds. Raúl Ruben, J.P. Groot, and E.V.K. Fitzgerald. Managua: Editorial Ciencias Sociales. 25–45.

Flores-Macías, Gustavo A. 2014. "Financing Security through Elite Taxation: The Case of Colombia's 'Democratic Security Taxes.'" *Studies in Comparative International Development* 49: 477–500.

2018. "The Consequences of Militarizing Anti-Drug Efforts for State Capacity in Latin America." *Comparative Politics* 51(1): 1–20.

Font, Juan Luis. 2002. "Ortega Menaldo perdió su visa estadounidense." *El Periódico*. March 19: 2.

GAM [Mutual Support Group]. 2010. *Los Obstáculos Estructurales de la Policía Nacional Civil en un context de Paz*. Guatemala City: Mutual Support Group.

GAO [US General Accounting Office]. 1989. *Central America: Impact of U.S. Assistance in the 1980s*. Report to the Chairman, Committee on Foreign Relations, U.S. Senate. Available at https://www.gao.gov/assets/150/147879.pdf.

Garay, Luis Jorge, Eduardo Salcedo-Albarán, Isaac de León-Beltrán, and Bernardo Guerrero. 2008. *La Captura y Reconfiguración del Estado en Colombia*. Bogotá: Grupo Metodo.

García, Jody. 2016. "Las 49 muertes del IGSS siguen impunes; hoy empiezan audiencias por Q18 millones." *Nómada*. Available at https://nomada.gt/las-49-muertes-del-igss-siguen-impunes-hoy-empiezan-audiencias-por-q18-millones/.

Garrard-Burnett, Virginia. 2010. *Terror in the Land of the Holy Spirit: Guatemala under General Efraín Ríos Montt, 1982–1983*. New York: Oxford University Press.

Gavigan, Patrick. 2009. "Organized Crime, Illicit Power Structures and Guatemala's Threatened Peace Process." *International Peacekeeping* 16(1): 62–76.

Geddes, Barbara. 1994. *Politician's Dilemma: Building State Capacity in Latin America*. Berkeley: University of California Press.

Gerschewski, Johannes. 2021. "Explanations of Institutional Change: Reflecting on a 'Missing Diagonal.'" *American Political Science Review* 115(1): 218–233.

Gilligan, Michael J., Benjamin J. Pasquale, and Cyrus Samii. 2014. "Civil War and Social Cohesion: Lab-in-the-Field Evidence from Nepal." *American Journal of Political Science* 58(3): 604–619.

Giraudy, Agustina, Eduardo Moncada, and Richard Snyder. 2019. *Inside Countries: Subnational Research in Comparative Politics*. New York: Cambridge University Press.

Glebbeek, Marie-Louise. 2001. "Police Reform and the Peace Process in Guatemala: The Fifth Promotion of the National Civilian Police." *Bulletin of Latin American Research* 20(4): 431–453.

Gleijeses, Piero. 1991. *Shattered Hope: The Guatemalan Revolution and the United States, 1944–1954*. Princeton, NJ: Princeton University Press.

González, Miguel. 2018. "Leasing Communal Properties…in 'Perpetuity': Post-Titling Scenarios on the Caribbean Coast of Nicaragua." In *Indigenous Struggles for Autonomy: The Caribbean Coast of Nicaragua*. Ed. Luciano Baracco. Lanham, MA: Lexington Books. 75–97.

González, Rolando. 2002. "Julio Girón." *El Periódico*. January 6: 7.

González, Yanilda María. 2020. *Authoritarian Police in Democracy: Contested Security in Latin America*. New York: Cambridge University Press.

González-Izás, Matilde. 2014. *Territorio, Actores Armados y Formación del Estado*. Guatemala City: Editorial Cara Parens.

González Moraga, Miguel. 1996. "El caso Cifuentes, sigue la depuración." *Crónica*. October 4: 23–24.

Goodfellow, William and James Morrell. 1991. "From Contadora to Esquipulas to Sapoá and Beyond." In *Revolution and Counterrevolution in Nicaragua*. Ed. Thomas W. Walker. Boulder, CO: Westview Press. 369–393.

Goodwin, Jeff. 2001. *No Other Way Out: States and Revolutionary Movements, 1945–1991*. New York: Cambridge University Press.

Gordon, Eleanor. 2017. "Crimes of the Powerful in Conflict-Affected Environments: False Positives, Transitional Justice, and Prospects for Peace in Colombia." *State Crime Journal* 6(1): 132–155.

Gossman, Patricia. 2000. "India's Secret Armies." In *Death Squads in Global Perspective: Murder with Deniability*. Eds. Bruce B. Campbell and Arthur D. Brenner. New York: St. Martin's Press. 261–286.

Government of Guatemala. 1996. "Acuerdo sobre aspectos socioeconómicos y situación agraria." Mexico City, May 6.

1996b. "Agreement on the Strengthening of Civilian Power and on the Role of the Armed Forces in Democratic Society." September.

Greif, Avner and David D. Laitin. 2004. "A Theory of Endogenous Institutional Change." *American Political Science Review* 98(4): 633–652.

Grieb, Kenneth J. 1979. *Guatemalan Caudillo: The Regime of Jorge Ubico: Guatemala, 1931–1944*. Athens, OH: Ohio University Press.

Grimes, Collin and David Pion-Berlin. 2019. "Power Relations, Coalitions, and Rent Control: Reforming the Military's Natural Resource Levies." *Comparative Politics* 51(4): 625–643.

Grzymala-Busse, Anna. 2008. "Beyond Clientelism: Incumbent State Capture and State Formation." *Comparative Political Studies* 41(4/5): 638–673.

2010. "The Best Laid Plans: The Impact of Informal Rules on Formal Institutions in Transitional Regimes." *Studies in Comparative International Development* 45: 311–333.

Guerra, Hermán. 1997. "La SAT controlará a quienes nunca han trasladado ni un centavo al fisco." *El Periódico*. October 27: 16.

2000. "Byron Barrientos a Gobernación. *El Periódico*. July 31: 4.

Guoz, Abner. 2002. "Julio Girón deja la Portuaria Quetzal." *El Periódico*. July 9: 3.

2004. "Carlos Vielman asume Ministerio de Gobernación." *El Periódico*. July 23: 3.

Gutiérrez, Iván. 1988. "La Política de Tierras de la Reforma Agraria Sandinista." In *El Debate sobre la Reforma Agraria en Nicaragua: transformación agraria y atención al campesinado en nueve años de reforma agraria (1979–1988)*. Eds. Raúl Ruben, J.P. Groot, and E.V.K. Fitzgerald. Managua: Editorial Ciencias Sociales. 113–128.

Gutiérrez-Sanín, Francisco and Elisabeth Jean Wood. 2017. "What Should We Mean by 'Pattern of Political Violence'? Repertoire, Targeting, Frequency, and Technique." *Perspectives on Politics* 15 (1): 21–41.

Hagopian, Frances. 1996. *Traditional Politics and Regime Change in Brazil*. New York: Cambridge University Press.

Handy, Jim. 1994. *Revolution in the Countryside: Rural Conflict & Agrarian Reform in Guatemala, 1944–1954*. Chapel Hill: The University of North Carolina Press.

Hanson, Jonathan K. and Rachel Sigman. 2013. "Leviathan's Latent Dimensions: Measuring State Capacity for Comparative Political Research." Presented at the World Bank Political Economy Lunch Series. Washington, DC. March 21.

Hartzell, Caroline A. and Matthew Hoddie. 2007. *Crafting Peace: Power-Sharing Institutions and the Negotiated Settlement of Civil Wars*. University Park, PA: Penn State University Press.

Hazelton, Jacqueline L. 2021. *Bullets Not Ballots: Success in Counterinsurgency Warfare*. Ithaca, NY: Cornell University Press.

Hazen, Jennifer M. 2013. *What Rebels Want: Resources and Supply Networks in Wartime*. Ithaca, NY: Cornell University Press.

Heathershaw, John and Edward Schatz. "The Logics of State Weaknes in Eurasia: An Introduction." In *Paradox of Power: The Logics of State Weakness in Eurasia*. Eds. John Heathershaw and Edward Schatz. Pittsburgh, PA: University of Pittsburgh Press. 3–23.

Hellman, Joel S., Geraint Jones, and Daniel Kaufmann. 2003. "Seize the State, Seize the Day: State Capture and Influence in Transition Economies." *Journal of Comparative Economics* 31: 751–773.

Helmke, Gretchen and Steven Levitsky. 2006. "Introduction." In *Informal Institutions and Democracy: Lessons from Latin America*. Eds. Gretchen Helmke and Steven Levitsky. Baltimore, MD: The Johns Hopkins University Press. 1–32.

Hendrix, Cullen S. 2010. "Measuring State Capacity: Theoretical and Empirical Implications for the Study of Civil Conflict." *Journal of Peace Research* 47 (3): 273–285.

Herbst, Jeffrey. 1990. "War and the State in Africa." *International Security* 14(4): 117–139.

2000. *States and Power in Africa: Comparative Lessons in Authority and Control*. Princeton, NJ: Princeton University Press.

Hernández Batres, Iduvina. 2014. "La Policía Nacional Civil de Guatemala: vida, pasión y muerte de una institución desdeñada." *Perspectivas* (July). Friedrich Ebert Stiftung.

Hernández, S. Ramón. 1996a. "Capturan a comerciante sindicado de contrabando y evasión fiscal." *Prensa Libre*. September 15: 6.

1996b. "Portillo y Letona fueron intermediarios entre Alfredo Moreno y empresario Peter Stolz." *Prensa Libre*. November 4: 2.

1996c. "Drogas y contrabando se mezclan en prontuario criminal de Moreno." Informe Especial. *Prensa Libre*. September 29: 7.

1996d. "Militares involucrados con el *capo* del contrabando serán sometidos al orden, asegura Pérez Aguilera." *Prensa Libre*. September 16: 6.

1996e. "Destituyen a militares, jefes policiacos y aduanales por estar involucrados con el *capo* del contrabando." *Prensa Libre*. September 18: 2.

Holden, Robert H. 2004. *Armies without Nations: Public Violence and State Formation in Central America, 1821–1960*. New York: Oxford University Press.

Holiday, David. 1997. "Guatemala's Long Road to Peace." *Current History* 96 (607): 68–74.

Holland, Alisha. 2017. *Forbearance as Redistribution: The Politics of Informal Welfare in Latin America*. New York: Cambridge University Press.

Hoover Green, Amelia. 2018. *The Commander's Dilemma: Violence and Restraint in Wartime*. Ithaca, NY: Cornell University Press.

Hope Sr., Kempe Ronald. 2010. "Liberia's Governance and Economic Management Assistance Program (GEMAP): An Impact Review and Analytical Assessment of a Donor Policy Intervention for Democratic State-building in a Post-conflict State." *South Africa Journal of International Affairs* 17(2): 243–263.

Horton, Lynn. 1999. *Peasant in Arms: War and Peace in the Mountains of Nicaragua, 1979–1994*. Athens, OH: Ohio University Press.

Huang, Reyko. 2016. *The Wartime Origins of Democratization: Civil War, Rebel Governance, and Political Regimes*. New York: Cambridge University Press.

Huggins, Martha K. 2000. "Modernity and Devolution: The Making of Police Death Squads in Modern Brazil." In *Death Squads in Global Perspective: Murder with Deniability*. Eds. Bruce B. Campbell and Arthur D. Brenner. New York: St. Martin's Press. 203–228.

Hui, Victoria Tin-bor. 2005. *War and State Formation in Ancient China and Early Modern Europe*. New York: Cambridge University Press.

Human Rights Watch. 2017. "'License to Kill': Philippine Police Killings in Duterte's 'War on Drugs.'" March. Available at www.hrw.org/sites/default/files/report_pdf/philippines0317_insert.pdf.

Huntington, Samuel. 1968. *Political Order in Changing Societies*. New Haven, CT: Yale University Press.

ICEFI [Central American Institute of Fiscal Studies]. 2007. Historia de la Tributación en Guatemala (Desde los Mayas hasta la Actualidad). Document prepared for the Superintendent of Tax Administration (SAT). Guatemala City. December.

*Imparcial*. 1974a. "Identificado Décimo Cuarto Escuadronado." April 5.

1974b. "Escuadrón de la Muerte Actúa, Esta Vez con Bala: Ha Ejecutado ya a Seis." February 2.

Invernizzi, Gabriele, Francis Pisani, and Jesús Ceberio. 1986. *Sandinistas: Entrevistas a Humberto Ortega Saavedra, Jaime Wheelock Román y Bayardo Arce*. Managua: Editorial Vanguardia.

IRAM [Institute for the Application of Research Methods and Development]. 2000. "Estudios sobre la Tenencia de la Tierra en Nicaragua." France. September.

Isaacs, Anita. 2010. "At War with the Past? The Politics of Truth Seeking in Guatemala." *International Journal of Transitional Justice* 4(2): 251–274.

Isaacs, Anita and Rachel A. Schwartz. 2020. "Guatemala: The Military in Politics." In *Oxford Research Encyclopedia of Politics*. Eds. William R. Thompson and Hicham Bou Nassif. New York: Oxford University Press. DOI: 10.1093/acrefore/9780190228637.013.1893.

Jonakin, Jon. 1996. "The Impact of Structural Adjustment and Property Rights Conflicts on Agrarian Reform Beneficiaries." *World Development* 24(7): 1179–1191.

Jonas, Susanne. 1991. *The Battle for Guatemala: Rebels, Death Squads, and U.S. Power*. Boulder, CO: Westview Press.

2000. *Of Centaurs and Doves: Guatemala's Peace Process*. Boulder, CO: Westview Press.

Juárez, Walter Martín. 1997. "Nuevo juicio contra Moreno." *El Periódico*. February 28: 4.

Kaimowitz, David. 1988. "La Planificación Agropecuaria en Nicaragua: de un Proceso de Acumulación Basado en el Estado a la Alianza Estratégica con el Campesinado." In *El Debate sobre la Reforma Agraria en Nicaragua: transformación agraria y atención al campesinado en nueve años de reforma agraria (1979–1988)*. Eds. Raúl Ruben, J.P. Groot, and E.V.K. Fitzgerald. Managua: Editorial Ciencias Sociales. 47–80.

Kaldor, Mary. 1999. *New and Old Wars: Organized Violence in a Global Era*. Stanford, CA: Stanford University Press.

Kalyvas, Stathis N. 2006. *The Logic of Violence in Civil War*. New York: Cambridge University Press.

Kalyvas, Stathis N. and Laia Balcells. 2010. "International System and Technologies of Rebellion: How the End of the Cold War Shaped Internal Conflict." *American Political Science Review* 104(3): 415–429.

Kang, David C. 2002. *Crony Capitalism: Corruption and Development in South Korea and the Philippines*. New York: Cambridge University Press.

Kannyo, Edward. 2000. "State Terrorism and Death Squads in Uganda (1971–79)." In *Death Squads in Global Perspective: Murder with Deniability*. Eds. Bruce B. Campbell and Arthur D. Brenner. New York: St. Martin's Press. 153–180.

Keefe, Eugene K. 1984. "National Security." In *Guatemala: A Country Study*. Ed. Richard Nyrop. Washington, DC: American University, Foreign Area Studies. 177–218.

Keen, David. 1998. *The Economic Functions of Violence in Civil Wars*. Adelphi paper. Oxford; New York: Oxford University Press for the International Institute for Strategic Studies.

Kelmendi, Pellumb and Amanda Rizkallah. 2018. "The Effects of Civil War on Post-War Political Development." *Oxford Research Encyclopedia of Politics*. DOI: 10.1093/acrefore/9780190228637.013.542.

Kim, Diana S. 2020. *Empires of Vice: The Rise of Opium Prohibition across Southeast Asia*. Princeton, NJ: Princeton University Press.

Kinzer, Stephen. 1984. "Soviet Help to Sandinistas: No Blank Check." *The New York Times*. March 28. Available at www.nytimes.com/1984/03/28/world/soviet-help-to-sandinistas-no-blank-check.html.

Klem, Bart. 2013. "In the Eye of the Storm: Sri Lanka's Front-Line Civil Servants in Transition." *Development and Change* 43(3): 695–717.

Klyachkina, Sasha. 2019. "Reconfiguration of Subnational Governance: Responses to Violence and State Collapse in the North Caucasus." Ph.D. diss. Evanston, IL: Northwestern University.

Knight, Jack. 1992. *Institutions and Social Conflict*. New York: Cambridge University Press.

Koivu, Kendra L. 2018. "Illicit Partners and Political Development: How Organized Crime Made the State." *Studies in Comparative International Development* 53: 47–66.

Kornbluh, Peter. 1991. "The U.S. Role in Counterrevolution." In *Revolution and Counterrevolution in Nicaragua*. Ed. Thomas W. Walker. Boulder, CO: Westview Press. 323–350.

Kruijt, Dirk. 2008. *Guerrillas: War and Peace in Central America*. London: Zed Books.

2011. "Revolución y contrarrevolución: el gobierno sandinista y la guerra de la Contra en Nicaragua, 1980–1990." *Desafíos* 23(2): 53–81.

Kurtenbach, Sabine and Angelika Rettberg. 2018. "Understanding the Relation between War Economies and Post-war Crime." *Third World Thematics* 3(1): 1–8.

*La República*. 1993. "'Escuadrones de la muerte' continúan vigentes en Guatemala." November 7: 6.

1996a. "Grupo Salvavidas el disfraz perfecto para todas las operaciones de Alfredo Moreno." October 6: 4.

1996b. "Moreno afirmó que Alfonso Portillo era miembro del Grupo Salvavidas desde 1991." October 6: 5.

1996c. "Intensa movilización militar y policíaca en cateos de allegados del capo Moreno." September 18: 4.

1996d. "Gabinete de Gobierno exige colaborar para descubrir a funcionarios corruptos." September 17: 5.

1996e. "Ejército destituye al general Letona Hora." November 11: 32.

*La Tarde.* 1980. "Dos Torturados, Baleados y Quemados." Guatemala City. February 2: 5.

Lacayo Oyanguren, Antonio. 2005. *La difícil transición nicaragüense en el gobierno de doña Violeta.* Managua: Fundación UNO.

Lake, David A. 2016. *The Statebuilder's Dilemma: On the Limits of Foreign Intervention.* Ithaca, NY: Cornell University Press.

Lake, Milli. 2017. "Building the Rule of War: Postconflict Institutions and the Micro-Dynamics of Conflict in Eastern DR Congo." *International Organization* 71: 281–315.

2022. "Policing Insecurity." *American Political Science Review* 116(3): 858–874.

Larra, Myriam and Byron Dardón. 1998. "Creada la Superintendencia de Administración Tributaria." *Prensa Libre.* January 13: 53.

Larson, Anne. 1993. "Nicaragua's Real Property Debate." *Envío.* No. 139. January. Managua: UCA.

Lauth, Hans-Joachim. 2000. "Informal Institutions and Democracy." *Democratization* 7(4): 21–50.

Lee, Melissa M. 2020. *Crippling Leviathan: How Foreign Subversion Weakens the State.* Ithaca, NY: Cornell University Press.

Lehoucq, Fabrice. 2012. *The Politics of Modern Central America: Civil War, Democratization, and Underdevelopment.* New York: Cambridge University Press.

Lemay-Hébert, Nicolas. 2009. "Statebuilding without Nationbuilding? Legitimacy, State Failures and the Limits of the Institutionalist Approach." *Journal of Intervention and Statebuilding* 3(1): 21–45.

Leogrande, William M. 1996. "Making the Economy Scream: US Economic Sanctions against Sandinista Nicaragua." *Third World Quarterly* 17(2): 329–348.

Levi, Margaret. 1988. *Of Rule and Revenue.* Berkeley: University of California Press.

Levitsky, Steven and María Victoria Murillo. 2013. "Lessons from Latin America: Building Institutions on Weak Foundations." *Journal of Democracy* 24(2): 93–107.

Lewis, Janet I. 2020. *How Insurgency Begins: Rebel Group Formation in Uganda and Beyond.* New York: Cambridge University Press.

Linz, Juan and Alfred J. Stepan. 1996. *Problems of Democratic Transition and Consolidation: Southern Europe, South America, and Post-Communist Europe.* Baltimore, MD: Johns Hopkins University Press.

Llorca, Juan Carlos. 2004. "Entrevista: Soy empresario y moriré siendo empresario." *El Periódico.* September 19: 16–17.

López, Anayansi and Ramón Hernández S. 1996. "Gobierno interviene Puerto Quetzal y Portuaria Santo Tomás de Castilla para eliminar corrupción." *Prensa Libre.* October 7: 2.

López Salinas, G. Enrique. 2011. *La guerra que no existió.* Managua: Editarte.

"Los contras: una derrota anunciada." 1987. *Envío* 68 (February).

Lu, Lingyu, and Cameron G. Thies. 2013. "War, Rivalry, and State Building in the Middle East." *Political Research Quarterly* 66(2): 239–253.

Lupu, Noam and Leonid Peisakhin. 2017. "The Legacy of Political Violence across Generations." *American Journal of Political Science* 61(4): 836–851.

Lyall, Jason. 2015. "Process Tracing, Causal Inference, and Civil War." In *Process Tracing: From Metaphor to Analytical Tool*. Eds. Andrew Bennett and Jeffrey T. Checkel. New York: Cambridge University Press. 186–208.

MacLachlan, Karolina. 2015. *Security Assistance, Corruption and Fragile Environments: Exploring the Case of Mali, 2001–2012*. Berlin, Germany: Transparency International.

Madariaga, Aldo. 2017. "Mechanisms of Neoliberal Resilience: Comparing Exchange Rates and Industrial Policy in Chile and Estonia." *Socio-Economic Review* 15(3): 637–660.

Mahoney, James. 2002. *The Legacies of Liberalism: Path Dependence and Political Regimes in Central America*. Baltimore, MD: Johns Hopkins University Press.

  2015. "Process Tracing and Historical Explanation." *Security Studies* 24(2): 200–218.

Mahoney, James and Kathleen Thelen. 2010. *Explaining Institutional Change: Ambiguity, Agency, and Power*. New York: Cambridge University Press.

Mampilly, Zachariah Cherian. 2011. "The Nexus of Militarisation and Corruption in Post-conflict Sri Lanka." In *Selling Peace: Post-conflict Peacebuilding and Corruption*. Eds. Dominik Zaum and Christine Cheng. New York: Routledge. 180–198.

Manion, Melanie. 2004. *Corruption by Design: Building Clean Government in Mainland China and Hong Kong*. Cambridge, MA: Harvard University Press.

Mann, Michael. 1984. "The Autonomous Power of the State: Its Origins, Mechanisms and Results." *European Journal of Sociology* 25(2): 185–213.

  1988. *States, War, and Capitalism: Studies in Political Sociology*. Oxford; New York: Basil Blackwell.

Manzetti, Luigi and Charles H. Blake. 1996. "Market Reforms and Corruption in Latin America: New Means for Old Ways." *Review of International Political Economy* 3(4): 662–697.

March, James G. and Johan P. Olsen. 2011. "Logic of Appropriateness." In *The Oxford Handbook of Political Science*. Ed. Robert E. Goodin. New York: Oxford University Press. 478–497.

Martí i Puig, Salvador. 1997. *Nicaragua 1977–1996: la revolución enredada*. Madrid: Libros de la Catarata.

  2008. "El regreso del FSLN al poder: ¿Es possible hablar de realineamiento electoral en Nicaragua?" *Política y Gobierno* 15(1): 75–112.

  2010. "The Adaptation of the FSLN: Daniel Ortega's Leadership and Democracy in Nicaragua." *Latin American Politics and Society* 52(4): 79–106.

Martí i Puig, Salvador and Eduardo Baumeister. 2017. "Agrarian Policies in Nicaragua: From Revolution to the Revival of Agro-exports, 1979–2016." *Journal of Agrarian Change* 17: 381–396.

Martí i Puig, Salvador, David Close, and Shelley McConnell (eds.). 2011. *The Sandinistas and Nicaragua since 1979*. Boulder, CO: Lynne Rienner Publishers.

Mason, T. David and Dale A. Krane. 1989. "The Political Economy of Death Squads: Toward a Theory of the Impact of State-Sanctioned Terror." *International Studies Quarterly* 33(2): 175–198.

Matanock, Aila M. 2014. "Governance Delegation Agreements: Shared Sovereignty as a Substitute for Limited Statehood." *Governance* 27(4): 589–612.

Matsuzaki, Reo. 2019. *Statebuilding by Imposition: Resistance and Control in Colonial Taiwan and the Philippines*. Ithaca, NY: Cornell University Press.

McClintock, Michael. 1985. *The American Connection: State Terror and Popular Resistance in Guatemala*. London: Zed Books.

McCreery, David. 1983. *Development and the State in Reforma Guatemala, 1871–1885*. Athens, OH: Ohio University Center for International Studies, Latin America Program.

McNeish, John-Andrew, Skarlleth Martinez Prado, and Hugo Frühling Ehrlich. 2019. "Community-Based Policing in Nicaragua: Do the Claims of Communtarian, Proactive, and Preventive Hold True?" *Journal of Human Security* 15(2): 7–20.

Meagher, Kate. 2012. "The Strength of Weak States? Non-State Security Forces and Hybrid Governance in Africa." *Development and Change* 43(5): 1073–1101.

Medrano, Mario. 2022. "Declaran culpables de conspiración a expresidente y exvicepresidente de consejo empresarial de Nicaragua." *CNN*. April 30. Available at https://cnnespanol.cnn.com/2022/04/30/nicaragua-declaran-culpables-de-conspiracion-a-expresidente-y-exvicepresidente-de-consejo-empresarial-orix/.

Meléndez, Javier and Roberto Orozco. 2013. "The Unsuspected Dimensions of Drug Trafficking in Nicaragua." *Insight Crime*. April 15. Available at www.insightcrime.org/news/analysis/unsuspected-dimensions-drug-trafficking-nicaragua/.

Méndez Arriaza, Claudia. 2001. "Ex empleados del Archivo y de la Guardia de Hacienda: Minugua detecta grupos armados clandestinos." *El Periódico*. September 5: 6.

Menjívar, Cecilia and Andrea Gómez Cervantes. 2018. "El Salvador: Civil War, Natural Disasters, and Gang Violence Drive Migration." *Migration Information Source*. September 29. Washington, DC: Migration Policy Institute. Available at https://www.migrationpolicy.org/article/el-salvador-civil-war-natural-disasters-and-gang-violence-drive-migration.

Merrill, Tim L. (ed.). 1994. *Nicaragua: A Country Study. Area Studies Handbook Series. Federal Research Division*. Washington, DC: Library of Congress.

Mitchell, Neil J. 2004. *Agents of Atrocity: Leaders, Followers, and the Violation of Human Rights in Civil War*. 1st Edition. London: Palgrave Macmillan.

Moe, Terry M. 2005. "Power and Political Institutions." *Perspectives on Politics* 3 (2): 215–233.

Moncada, Eduardo. 2022. *Resisting Extortion: Victims, Criminals, and States in Latin America*. New York: Cambridge University Press.

Montenegro Lima, Gerardo R. 1996. "Gobernación destituye a doce jefes policiacos por tener vínculos con Moreno." *La República*. September 25: 2.

Morales Carazo, Jaime. 1989. *La Contra: Anatomía de una múltiple traición*. Mexico: Planeta.

Mukhopadyay, Dipali. 2014. *Warlords, Strongman Governors, and the State in Afghanistan*. New York: Cambridge University Press.

Murdoch, James and Todd Sandler. 2002. "Economic Growth, Civil Wars, and Spatial Spillovers." *Journal of Conflict Resolution* 46(1): 91–110.

Murtazashvili, Jennifer Brick. 2016. *Informal Order and the State in Afghanistan*. New York: Cambridge University Press.

Murthy, R. Srinivasa and Rashmi Lakshminarayana. 2006. "Mental Health Consequences of War: A Brief Review of Research Findings." *World Psychiatry* 5(1): 25–30.

Najarro, Oneida. 1997. "Exagente del DIC fue condenado a 18 años de prisión por secuestro." *Prensa Libre*. April 17: 9.

Navarrete, Felix. 1991. "Piñata escandaliza." *La Prensa*. June 26: 1.

Nilsson, Manuela. 2018. "Civil Society Actors in Peace Negotiations in Central America." *Journal of Civil Society* 14(2): 135–152.

Nordstrom, Carolyn. 2004. *Shadows of War: Violence, Power, and International Profiteering in the Twenty-first Century*. Berkeley: University of California Press.

North, Douglass C. 1990. *Institutions, Institutional Change, and Economic Performance*. New York: Cambridge University Press.

NSA [National Security Archive]. 2018. "Guatemala Police Archive Under Threat." August 13. Available at https://nsarchive.gwu.edu/news/guatemala/2018-08-13/guatemala-police-archive-under-threat.

Núñez de Escorcia, Vilma. 1985. "Justice and the Control of Crime in the Sandinista Popular Revolution." *Crime and Social Justice* 1985(23): 5–28.

Núñez Soto, Orlando (ed.). 1991. *La guerra en Nicaragua*. Managua: CIPRES.

Núñez Soto, Orlando, Gloria Cardenal, Amanda Lorío, S. Agurto, J. Morales, J. Pasquier, J. Matus, and R. Pasos. 1998. *La guerra y el campesinado en Nicaragua*. Managua: Centro para la Investigación, la Promoción y el Desarrollo Rural y Social.

Nygren, Anja. 2004. "Competing Claims on Disputed Lands: The Complexity of Resource Tenure in the Nicaraguan Interior." *Latin American Research Review* 39(1): 123–153.

O'Donnell, Guillermo. 1993. "On the State, Democratization, and Some Conceptual Problems (A Latin American View with Glances at Some Post-Communist Countries)." Working Paper #192 (April). South Bend, IN: Kellogg Institute.

ODHAG (Oficina de Derechos Humanos del Arzobispado de Guatemala). 1998. *Guatemala: Nunca más* [Guatemala, Never Again]. Guatemala City, Guatemala: Oficina de Derechos Humanos del Arzobispado de Guatemala, ODHAG.

OECD. 2011. *Supporting Statebuilding in Situations of Conflict and Fragility: Policy Guidelines*. DAC Guidelines and Reference Series. Washington, DC: OECD Publishing.

Olivares, Iván. 2018. "Invasión de tierras es por razones políticas." *Confidencial.* July 8. Available at https://confidencial.com.ni/economia/invasion-de-tierras-es-por-razones-politicas/.

Open Society Justice Initiative. 2016. "Against the Odds: CICIG in Guatemala." New York: Open Society Foundation.

Ortega, Marvin. 1988. "Las Cooperativas Sandinistas: Entre la Democracia y el Verticalismo." In *El Debate sobre la Reforma Agraria en Nicaragua: transformación agraria y atención al campesinado en nueve años de reforma agraria (1979–1988).* Eds. Raúl Ruben, J.P. Groot, and E.V.K. Fitzgerald. Managua: Editorial Ciencias Sociales. 199–224.

Paige, Jeffrey M. 1975. *Agrarian Revolution.* New York: The Free Press.

   1997. *Coffee and Power: Revolution and the Rise of Democracy in Central America.* Cambridge, MA: Harvard University Press.

Palacios, Edwin. 2000. "Confirman prisión para agente por ejecución extrajudicial." *El Periódico.* August 12: 5.

Palma, Claudia. 2004. "Persiste la red que Abadío llevó de la CGCN a la SAT." *El Periódico.* March 16: 4.

Paris, Roland. 2004. *At War's End: Building Peace After Civil Conflict.* New York: Cambridge University Press.

PDH [Human Rights Ombudsman's Office]. 2006a. ¿Estado de Derecho o Impunidad? Hechos acaecidos en la Granja Modelo de Rehabilitación Pavón el 25 de septiembre de 2006." Presentation. Guatemala City. December.

   2006b. "Las Características de las Muertes Violentas en el País." February.

Peacock, Susan C. and Adriana Beltrán. 2003. "Poderes Ocultos: Grupos ilegales armados en la Guatemala post conflicto y las fuerzas detrás de ellos." Washington, DC: Washington Office on Latin America (WOLA).

Perera, Victor. 1993. *Unfinished Conquest: The Guatemalan Tragedy.* Berkeley: University of California Press.

Pérez, Francisco J. and Sandrine Fréguin-Gresh. 2014. "Nicaragua: evoluciones y perspectivas." In *Políticas públicas y agriculturas familiares en América Latina y el Caribe: Balance, desafíos y perspectivas.* Eds. Eric Sabourin, Mario Samper, and Octavio Sotomayor. Santiago, Chile: CEPAL. 231–256.

Pierson, Paul. 2000. "The Limits of Design: Explaining Institutional Origins and Change." *Governance: An International Journal of Policy and Administration* 13(4): 475–499.

Pion-Berlin, David. 2010. "Informal Civil-Military Relations in Latin America: Why Politicians and Soldiers Choose Unofficial Venues." *Armed Forces & Society* 36(3): 526–544.

Prasad, Monica, Mariana Borges Martins da Silva, and Andre Nickow. 2018. "Approaches to Corruption: A Synthesis of the Scholarship." *Studies in Comparative International Development* 54: 96–132.

*Prensa Libre.* 1981. "Valiente Téllez acusa al jefe de detectives." July 8: 2.

   1996a. "De León Carpio sabía de las actividades de contrabandista." October 23: 3.

   1996b. "Sindicato de la PN conocía vínculos de comisarios con Moreno." September 21: 2.

1997. "Por nuevos delitos de plagio indagan a exjefe del Comando Antisecuestros." April 16: 3.

Presidencia de la República de Guatemala. 1997. *De las palabras a las obras: Crónica de Gobierno 1996–2000, primer año.* Guatemala City: Unidad de Crónica Presidencial, Presidencia de la República de Guatemala.

Presidencia de la República de Nicaragua. 1990. "Créase la Comisión Nacional Agraria." Decreto No. 54-90. La Gaceta No. 197. October 5. Available at http://legislacion.asamblea.gob.ni/normaweb.nsf/($All)/B30316356C5F1C02062570A10057B476?OpenDocument.

Prevost, Gary. 1996. "The Nicaraguan Revolution – Six Years after the Sandinista Electoral Defeat." *Third World Quarterly* 17(2): 307–327.

Ramírez, Sergio. 2011. *Adiós Muchachos: A Memoir of the Sandinista Revolution.* Durham, NC: Duke University Press. Kindle Version.

Ramírez Espada, Alberto. 1996. "Gobierno destituye a altos jefes militares y policíacos." *El Gráfico.* September 18: 3.

Rasler, Karen and William R. Thompson. 1985. "War Making and State Making: Governmental Expenditures, Tax Revenues, and Global War." *The American Political Science Review* 79(2): 491–507.

2017. "War Making and the Building of State Capacity: Expanding the Bivariate Relationship." *Oxford Research Encyclopedia of Politics.* DOI: 10.1093/acrefore/9780190228637.013.642

Reeves, René. 2006. *Ladinos with Ladinos, Indians with Indians: Land, Labor, and Regional Ethnic Conflict in the Making of Guatemala.* Stanford, CA: Stanford University Press.

Reno, William. 1995. *Corruption and State Politics in Sierra Leone.* New York: Cambridge University Press.

2000a. "Shadow States and the Political Economy of Civil War." In *The Political Economy of Armed Conflict: Beyond Greed and Grievance.* Eds. K. Ballentine and J. Sherman. Boulder, CO: Lynne Rienner Publishers. 43–68.

2000b. "Clandestine Economies, Violence, and States in Africa." *Journal of International Affairs* 53(2): 433–459.

Rettberg, Angelika. 2007. "The Private Sector and Peace in El Salvador, Guatemala, and Colombia." *Journal of Latin American Studies* 39: 463–494.

Reyes, Kenia. 2004a. "Napoleón Rojas declarará ante la Fiscalía contra la Corrupción." *El Periódico.* May 25: 3.

2004b. "Ortega Menaldo, a punto de conseguir que se archive su caso." *El Periódico.* March 19: 4.

Ripoll, Santiago. 2018. "As Good as It Gets? The New Sandinismo and the Co-optation of Emancipatory Rural Politics in Nicaragua." Conference paper No. 46. ERPI 2018 International Conference: Authoritarian Populism and the Rural World. The Hague, Netherlands.

Robles Montoya, Jaime. 2002. *El "Poder Oculto."* Guatemala City: Fundación Myrna Mack.

Rocha, José Luis. 2019. "Agrarian Reform in Nicaragua in the 1980s: Lights and Shadows of a Legacy." In *A Nicaraguan Exceptionalism? Debating the*

*Legacy of the Sandinista Revolution.* Ed. Hilary Francis. London: University of London Press. 103–125.

Roche, Michael. 2006. "Competing Claims: The Struggle for Title in Nicaragua." *Vanderbilt Journal of Transnational Law* 39: 577–606.

Rodríguez-Franco, Diana. 2016. "Internal Wars, Taxation, and State Building." *American Sociological Review* 81(1): 190–213.

Rosada-Granados, Héctor. 1999. *Soldados en el Poder: Proyecto Militar en Guatemala, 1944–1990.* Amsterdam: Thela Latin America Series.

Rose-Ackerman, Susan. 1999. *Corruption and Government: Causes, Consequences, and Reform.* New York: Cambridge University Press.

Rotberg, Robert I. 2004. *When States Fail: Causes and Consequences.* Princeton, NJ: Princeton University Press.

Ruhl, J. Mark. 2003. "Civil-Military Relations in Post-Sandinista Nicaragua." *Armed Forces & Society* 30(Fall): 117–139.

Salazar, Maynor. 2018. "¿Quiénes son los tomatierras?" *Confidencial.* December 8. Available at https://confidencial.com.ni/principal/quienes-son-los-tomatierras/.

Sánchez, Omar. 2009. "Tax Reform Paralysis in Post-Conflict Guatemala." *New Political Economy* 14(1): 101–131.

Santos, Julio E. 2015. "Empresas de miembro de la red Moreno lavaron dinero con 'Chico Dólar.'" *El Periódico.* July 27. Available at https://elperiodico.com.gt/nacion/2015/07/27/empresas-de-miembro-de-la-red-moreno-lavaron-dinero-con-chico-dolar/.

Sas, Luis Ángel. 2005. "Investigaciones de la PNC son guiadas por Inteligencia Militar." *El Periódico.* October 20: 3.

SAT [Superintendent of Tax Administration]. 2016. *Informe Circunstanciado y Memoria de Labores 2016.* Guatemala City: SAT.

Schamis, Hector E. 1999. "Distributional Coalitions and the Politics of Economic Reform in Latin America." *World Politics* 51(2): 236–268.

Schirmer, Jennifer G. 1991. "The Guatemalan Military Project: An Interview with Gen. Héctor Gramajo." *Harvard International Review* 13(3): 10–13.

1998a. *The Guatemalan Military Project: A Violence Called Democracy.* Philadelphia: University of Pennsylvania Press.

1998b. "Prospects for Compliance: The Guatemalan Military and the Peace Accords." In *Guatemala After the Peace Accords.* Ed. Rachel Sieder. London: University of London Institute for Latin American Studies. 21–32.

Schlichte, Klaus. 2003. "State Formation and the Economy of Intra-state Wars." In *Shadow Globalization, Ethnic Conflicts and New Wars.* Ed. D. Jung. London: Routledge. 27–44.

2017. "The International State: Comparing Statehood in Central Asia and Sub-Saharan Africa." In *Paradox of Power: The Logics of State Weakness in Eurasia.* Eds. John Heathershaw and Edward Schatz. Pittsburgh, PA: University of Pittsburgh Press. 105–119.

Schmitt, Carl. 2005. *Political Theology: Four Chapters on the Concept of Sovereignty.* Translated by G. Schwab. Chicago: University of Chicago Press.

Schneider, Aaron. 2012. *State-Building and Tax Regimes in Central America.* New York: Cambridge University Press.

Schroeder, Michael J. 2000. "'To Induce a Sense of Terror': Caudillo Politics and Political Violence in Northern Nicaragua, 1926-1934 and 1981–1985." In *Death Squads in Global Perspective: Murder with Deniability.* Eds. Bruce B. Campbell and Arthur D. Brenner. New York: St. Martin's Press. 27–56.

Schulz, Donald E. and Deborah Sundloff Schulz. 2018. *The United States, Honduras, and the Crisis in Central America.* New York: Routledge.

Schwartz, Rachel A. 2019. "Guatemala's Anti-Corruption Struggle Teeters on the Edge." *NACLA – Report on the Americas* 51(2): 200–205.

2020. "Civil War, Institutional Change, and the Criminalization of the State: Evidence from Guatemala." *Studies in Comparative International Development* 55: 381–401.

2021a. "How Predatory Informal Rules Outlast State Reform: Evidence from Postauthoritarian Guatemala." *Latin American Politics and Society* 63(1): 48–71.

2021b. "Conjuring the Criminal State: The 'State-Idea' in Post-Conflict Reconstruction and International Statebuilding." *Journal of Global Security Studies* 6(2). DOI: 10.1093/jogss/ogaa031.

2022. "Rewriting the Rules of Land Reform: Counterinsurgency and the Property Rights Gap in Wartime Nicaragua." *Small Wars and Insurgencies.* Advanced article.

Schwartz, Rachel A. and Scott Straus. 2018. "What Drives Violence against Civilians in Civil War? Evidence from Guatemala's Conflict Archives." *Journal of Peace Research* 55(2): 222–235.

Seelke, Clare Ribando. 2007. "Anti-Gang Efforts in Central America: Moving Beyond Mano Dura?" Report for Center for Hemispheric Policy. April 10. Miami, FL: Center for Hemispheric Policy, University of Miami.

SEPAZ [Secretariat of Peace]. 2009. Las adopciones y los derechos humanos de la niñez guatemalteca, 1977–1989. Dirección de los Archivos de Paz. Available at www.plazapublica.com.gt/sites/default/files/t-informe-adopciones_cpaz .pdf.

Shetemul, Haroldo. 1996a. "Alfonso Portillo: 'Moreno contribuyó cuatro o cinco veces con 15 mil quetzales cada vez.'" *Crónica.* September 27: 38.

1996b. "Entrevista: Vinicio Cerezo Arevalo, Ex presidente de la República." *Crónica.* October 4: 31.

Shifter, Michael. 2012. *Countering Criminal Violence in Central America.* Center for Preventive Action. New York: Council on Foreign Relations.

Sierakowski, Robert. 2020. "'We Didn't Want to Be Like Somoza's Guardia': Policing, Crime, and Nicaraguan Exceptionalism." In *A Nicaraguan Exceptionalism? Debating the Legacy of the Sandinista Revolution.* Ed. Hilary Francis. London: University of London Press. 21–44.

*Siglo Veintiuno.* 1996a. "Capturan a presunto capo máximo de Aduanas." September 15: 3.

1996b. "Nuevas evidencias de más aportes de Moreno a Portillo." September 24: 3.

1996c. "El origen de Alfredo Moreno Molina." September 17: 3.

1996d. "Anuncian desaparición de Rentas Internas y Aduanas." November 9: 6.

1996e. "Ministro de Comunicaciones dice que en portuarias falsificaban documentos." October 8: 3.

1996f. "Arzú prevé represalias por caso Moreno, pero reafirma determinación de actuar." September 18: 3.

Silva Ávalos, Héctor. 2014. *Infiltrados: Crónica de la Corrupción de la PNC (1992–2013)*. San Salvador: UCA Editores.

Simmons, Erica S. and Nicholas Rush Smith. 2017. "Comparison with an Ethnographic Sensibility." *PS: Political Science & Politics* 50(1): 126–130.

Simmons, Erica S., Nicholas Rush Smith, and Rachel A. Schwartz. 2018. "Rethinking Comparison in the Social Sciences." *Qualitative and Multi-Method Research* 16(1): 1–7.

Sisk, Timothy. 2013. *Statebuilding*. Cambridge, UK: Polity.

Slater, Dan. 2010. *Ordering Power: Contentious Politics and Authoritarian Leviathans in Southeast Asia*. New York: Cambridge University Press.

2020. "Violent Origins of Authoritarian Variation: Rebellion Type and Regime Type in Cold War Southeast Asia." *Government and Opposition* 55(1): 21–40.

Smith Rotabi, Karen. 2014. "Child Adoption and War: 'Living disappeared' Children and Social Worker's Post-conflict Role in El Salvador and Argentina." *International Social Work* 57(2): 169–180.

Sobek, David. 2010. "Masters of Their Domains: The Role of State Capacity in Civil Wars: Introduction." *Journal of Peace Research* 47(3): 267–271.

Soifer, Hillel David. 2015. *State Building in Latin America*. New York: Cambridge University Press.

Soifer, Hillel David and Mathias vom Hau. 2008. "Unpacking the *Strength* of the State: The Utility of State Infrastructural Power." *Studies in Comparative International Development* 43(3–4): 219–230.

Soifer, Hillel David and Everett A. Vieira III. 2019. "The Internal Armed Conflict and State Capacity: Institutional Reforms and the Effective Exercise of Authority." In *Politics after Violence: Legacies of the Shining Path Conflict in Peru*. Eds. Hillel David Soifer and Alberto Vergara. Austin: University of Texas Press. 109–131.

Spalding, Rose J. 1994. *Capitalists and Revolution in Nicaragua: Opposition and Accommodation, 1979–1993*. Chapel Hill: The University of North Carolina Press.

2017. "Los empresarios y el estado posrevolucionario: el reordenamiento de las élites y la nueva estrategia de colaboración en Nicaragua." *Anuario de Estudios Centroamericanos* 43: 149–188.

Speck, Mary. 1990. "Nicaragua, Contras Sign Peace Accords." *Chicago Tribune*. April 20. Available at www.chicagotribune.com/news/ct-xpm-1990-04-20-9002020146-story.html.

Spoor, Max. 1994. "Neo-Liberalism and Institutional Reform in Post-1990 Nicaragua: The Impact on Grain Markets." *Bulletin of Latin American Research* 13(2): 185–202.

Stanfield, J. David. 1995. "Insecurity of Land Tenure in Nicaragua." LTC Research Paper 120. Land Tenure Center. Madison: University of Wisconsin–Madison.

Staniland, Paul. 2012. "States, Insurgents, and Wartime Political Order." *Perspectives on Politics* 10(2): 243–264.

2021. *Ordering Violence: Explaining Armed Group-State Relations from Conflict to Cooperation.* Ithaca, NY: Cornell University Press.

Stanley, William. 1996. *The Protection Racket State: Elite Politics, Military Extortion, and Civil War in El Salvador.* Philadelphia: Temple University Press.

2013. *Enabling Peace in Guatemala: The Story of MINUGUA.* 1st Edition. Boulder, CO: Lynne Rienner Publishers, Inc.

Stedman, Stephen John. 1997. "Spoiler Problems in Peace Processes." *International Security* 22(2): 5–53.

Steele, Abbey. 2017. *Democracy and Displacement in Colombia's Civil War.* Ithaca, NY: Cornell University Press.

Steenkamp, Christina. 2009. *Violence and Post-war Reconstruction: Managing Insecurity in the Aftermath of Peace Accords.* London: I.B.Tauris.

Streeck, Wolfgang and Kathleen Thelen. 2005. *Beyond Continuity: Institutional Change in Advanced Political Economies.* Oxford: Oxford University Press.

Subotić, Jelena. 2021. "Ethics of Archival Research on Political Violence." *Journal of Peace Research* 58(3): 342–354.

Sullivan, Christopher Michael. 2012. "Blood in the Village: A Local-Level Investigation of State Massacres." *Conflict Management and Peace Science* 29(4): 373–396.

2016a. "Undermining Resistance: Mobilization, Repression, and the Enforcement of Political Order." *Journal of Conflict Resolution* 60(7): 1160–1190.

2016b. "Political Repression and the Destruction of Dissident Organizations: Evidence from the Guatemalan Police Archives." *World Politics* 68(4): 645–676.

Sweet, Rachel. 2020. "Bureaucrats at War: The Resilient State in the Congo." *African Affairs* 119(475): 224–250.

2021. "Concealing Conflict Markets: How Rebels and Firms Use State Institutions to Launder Wartime Trade." *International Organization* 75(4): 1109–1132.

Tapscott, Rebecca. 2021. *Arbitrary States: Social Control and Modern Authoritarianism in Museveni's Uganda.* Oxford: Oxford University Press.

Thaler, Kai M. 2017. "Nicaragua: A Return to Caudillismo." *Journal of Democracy* 28(2): 157–169.

2018. "From Insurgent to Incumbent: State Building and Service Provision After Rebel Victory in Civil Wars." Ph.D. diss. Cambridge, MA: Harvard University.

*The New York Times.* 1970. "Kidnapping Diplomats is Becoming a Latin Custom." March 15: 176.

Thelen, Kathleen. 2004. *How Institutions Evolve: The Political Economy of Skills in Germany, Britain, the United States, and Japan.* New York: Cambridge University Press.

2014. *Varieties of Liberalization and the New Politics of Social Solidarity.* New York: Cambridge University Press.

Thies, Cameron G. 2005. "War, Rivalry, and State Building in Latin America." *American Journal of Political Science* 49(3): 451–465.

2006. "Public Violence and State-Building in Central America." *Comparative Political Studies* 39(10): 1263–1282.

2010. "Of Rulers, Rebels, and Revenue: State Capacity, Civil War Onset, and Primary Commodities." *Journal of Peace Research* 47(3): 321–332.

Tilly, Charles (ed.). 1975. *Formation of National States in Western Europe.* Princeton, NJ: Princeton University Press.

1985. "War Making and State Making as Organized Crime." In *Bringing the State Back In.* Eds. D. R. Peter Evans, and Theda Skocpol. New York: Cambridge University Press. 169–191.

1990. *Coercion, Capital, and European States, AD 990–1990.* Cambridge, MA: B. Blackwell.

Trackman, Brian, William Fisher, and Luis Salas. 1999. "The Reform of Property Registration Systems in Nicaragua: A Status Report." Harvard University. June 11. Available at https://cyber.harvard.edu/prs/Nicar.html.

Treisman, Daniel. 2000. "The Causes of Corruption: A Cross-national Study." *Journal of Public Economics* 76: 399–457.

Trejo, Alba. 2001. "Querían que repartiera aduanas, no lo hice y se molestaron." *El Periódico.* July 23: 13.

Trejo, Marco Tulio. 1994. "Salguero: Alcaide y guardia manejan al escuadrón de la muerte en Pavón." *Siglo Veintiuno.* May 19: 6.

Trejo, Guillermo, Juan Albarracín, and Lucía Tiscornia. 2018. "Breaking State Impunity in Post-authoritarian Regimes: Why Transitional Justice Processes Deter Criminal Violence in New Democracies." *Journal of Peace Research* 55 (6): 787–809.

Trejo, Guillermo and Sandra Ley. 2020. *Votes, Drugs, and Violence: The Political Logic of Criminal Wars in Mexico.* New York: Cambridge University Press.

Tsai, Kellee S. 2006. "Adaptive Informal Institutions and Endogenous Institutional Change in China." *World Politics* 59(1): 116–141.

United Nations. 1994. "Informe del Grupo Conjunto para la Investigación de Grupos Armados Ilegales con Motivaciones Políticas." San Salvador. July 28.

Van de Velde, Brenda. 2011. "Revolutionary Policing: A Case Study about the Role of la Mística and el Espíritu in the Nicaraguan Police Institution and in the Lives of Its Fundadores." Master's Thesis. Department of Cultural Anthropology. Utrecht: Utrecht University.

Vela, Manolo. 2002. "De perras y olmos: La reforma de los servicios de inteligencia en Guatemala." *Revista de la Secretaría de Análisis Estratégico de la Presidencia de la República* 1(1): 67–100.

Vilas, Carlos M. 1984. *Perfiles de la Revolución Sandinista.* Buenos Aires: Editorial Legasa.

Wade, Christine J. 2016. *Captured Peace: Elites and Peacebuilding in El Salvador.* Athens, OH: Ohio University Press.

Walker, Thomas W. 2003. *Nicaragua: Living in the Shadow of the Eagle.* 4th Edition. Boulder, CO: Westview Press.

Walter, Barbara F. 2002. *Committing to Peace: The Successful Settlement of Civil Wars.* Princeton, NJ: Princeton University Press.

2010. "Conflict Relapse and the Sustainability of Post-Conflict Peace." World Development Report Background Paper. Washington, DC: The World Bank.

2015. "Why Bad Governance Leads to Repeat Civil War." *Journal of Conflict Resolution* 59: 1242–1272.

Weaver, Eric and William Barnes. 1991. "Opposition Parties and Coalitions." In *Revolution and Counterrevolution in Nicaragua*. Ed. Thomas W. Walker. Boulder, CO: Westview Press. 117–142.

Weinstein, Jeremy M. 2005. "Autonomous Recovery and International Intervention in Comparative Perspective." Working Paper No. 57. Washington, DC: Center for Global Development. April.

2007. *Inside Rebellion: The Politics of Insurgent Violence*. New York: Cambridge University Press.

Whalan, Jeni. 2010. "The Power of Friends: The Regional Assistance Mission to Solomon Islands." *Journal of Peace Research* 47(5): 627–637.

Wheelock Román, Jaime. 1991. *La verdad sobre la Piñata*. Managua: Instituto para el Desarrollo de la Democracia.

Wilkinson, Daniel. 2002. *Silence on the Mountain: Stories of Terror, Betrayal, and Forgetting in Guatemala*. Boston, MA: Houghton Mifflin.

Williams, Philip J. 1994. "Dual Transitions from Authoritarian Rule: Popular and Electoral Democracy in Nicaragua." *Comparative Politics* 26(2): 169–185.

Wisser, Katherine M. and Joel A. Blanco-Rivera. 2016. "Surveillance, Documentation and Privacy: An International Comparative Analysis of State Intelligence Records." *Archival Science* 16: 125–147.

Wittenberg, Jason. 2015. "Conceptualizing Historical Legacies." *Eastern European Politics and Societies* 29(2): 366–378.

WOLA [Washington Office on Latin America]. 2009. "Protect and Serve? The Status of Police Reform in Central America." June. Washington, DC. Available at https://www.wola.org/analysis/protect-and-serve-the-status-of-police-reform-in-central-america/.

WOLA and Fundación Mack. 2019. Guatemala's Justice System: Evaluating Capacity Building and Judicial Independence. Washington, DC. Available at www.wola.org/wp-content/uploads/2019/07/Informe_cam_english_final7.1.pdf.

Wood, Elisabeth. 2003. *Insurgent Collective Action and Civil War in El Salvador*. New York: Oxford University Press.

World Bank. 2011. *World Development Report 2011: Conflict, Security, and Development*. Washington, DC: The International Bank for Reconstruction and Development, World Bank.

Wright, Bruce E. 1990. "Pluralism and Vanguardism in the Nicaraguan Revolution." *Latin American Perspectives* 17(3): 38–54.

Yashar, Deborah J. 1997. *Demanding Democracy: Reform and Reaction in Costa Rica and Guatemala, 1870s–1950s*. Stanford, CA: Stanford University Press.

2018. *Homicidal Ecologies: Illicit Economies and Complicit States in Latin America*. New York: Cambridge University Press.

Young, Crawford. 1988. *The African Colonial State in Comparative Perspective*. New Haven, CT: Yale University Press.

Zamora, José Rubén. 2002. "El crimen organizado, el Ejército y el futuro de los guatemaltecos." *El Periódico*. November 12: 2–4.

Zelada, Rodolfo. 2000. "Más señalamientos a la PNC: Cambios fueron ilegales." *El Periódico*. February 15: 6.

## Archival Documents

AHPN [Historical Archive of the National Police]. 1971. GT PN 50 S007. Departamento de Investigaciones Criminológicas, Expedientes de juzgados de paz ramo criminal. 8574 /Of.30.- jidg.-. Expediente No. (11.1207.1108) 1672, Doc. No. 1. July 27. Guatemala City.

    1973. GT PN 50 S002. Departamento de Investigaciones Criminológicas, Expedientes del Cuerpo de Detectives. Expediente No. (11.1207.1239) 5487. May 26. Guatemala City.

    1974. GT PN 50 S002. Departamento de Investigaciones Criminológicas, Expedientes del Cuerpo de Detectives. Expediente No. (11.1207.1226) 2218, Doc. 1. July 9. Guatemala City.

    1980. GT PN 51-01 S011. Centro de Operaciones Conjuntas de la Policía Nacional, Jefatura. Memorias, informes y análisis realizadas por el COCP. "Inteligencia Policial." Guatemala City. Internal Reference CUIT 3060247.

    1981. GT PN 50 S020. Departamento de Investigaciones Criminológicas, Expedientes de denuncias. (11.1207.1208)077. January 3. Guatemala City.

    1982. GT-PN 51-01 S002. Centro de Operaciones Conjuntas de la Policía Nacional, JEFATURA, Correspondencia confidencial enviada y recibida. Expediente No. (11.0329.1115)51-104, Doc. No. 2. February 26. Guatemala City.

    1983. GT PN 30-01 S009. Oficio No. 201/83.-SEM. Dirección General, Director General, Expedientes de informes [Reference No. 5114058]. Guatemala City.

    1984. GT PN 30-01 S009. Oficio No. 001-SEM-MEAM-84. Dirección General, Director General, Expedientes de informes [Reference 5119396]. Guatemala City.

    1986. GT 50 S028. Oficio No. 07-86 UOP SEM. Departamento de Investigaciones Criminológicas, Expedientes de ministerios. [Reference 4248230]. Guatemala City.

    1988. GT 50-21 S001. Departamento de Investigaciones Criminológicas, Sección de Antisecuestros, Extorsiones. Documentos de la Sección de Antisecuestros y Extorsiones. "Memorandum." March 10. Internal Reference CUIT 5292800.

    n.d. GT PN 30 DSC. Dirección General , Documentos sin clasificar. Expediente No. (14.0801.0957)30-1015. Guatemala City.

Bureau of Intelligence and Research. 1970. "Guatemala: Violence from the Right." Intelligence Note. May 26. US Department of State. *Proquest* Digital National Security Archive.

CIA [United States Central Intelligence Agency]. 1983. "[The Archivo and Government-Sponsored Violence]." February. *ProQuest* Digital National Security Archive.

CIERA [Centro de Investigación y Estudios de Reforma Agraria]. 1980. "Evaluación de la Política Económica en el Sector Agropecuario." Ministerio de Desarrollo Agropecuario y Reforma Agraria (MIDINRA). Documento No. 3. Managua.

1986. "Políticas agrarias y económicas en el Bolsón: las transformaciones en condiciones de guerra. Estudio del bolsón interno de las Segovias." Anexo 4. *Campesinado y Reforma Agraria.* Volume 68 (December). Managua.

1988. "Consideraciones sobre la Situación Económica del Campesinado." CIERA Análisis Económico. Volume 87. Managua.

1989. *Cifras y Referencias Documentales.* Ministerio de Desarrollo Agropecuario y Reforma Agraria. Managua.

DGFCRA [Dirección General de Fomento Campesino y Reforma Agraria]. 1982. Plan de Trabajo de 1982. MIDINRA-DGFCRA. Managua.

1983a. "Informe presentado al comandante de la revolución Tomás Borge Martínez, en ocasión del acto de entrega de títulos de Reforma Agraria el 9 de julio, Daraylí, Región I." MIDINRA-DGFCRA. Managua.

1983b. "Acto de Entrega de Títulos en Conmemoración a la caída del "Comandante Félix Pedro Carrillo", enmarcado en la Jornada IV Aniversario." MIDINRA-DGFCRA. Managua.

1983c. "Informe al Comandante de la Revolución Jaime Wheelock Román, en ocasión del acto de entrega de títulos de Reforma Agraria el 10 de julio en San Francisco Libre, Región III." MIDINRA-DGFCRA. Managua.

1983d. "Información básica para la entrega de títulos de Reforma Agraria en San Rafael del Sur." MIDINRA-DGFCRA. January. Managua.

1984a. "Síntesis de Problemas Señalados en las Visitas a las Regiones." Managua.

1984b. "Informe sobre la situación actual del campesinado de la Región VI." MIDINRA-DGFCRA. April. Managua.

1984c. "Datos básicos sobre entrega de títulos de Reforma Agraria en Río Blanco y El Cuá, Región VI." MIDINRA-DGFCRA. February. Managua.

1985. "Evaluación Primer Trimestre." MIDINRA-DGFCRA. April. Managua.

1986a. "Acercamiento a la problemática del Movimiento Cooperativo." MIDINRA-DGFCRA. May 3. Managua.

1986b. "La transición de asentamientos de guerra a pueblos rurales: Elementos de discusión en base a estudios de caso en los asentamientos de Panalí y El Coco, Quilalí, Nueva Segovia, Región I." MIDINRA-DGFCRA. April. Managua.

DIA [United States Defense Intelligence Agency]. 1972. "Armed Forces: Army G2 Organization." June 13. *ProQuest* Digital National Security Archive.

1991. "Corruption in the Guatemalan Customs Service." April 8. *ProQuest* Digital National Security Archive.

Dirección de Inteligencia Militar (EMG-EPS). 1987. "Reseña Histórica de la Organización C/R F.D.N." Ministerio de Defensa miscellaneous records, 1985-1987. Hoover Institution Archives.

FDN [Fuerza Democrática Nacional]. 1982. "Informe del Estado de Fuerza." November 20. Folder 4.4. Enrique Bermúdez Varela papers. Hoover Institution Archives.

1984. "Informe del Estado de Fuerza." February 20. Folder 4.4. Enrique Bermúdez Varela papers. Hoover Institution Archives.

"[Former Members of Guatemala National Police and Civilians Kill Criminals]." 1989. February. *Proquest* Digital National Security Archive.

FSLN [Frente Sandinista de Liberación Nacional]. 1980. "Preparación Política 80 – Estructura y Funcionamiento de la Junta de Gobierno de Reconstrucción Nacional." Managua, Nicaragua: Instituto de Historia de Nicaragua y Centroamérica (IHNCA).

International Cooperation Administration. 1956. "Report on the National Police in the Republic of Guatemala." US Department of State. April 9. *Proquest* Digital National Security Archive.

JGRN [Junta de Gobierno de Reconstrucción Nacional]. 1983. *Ley de Servicio Militar Patriótico*. Decreto No. 1327. May 2. Managua.

MIDINRA. 1980. "Estado y Agro Durante el Somocismo." Managua

1983a. Plan Anual de Trabajo 1983. MIDINRA. Managua.

1983b. Informe de Nicaragua a la Conferencia de la FAO 1983, sobre los avances en la Reforma Agraria y Desarrollo Rural. MIDINRA-CIERA. March. Managua.

1984. "Balance de la Reforma Agraria 1979/83." CIERA-MIDINRA. Managua.

1985a. "Los Comités de Defensa Sandinista." Centro de Investigación y Estudios de la Reforma Agraria, CIERA-MIDINRA. Trabajos FLACSO. Managua.

1985b. "Impacto Político de la Reforma Agraria." Campesinado y Reforma Agraria. Tomo 3.9. Volume 71. MIDINRA-CIERA. Managua.

1985c. "Matiguás: Campesinado y Formas Organizativas, Sintesis." MIDINRA-CIERA. Managua.

1986. "Avance y Perspectivas de la Reforma Agraria." Dirección General de Reforma Agraria. January. Managua.

1987a. "Informe de Nicaragua a la FAO 1986. Balance: Logros alcanzados en materia de Reforma Agraria y Desarrollo Rural." CIERA-MIDINRA. Managua.

1987b. "Política de Reforma Agraria para 1987." CIERA-MIDINRA. Managua.

Organismo Judicial. 2003. Expediente No. 22023-2003-00048. Tribunal Décimo de Sentencia Penal, Narcoactividad y Delitos Contra el Ambiente.

Ratliff, William. n.d. Interview transcripts with Roger Miranda Bengochea. Chapters 4 and 5. Roger Miranda Collection, Miranda-Ratliff papers, 1987-2000. Hoover Institution Archives.

RN [Resistencia Nicaragüense]. n.d. List of RN Comandos. Box 2.3. Resistencia Nicaragüense Ejército Records, 1979-1993. Hoover Institution Archives.

Secretaría del Estado Mayor Presidencial. 1979-1982. Nóminas y Planillas. Doc. C.2.1.6.2-5-S001–0040; C.2.1.6.2-5-S001–0042. Archivo General de Centroamérica. Guatemala City.

1983. Nóminas y Planillas Nóminas. Doc. C.2.1.6.2-5-S001–0049. Archivo General de Centroamérica. Guatemala City.

1984. Fichas de Ascenso, Letra L. Doc. C.2.1.6.2.-5-S005–0013. Archivo General de Centroamérica. Guatemala City.

Secretaría del Estado Mayor Presidencial, División de Comunicaciones. 1982. Memoria de Labores. Doc. C.2.1.6.2-5-S042–0003. Archivo General de Centroamérica. Guatemala City.

1982. Memoria de Labores. Doc. C.2.1.6.2-5-S042–0005. Archivo General de Centroamérica. Guatemala City.

Secretaría del Estado Mayor Presidencial, Sistema de Comunicaciones. 1983. Memoria de Labores. Doc. C.2.1.6.2-5-S042–0011. Archivo General de Centroamérica. Guatemala City.

Serafino, Nina M. 1989. "Contra Aid: Summary and Chronology of Major Congressional Action, 1981–1989." November. Washington, DC: Congressional Research Service. *Proquest* Digital National Security Archive.

USAID (United States Agency for International Development), Bureau for Latin America, Mission to Guatemala, Public Safety Division. 1968. "Guatemalan Military Intelligence Organization; Includes Annex." December. *Proquest* Digital National Security Archive.

US Department of Defense. 1988. "VCSA Visit to Guatemala." June 17. *ProQuest* Digital National Security Archive.

1991. "Why the 'Tanda' Phenomenon Does Not Exist in the Guatemala Military." August 27. *ProQuest* Digital National Security Archive.

1993. "Influencing the Appointment of a New Director of Guatemalan Customs – A Family Affair?" January 20. *ProQuest* Digital National Security Archive.

US Department of State. 1967. "Guatemala: Vigilantism Poses Threat to Stability." Intelligence Note from Office of Director of Intelligence and Research. May 12. *Proquest* Digital National Security Archive.

1968. "Action Plan for Guatemala." Memo from John R. Breen to the Executive Chairman. November 5. *Proquest* Digital National Security Archive.

1969. "Study in Anticipation of a Crisis in Guatemala." Washington, DC. April 21. *Proquest* Digital National Security Archive.

1970. "Assistance to Elite Police Corps." Memorandum from Political Affairs Officer Pezzullo to USAID Director Culbertson. April 20. *Proquest* Digital National Security Archive.

1986. "Demarche to President Cerezo on Possible Death Squad Resurgence." Memo to US Embassy in Guatemala. December 18. *Proquest* Digital National Security Archive.

US Department of State and Department of Defense. 1987. "The Sandinista Military Build-up: An Update." Department of State Publication 9432. October. Washington, DC. *Proquest* Digital National Security Archive.

US Embassy in Guatemala. 1956. "Establishment of General Office of National Security." Foreign Service Dispatch. March 6. *Proquest* Digital National Security Archive.

1961. "Internal Security Situation and Needs." Memo to the US Department of State. May 22. *Proquest* Digital National Security Archive.

1962. "Assessment of Local Police Forces." Airgram to the US Department of State. May 29. *Proquest* Digital National Security Archive.

1963. "Guatemala Internal Defense Plan – Progress Report." Memorandum to the Office of Public Safety. September 25. Washington, DC. *Proquest* Digital National Security Archive.

1964. "Internal Defense Plan for Guatemala: Progress Report and Prospects."
    Airgram to US Department of State. March 6. Washington, DC. *Proquest*
    Digital National Security Archive.
1966. "Guatemalan Police Powers Expanded." Airgram to US Department of
    State. December 24. *Proquest* Digital National Security Archive.
1967. "Internal Security Assessment." Memo to the US Secretary of State.
    October 10. *Proquest* Digital National Security Archive.
1968. "Terrorism in Guatemala: New Myths and Hard Realities." Airgram to
    US Department of State. February 17. *Proquest* Digital National Security
    Archive.
1979a. "Acting President Comments on Continuing High Level of Violence."
    Memo to Secretary of State and Central American Embassies. February 16.
    *Proquest* Digital National Security Archive.
1979b. "Right-Wing Terrorism." Memo to Secretary of State. January 22.
    *Proquest* Digital National Security Archive.
1986a. "The Secret Anti-Communist Army." Memo to Secretary of State and
    Central American Embassies. January 22. *Proquest* Digital National Security
    Archive.
1986b. "Human Rights Abuses and Possible Death Squad Resurgence." Memo
    to Secretary of State. December 23. *Proquest* Digital National Security
    Archive.
1987a. "Meeting with Cerezo on Posible Death Squad Resurgence." Memo to
    Secretary of State. January 19. *Proquest* Digital National Security Archive.
1987b. "Alleged Resurgence of Death Squads on Pacific Coast Denounced."
    Memo to Secretary of State and Central American Embassies. March 11.
    *Proquest* Digital National Security Archive.
1987c. "Rising Violence in Guatemala Again Causing Concern." Memo to
    Secretary of State and Central American Embassies. December 12. *Proquest*
    Digital National Security Archive.
1993. "National Police Director on his Plans." Memo to Secretary of State.
    August 19. *Proquest* Digital National Security Archive.
US Embassy in Managua. 1983. "Agrarian Reform's New Focus: The Armed
    Cooperative." June 14. *Proquest* Digital National Security Archive.

# Index

For EU product safety concerns, contact us at Calle de José Abascal, 56–1°,
28003 Madrid, Spain or eugpsr@cambridge.org.

www.ingramcontent.com/pod-product-compliance
Ingram Content Group UK Ltd.
Pitfield, Milton Keynes, MK11 3LW, UK
UKHW010249140625
459647UK00013BA/1747